THE EMOTIONALLY
INTELLIGENT WORKPLACE

A volume in the series *Advances in Emotional Intelligence: Research and Practice,* edited by Cary Cherniss, Richard E. Boyatzis, and Maurice Elias

THE EMOTIONALLY INTELLIGENT WORKPLACE

How to Select for, Measure, and Improve Emotional Intelligence in Individuals, Groups, and Organizations

Cary Cherniss
Daniel Goleman
Editors

Foreword by Warren Bennis

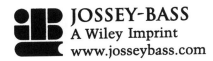

JOSSEY-BASS
A Wiley Imprint
www.josseybass.com

Published by Jossey-Bass
A Wiley Imprint
989 Market Street, San Francisco, CA 94103-1741   www.josseybass.com

Jossey-Bass books and products are available through most bookstores. To contact Jossey-Bass directly call our Customer Care Department within the U.S. at 800-956-7739, outside the U.S. at 317-572-3986, or fax 317-572-4002.

Jossey-Bass also publishes its books in a variety of electronic formats. Some content that appears in print may not be available in electronic books.

Library of Congress Cataloging-in-Publication Data
   The emotionally intelligent workplace : how to select for, measure, and improve emotional intelligence in individuals, groups, and organizations / by Cary Cherniss, Daniel Goleman, editors.—1st ed.
       p. cm.—(The Jossey-Bass business & management series)
Includes bibliographical references and index.
   ISBN 978-1-118-30879-0
  1. Emotional intelligence. 2. Emotional intelligence tests.
3. Work—Psychological aspects. 4. Success in business. I.
Cherniss, Cary. II. Goleman, Daniel. III. Series.
   BF576 .E467 2001
   658.3—dc21

2001000675

FIRST EDITION
HB Printing   15 14 13 12 11 10 9

CONTENTS

TABLES, FIGURES, & EXHIBITS

Tables

Figures

Exhibits

FOREWORD

Intellect still matters, certainly. You generally need a certain number of IQ points just to get in the game. But Daniel Goleman's great contribution has been to make clear the astonishing degree to which, once you're in the game, becoming a star is largely attributable to factors beyond intellect—factors such as maturity, emotional health, and *grownupness*. If you will, it comes down to character. In demonstrating this with clarity and convincing data, Goleman has proved beyond a doubt something we may have known deep down in our bones yet which has largely been ignored in American organizational life in recent decades.

The essence of his findings can be summed up fairly simply. Emotional intelligence (EI), more than any other asset, more than IQ or technical expertise, is the most important overall success factor in careers. And the higher one's position in an organization, the more important EI is; EI accounts for 85 to 90 percent of the success of organizational leaders.

Anyone who followed the 2000 presidential election will recall the mini-drama surrounding the scheduling of the debates. From all appearances, Al Gore wanted as many debates and as wide an audience as possible; for his part, George W. Bush seemed quite reluctant to step into the fray. Experts asserted that Gore's sharp mind made him far more suited than Bush to success in debating. Yet in the end, Bush gained more from the debates than did Gore. Why? Because he displayed more emotional intelligence.

Journalists and campaign professionals alike have spoken of the magical ability of the television camera to strip a politician bare and expose the personality strengths and weaknesses that lie beneath the fine arguments and well-chosen words. Those unfamiliar with Goleman's research may see this as a regrettable sign that style triumphs over substance. But to the initiated it is a powerful reminder of the centrality of EI.

Now Goleman and coeditor Cary Cherniss have advanced work in EI in a remarkable way, through this volume of essays that will contribute immeasurably to organizations of every stripe. *The Emotionally Intelligent Workplace* allows people in business, academia, and government to apply the lessons learned about EI to actual institutions and the women and men contained within them. Beyond being rigorous and comprehensive, it is a wonderfully practical book—complete with insights into how to nurture the emotional competencies of both individuals and groups and how to use EI to dramatically improve the screening and recruitment of top-level executives.

Recently I had the privilege of conducting a leadership development program that allowed a team of world-class experts and executives to spend a week mentoring and teaching hundreds of emerging leaders from top corporations around the globe. The influence of Daniel Goleman's work was obvious in many of the themes and messages offered during the week. A personal note of sadness sounded on the last day, however, when I reflected on what happens all too often after such conferences. Changed people return to unchanged organizations; they come down from a majestic mountaintop into an arid Death Valley that is hostile to a better way of looking at things. They may frequently thrive in their own careers, but their organizations remain largely what they were before.

The problem is that real change involves getting an entire organization, not simply a few managers, to adequately grasp the importance of building up emotional competencies in addition to intellectual ones. Even today the bulk of executive training and development coursework is devoted to work that employs the cognitive area of the brain, the neocortex. These courses are much like the ones we all took in college, favoring the "thinking brain." And indeed, fitting new insights and data into people's neural circuitry may be helpful for many technical jobs. What Goleman calls "the billion-dollar mistake," however, occurs in too many organizations—they neglect to engage people's emotional circuitry. In fact the penalty is worse than that: it's a $250 billion mistake, the amount spent annually (according to Linkage Inc., a management consulting firm) on executive development. I now think of this mistake as the Great Training Robbery.

My first significant insight into the neglect of the emotional life of leaders came some time ago, when I was asked to evaluate the number two executive in a large global corporation for the firm's top post. Let's call this executive Ed. He seemed ideal: energetic, ambitious, and super smart. It took me about six months to come to the conclusion that though Ed looked perfect, he lacked a crucial ingredient of leadership—integrity. Nobody trusted him, and I couldn't help him. But the board ignored my advice, and when the incumbent chief executive officer had a heart attack, in a collective panic the board elevated Ed. He was summarily discharged only twelve months later. A conservative estimate of his cost to the company was over $5 million.

I included this anecdote in one of my books, and to this day I get letters telling me, "Ed's my boss." If *The Emotionally Intelligent Workplace* had been available back then, I could have saved that company $5 million for a small cost. Maybe Ed could have been saved too. Today I recommend this book to anyone who knows an Ed and anyone who is interested in leadership and the health of human institutions; I especially recommend it to those who want to see their organizations in the telephone book in the year 2010.

April 2001
Los Angeles, California

Warren Bennis
Distinguished Professor of Business Administration
and Founding Chairman of the Leadership Institute,
University of Southern California

PREFACE

What is emotional intelligence? What difference does it make? And what is the best way to promote it in the workplace? *The Emotionally Intelligent Workplace* explores these three questions. It presents thoughtful and practical perspectives on how to measure emotional intelligence, use it as a basis for personnel selection, and improve it for the individual, the group, and the organization. Although this is not a how-to book, several chapters offer concrete guidelines for practitioners. At the same time, this book is designed to meet the growing need among researchers, graduate students, and professionals for a sophisticated yet readable analysis of the emotional intelligence concept. It provides a much deeper understanding of the concept's theoretical and empirical foundations than can be found in most other books on the topic. Among those who will find this book of value are human resource managers and executives, general managers and executives, consultants, academics in both psychology and business schools, and students in management and applied psychology courses.

Our primary objective in this book is to advance the understanding of emotional intelligence and its role in promoting superior performance at work. Following the publication of Daniel Goleman's best-selling books *Emotional Intelligence* and *Working with Emotional Intelligence,* there has been keen interest in enhancing emotional intelligence in the workplace. Emotional intelligence (EI) is linked to abilities that involve skill in managing emotion in oneself and others and that are predictive of superior performance in work roles. Research during the last twenty-five years has consistently pointed to a set of competencies such as Self-Confidence, Initiative, and Teamwork, for example—that make a significant difference to the performance of individuals and organizations. A few of these competencies are purely cognitive, but most are emotional. This book explores how these competencies are linked to EI and how they contribute to superior performance in individuals and organizations.

Another objective of this volume is to consider emotional intelligence as a group and organizational phenomenon as well as an individual one. Most writers and researchers have conceived of emotional intelligence as a characteristic of individuals. The contributors to this volume show how analogous EI qualities and processes occur at the group level. Some of them also describe how individual EI and group EI are vital for organizational effectiveness. In addition the chapter authors explore how emotional competence in an organization depends on the interplay of such factors as how organizational members are selected, how they are trained, and how the organization structures its subsystems.

Origins of This Book

The Emotionally Intelligent Workplace is based largely on the work of the Consortium for Research on Emotional Intelligence in Organizations. This group, initially funded by the Fetzer Institute, now consists of thirty members representing four universities, two large corporations, two federal agencies, and two large consulting firms. A number of the individual members are internationally recognized experts who have extensive careers in both research and practice. Since 1996, they have met together at least twice a year to exchange ideas, share information with one another, and coordinate the work of the consortium's research staff.

Daniel Goleman formed the consortium in 1996 after he discovered that many managers and consultants wanted to apply the ideas surrounding emotional intelligence but needed guidance in order to make good decisions about how to proceed. The mission of the consortium was to assess all that is known about promoting emotional intelligence competencies in the workplace and to develop guidelines for practice. In addition the consortium identified empirically sound models of good practice in this field.

The members of the consortium spent the first three years studying a large number of the programs and organizations that have sought to enhance the social and emotional competencies of workers. These have included any effort that targeted one or more of the four domains of emotional intelligence described by Goleman in his books: Self-Awareness, Self-Management, Social Awareness, and

Relationship Management. As a result of this work, the consortium has identified fifteen best practice models that have been tested and empirically validated in countless organizations.

In a second important project, the consortium developed twenty-two guidelines for promoting emotional intelligence in organizations. These guidelines are based on an exhaustive review of the empirical literature concerning training and development, counseling, and behavioral change. Yet another project undertaken by the group involved a review of the different measures and measurement strategies for assessing emotional and social competence in organizations. The U.S. Office of Personnel Management, a member of the consortium, spearheaded this project.

Most of the contributors to this volume are members of the consortium. Many of the ideas discussed here evolved during the semiannual, day-long meetings of that group. In addition an early draft of each chapter was read by at least two other members of the consortium in order to help the chapter authors further refine their thinking.

Finally, *The Emotionally Intelligent Workplace* is the first volume in a series titled *Advances in Emotional Intelligence: Research and Practice.* Some future volumes will explore various facets of emotional intelligence in different settings (for example, schools, the family, colleges and universities, the workplace) and among different populations (children, adolescents, adults). Some volumes will be devoted to specific topics, such as assessment and measurement issues. Yet other volumes will focus on particular applications of EI, in the field of health for example. Cary Cherniss of Rutgers University, Richard E. Boyatzis of Case Western Reserve University, and Maurice Elias of Rutgers University edit this series. A distinguished editorial board composed of both scholars and practitioners assists them.

Overview of the Contents

This book is divided into three parts. The first part (Chapters One through Six) looks at emotional intelligence as a concept, exploring issues related to EI definition and measurement. The first chapter, by Cary Cherniss, begins by discussing how and why the promotion of emotional intelligence in the workplace has become so important for the well-being of our society. What are the current challenges facing public and private sector organizations today? What are the ways in which organizations are attempting to cope with those challenges? And what role does emotional intelligence play in all of this? These are the primary questions that Chapter One addresses. Cherniss also presents a model depicting how emotional intelligence influences organizational effectiveness. It illustrates how the expression of individual and group competence depends on the interplay of member selection, member training, and the structure of organizational subsystems (rewarding and valuing, decision making, communicating and feeding back, and so forth). The chapter concludes with a discussion of some unresolved issues and dilemmas currently facing the EI field, including concerns about how best to define and measure the concept of emotional intelligence and questions about its significance as a predictor of performance.

The second chapter, by Daniel Goleman, a leading thinker and author in the EI field today, returns to the question of definition. Goleman begins by going back to the early part of the twentieth century to review the historical roots of EI theory and research. He next describes how his conception of EI differs from the conceptions of Reuven Bar-On, John Mayer, and Peter Salovey, the other major EI theorists, in that it is a *theory of performance*. Goleman concludes this chapter with a discussion of the relative influence of EI and IQ in predicting career success. He offers a more nuanced view than do those who claim that EI is all that matters, and he summarizes the data suggesting that EI is a significant predictor of the individuals in a particular job category who will rise to the top.

In Chapter Three, Goleman presents in detail his EI-based theory of performance. He begins by distinguishing between emotional intelligence and the specific competencies based on it. He then presents, first, a more detailed view of the neural substrates of his theory, drawing on recent advances in neuroscience, and next, the business case for focusing on the EI-based competencies his model comprises, describing data linking the EI competencies to workplace performance and organizational effectiveness. Goleman concludes this chapter by discussing some implications for education. He notes that social and emotional learning programs are increasingly offered during the early school years but not during higher education. Few courses at the college or professional level teach the competencies associated with EI and superior performance in the workplace.

Lyle Spencer begins Chapter Four by making a compelling case that researchers and practitioners should base their practices on sound scientific data. He then demonstrates the analytical tools one can use to estimate the economic value added of any human resource (HR) practice. He presents data demonstrating the economic utility of selection, training, and development based on emotional intelligence competencies (EIC). In fact he shows that carefully designed and implemented training in emotional competencies can produce as much as 1.7 times the effect size shift and 8 times the return on investment of non-EIC-based training. Finally, Spencer introduces a seven-step protocol for developing business cases for EIC-based HR interventions and for evaluating these interventions, presenting a recent case study to illustrate the use of this protocol.

Marilyn Gowing focuses in Chapter Five on the assessment and measurement of emotional intelligence. She provides an update on the latest measures of emotional intelligence and describes their intended purposes. She also summarizes the scientific literature supporting these instruments and further clarifies the conceptual distinctions between the different models of EI that have become popular among managers and HR professionals. She closes her chapter with a forecast of some new directions for the measurement of emotional intelligence, including the use of computer-based simulations to assess EI competencies.

Chapter Six shifts the focus from individuals to groups. If one can think of emotionally intelligent individuals, is it possible to think also of emotionally intelligent groups? Is the emotional competence of a group simply the sum of the emotional competence of its individual members? Vanessa Druskat and Steven Wolff argue that one *can* think of emotional competence on a group level and that the emotional intelligence of a group is more than the sum of group members' EI. The authors present a model that defines the components of emotional competence in groups, integrates several streams of research on emotions and on group effectiveness, and describes the process through which team-level emotional intelligence influences team effectiveness.

The second part of this volume (Chapters Seven and Eight) examines human resource applications in more depth. In Chapter Seven, Ruth Jacobs introduces ways that organizations can increase their EI as they carry out standard HR functions such as hiring, training and development, and managing performance. She begins by showing how HR professionals can use Goleman's EI-based theory of performance to improve the precision with which they select people for important positions in an organization. She then presents data showing that although star performers do not need to excel in every EI competence, scoring above a given tipping point on at least some competencies in each of the four major clusters, or domains, greatly increases the likelihood that an individual will succeed. She also shows how a particular selection tool, the behavioral event interview, can be used to select individuals who possess EI competencies. And she presents guidelines for those who wish to increase EI through training and development interventions. In closing, Jacobs describes how managers can increase the EI of their employees through the normal performance management function.

Chapter Eight, by Claudio Fernández-Aráoz, focuses on the relevance of EI for hiring at the highest levels of organizations. After pointing out the enormous impact that hiring decisions have on an organization when those decisions involve top-level positions, Fernández-Aráoz discusses how the dynamics of the selection process make such decisions particularly difficult. He then describes the usual process followed in selecting top-level executives, which emphasizes technical skill and measures of cognitive ability, and shows how it is deficient. Using data from three different continents that reflects over five hundred top-level executive hires, Fernández-Aráoz shows that emotional competencies are better predictors of success than other commonly used predictors are. He concludes with specific recommendations for how to improve senior-level hiring practices.

The third and last part of the book (Chapters Nine through Twelve) focuses on training and development interventions. Can people working in organizations be helped to improve the competencies associated with EI that are so crucial for success? These final chapters suggest that they can, and the chapter authors examine some of the issues that must be addressed in achieving this improvement. Chapter Nine, by Cherniss and Goleman, begins the discussion by describing three training and development interventions that have been conducted in organizations, rigorously evaluated, and replicated. The research on these interventions strongly supports the notion that it is possible to help people in the workplace become more emotionally competent and effective. This chapter also presents specific techniques that have been used to help people develop competencies in each of the domains of EI initially identified by Goleman: Self-Awareness, Self-Management, Social Awareness, and Relationship Management. The last part of the chapter presents a model for designing effective programs, derived from research on social and emotional learning (SEL) in a variety of contexts.

Chapter Ten offers a different way of thinking about EI training and development activities. Richard Boyatzis presents a model of individual change based on years of research. One part of this research is a series of longitudinal studies now under way at the Weatherhead School of Management at Case Western Reserve University. As Boyatzis discusses, although still in their early stages, these studies show that people can change on the competencies associated with EI. The model Boyatzis presents is also based on a fundamental premise about human behavior: significant and lasting change in adults occurs only when they *want* to change. Thus only learning that is *self-directed* is likely to lead to lasting improvement. The remainder of the chapter discusses the implications of this model of self-directed learning for EI training and development efforts.

Chapter Eleven, by Kathy Kram and Cary Cherniss, presents a different perspective on the development of EI in the workplace. The chapter authors show how relationships in the workplace provide a natural arena for the promotion of emotional intelligence. Because time and budgets for training are increasingly scarce resources, it is vital that we learn how to use these relationships to help people become more emotionally competent. Not all relationships are equally productive of emotional competence. Some may even be destructive. Kram and Cherniss consider the factors that influence the capacity of relationships to promote social and emotional learning. These factors include the level of emotional competence and psychological development that each person brings to the relationship and the group memberships (especially race, ethnicity, and gender) each brings. Also important are routinized patterns of behavior that can facilitate learning through social interaction. Finally, two organizational factors can have a significant influence: formal human resource systems and leadership.

The final chapter, by Cary Cherniss and Robert Caplan, describes how a large U.S. corporation, American Express Financial Advisors, applied many of the guidelines discussed earlier in the successful development of a training program in "emotional competence." What was especially intriguing about this case is that the program was conceived, developed, and implemented several years before Goleman's *Emotional Intelligence* was first published. The authors suggest that the program's success was due primarily to two factors. The first is that the program planners did a sound job of navigating three critical stages in the successful implementation of any innovation: exploration, mutual adaptation, and institutionalization. The second factor is the high level of emotional intelligence of those who implemented the program. This chapter concludes with a number of specific lessons and guidelines for those who wish to implement emotional intelligence programs in their own or others' organizations.

In sum, this book shows the various ways in which EI contributes to greater individual and organizational effectiveness. It also presents the latest thinking and research on how organizational leaders can use EI to improve results. Finally, it points to new directions for EI research, theory, and practice in the future.

April 2001   Cary Cherniss
                                                                   Piscataway, New Jersey

                                                                   Daniel Goleman
                                                                   Williamsburg, Massachusetts

THE CONTRIBUTORS

Cary Cherniss is professor of applied psychology at Rutgers University. He earned a B.A. degree in psychology from the University of California, Berkeley, in 1969 and his Ph.D. degree in psychology from Yale University in 1972. He then went on to teach at the University of Michigan in Ann Arbor, the University of Illinois in Chicago, the Chicago Medical School, and the Illinois Institute of Technology. In 1983, he came to Rutgers to create the Organizational Psychology program in the Graduate School of Applied and Professional Psychology.

Cherniss is a specialist in the areas of emotional intelligence, work stress and burnout, management training and development, planned organizational change, and career development. He has published over forty scholarly articles on these topics, as well as five books: *Promoting Emotional Intelligence in Organizations: Guidelines for Practitioners* (2000, with Mitchel Adler), *The Human Side of Corporate Competitiveness* (1990, with Daniel Fishman), *Professional Burnout in Human Service Organizations* (1980), *Staff Burnout* (1980), and *Beyond Burnout: Helping Teachers, Nurses, Therapists, and Lawyers Recover from Stress and Disillusionment* (1995).

Cherniss has consulted with many organizations in the public and private sectors, including American Express Financial Advisors, Johnson & Johnson, AT&T, Colgate Palmolive, the U.S. Office of Personnel Management, and Marriott. He is director and cochair (with Daniel Goleman) of the Consortium for Research on Emotional Intelligence in Organizations. He is a Fellow of the American

Psychological Association, a member of the Academy of Management, and president of the Society for Community Research and Action (Division 27 of the American Psychological Association).

Daniel Goleman consults internationally and lectures frequently to business, professional, and college audiences. A psychologist who for many years reported on the brain and the behavioral sciences for the *New York Times,* Goleman has also held an appointment as visiting faculty member at Harvard. He received his undergraduate degree from Amherst College, where he was an Alfred P. Sloan Scholar and graduated magna cum laude. His graduate education was at Harvard, where he was a Ford Fellow and received his M.A. and Ph.D. degrees in clinical psychology and personality development (1974).

Goleman is a cofounder of the Collaborative for Social and Emotional Learning (originally based at the Child Studies Center at Yale University and now at the University of Illinois at Chicago), which has a mission to help schools introduce emotional literacy courses. Thousands of schools around the world have begun to implement such programs. He is cochair of the Consortium for Research on Emotional Intelligence in Organizations (based at the Graduate School of Applied and Professional Psychology at Rutgers University), which seeks to recommend best practices for developing emotional competence.

His book *Emotional Intelligence* (1995) was on the *New York Times* bestseller list for a year and a half. With more than five million copies in print worldwide, it has been a best-seller throughout Europe, Asia, and Latin America and has been translated into thirty-three languages. *Working with Emotional Intelligence* (1998) also made the *New York Times* best-seller list, just three weeks after the book's release. Goleman has also received many awards for his writing, including two nominations for the Pulitzer Prize for his articles in the *Times* and a career achievement award for journalism from the American Psychological Association. In recognition of his efforts to communicate the work of the behavioral sciences to the public, he was elected a Fellow of the American Association for the Advancement of Science.

Richard E. Boyatzis is professor of organizational behavior and chair of the Department of Organizational Behavior in the Weatherhead School of Management at Case Western Reserve University. His main areas of research are adult development and leadership. Prior to joining the faculty at CWRU, he was president and CEO of McBer Company. He has also served as an executive with Yankelovich, Skelly and White and has served on the board of that company and the boards of the Reliance Consulting Group and the Hay Group. He has consulted to many Fortune 500 companies, governmental agencies, and companies in Europe in such areas as executive and management selection, appraisal, and development; organizational structure; culture change; R&D productivity; and economic development. He is the author of numerous articles on topics including motivation, self-directed behavioral change, leadership, and managerial competencies and the author of the books *The Competent Manager: A Model for Effective Performance* and *Transforming Qualitative Information: Thematic Analysis and Code Development*. Boyatzis is a coeditor of *Innovations in Professional Education: Steps on a Journey from Teaching to Learning* (with Scott S. Cowen and David A. Kolb). He has a B.S. degree in aeronautics and astronautics from the Massachusetts Institute of Technology (MIT) and M.A. and Ph.D. (1973) degrees in social psychology from Harvard University.

Robert D. Caplan is program research administrator for the Beach Cities Health District, a governmental organization that promotes social and emotional as well as physical wellness in the communities it serves. Previously he directed the doctoral program in applied social and organizational psychology at George Washington University and was a senior program director at the University of Michigan's Survey Research Center in the Institute for Social Research. His research interests include exploring models of the ways human service organizations and their staffs gain and maintain the social and emotional competencies required to be client-focused continuous learning organizations. He is also interested in practical methods of program evaluation that contain self-correcting elements to produce immediate service improvement. Caplan has held National Science Foundation and Fulbright Senior Research Fellowships to India, and his research team won the National Mental Health Association's Lela Rowland Prevention Award for its field experiments on preventive interventions for the unemployed. The coauthor of *Job Demands and Worker Health* (with John R. P. French Jr., Sidney Cobb, Samuel R. Pinneau, and R. Van Harrison) and *The Mechanisms of Stress and Strain* (with John R. P. French Jr. and R. Van Harrison), he holds a Ph.D. degree (1971) in organizational psychology from the University of Michigan.

Vanessa Urch Druskat is an assistant professor in the Department of Organizational Behavior of the Weatherhead School of Management, Case Western Reserve University. Her research focuses on factors that influence the effectiveness of empowered or self-managing work teams. Her writings on required competencies for self-managing work teams, the organizational antecedents of team competencies, the formal and informal leadership of self-managing teams, and the role of emotion in group dynamics and group effectiveness have appeared in such periodicals as the *Journal of Applied Psychology, Leadership Quarterly,* and *Small Group Research;* the book *Research on Managing Groups and Teams* (edited by D. H. Gruenfeld, B. Mannix, and M. Neale); and *The Academy of Management Best Paper Proceedings.* She and her colleague Jane V. Wheeler received the 1999 Walter F. Ulmer Applied Research Award from the Center for Creative Leadership for their paper on the leadership of self-managing teams, and she received the 1992 Kenneth E. Clark Research Award from the Center for Creative Leadership for her paper on gender and leadership style. She received her B.A. degree in psychology from Indiana University, her M.A. degree in organizational psychology from Teachers College, Columbia University, and her Ph.D. degree (1995) in social and organizational psychology from Boston University.

Claudio Fernández-Aráoz is a partner at the executive search firm Egon Zehnder International, a member of that firm's executive committee, and the leader of the firm's internal professional development for its fifty-eight offices worldwide. Since 1986, he has focused on senior executive search assignments. He is also conducting research on the relevance of emotional intelligence and the various competencies for top leadership and managerial positions, and he is the author of the 1999 *Harvard Business Review* article "Hiring Without Firing." Before joining Egon Zehnder International, Fernández-Aráoz worked as an engagement manager for McKinsey and Company in Spain and Italy. He was born and presently lives in Argentina. He was at the top of his class at the Catholic University of Argentina and earned an M.S. degree in industrial engineering from that institution. After a period of working in Argentina in operations and logistics, he obtained his M.B.A. degree at Stanford University in 1983, where he graduated with honors as an Arjay Miller Scholar, financing his studies with an ITT International Fellowship.

Marilyn K. Gowing is vice president–public sector consulting services at Assessment Solutions Incorporated. Previously she was the chief industrial/organizational psychologist in the federal government, managing the Personnel Resources and Development Center, a preeminent psychological research center, which conducts basic, applied, and innovative research in every area of human resource management. She has written numerous journal articles and book chapters and is coauthor of the book *Taxonomies of Human Performance: The Description of Human Tasks* (with Edwin A. Fleishman). Her most recent book is *The New Organizational Reality: Downsizing, Restructuring and Revitalization* (with John Kraft and James Campbell Quick). She has served on the editorial boards of several journals. Gowing has worked in psychological research organizations, a professional association, and several organizational consulting firms as well as for the federal government. She has won numerous awards for her assistance in improving agencies' human resource capacities, including awards from the U.S. Department of Housing and Urban Development, the Office of Personnel Management, and the Secretary of the U.S. Department of Veterans' Affairs. She was named Distinguished Psychologist in Management for the Year 2000 by the Society for Psychologists in Management. She received a B.A. degree in psychology from the College of William and Mary and M.A. and Ph.D. (1982) degrees summa cum laude in industrial and organizational psychology from George Washington University.

Ruth L. Jacobs is a senior consultant and research scientist at Hay/McBer. She received her Ph.D. degree (1992) in psychology from Boston University, where she was a student of David McClelland's. She has done research in the areas of women and leadership. She has been involved in dozens of competency studies during the last decade, and she has consulted to many of the largest firms in the world, including PepsiCo, Compaq, IBM, State Farm, L'Oreal, Unilever, and Toyota.

Kathy E. Kram is a professor in the Department of Organizational Behavior, teaching courses in global management, leadership, team dynamics, and organizational change, and formerly was faculty director of the Executive MBA Program at the Boston University School of Management. Her primary areas of interest are adult development, mentoring and relational learning, diversity in executive development and leadership, and organizational change processes. She is currently studying the nature of the midlife transition for high-achieving women, and investigating individual and organizational conditions that promote emotional competence in work settings. In addition to her book, *Mentoring at Work*, Kram has published in a wide range of journals including *Organizational Dynamics, Academy of Management Journal, Academy of Management Review, Business Horizons, Qualitative Sociology, Mentoring International, Journal of Management Development, Journal of Management Education, Journal of Management, Organizational Behavior and Human Performance,* and *Psychology of Women Quarterly*. She also consults with private and public sector organizations on a variety of human resource management concerns. She received her B.S. and M.S. degrees from MIT's Sloan School of Management, and her Ph.D. degree from Yale University (1980).

Lyle M. Spencer is president of Spencer Research and Technology, and Research Fellow with Competency International, Cybertronics, Hay Group, and LdrGroup. From 1990 to 1994, as president and CEO of the Hay Group subsidiary McBer Company, he established Hay/McBer offices in twenty-four countries. In twenty-five years with McBer, he developed competency models and conducted cost-benefit studies for such clients as AT&T, General Electric, General Motors, IBM, Merck, Mobil, Nortel, the U.S. Army and Navy, and the United Nations Industrial Development Organization (UNIDO). He has trained more than one thousand human resource professionals in competency modeling, cost-benefit evaluation, and reengineering methods. Spencer's books include *Reengineering*

Human Resources, Competence at Work (with S. M. Spencer), and *Calculating Human Resource Costs and Benefits.* He has published more than fifty chapters and articles in such references as the American Management Association's handbooks on recruitment and selection, training and development, compensation, and change management. He also developed the human resource expert system software Cost Benefit Analyst and Hay/McBer Xcel. A graduate of Harvard College, Spencer received his M.B.A. degree from Harvard Business School and his Ph.D. degree (1970) in human development from the University of Chicago.

Steven B. Wolff is assistant professor of management at Marist College in Poughkeepsie, New York. He has over fifteen years of experience in the high-tech industry as an engineer and manager. Wolff has conducted research in the areas of managing performance in self-managed teams, the role of caring behavior in creating team effectiveness, peer feedback, organizational learning, and partnerships between business and public schools. He is also the coauthor of *OB in Action: Cases and Exercises* (with Janet Wohlberg). He is a member of the Academy of Management and the management and engineering honor societies, Beta Gamma Sigma and Tau Beta Pi, respectively. He has worked with the Boston Public Schools to provide training and consultation to school-site councils, a form of self-managed team, and has provided leadership training to principals and headmasters. One school with which he has worked won the National Blue Ribbon Award. Wolff holds an M.S. degree in electrical engineering from Northeastern University and an M.B.A. degree from Babson College. He received his D.B.A. degree (1998) from Boston University, with a concentration on organizational behavior and a minor in adult learning and development.

PART ONE

DEFINING AND ASSESSING EMOTIONAL INTELLIGENCE

CHAPTER ONE

EMOTIONAL INTELLIGENCE AND ORGANIZATIONAL EFFECTIVENESS

Cary Cherniss

In 1981, James Dozier discovered the power of emotional intelligence. It saved his life. Dozier was a U.S. Army brigadier general who was kidnapped by the Red Brigades, an Italian terrorist group. He was held for two months before he was rescued. During the first few days of his captivity, his captors were crazed with the excitement surrounding the event. As Dozier saw them brandishing their guns and becoming increasingly agitated and irrational, he realized his life was in danger. Then he remembered something he had learned about emotion in an executive development program at the Center for Creative Leadership in Greensboro, North Carolina. Emotions are contagious, and a single person can influence the emotional tone of a group by modeling.

Dozier's first task was to get his own emotions under control—no easy feat under the circumstances. But with effort he managed to calm himself. Then he tried to express his calmness in a clear and convincing way through his actions. Soon he noticed that his captors seemed to be "catching" his calmness. They began to calm down themselves and became more rational. When Dozier later looked back on this episode, he was convinced that his ability to manage his own emotional reactions and those of his captors literally saved his life (Campbell, 1990).

The term *emotional intelligence* (EI) had not been coined in 1981, but James Dozier provided a vivid example of what it is: "The ability to perceive and express emotion, assimilate emotion in thought, understand and reason with emotion, and regulate emotion in the self and others" (Mayer, Salovey, & Caruso,

2000, p. 396; for an extended discussion of the varied definitions of emotional intelligence, see Chapter Two). Dozier's experience illustrates emotional intelligence in action. He perceived accurately the emotional reactions of his captors, and he understood the danger that those reactions posed for him. He then was able to regulate his own emotions, and by expressing those emotions effectively, he was able to regulate the emotions of his captors.

Not only does Dozier's experience illustrate what the contributors to this book mean by emotional intelligence, it also demonstrates how emotional intelligence can help people to be more effective at work. However, Dozier's predicament was an extreme and unusual work situation. To what extent is emotional intelligence important for the more typical jobs and work situations that people encounter? What is the connection between emotional intelligence and organizational effectiveness? And finally, can emotional intelligence be taught? And if so, how?

The Impact of EI on Organizational Effectiveness

Look deeply at almost any factor that influences organizational effectiveness, and you will find that emotional intelligence plays a role. For instance, as this volume is being completed, the United States continues an unprecedented period of economic prosperity and growth. The downside of this fortunate circumstance for many organizations is that it has become increasingly more difficult to retain good employees, particularly those with the skills that are important in the high-tech economy. So what aspects of an organization are most important for keeping good employees? A Gallup Organization study of two million employees at seven hundred companies found that how long an employee stays at a company and how productive she is there is determined by her relationship with her immediate supervisor (Zipkin, 2000). Another study quantified this effect further. Spherion, a staffing and consulting firm in Fort Lauderdale, Florida, and Lou Harris Associates, found that only 11 percent of the employees who rated their bosses as excellent said that they were likely to look for a different job in the next year. However, 40 percent of those who rated their bosses as poor said they were likely to leave. In other words, people with good bosses are four times less likely to leave than are those with poor bosses (Zipkin, 2000).

What is it about bosses that influences their relationship with employees? What skills do bosses need to prevent employees from leaving? The most effective bosses are those who have the ability to sense how their employees feel about their work situation and to intervene effectively when those employees begin to feel discouraged or dissatisfied. Effective bosses are also able to manage their own emotions, with the result that employees trust them and feel good about working with them. In short, bosses whose employees stay are bosses who manage with emotional intelligence.

When I ask employees and their bosses to identify the greatest challenges their organizations face, they mention these concerns:

- People need to cope with massive, rapid change.
- People need to be more creative in order to drive innovation.
- People need to manage huge amounts of information.
- The organization needs to increase customer loyalty.
- People need to be more motivated and committed.
- People need to work together better.
- The organization needs to make better use of the special talents available in a diverse workforce.
- The organization needs to identify potential leaders in its ranks and prepare them to move up.
- The organization needs to identify and recruit top talent.
- The organization needs to make good decisions about new markets, products, and strategic alliances.
- The organization needs to prepare people for overseas assignments.

These are the intense needs that face all organizations today, both public sector and private. And in virtually every case, emotional intelligence must play an important role in satisfying the need. For instance, coping with massive change involves, among other things, the ability to perceive and understand the emotional impact of change on ourselves and others. To be effective in helping their organizations manage change, leaders first need to be aware of and to manage their own feelings of anxiety and uncertainty (Bunker, 1997). Then they need to be aware of the emotional reactions of other organizational members and act to help people cope with those reactions. At the same time in this process of coping effectively with massive change, other members of the organization need to be actively involved in monitoring and managing their emotional reactions and those of others.

Let us consider one other challenge, one that might seem less emotional than many of the others in the list. How might emotional intelligence play a role in helping organizational leaders make good decisions about new products, markets, and strategic alliances? Making such decisions involves much more than emotional intelligence. Good data must be assembled, and these data must be analyzed using the most sophisticated tools available. However, in the end, data almost never produce a clear-cut answer. Many important variables can be quantified but not all. Analytical tools can organize most of the information needed for a clear and coherent picture, but almost always there is also some ambiguity and guesswork involved. There comes a point when organizational leaders must rely on their intuition or gut feeling. Such feelings will sometimes point in the right direction and sometimes in the wrong direction. The leaders who are most likely to have feelings that point in the right direction are the ones who have a good sense of why they are reacting as they are. They have learned to discriminate between feelings that are irrelevant and misleading and feelings that are on target. In other words, emotional intelligence enables leaders to tune into the gut feelings that are most accurate and helpful in making difficult decisions.

Emotional intelligence influences organizational effectiveness in a number of areas:

- Employee recruitment and retention
- Development of talent
- Teamwork
- Employee commitment, morale, and health
- Innovation
- Productivity
- Efficiency
- Sales
- Revenues
- Quality of service
- Customer loyalty
- Client or student outcomes

The influence of EI begins with the retention and recruitment of talent. For instance, as Claudio Fernández-Aráoz points out in Chapter Eight, the extent to which candidates' emotional intelligence is considered in making top executive hiring decisions has a significant impact on the ultimate success or failure of those executives. The emotional intelligence of the persons doing the hiring is also crucial for good hiring decisions.

Emotional intelligence also affects the development of talent. For instance, Kathy Kram and I (Chapter Eleven) show how relationships at work can contribute to the development of talent. However, not all relationships are equally effective in doing so. The emotional intelligence of the mentor, boss, or peer will influence the potential of a relationship with that person for helping organizational members develop and use the talent that is crucial for organizational effectiveness. (See Chapter Ten for further discussion of emotional intelligence and the development of talent.)

Thus far I have been discussing individual emotional intelligence. However, it is also possible to think of emotional intelligence as a group-level phenomenon. As Vanessa Druskat and Steven Wolff explain in Chapter Six, there are emotionally intelligent groups as well as emotionally intelligent individuals. Druskat and Wolff suggest that emotionally intelligent teams display the kinds of cooperation, commitment, and creativity that are increasingly important for organizational effectiveness. Furthermore, they show that although the emotional intelligence of individual members contributes to the level of emotional intelligence found in the team, there are other sources of group EI as well. Also, just as individual EI contributes to the EI of the group, group EI contributes to the EI of group members. People who are members of emotionally intelligent groups become more emotionally intelligent individuals.

Many of these ways that EI influences organizational effectiveness are subtle and difficult to measure. However, as Lyle Spencer shows in Chapter Four, we now are able to estimate more precisely than ever before the economic utility of EI in organizations. And the results of these analyses are consistent with commonsense notions: competencies associated with EI play an important role in determining the effectiveness of organizations.

Sources of EI in Organizations

If individual and group emotional intelligence contribute to organizational effectiveness, what in the organization contributes to individual and group emotional intelligence? Such a question is especially important for anyone who wishes to harness the power of emotional intelligence for organizational improvement. Figure 1.1 presents a model that points to some broad factors in organizations that contribute to emotional intelligence. Those who wish to help individuals and groups become more emotionally intelligent can use this model as a starting point.

Emotional intelligence, as Goleman (1995a) pointed out in his first book on the topic, emerges primarily through relationships. At the same time, emotional intelligence affects the quality of relationships. Kram and I (Chapter Eleven) note that both formally arranged relationships and naturally occurring relationships in organizations contribute to emotional intelligence. Relationships can help people become more emotionally intelligent even when they are not set up for that purpose. The model suggests that ultimately any attempts to improve emotional intelligence in organizations will depend on relationships. Even formal training interventions or human resource policies will affect emotional intelligence through their effect on relationships among individuals and groups in the organization.

FIGURE 1.1. A MODEL OF EMOTIONAL INTELLIGENCE AND ORGANIZATIONAL EFFECTIVENESS.

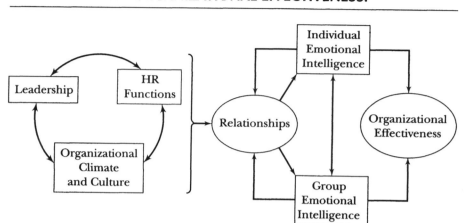

The left-hand portion of the model (Figure 1.1), illustrates three organizational factors that are interrelated. Each of these factors influences emotional intelligence through its impact on relationships, and each factor influences the other two. For instance, in Chapter Three Goleman presents data showing how the emotional intelligence of organizational leadership influences organizational effectiveness through its impact on organizational climate. At the same time, the HR functions of recruitment and selection, training and development, and management performance have a strong impact on leadership EI (as Ruth Jacobs points out in Chapter Seven). However, leadership in turn will influence the extent to which HR functions are effective in helping organizational members increase their EI. As several chapters in this book show, leaders who lack EI provide poor models for the development of EI in others, and they are unlikely to provide the kind of support and encouragement necessary for effective EI promotion efforts.

The model suggests two important implications for practice. First, any effort to improve the EI of organizational members will ultimately fail unless it affects naturally occurring relationships among those members. Formal, off-site training programs can have value, for example, but only if they lead to sustained changes in interpersonal and intergroup relationships back in the organization (see Chapters Nine and Ten for more on this point). The second important implication is that interventions that focus on only one part of the model are not likely to be very effective. So, for instance, a training program designed to help organizational members become more emotionally intelligent will be of limited value by itself because it targets only one part of the model—HR functions. Such training efforts will succeed only if the organizational leadership and culture support them (see Chapter Twelve for a case study that illustrates this point).

All models are necessarily incomplete. This one captures some but not all of the important forces that contribute to the development of individual and group EI in organizations. For instance, as Boyatzis (Chapter Ten) and Kram and I (Chapter Eleven) note, individuals bring into the organization values, aspirations, and developmental histories that influence their response to EI promotion efforts. Moreover this model does not begin to suggest the rich and complex ways in which HR functions, to take just one example, can influence the level of organizational EI (see Chapter Seven). Subsequent chapters of this book, however, flesh out different parts of the model and the relationships between those parts and organizational effectiveness.

Some Unresolved Issues and Dilemmas

Although psychologists have been studying aspects of emotional intelligence in organizations for decades (without using that term), the concept as it is now understood is relatively new. There still is much that is unclear about the nature of emotional intelligence, the way in which it should be measured, and its impact on individual performance and organizational effectiveness. In some cases this lack of clarity has led to conflict and controversy among researchers and practitioners.

One of the most basic controversies involves the definition of the concept itself. The term *emotional quotient* (EQ), as Goleman notes in Chapter Two, was first coined by Bar-On (1988) as a counterpart to *intelligence quotient* (IQ), that is, to cognitive ability. Bar-On thought of EQ as representing a set of social and emotional abilities that help individuals cope with the demands of daily life. Salovey and Mayer (1990) had something different and more restricted in mind when they introduced the term *emotional intelligence* several years later. For them, EI concerned the way in which an individual processes information about emotion and emotional responses. Finally, Goleman (1995a) initially saw EI as an idea or theme that emerged from a large set of research findings on the role of the emotions in human life. These findings pointed to different ways in which competencies such as Empathy, Learned Optimism, and Self-Control contributed to important outcomes in the family, the workplace, and other life arenas.

Fortunately, there seems to be some progress in clarifying the concept of emotional intelligence. Goleman has recently made a distinction between emotional intelligence and emotional competencies (see Chapter Two). According to this view, emotional intelligence provides the bedrock for the development of a large number of competencies that help people perform more effectively. For instance, managers who possess a high level of what Salovey and Mayer (1990) think of as EI will not necessarily be more effective than other managers in dealing with conflict among their employees. However, they will be able to learn and to use conflict management skills more readily than will individuals who bring less EI to the job. This recent formulation helps clarify the relationship between the three definitions of EI that are used most frequently in the field. Nevertheless, it probably will be some time before there is real clarity and consensus concerning the nature of emotional intelligence.

A related area of controversy is the measurement of emotional intelligence. As Gowing shows in Chapter Five, several different instruments are now available that claim to measure EI. All are of recent vintage except for Bar-On's EQ-i, which was developed in the mid-eighties, and all have both strengths and weaknesses. Gowing clarifies how the different instruments overlap and how they diverge in what they measure. Although much progress has been made and all the current measures show promise, there still is much work to be done in clarifying and refining measurement methodology.

Another unresolved issue concerns the relative predictive power of EI and IQ. Although Goleman (1998b) has argued that EI accounts for more of the variance in individual and group performance than purely cognitive ability does, in Chapter Three he concedes that the issue is complex. Part of the problem is that these abilities are not mutually exclusive: emotional intelligence by any definition is really a combination of cognitive and emotional abilities. As Goleman has suggested elsewhere, the essence of emotional intelligence is the integration of the emotional centers of the brain (the limbic system) and the cognitive centers (prefrontal cortex). Similarly, Mayer, Salovey, and Caruso (2000) conceive of EI as a set of skills that involve processing information about emotion.

Empirical research leaves little doubt that (1) IQ and other measures of cognitive ability are limited in their power to predict who will succeed and (2) measures of EI are strongly correlated with performance in certain situations (see Chapter Four for data supporting this notion). However, there has been little good research that compares the predictive power of IQ and EI. As Goleman (Chapter Two) notes, what is needed now is a good longitudinal study using sound measures of both cognitive and emotional skills.

An often overlooked fact is that EI is composed of varied competencies, and it still is unclear exactly how they are related. Both Mayer et al. (2000) and Goleman (1998b) have developed models suggesting how different competencies may be related. For instance, Goleman proposes that Self-Awareness is the foundation for two other EI abilities: Self-Control and Social Awareness. Self-Control and

Social Awareness, in turn, are the foundation for Social Skills. Although some research provides support for this model, other research suggests some of the abilities may be inversely related. To take but one example, Self-Control (the ability to inhibit one's impulses and actions) would seem to be antagonistic to Initiative (the propensity to take action without strong external pressure to do so) (Boyatzis, 1999a). Such issues may ultimately be settled when researchers begin to explore the possibility of nonlinear relationships between the different dimensions and competencies. It may be, for example, that the relationship between Self-Control and Initiative is curvilinear: increases in Self-Control may contribute to the capacity to show Initiative up to a certain point, whereas increased Self-Control beyond that point may inhibit Initiative. (See Chapter Seven for a discussion of Boyatzis's ideas on this issue and more examples of the ways in which EI abilities may be related.)

The relationship between individual and group emotional intelligence presents us with yet another unresolved issue. Druskat and Wolff argue in Chapter Six that group EI is not simply the sum total of the individual EI of group members. Having a few people with high individual EI is not enough to generate the conditions necessary for teamwork and group effectiveness. Groups also need norms and enduring processes that support awareness and regulation of emotion within the group. According to Druskat and Wolff's model, it is these norms and processes that are the essence of group EI.

Although Druskat and Wolff present a compelling case for making a distinction between individual and group EI, there are currently few data directly supporting it. What we need is a study that measures both individual EI and group EI and then examines whether adding group EI increases our ability to predict group effectiveness. Before we can conduct such a study, we need good measures of both group EI as Druskat and Wolff define it and individual EI.

I conclude this overview of the issues by noting two dilemmas, one involving practice and the other research. The first dilemma is that the same conditions that make emotional intelligence so vital for organizational effectiveness also make EI difficult to nurture in organizations. This dilemma results from the current climate in contemporary organizations. As Kram and I (Chapter Eleven) note, the highly turbulent, dynamic, and competitive environment that has come to characterize the U.S. economic system at the dawn of the new millennium makes emotional intelligence more vital than ever before. Rapid technological change, an increasingly diverse workforce, and global markets also contribute to a growing need for EI. Yet these factors are also creating a climate in which it is increasingly difficult for people to develop and use the emotional intelligence that is so necessary for organizational effectiveness. Even senior executives find it difficult to focus on anything other than short-term results. Yet the development of emotional intelligence requires sustained reflection and learning. People must step back from the day-to-day focus on getting more done and instead concentrate on personal development. Carving out time each week for such activity seems to many an unaffordable luxury. Only the most emotionally intelligent have the insight and determination to do so. It is not clear how those who lack this level of EI can be helped to change their priorities in ways that enable them to develop it.

The second dilemma results from the fact that much of the research on which the field is now based has been conducted by firms that have little incentive to publish their work and considerable incentive not to. For instance, much of the most exciting and compelling research comes from consulting firms such as Hay/McBer (see Chapters Two, Three, Four, and Seven). These firms conduct studies for corporate clients that want to use the research for their own purposes. These clients are not willing to pay the firms to prepare articles about the study findings for publication in scientific journals, and so it is difficult for the researchers employed at these firms to take the time to prepare such articles.

Perhaps more crucial, the data collected in these studies are proprietary. The clients would prefer that the details of the research be known to as few as possible, particularly not to their corporate competitors. Yet unpublished research is of uncertain validity. The essence of the scientific enterprise is full and open communication not only of the results of research but also of the ways in which the data were collected and analyzed. The peer review process that occurs when a study is submitted for publication in a scientific journal is an imperfect process, but it does provide an opportunity to scrutinize both the methods and results of research. Until more research on EI in organizations finds its way into the scientific literature, practice will not be based on a firm foundation. It is the hope of the editors that this volume will inspire not only more good research on the topic of EI in organizations but also the publication of that research in peer-reviewed scientific journals. However, finding support for such efforts in the current business climate is yet another dilemma facing the field.

CHAPTER TWO

EMOTIONAL INTELLIGENCE

Issues in Paradigm Building

Daniel Goleman

It was Super Bowl Sunday, that sacrosanct day when most American men are to be found watching the biggest football game of the year. The flight from New York to Detroit was delayed two hours in departing, and the tension among the passengers—almost entirely businessmen—was palpable. As they finally arrived at Detroit, a mysterious glitch with the boarding ramp made the plane stop some one hundred feet from the gate. Frantic about arriving late, people on the plane leapt to their feet anyway.

One of the flight attendants went to the intercom. How could she most effectively get all the passengers to comply with federal regulations requiring they all be seated before the plane could finish taxiing to the gate?

She did *not* announce in a stern voice, "Federal regulations require that you be seated before we can move to the gate."

Instead, she warbled in a singsong tone, suggestive of a playful warning to an adorable small child who has done something naughty but forgivable, "You're staaanding!"

At that, everyone laughed and sat back down until the plane had finished taxiing to the gate. And given the circumstances, the passengers got off the plane in a surprisingly good mood [Goleman, 1998b].

The flight attendant's adept intervention speaks to the great divide in human abilities that lies between the mind and heart, or more technically, between cognition and emotion. Some abilities are purely cognitive, like IQ or technical expertise. Other abilities integrate thought and feeling and fall within the domain of *emotional intelligence,* a term that highlights the crucial role of emotion in their performance.

All emotional intelligence abilities involve some degree of skill in the affective domain, along with skill in whatever cognitive elements are also at play in each ability. This stands in sharp contrast to purely cognitive aspects of intelligence, which, to a large degree, computers can be programmed to execute about as well as a person can: on that Sunday flight a digitized voice could have announced, "Federal regulations require that all passengers be seated before we proceed to the gate." But although the basic content of the digitized and "live" messages might have been the same, lacking the flight attendant's sense of timing, artful wit, and affect, the computerized version would have fallen flat. People might have grudgingly complied with the firm directive but would have undergone nothing like the positive mood shift the attendant accomplished. She was able to hit exactly the right *emotional* note—something cognitive capabilities alone are insufficient for, because by definition they lack the human flair for feelings.

Peter Salovey and John Mayer first proposed their theory of emotional intelligence (EI) in 1990. Over the intervening decade, theorists have generated several distinctive EI models, including the elaborations by Salovey and Mayer on their own theory. The theory as formulated by Salovey and Mayer (1990; Mayer, Salovey, & Caruso, 2000) framed EI within a model of intelligence. Reuven Bar-On (1988) has placed EI in the context of personality theory, specifically a model of well-being. My own model formulates EI in terms of a *theory of performance* (Goleman, 1998b). As I will show in this chapter and Chapter Three, an EI-based theory of performance has direct applicability to the domain of work and organizational effectiveness, particularly in predicting excellence in jobs of all kinds, from sales to leadership.

All these EI models, however, share a common core of basic concepts. Emotional intelligence, at the most general level, refers to the *abilities to recognize and regulate emotions in ourselves and in others.* This most parsimonious definition suggests four major EI domains: *Self-Awareness, Self-Management, Social Awareness,* and *Relationship Management.* (As theories develop, the terms they use develop too. As I discuss in Chapter Three, these are the domain names in the most recent version of my model. Some readers may be familiar with earlier versions of these names.)

These four domains are shared by all the main variations of EI theory, though the terms used to refer to them differ. The domains of Self-Awareness and Self-Management, for example, fall within what Gardner (1983) calls *intrapersonal intelligence,* and Social Awareness and Relationship Management fit within his definition of *interpersonal intelligence.* Some make a distinction between *emotional intelligence* and *social intelligence*, seeing EI as personal self-management capabilities like impulse control and social intelligence as relationship skills (see, for example, Bar-On, 2000a). The movement in education that seeks to implement curricula that teach EI skills uses the general term *social and emotional learning*, or SEL (Salovey & Sluyter, 1997).

The EI model seems to be emerging as an influential framework in psychology. The span of psychological fields that are now informed by (and that inform) the EI model ranges from neuroscience to health psychology. Among the areas with the strongest connections to EI are developmental, educational, clinical and counseling, social, and industrial and organizational psychology. Indeed, instructional segments on EI are now routinely included in many college-level and graduate courses in these subjects.

One main reason for this penetration seems to be that the concept of emotional intelligence offers a language and framework capable of integrating a wide range of research findings in psychology. Beyond that, EI offers a positive model for psychology. Like other positive models, it has implications for the ways we might tackle many problems of our day—for prevention activities in physical and mental health care and for effective interventions in schools and communities, businesses, and organizations (Seligman & Csikszentmihalyi, 2000). Our increasing understanding of EI also suggests a promising scientific agenda, one that goes beyond the borders of personality, IQ, and academic achievement to study a broader spectrum of the psychological mechanisms that allow individuals to flourish in their lives, their jobs, and their families and as citizens in their communities.

In this chapter and the next I seek to explore the implications of the EI framework for the workplace, and particularly for identifying the active ingredients in outstanding performance, and to review the business case for the utility to an organization of selecting, promoting, and training people for EI. Specifically, this chapter offers a brief history of the EI concept and the increasing interest it is generating, discusses concerns about definitions and means of distinguishing EI abilities from other abilities, and introduces some ideas and data for comparing EI and IQ as predictors of how well a person will perform in a job.

The EI Paradigm Evolves

A paradigm, writes Thomas Kuhn, in his landmark work *The Structure of Scientific Revolutions* (1970), "is an object for further articulation and specification under new or more stringent conditions" (p. 23). He adds that once a model or paradigm has been articulated, the signs of scientific vigor include "the proliferation of competing articulations, the willingness to try anything, the expression of explicit discontent, the recourse to philosophy and to debate over fundamentals" (p. 91). By Kuhn's criteria, the emotional intelligence paradigm shows signs of having reached a state of scientific maturity.

It has taken decades to reach this point. In the field of psychology the roots of EI theory go back at least to the beginnings of the intelligence testing movement. E. L. Thorndike (1920), professor of educational psychology at Columbia University Teachers College, was one of the first to identify the aspect of EI he called *social intelligence*. In 1920 he included it in the broad spectrum of capacities that individuals possess, their "varying amounts of different intelligences." Social intelligence, wrote Thorndike, is "the ability to understand and manage men and women, boys and girls—to act wisely in human relations" (p. 228). It is an ability that "shows itself abundantly in the nursery, on the playground, in barracks and factories and salesrooms, but it eludes the formal standardized conditions of the testing laboratory" (p. 231). Although Thorndike did once propose a means of evaluating social intelligence in the laboratory—a simple process of matching pictures of emotive faces with descriptions of emotions—he also maintained that because social intelligence manifests in social interaction, "genuine situations with real persons" would be necessary to accurately measure it.

In 1937, Robert Thorndike and Saul Stern reviewed the attempts to measure the social intelligence E. L. Thorndike had discussed, identifying three different areas "adjacent to social intelligence, perhaps related to it, and often confused with it" (p. 275). The first area encompassed primarily an individual's attitude toward society and its various components: politics, economics, and values such as honesty. The second involved social knowledge: being well versed in sports, contemporary issues, and general "information about society." This area seemed often conflated with the first. The third form of social intelligence was an individual's degree of social adjustment: introversion and extroversion were measured by individuals' responses to questionnaires (p. 276). One widely known questionnaire of the time that Thorndike and Stern reviewed was the George Washington Social Intelligence Test, developed in 1926. It measured, for example, an individual's judgment in social situations and in relationship problems; recognition of the "mental state" of a speaker (measured through ability to match the person's words with the names of emotions), and ability to identify emotional expression (measured through ability to match pictures of faces with the corresponding emotions).

But Thorndike and Stern concluded that the attempts to measure the "ability to deal with people" had more or less failed: "It may be that social intelligence is a complex of several different abilities, or a complex of an enormous number of specific social habits and attitudes." And they added, "We hope that further investigation, via situation tests, movies, etc., getting closer to the actual social reaction and further from words, may throw more light on the nature of ability to manage and understand people" (p. 284).

The next half century of psychology, dominated as it was by the behaviorist paradigm on one hand and the IQ testing movement on the other, turned its back on the EI idea. Still, even David Wechsler (1952), as he continued to develop his widely used IQ test, nodded to "affective capacities" as part of the human repertoire of capabilities.

Howard Gardner (1983) had a major hand in resurrecting EI theory in psychology. His influential model of multiple intelligence includes two varieties of *personal intelligence,* the *interpersonal* and *intrapersonal intelligences;* EI, as mentioned earlier, can be seen as elaborating on the role of emotion in these domains.

Reuven Bar-On (1988) developed perhaps the first attempt to assess EI in terms of a measure of well-being. In his doctoral dissertation he used the term *emotional quotient* ("EQ"), long before it gained widespread popularity as a name for emotional intelligence and before Salovey and Mayer had published their first model of emotional intelligence. Bar-On (2000a) now defines EI in terms of an array of emotional and social knowledge and abilities that influence our overall ability to effectively cope with environmental demands. This array includes (1) the ability to be aware of, to understand, and to express oneself; (2) the ability to be aware of, to understand, and to relate to others; (3) the ability to deal with strong emotions and control one's impulses; and (4) the ability to adapt to change and to solve problems of a personal or a social nature. The five main domains in his model are *intrapersonal skills, interpersonal skills, adaptability, stress management,* and *general mood* (Bar-On, 1997b).

Finally, in 1990, Peter Salovey at Yale and his colleague John Mayer, now at the University of New Hampshire, published the seminal article "Emotional Intelligence," the most influential statement of EI theory in its current form. Salovey and Mayer's original model (1990) identified emotional intelligence as the "ability to monitor one's own and other's feelings and emotions, to discriminate among them, and to use this information to guide one's thinking and action" (p. 189). Citing a need to distinguish emotional intelligence abilities from social traits or talents, Salovey and Mayer evolved a model with a cognitive emphasis. It focused on specific mental aptitudes for recognizing and marshalling emotions (for example, knowing what someone is feeling is a mental aptitude, whereas being outgoing and warm is a behavior). A comprehensive EI model, they argued, must include some measure of "thinking about feeling," an aptitude lacked by models that focus on simply perceiving and regulating feelings.

Their current model is decidedly cognitive in focus (Mayer & Salovey, 1997). In this model, emotional intelligence comprises four tiers of abilities that range from basic psychological processes to more complex processes integrating emotion and cognition. In the first tier of this "mental ability model" is the complex of skills that allow an individual to perceive, appraise, and express emotions. Abilities here include identifying one's own and other's emotions, expressing one's own emotions, and discriminating the expressions of emotion in others. The second tier abilities involve using emotions to facilitate and prioritize thinking: employing the emotions to aid in judgment, recognizing that mood swings can lead to a consideration of alternative viewpoints, and understanding that a shift in emotional state and perspective can encourage different kinds of problem solving. In the third tier are skills such as labeling and distinguishing between emotions (differentiating liking and loving, for instance), understanding complex mixtures of feelings (such as love and hate), and formulating rules about feelings: for example, that anger often gives way to shame and that loss is usually accompanied by sadness. The fourth tier of the model is the general ability to marshal the emotions in support of some social goal. In this more complex level of emotional intelligence are the skills that allow individuals to selectively engage in or detach from emotions and to monitor and manage emotions in themselves and in others.

Salovey and Mayer's 1997 model is developmental: the complexity of emotional skill grows from the first tier to the fourth. However, all the mental aptitudes they describe fit within the general matrix of self-other recognition or regulation.

The Increasing Interest in EI

My primary role as an EI theorist has been to propose a theory of performance that builds on the basic EI model, adapting it to predict personal effectiveness at work and in leadership (Goleman, 1998b). As I have done so, my role has also been that of a synthesizer, bringing together a broad array of findings and theories in psychology and integrating them into the emotional intelligence framework.

In my role as a science journalist, I have aimed to disseminate the EI concept, primarily through my book *Emotional Intelligence* (Goleman, 1995a) but also through other publications (for example, Goleman, 1998a, 1998b, 2000a, 2000b). The EI concept has found remarkably receptive audiences throughout the world: the 1995 book has, at this writing, been published in thirty-three foreign editions, is available in more than fifty countries, and has more than five million copies in print worldwide. Howard Gardner (1999) contends that *Emotional Intelligence* is now the most widely read social science book in the world. Amazon.com now lists more than seventy titles on emotional intelligence.

My 1998 follow-up book, *Working with Emotional Intelligence*, articulated my EI-based theory of performance, made the business case for the importance of EI at work, and set forth guidelines for effective individual development of the key EI-based competencies. That book has also been widely published, as of this writing going into print in twenty-nine foreign editions and becoming a best-selling business book in many countries.

Although this wave of interest has, perhaps inevitably, given rise to many questionable claims for EI—particularly in the business realm—that should not detract from the solid science that supports EI or from its implications for psychology. As a theoretical construct the EI model is very new. Yet in the last few years psychologists have begun the process of establishing validity for measurement tools (Davies, Stankov, & Roberts, 1998). There have been some detours in this process. One of the stranger ones came when a group of Australian psychologists seized on an informational quiz I had compiled in 1995, somewhat in the spirit of the satirical *Journal of Irreproduceable Results,* for a popular magazine (Goleman, 1995b). Without contacting me, the psychologists treated the quiz as though it were a serious measure (Davies et al., 1998). They were apparently oblivious to my warning preceding the quiz that there were as yet (in 1995) no well-validated paper-and-pencil assessments of EI. They also missed the pointed humor in the quiz scoring key, which rated answers on a scale where the low end was "Newt" and the high end "Gandhi." And they earnestly reported that the quiz had abysmal reliability and validity!

Despite such digressions, the EI construct has now passed several validation benchmarks. In terms of formal theory, EI meets traditional criteria for an intelligence (Mayer, Caruso, & Salovey, 2000a). As I have discussed, in the influential framework of multiple intelligences formulated by Howard Gardner (1999), EI fits squarely within the spectrum of personal intelligence, elaborating on the role of emotions in the intrapersonal and interpersonal intelligences. And there is now an array of validated instruments for assessing aspects of EI (see, for example, Bar-On, 2000a; Mayer, Caruso, & Salovey, 2000b; Boyatzis, Goleman, & Rhee, 2000).

In addition, the EI model is already influential in the business community, unusually so for such a recently proposed theory. Organizations are applying an array of EI-based instruments for predicting on-the-job performance (as Marilyn Gowing discusses in Chapter Five). A strong interest in the professional applications of the EI concept is apparent in the field of industrial and organizational psychology. The American Society for Training and Development, for example, has published a volume describing "best practice" guidelines for helping people in organizations cultivate the EI-based competencies that distinguish outstanding performers from average ones (Cherniss & Adler, 2000). An article I published in the *Harvard Business Review* on the role of emotional intelligence in effective leadership (Goleman, 1998a) immediately became the review's most requested reprint. This response also suggests high levels of interest in EI in the business community.

And there are other signs of considerable interest: for example, the first annual conference on EI and the workplace, sponsored by conference promoter Linkage, Inc., in 1999, was the most heavily enrolled of Linkage's many professional conferences that year.

The model of EI as a variety of intelligence has a wide range of implications. But I believe that when it comes to applications in the workplace and organizational life, the EI-based theory of performance I articulate in the next chapter has more direct implications—and applications—particularly in predicting and developing the hallmarks of outstanding performers in jobs of every kind and at every level.

Issues in EI Theory

Arguing from their framework of EI as a theory of intelligence, Mayer, Salovey, and Caruso (2000) make a distinction between EI models that are *mixed* and those that are *pure* models, or *ability* models, focusing exclusively on cognitive aptitudes. Mixed models, they argue, contain a melange of abilities, behaviors, and general disposition and conflate personality attributes—such as optimism and persistence—with mental ability.

Based on their reading of my 1995 book, Mayer, Salovey, and Caruso (2000) contend that my EI model is mixed. But the point of that book was to explore EI as a groundbreaking conception of intelligence rather than to systematically articulate an EI model. The EI-based theory of performance I first described in *Working with Emotional Intelligence* in 1998 is a formulation that seems to meet Mayer et al.'s criteria for a pure model. It is competency based, comprising a discrete set of abilities that integrate affective and cognitive skills but are distinct from abilities measured by traditional IQ tests.

For example, I agree with Mayer, Salovey, and Caruso's critique that a "warm and outgoing nature" is not an EI competence. It may be seen as a personality trait. However, it may also be a reflection of a specific set of EI competencies, chiefly those involving the ability to relate positively to others—that is, those found in the Social Awareness and Relationship Management clusters. Likewise, optimism, although it may be seen as a personality trait, may also refer to specific behaviors that contribute to the competence I label Achievement Drive.

Mayer, Salovey, and Caruso's model draws upon a psychometric tradition that an intelligence must meet three criteria to be defined as such. The proposed intelligence must be conceptual (that is, it must reflect mental aptitudes rather than behaviors), it must be correlational (that is, it must share similarities with yet remain distinct from other established intelligences), and it must be developmental (that is, the aptitudes that characterize it must increase with an individual's experience and age). Mayer et al. demonstrate that emotional intelligence meets these criteria.

Arguing from a different perspective, Howard Gardner (1983, 1999) has proposed broadening our notion of intelligence so that it incorporates many significant faculties that have traditionally been beyond its scope. The psychometric tradition invoked by Mayer, Salovey, and Caruso (2000), Gardner argues, is too narrow. The psychometric tradition focuses on intellectual aptitudes that can be measured by standardized tests, but performance on such tests does not necessarily translate into success in school or in life. In expanding the range of significant aptitudes for such success, Gardner (1999) defines an intelligence as "the biopsychological potential to process information that can be activated in a cultural setting to solve problems or create products that are of value in a culture" (pp. 33–34).

Gardner thus adds several new items to the standard list of criteria for an intelligence. His criteria suggest further arguments for considering EI a distinct variety of intelligence.

- *Potential for isolation by brain damage, making it separable from other abilities in the functioning of the brain.* Studies have indicated that trauma to the brain's emotional circuitry and that circuitry's connections to the prefrontal areas can have significant consequences for the performance of competencies associated with EI, such as Empathy or Collaboration, yet can leave abilities associated with pure intellect entirely intact (Damasio, 1994).
- *An evolutionary history and evolutionary plausibility.* The limbic structures in the brain that govern emotion integrate with neocortical structures, particularly the prefrontal areas, in producing the instinctual emotional responses that have been essential for our survival throughout human evolution (Lewis, Amini, & Lannon, 2000). These prefrontal limbic structures appear to be the underlying circuits for the bulk of the EI competencies.
- *An identifiable core operation or set of operations.* A universal characteristic of EI models is a 2 × 2 core set of operations constituting the overall ability to recognize and regulate emotions in oneself and others. (Figure 3.1 is an example of this core set of operations.)
- *Susceptibility to encoding in a symbol system.* We are able to articulate our feelings and the operations of the core EI abilities. (The EI theory of performance discussed in Chapter Three represents one form of this encoding.)
- *A distinct developmental history, along with a definable set of expert, or end state, performances.* Emotional skills range from the simple (recognizing that you're upset) to the complex (artfully calming down an upset colleague). Emotional skills

tend to develop in children at specific and recognizable stages: for example, there is a point at which young children become able to label emotions and talk about their feelings, and this ability precedes the ability to recognize feelings in others and to soothe them (see, for example, Saarni, 1997). Experts, such as high performers in the workplace, exhibit this developmental dimension in their set of learned EI competencies (Goleman, 1998b).

EI Versus IQ as a Predictor of Workplace Performance

Does EI predict success more strongly than IQ? In one sense, this question is purely academic: in life, cognitive abilities and emotional intelligence always interplay. But in another sense, it has practical implications for significant workplace decisions. For example, in Chapter Eight Claudio Fernández-Aráoz offers qualitative data suggesting that basing the selection of high-level executives solely on their academic intelligence and business expertise and ignoring their emotional intelligence often leads to poor choices that can be disastrous for an organization. Data establishing the relative contribution of EI and IQ to effective performance would be of both theoretical and practical importance—for instance, providing a scientific rationale for making more balanced decisions in hiring and promotions.

There is good reason to expect that EI and IQ make separate and discrete contributions to performance. For one thing, early studies of the correlation between IQ and EI show a range from 0 to .36, depending on the measures used. John Mayer, using his own EI measure, reports a zero correlation with fluid intelligence and a .36 correlation with verbal IQ; Reuven Bar-On, using his own measure, finds correlations ranging from .06 to .12—positive but not significant (Mayer, 2000; Bar-On, 2000a).

However, the EI concept has been articulated relatively recently, and there has not yet been time to conduct a longitudinal study designed to assess the predictive power of EI relative to IQ in distinguishing workplace performance over the course of a career. My belief is that if such a study were done, IQ would be a much stronger predictor than EI of which jobs or professions people can enter. Because IQ stands as a proxy for the cognitive complexity a person can process, it should predict what technical expertise that person can master. Technical expertise, in turn, represents the major set of threshold competencies that determine whether a person can get and keep a job in a given field. IQ, then, plays a sorting function in determining what jobs people can hold. However, having enough cognitive intelligence to hold a given job does not by itself predict whether one will be a star performer or rise to management or leadership positions in one's field.

In my own analysis of competency data for outstanding performers within a given field, an emphasis on emotional intelligence–based abilities emerged. These data were gathered from several hundred organizations (Goleman, 1998b). Mostly proprietary and so not typically shared outside companies, they reveal the competencies that a given organization has concluded distinguish star performers from average ones in a specific job or role. Such studies are undertaken for competitive, strategic reasons: companies want to identify these key capabilities so that they can hire and promote people who have them or develop them in their employees (Spencer & Spencer, 1993).

The competencies in these models generally fall into one of three domains: technical skills (for example, software programming), purely cognitive abilities (for example, analytical reasoning), and abilities in the EI range (such as customer service or conflict management abilities). These EI-based competencies combine both cognitive and emotional skills, and so are distinguished from purely cognitive abilities like IQ and from technical skills, which have no such emotional component.

Comparing the three domains, I found that for jobs of all kinds, emotional competencies were twice as prevalent among distinguishing competencies as were technical skills and purely cognitive abilities combined (Goleman, 1998b). In general the higher a position in an organization, the more EI mattered: for individuals in leadership positions, 85 percent of their competencies were in the EI domain. These competency models reflect the perceived value of EI competencies relative to technical and cognitive abilities and so are highly consequential. They already guide decisions about who is hired, who is put on a fast track for promotion, and where to focus development efforts—particularly for leadership—in many of the largest organizations throughout the world (Spencer & Spencer, 1993).

EI may so strongly outstrip intellect alone in this context because those in the pools that were evaluated had had to clear relatively high entry hurdles for IQ and technical competence. For most positions, particularly those at the higher levels of an organization, competencies in technical and cognitive realms are *threshold* skills, essential requirements for entry into fields like engineering, law, or the executive management of an organization. Because everyone in a given field has its threshold skills, these basic abilities lose their power as *distinguishing* competencies, the capabilities that set outstanding performers apart from average.

IQ, then, mainly predicts what profession an individual can hold a job in— for instance, it takes a certain mental acumen to pass the bar exam or the MCATs. Estimates are that in order to pass the requisite cognitive hurdles such as exams or required coursework or mastery of technical subjects and enter a profession like law, engineering, or senior management, individuals need an IQ in the 110 to 120 range (Spencer & Spencer, 1993). That means that once one is in the pool of people in a profession, one competes with people who are also at the high end of the bell curve for IQ. This is why, even though IQ is a strong predictor of success among the general population, its predictive power for outstanding performance weakens greatly once the individuals being compared narrow to a pool of people in a given job in an organization, particularly at its higher levels (Goleman, 1998b).

In contrast, there is less systematic selection pressure for emotional intelligence along the way to entering the ranks of such professions. Of course some minimal level of EI is needed to be successful in school and to enter a profession, but because there is no specific EI hurdle one must clear to enter a profession, there is a much wider range of EI abilities among those one competes with in one's field. For that reason, once people are in a given job, role, or profession, EI emerges as a more powerful predictor of who succeeds and who does not—for instance, who is promoted to the upper echelons of management and who passed over.

In short, my position is that IQ will be a more powerful predictor than EI of individuals' career success in studies of large populations over the career course because it sorts people before they embark on a career, determining which fields or professions they can enter. But when studies look *within* a job or profession to learn which individuals rise to the top and which plateau or fail, EI should prove a more powerful predictor of success than IQ.

IQ Versus EI: The Data

My position on this question has been misrepresented by John Mayer and his colleagues (Mayer, Salovey, and Caruso, 2000), apparently based on a misreading of my 1995 book, in which I state that EI "can be as powerful, and at times more powerful, than IQ" in predicting success at a variety of life tasks (p. 34). They infer that I was asserting that EI should predict success at levels higher than $r = .45$, the figure that many studies have found for IQ as a predictor of success in fields such as academics. However, as I have since pointed out to Mayer, my statement pertained to areas in life where IQ predicts not at that strong level but at weaker ones—areas such as health or marital success. With regard to work performance, as I have just explained, my prediction is that in distinguishing successful people *within* a job category or profession, EI will also emerge as a stronger predictor than IQ of who, for instance, will become a star salesperson, team head, or top-rank leader.

The resolution of this issue awaits the appropriate research. The existing data that speak to the relative contribution of EI and IQ to career success are sparse and largely indirect. For example, among the measures taken of eighty graduate students at the University of California-Berkeley in 1950, Feist and Barron (1996) identified measures that in retrospect seemed to reflect EI—for example, measures of emotional balance and interpersonal effectiveness. Feist and Barron report these surrogate measures of EI accounted for 13 percent of variance over and above IQ scores in predicting the students' career success forty years later, whereas IQ added no variance over and above the EI measures. Although these surrogate measures do appear to fall within the EI domain, they reflect only a slim portion of the EI spectrum.

One of the few longitudinal studies to directly compare the contribution to work performance (as gauged by promotions) of cognitive competencies and EI competencies was done by Dulewicz and Higgs (1998). They reanalyzed data from a seven-year study of the career progress of fifty-eight general managers in the United Kingdom and Ireland, assessing three domains of ability—emotional skill (which they call EQ), intellectual aptitude (IQ), and managerial competency (MQ) that contributes to on-the-job performance. The emotional skill category included abilities like Resilience, Influence, Assertiveness, Integrity, and Leadership. The IQ domain was not assessed by intelligence test scores but by competencies used as surrogate measures, such as Analysis, Judgment, Planning, Creativity, and Risk-Taking. MQ included Supervision, Oral Communication, Business Sense, Self-Management, and Initiative and Independence.

Dulewicz and Higgs found that their measure of emotional intelligence accounted for 36 percent of the variance in organizational advancement whereas IQ accounted for 27 percent and MQ 16 percent. This suggests that EI contributes slightly more to career advancement than does IQ. However, there are several limitations to this study. One is that the measure of IQ involves surrogates—such as Judgment, Creativity, and Risk-Taking—that have questionable or uncertain relationships to standard measures of intelligence. Another limitation is that some competencies classified in the IQ and MQ domains—such as Self-Management, Initiative, and Risk-Taking—arguably belong in the EQ category. In addition, compared to the generic EI model described in this chapter, the study's EQ model fails to reflect the full spectrum of EI, omitting several key competencies, including any measure of Self-Awareness, a cluster of competencies that some research suggests is the cornerstone of emotional intelligence (Boyatzis, Goleman, & Rhee, 2000). For all these reasons, this study seems to underestimate the effect of emotional intelligence on success.

The relative significance of emotional competencies compared to cognitive abilities has also been borne out by several converging analyses using different data sets. A competency study drawing on models from forty companies revealed that strengths in purely cognitive capacities were 27 percent more frequent in the stars than in the average performers, whereas greater strengths in emotional competencies were 53 percent more frequent (Goleman, 1998b). In Boyatzis's classic

1982 study of more than two thousand supervisors, middle managers, and executives at twelve organizations, all but two of the sixteen abilities setting the star apart from the average performers were emotional competencies. And an analysis of job competencies at 286 organizations worldwide by Spencer and Spencer (1993) indicated that eighteen of the twenty-one competencies in their generic model for distinguishing superior from average performers were EI based. However, a more definitive analysis—particularly a multiple regression using such a data set—remains to be done. My prediction is that when such a study is done, EI-based competencies will have greater power than IQ-based measures in predicting which individuals in a given job pool will be outstanding.

CHAPTER THREE

AN EI-BASED THEORY OF PERFORMANCE

Daniel Goleman

In 1998, in *Working with Emotional Intelligence*, I set out a framework of emotional intelligence (EI) that reflects how an individual's potential for mastering the skills of Self-Awareness, Self-Management, Social Awareness, and Relationship Management translates into on-the-job success. This model is based on EI competencies that have been identified in internal research at hundreds of corporations and organizations as distinguishing outstanding performers. Focusing on EI as a theory of performance, this chapter presents a new version of that model, looks at the physiological evidence underlying EI theory, and reviews a number of studies of the drivers of workplace performance and the factors that distinguish the best individuals from the average ones.

As I define it, an *emotional competence* is "a learned capability based on emotional intelligence that results in outstanding performance at work" (Goleman, 1998b). To be adept at an emotional competence like Customer Service or Conflict Management requires an underlying ability in EI fundamentals, specifically, Social Awareness and Relationship Management. However, emotional competencies are learned abilities: having Social Awareness or skill at managing relationship does not guarantee we have *mastered* the additional learning required to handle a customer adeptly or to resolve a conflict—just that we have the *potential to become skilled* at these competencies.

Emotional competencies are job skills that can, and indeed must, be learned. An underlying EI ability is necessary, though not sufficient, to manifest competence in any one of the four EI domains, or clusters that I introduced in Chapter Two. Consider the IQ corollary that a student can have excellent spatial abilities yet never learn geometry. So too can a person be highly empathic yet poor at handling customers if he or she has not learned competence in customer service. Although our emotional *intelligence* determines our potential for learning the practical skills that underlie the four EI clusters, our emotional *competence* shows how much of that potential we have realized by learning and mastering skills and translating intelligence into on-the-job capabilities.

Figure 3.1 presents the current version of my EI framework. Twenty competencies nest in four clusters of general EI abilities. The framework illustrates, for example, that we cannot demonstrate the competencies of Trustworthiness and Conscientiousness without mastery of the fundamental ability of Self-Management or the competencies of Influence, Communication, Conflict Management, and so on without a handle on Managing Relationships.

This model is a refinement of the model I used in 1998. That earlier framework identified five domains, or dimensions, of emotional intelligence that comprised twenty-five competencies. Three dimensions—Self-Awareness, Self-Regulation, and Motivation—described personal competencies, that is, knowing and managing emo-

FIGURE 3.1. A FRAMEWORK OF EMOTIONAL COMPETENCIES.

	Self (Personal Competence)	Other (Social Competence)
Recognition	**Self-Awareness** • Emotional self-awareness • Accurate self-assessment • Self-confidence	**Social Awareness** • Empathy • Service orientation • Organizational awareness
Regulation	**Self-Management** • Emotional self-control • Trustworthiness • Conscientiousness • Adaptability • Achievement drive • Initiative	**Relationship Management** • Developing others • Influence • Communication • Conflict management • Visionary leadership • Catalyzing change • Building bonds • Teamwork and collaboration

tions in oneself. Two dimensions—Empathy and Social Skills—described social competencies, that is, knowing and managing emotions in others. The current model reflects recent statistical analyses by my colleague Richard Boyatzis that supported collapsing the twenty-five competencies into twenty, and the five domains into the four seen here: Self-Awareness, Self-Management, Social Awareness, and Relationship Management (Boyatzis, Goleman, & Rhee, 2000). Boyatzis, Goleman, and Rhee administered the Emotional Competence Inventory, a questionnaire designed to assess the twenty EI competencies just described, to nearly six hundred corporate managers and professionals and engineering, management, and social work graduate students. Respondents were asked to indicate the degree to which statements about EI-related behaviors—for instance, the ability to remain calm under pressure—were characteristic of themselves. Their ratings of themselves were then compared to ratings of them made by those who worked with them. Three key clusters into which the twenty EI competencies were grouped emerged: Self-Awareness, Self-Management, and Relationship Management, which, in the statistical analysis, subsumed the Social Awareness cluster. While the analysis verifies that the competencies nest within each EI domain, it also suggests that the distinction between the Social Awareness cluster and the Relationship Management cluster may be more theoretical than empirical in some contexts.

In this process the competence called Innovation was collapsed into Initiative; Optimism was integrated with Achievement Drive; Leveraging Diversity and Understanding Others combined to become Empathy; Organizational Commitment was collapsed into Visionary Leadership; and the competencies Collaboration and Team Capabilities became one, called Teamwork and Collaboration. Political Awareness was renamed Organizational Awareness, and Emotional Awareness became Emotional Self-Awareness.

Neurological Substrates of EI

The competencies named in Figure 3.1 have long been recognized as adding value to performance; however, one of the functions of the EI framework is to reflect the neurological substrates of this set of human abilities. An understanding of these neurological substrates has critical implications for how people can best learn to develop strengths in the EI range of competencies.

The EI theory of performance posits that each of the four domains of EI derives from distinct neurological mechanisms that distinguish each domain from the others and all four from purely cognitive domains of ability. In turn, at a higher level of articulation, the EI competencies nest within these four EI domains. This distinction between EI-based competencies and purely cognitive abilities like IQ can now be drawn more clearly than before owing to recent findings in neuroscience. Research in the newly emerging field of *affective neuroscience* (Davidson, Jackson, & Kalin, 2000) offers a fine-grained view of the neural substrates of the EI-based range of behavior and allows us to see a bridge between brain function and the behaviors described in the EI model of performance.

From the perspective of affective neuroscience, the defining boundary in brain activity between emotional intelligence and cognitive intelligence is the distinction between capacities that are purely (or largely) neocortical and those that *integrate* neocortical and limbic circuitry. Intellectual abilities like verbal fluency, spatial logic, and abstract reasoning—in other words, the components of IQ—are based primarily in specific areas of the neocortex. When these neocortical areas are damaged, the corresponding intellectual ability suffers. In contrast, emotional intelligence encompasses the behavioral manifestations of underlying neurological circuitry that primarily links the limbic areas for emotion, centering on the amygdala and its extended networks throughout the brain, to areas in the prefrontal cortex, the brain's executive center.

Key components of this circuitry include the dorsolateral, ventromedial, and orbitofrontal sectors of the prefrontal cortex (with important functional differences between left and right sides in each sector) and the amygdala and hippocampus (Davidson, Jackson, & Kalin, 2000). This circuitry is essential for the development of skills in each of the four main domains of emotional intelligence. Lesions in these areas produce deficits in the hallmark abilities of EI—Self-Awareness, Self-Management (including Motivation), Social Awareness skills such as Empathy, and Relationship Management, just as lesions in discrete areas of the neocortex selectively impair aspects of purely cognitive abilities such as verbal fluency or spatial reasoning (Damasio, 1994, 1999).

The first component of emotional intelligence is *Emotional Self-Awareness,* knowing what one feels. John Mayer (see, for example, Mayer & Stevens, 1994) uses the term *meta-mood,* the affective analogue of *meta-cognition,* for key aspects of Emotional Self-Awareness. The neural substrates of Emotional Self-Awareness have yet to be determined with precision. But Antonio Damasio (1994), on the basis of neuropsychological studies of patients with brain lesions, proposes that the ability to sense, articulate, and reflect on one's emotional states hinges on the neural circuits that run between the prefrontal and verbal cortex, the amygdala, and the viscera. Patients with lesions that disconnect the amygdala from the prefrontal cortex, he finds, are at a loss to give words to feelings, a hallmark of the disorder alexithymia. In some ways, alexithymia and Emotional Self-Awareness may be mirror concepts, one reflecting a deficiency in the workings of these neural substrates, the other efficiency (Taylor, Parker, & Bagby, 1999).

The second component of EI, *Emotional Self-Management,* is the ability to regulate distressing affects like anxiety and anger and to inhibit emotional impulsivity. PET (positron-emission tomography) measurements of glucose metabolism reveal that individual differences in metabolic activity in the amygdala are associated with levels of distress or dysphoria—the more activity, the greater the negative affect (Davidson, Jackson, & Kalin, 2000). In contrast, metabolic activity in the left medial prefrontal cortex is inversely related to levels of activity in the amygdala—an array of inhibitory neurons in the prefrontal area, animal studies have shown, regulate activation of the amygdala. In humans, the greater the activity level in the left medial prefrontal cortex, the more positive the person's emotional state. Thus a major locus of the ability to regulate negative affect appears to be the circuit between the amygdala and the left prefrontal cortex.

This circuitry also appears instrumental in the motivational aspect of Emotional Self-Management; it may sustain the residual affect that propels us to achieve our goals. David McClelland (1975) has defined motivation as "an affectively toned associative network arranged in a hierarchy of strength and importance in the individual," which determines what goals we seek (p. 81). Davidson proposes that the left medial prefrontal cortex is the site of "affective working memory." Damage to this region is associated with a loss of the ability to sustain goal-directed behavior; loss of the capacity to anticipate affective outcomes from accomplishing goals diminishes the ability to guide behavior adaptively (Davidson, Jackson, & Kalin, 2000). In other words, Davidson proposes that the prefrontal cortex allows us to hold in mind or remind ourselves of the positive feelings that will come when we attain our goals and at the same time allows us to inhibit the negative feelings that would discourage us from continuing to strive toward those goals.

Social Awareness, the third EI component, which encompasses the competency of Empathy, also involves the amygdala. Studies of patients with discrete lesions to the amygdala show impairment of their ability to read nonverbal cues for negative emotions, particularly anger and fear, and to judge the trustworthiness of other people (Davidson, Jackson, & Kalin, 2000). Animal studies suggest a key role in recognizing emotions for circuitry running from the amygdala to the visual cortex; Brothers (1989), reviewing both neurological findings and comparative studies with primates, cites data showing that certain neurons in the visual cortex respond only to specific emotional cues, such as a threat. These emotion-recognition cortical neurons have strong connections to the amygdala.

Finally, *Relationship Management,* or Social Skill, the fourth EI component, poses a more complex picture. In a fundamental sense, the effectiveness of our relationship skills hinges on our ability to attune ourselves to or influence the emotions of another person. That ability in turn builds on other domains of EI, particularly Self-Management and Social Awareness. If we cannot control our emotional outbursts or impulses and lack empathy, there is less chance we will be effective in our relationships.

Indeed, in an analysis of data on workplace effectiveness, Michelle Burckle at HayGroup found that Emotional Self-Awareness is a prerequisite for effective Self-Management, which in turn predicts greater Social Skill. A secondary pathway runs from Self-Awareness to Social Awareness (particularly Empathy) to Social Skill. Managing relationships well, then, depends on a foundation of Self-Management and Empathy, each of which in turn requires Self-Awareness.

This evidence that Empathy and Self-Management are foundations for social effectiveness finds support at the neurological level. Patients with lesions in the prefrontal-amygdala circuits that undergird both Self-Management and Empathy show marked deficits in relationship skills, even though their cognitive abilities remain intact (Damasio, 1994). When Damasio administered an EI measure to one such patient, he found that though the patient had an IQ of 140, he showed marked deficits in Self-Awareness and Empathy (Bar-On, 2000b). Primate studies find parallel effects. Monkeys in the wild who had this prefrontal-amygdala circuitry severed were able to perform food gathering and similar tasks to maintain themselves but lacked all sense of how to respond to other monkeys in the band, even running away from those who made friendly gestures (Brothers, 1989).

The Business Case for EI Competencies

The data documenting the importance for outstanding performance of each of the twenty emotional intelligence competencies have been building for more than two decades. I have reviewed the data for each competence (Goleman, 1998b), as have Cherniss and Adler (2000). Moreover the data continue to build, both informally, as organizations worldwide do internal studies to identify the competencies that distinguish outstanding from average performers, and formally, as academic researchers continue to focus studies on one or another of these capabilities.

David McClelland (1975) was perhaps the first to propose the concept of competence as a basis for identifying what differentiates outstanding from average performers at work. McClelland (1998) reviewed data from more than thirty different organizations and for executive positions in many professions, from banking and managing to mining geology, sales, and health care. He showed that a wide range of EI competencies (and a narrow range of cognitive ones) distinguished top performers from average ones. Those that distinguished most powerfully were Achievement Drive, Developing Others, Adaptability, Influence,

Self-Confidence, and Leadership. The one cognitive competence that distinguished as strongly was Analytic Thinking.

Although each competence contributes on its own to workplace effectiveness, I believe it is less useful to consider them one by one than it is to examine them in their clusters, where one can also assess the synergies of strengths in several competencies that enable outstanding performance, as McClelland (1998) has shown. For that reason, I review here only selected examples of data linking the EI competencies to workplace performance. Readers who seek a fuller review should consult Goleman (1998b) or the classic work of Boyatzis (1982) and Spencer and Spencer (1993).

The Self-Awareness Cluster:
Understanding Feelings and Accurate Self-Assessment

The first of the three Self-Awareness competencies, *Emotional Self-Awareness*, reflects the importance of recognizing one's own feelings and how they affect one's performance. At a financial services company Emotional Self-Awareness proved crucial in financial planners' job performance (Goleman, 1998b). The interaction between a financial planner and a client is delicate, dealing not only with hard questions about money but also, when life insurance comes up, the even more discomforting issue of mortality; the planners' Self-Awareness apparently helped them handle their own emotional reactions better.

At another level, Self-Awareness is key to realizing one's own strengths and weaknesses. Among several hundred managers from twelve different organizations, *Accurate Self-Assessment* was the hallmark of superior performance (Boyatzis, 1982). Individuals with the Accurate Self-Assessment competence are aware of their abilities and limitations, seek out feedback and learn from their mistakes, and know where they need to improve and when to work with others who have complementary strengths. Accurate Self-Assessment was the competence found in virtually every "star performer" in a study of several hundred knowledge workers—computer scientists, auditors and the like—at companies such as AT&T and 3M (Kelley, 1998). On 360-degree competence assessments, average performers typically overestimate their strengths, whereas star performers rarely do; if anything, the stars tended to underestimate their abilities, an indicator of high internal standards (Goleman, 1998b).

The positive impact of the *Self-Confidence* competence on performance has been shown in a variety of studies. Among supervisors, managers, and executives, a high degree of Self-Confidence distinguishes the best from the average performers (Boyatzis, 1982). Among 112 entry-level accountants, those with the highest sense of Self-Efficacy, a form of Self-Confidence, were rated by their supervisors ten months later as having superior job performance. The level of Self-Confidence was in fact a stronger predictor of performance than the level of skill or previous training (Saks, 1995). In a sixty-year study of more than one thousand high-IQ men and women tracked from early childhood to retirement, those who possessed Self-Confidence during their early years were most successful in their careers (Holahan & Sears, 1995).

The Self-Management Cluster:
Managing Internal States, Impulses, and Resources

The Self-Management cluster of EI abilities encompasses six competencies. Heading the list is the *Emotional Self-Control* competence, which manifests largely as the absence of distress and disruptive feelings. Signs of this competence include being unfazed in stressful situations or dealing with a hostile person without lashing out in return. Among small business owners and employees, those with a stronger sense of control over not only themselves but the events in their lives are less likely to become angry or depressed when faced with job stress, or to quit (Rahim & Psenicka, 1996). Among counselors and psychotherapists, superior performers tend to respond calmly to angry attacks by a patient, as do outstanding flight attendants dealing with disgruntled passengers (Boyatzis & Burrus, 1995; Spencer & Spencer, 1993). And among managers and executives, top performers are able to balance their drive and ambition with Emotional Self-Control, harnessing their personal needs in the service of the organization's goals (Boyatzis, 1982). Those store managers who are best able to manage their own stress and stay unaffected have the most profitable stores, by such measures as sales per square foot, in a national retail chain (Lusch & Serkenci, 1990).

The *Trustworthiness* competence translates into letting others know one's values and principles, intentions and feelings, and acting in ways that are consistent with them. Trustworthy individuals are forthright about their own mistakes and confront others about their lapses. A deficit in this ability operates as a career derailer (Goleman, 1998b).

The signs of the *Conscientiousness* competence include being careful, self-disciplined, and scrupulous in attending to responsibilities. Conscientiousness distinguishes the model organizational citizens, the people who keep things running as they should. In studies of job performance, outstanding effectiveness in virtually all jobs—from the bottom to the top of the corporate ladder—depends on Conscientiousness (Barrick & Mount, 1991). Among sales representatives for a large U.S. appliance manufacturer, those who were most conscientious had the largest volume of sales (Barrick, Mount, & Strauss, 1993).

If there is any single competence our present times call for, it is *Adaptability.* Superior performers in management ranks exhibit this competence (Spencer & Spencer, 1993). They are open to new information and can let go of old assumptions and so adapt how they operate. Emotional resilience allows an individual to remain comfortable with the anxiety that often accompanies uncertainty and to think "out of the box," displaying on-the-job creativity and applying new ideas to achieve results. Conversely, people who are uncomfortable with risk and change become naysayers who can undermine innovative ideas or be slow to respond to a shift in the marketplace. Businesses with less formal and more ambiguous, autonomous, and flexible roles for employees open flows of information, and multidisciplinary team-oriented structures experience greater innovation (Amabile, 1988).

David McClelland's landmark work *The Achieving Society* (1961) established Achievement Orientation as the competence that drives the success of entrepreneurs. In its most general sense, this competence, which I call *Achievement Drive,* refers to an optimistic striving to continually improve performance. Studies that compare star performers in executive ranks to average ones find that stars display classic achievement-oriented behaviors—they take more calculated risks, they support enterprising innovations and set challenging goals for their employees, and so forth. Spencer and Spencer (1993) found that the need to achieve is the competence that most strongly sets apart superior and average executives. Optimism is a key ingredient of achievement because it can determine one's reaction to unfavorable events or circumstances; those with high achievement are proactive and persistent, have an optimistic attitude toward setbacks, and operate from hope of success. Studies have shown that optimism can contribute significantly to sales gains, among other accomplishments (Schulman, 1995).

Those with the *Initiative* competence act before being forced to do so by external events. This often means taking anticipatory action to avoid problems before they happen or taking advantage of opportunities before they are visible to anyone else. Individuals who lack Initiative are reactive rather than proactive, lacking the farsightedness that can make the critical difference between a wise decision and a poor one. Initiative is key to outstanding performance in industries that rely on sales, such as real estate, and to the development of personal relationships with clients, as is critical in such businesses as financial services or consulting (Crant, 1995; Rosier, 1996).

The Social Awareness Cluster: Reading People and Groups Accurately

The Social Awareness cluster manifests in three competencies. The *Empathy* competence gives people an astute awareness of others' emotions, concerns, and needs. The empathic individual can read emotional currents, picking up on nonverbal cues such as tone of voice or facial expression. Empathy requires Self-Awareness; our understanding of others' feelings and concerns flows from awareness of our own feelings. This sensitivity to others is critical for superior job performance whenever the focus is on interactions with people. For instance, physicians who are better at recognizing emotions in patients are more successful than their less sensitive colleagues at treating them (Friedman & DiMatteo, 1982). The ability to read others' needs well comes naturally to the best managers of product development teams (Spencer & Spencer, 1993). And skill in Empathy correlates with effective sales, as was found in a study among large and small retailers (Pilling & Eroglu, 1994). In an increasingly diverse workforce, the Empathy competence allows us to read people accurately and avoid resorting to the stereotyping that can lead to performance deficits by creating anxiety in the stereotyped individuals (Steele, 1997).

Social Awareness also plays a key role in the *Service* competence, the ability to identify a client's or customer's often unstated needs and concerns and then match them to products or services; this empathic strategy distinguishes star sales performers from average ones (Spencer & Spencer, 1993). It also means taking a long-term perspective, sometimes trading off immediate gains in order to preserve customer relationships. A study of an office supply and equipment vendor indicated that the most successful members of the sales team were able to combine taking the customer's viewpoint and showing appropriate assertiveness in order to steer the customer toward a choice that satisfied both the customer's and the vendor's needs (McBane, 1995).

Organizational Awareness, the ability to read the currents of emotions and political realities in groups, is a competence vital to the behind-the-scenes networking and coalition building that allows individuals to wield influence, no matter what their professional role. Insight into group social hierarchies requires Social Awareness on an organizational level, not just an interpersonal one. Outstanding performers in most organizations share this ability; among managers and executive generally, this emotional competence distinguishes star performers. Their ability to read situations objectively, without the distorting lens of their own biases and assumptions, allows them to respond effectively (Boyatzis, 1982).

The Relationship Management Cluster: Inducing Desirable Responses in Others

The Relationship Management set of competencies includes essential Social Skills. *Developing Others* involves sensing people's developmental needs and bolstering their abilities—a talent not just of excellent coaches and mentors, but also outstanding leaders. Competence in developing others is a hallmark of superior managers; among sales managers, for example, it typifies those at the top of the field (Spencer & Spencer, 1993). Although this ability is crucial for those managing front-line work, it has also emerged as a vital skill for effective leadership at high levels (Goleman, 2000b).

We practice the essence of the *Influence* competence when we handle and manage emotions effectively in other people, and so are persuasive. The most effective people sense others' reactions and fine-tune their own responses to move interaction in the best direction. This emotional competence emerges over and over again as a hallmark of star performers, particularly among supervisors, managers, and executives (Spencer & Spencer, 1993). Star performers with this competence draw on a wider range of persuasion strategies than others do, including impression management, dramatic arguments or actions, and appeals to reason. At the same time, the Influence competence requires them to be genuine and put collective goals before their self-interests; otherwise what would manifest as effective persuasion becomes manipulation.

Creating an atmosphere of openness with clear lines of communication is a key factor in organizational success. People who exhibit the *Communication* competence are effective in the give-and-take of emotional information, deal with difficult issues straightforwardly, listen well and welcome sharing information fully, and foster open communication and stay receptive to bad news as well as good. This competence builds on both managing one's own emotions and empathy; a healthy dialogue depends on being attuned to others' emotional states and controlling the impulse to respond in ways that might sour the emotional climate. Data on managers and executives show that the better people can execute this competence, the more others prefer to deal with them (Goleman, 1998b).

A talent of those skilled in the *Conflict Management* competence is spotting trouble as it is brewing and taking steps to calm those involved. Here the arts of listening and empathizing are crucial to the skills of handling difficult people and situations with diplomacy, encouraging debate and open discussion, and orchestrating win-win situations. Effective Conflict Management and negotiation are important to long-term, symbiotic business relationships, such as those between manufacturers and retailers. In a survey of retail buyers in department store chains, effectiveness at win-win negotiating was an accurate barometer of the health of the manufacturer-retailer relationship (Ganesan, 1993).

Those adept at the *Visionary Leadership* competence draw on a range of personal skills to inspire others to work together toward common goals. They are able to articulate and arouse enthusiasm for a shared vision and mission, to step forward as needed, to guide the performance of others while holding them accountable, and to lead by example. Outstanding leaders integrate emotional realities into what they see and so instill strategy with meaning and resonance. Emotions are contagious, particularly when exhibited by those at the top, and extremely successful leaders display a high level of positive energy that spreads throughout the organization. The more positive the style of a leader, the more positive, helpful, and cooperative are those in the group (George & Bettenhausen, 1990). And the emotional tone set by a leader tends to ripple outward with remarkable power (Bachman, 1988).

The acceleration of transitions as we enter the new century has made the *Change Catalyst* competence highly valued—leaders must be able to recognize the need for change, remove barriers, challenge the status quo, and enlist others in pursuit of new initiatives. An effective change leader also articulates a compelling vision of the new organizational goals. A leader's competence at catalyzing change brings greater efforts and better performance from subordinates, making their work more effective (House, 1988).

The *Building Bonds* competence epitomizes stars in fields like engineering, computer science, biotechnology, and other knowledge work fields in which networking is crucial for success; these stars tend to choose people with a particular expertise or resource to be part of their networks (Kelley, 1998). Outstanding performers with this competence balance their own critical work with carefully chosen favors, building accounts of goodwill with people who may become crucial resources down the line. One of the virtues of building such relationships is the reservoir of trust and goodwill that they establish; highly effective managers are adept at cultivating these relationships, whereas less effective managers generally fail to build bonds (Kaplan, 1991).

The *Collaboration and Teamwork* competence has taken on increased importance in the last decade with the trend toward team-based work in many organizations. Teamwork itself depends on the collective EI of its members; the most productive teams are those that exhibit EI competencies at the team level (as Druskat and Wolff discuss in Chapter Six). And Collaboration is particularly crucial to the success of managers; a deficit in the ability to work cooperatively with peers was, in one survey, the most common reason managers were fired (Sweeney, 1999). Team members tend to share moods, both good and bad—with better moods improving performance (Totterdell, Kellett, Teuchmann, & Briner, 1998). The positive mood of a team leader at work promotes both worker effectiveness and retention (George & Bettenhausen, 1990). Finally, positive emotions and harmony on a top-management team predict its effectiveness (Barsade & Gibson, 1998).

Competence Comes in Multiples

Although there is theoretical significance in showing that each competence in itself has a significant impact on performance, it is also in a sense an artificial exercise. In life—and particularly on the job—people exhibit these competencies in groupings, often across clusters, that allow competencies to support one another. Emotional competencies seem to operate most powerfully in synergistic groupings, with the evidence suggesting that mastery of a "critical mass" of competencies is necessary for superior performance (Boyatzis, Goleman, & Rhee, 2000).

Along with competency clusters comes the notion of a *tipping point*—the point at which strength in a competence makes a significant impact on performance. Each competence can be viewed along a continuum of mastery; at a certain point along each continuum there is a major leap in performance impact. In McClelland's analysis (1998) of the competencies that distinguish star performers from average ones, he found a tipping point effect when people exhibited excellence in six or more competencies. McClelland argues that a critical mass of competencies above the tipping point distinguishes top from average performers. The typical pattern is that stars are above the tipping point on at least six EI competencies and demonstrate strengths in at least one competency from each of the four clusters.

This effect has been replicated in Boyatzis's research (1999b), which demonstrated that meeting or surpassing the tipping point in at least three of the four EI clusters was necessary for success among high-level leaders in a large financial services organization. Boyatzis found that both a high degree of proficiency in several aptitudes in the same cluster and a spread of strengths across clusters are found among those who exhibit superior organizational performance.

Using information about the profit produced by partners at a large financial services company, Boyatzis (1999a) was able to analyze the financial impact of having a critical mass of strengths above the tipping point in different EI clusters. At this company, strengths in the Self-Awareness cluster added 78 percent more incremental profit; in the Self-Management cluster, 390 percent more profit, and the Relationship Management cluster, 110 percent more. The extremely large effect from strengths in the Self-Management competencies suggests the importance of managing one's emotions—using abilities such as self-discipline, integrity, and staying motivated toward goals—for individual effectiveness.

Organizations and individuals interface in ways that require a multitude of EI abilities, each most effective when used in conjunction with others. Emotional Self-Control, for instance, supports the Empathy and the Influence competencies.

Finding a comfortable fit between an individual and an organization is easier when important aspects of organizational culture (rapid growth, for example) link to a grouping of competencies rather than a single competency.

Other researchers have reported that competencies operate together in an integrated fashion, forming a meaningful pattern of abilities that facilitates successful performance in a given role or job (Nygren & Ukeritis, 1993). Spencer and Spencer (1993) have identified distinctive groupings of competencies that tend to typify high-performing individuals in specific fields, including health care and social services, technical and engineering, sales, client management, and leadership at the executive level.

EI Leadership, Climate, and Organizational Performance

I have indicated how EI can affect an individual's success in an organization. But how does it affect organizational success overall? The evidence suggests that emotionally intelligent leadership is key to creating a working climate that nurtures employees and encourages them to give their best. That enthusiasm, in turn, pays off in improved business performance. This trickle-down effect emerged, for example, in a study of CEOs in U.S. insurance companies. Given comparable size, companies whose CEOs exhibited more EI competencies showed better financial results as measured by both profit and growth (Williams, 1994).

A similar relationship between EI strengths in a leader and business results was found by McClelland (1998) in studying the division heads of a global food and beverage company. The divisions of the leaders with a critical mass of strengths in EI competencies outperformed yearly revenue targets by a margin of 15 to 20 percent. The divisions of the leaders weak in EI competencies underperformed by about the same margin (Goleman, 1998b).

The relationship between EI strengths in a leader and performance of the unit led appears to be mediated by the climate the leader creates. In the study of insurance CEOs, for example, there was a significant relationship between the EI abilities of the leader and the organizational climate (Williams, 1994). Climate reflects people's sense of their ability to do their jobs well. Climate indicators include the degree of clarity in communication; the degree of employees' flexibility in doing their jobs, ability to innovate, and ownership of and responsibility for their work; and the level of the performance standards set (Litwin & Stringer, 1968; Tagiuri & Litwin, 1968). In the insurance industry study, the climate created by CEOs among their direct reports predicted the business performance of the entire organization, and in three-quarters of the cases climate alone could be used to correctly sort companies by profits and growth.

Leadership style seems to drive organizational performance across a wide span of industries and sectors and appears to be a crucial link in the chain from leader to climate to business success. A study of the heads of forty-two schools in the United Kingdom suggests that leadership style drove up students' academic achievement by directly affecting school climate. When the school head was flexible in leadership style and demonstrated a variety of EI abilities, teachers attitudes were more positive and students' grades higher; when the leader relied on fewer EI competencies, teachers tended to be demoralized and students underperformed academically (Hay/McBer, 2000). Effective school leaders not only created a working climate conducive to achievement but were more attuned to teachers' perceptions of such aspects of climate and organizational health as clarity of vision and level of teamwork.

The benefits of an understanding and empathic school leader were reflected in the teacher-student relationship as well. In a related follow-up analysis, Lees and Barnard (1999) studied the climates of individual classrooms, concluding that teachers who are more aware of how students feel in the classroom are better able to design a learning environment that suits students and better able to guide them toward success. Teachers who have a leader who has created a positive school climate will be better equipped to do the same in their own classrooms. Indeed, several dimensions of school climate identified in the earlier study correspond to dimensions of classroom climate. For instance, clarity of vision in a school's purpose parallels clarity of purpose in class lessons; challenging yet realistic performance standards for teachers translate into like standards for students.

A similar effect of EI-based leadership on climate and performance was demonstrated in a study of outstanding leaders in health care (Catholic Health Association, 1994). For this study, 1,200 members of health care organizations were asked to nominate outstanding leaders based on criteria such as organizational performance and anticipation of future trends. The members were then asked to evaluate the effectiveness of the nominees in fifteen key situations that leaders face—among them organizational change, diversity, and institutional integrity. The study revealed that the more effective leaders in the health care industry were also more adept at integrating key EI competencies such as Organizational Awareness and relationship skills like Influence.

The link between EI strengths in a leader and the organization's climate is important for EI theory. A Hay/McBer analysis of data on 3,781 executives, correlated with climate surveys filled out by those who worked for them, suggests that 50 to 70 percent of employees' perception of working climate is linked to the EI characteristics of the leader (Goleman, 2000b). Research drawing on that same database sheds light on the role of EI competencies in leadership effectiveness, identifying how six distinct styles of EI-based leadership affect climate. Four styles—the visionary (sometimes called the "authoritative"), the affiliative, the democratic, and the coaching—generally drive climate in a positive direction. Two styles—the coercive and the pacesetting—tend to drive climate downward, particularly when leaders overuse them (though each of these two can have positive impact if applied in appropriate situations). Table 3.1. summarizes these effects.

Visionary leaders are empathic, self-confident, and often act as agents of change. Affiliative leaders, too, are empathic, with strengths in building relationships and managing conflict. The democratic leader encourages collaboration and teamwork and communicates effectively—particularly as an excellent listener. And

TABLE 3.1. LEADERSHIP STYLE, EI, AND ORGANIZATIONAL EFFECTIVENESS.

Leadership Style	EI Competencies	Impact on Climate	Objective	When Appropriate
Visionary	Self-Confidence, Empathy, Change Catalyst, Visionary Leadership	Most strongly positive	Mobilize others to follow a vision	When change requires a new vision or when a clear direction is needed
Affiliative	Empathy, Building Bonds, Conflict Management	Highly positive	Create harmony	To heal rifts in a team or to motivate during stressful times
Democratic	Teamwork and Collaboration, Communication	Highly positive	Build commitment through participation	To build buy-in or consensus or to get valuable input from employees
Coaching	Developing Others, Empathy, Emotional Self-Awareness	Highly positive	Build strengths for the future	To help an employee improve performance or develop long-term strengths
Coercive	Achievement Drive, Initiative, Emotional Self-Control	Strongly negative	Immediate compliance	In a crisis, to kick-start a turn around, or with problem employees
Pacesetting	Conscientiousness, Achievement Drive, Initiative	Highly negative	Perform tasks to a high standard	To get quick results from a highly motivated and competent team

the coaching leader is emotionally self-aware, empathic, and skilled at identifying and building on the potential of others.

The coercive leader relies on the power of his position, ordering people to execute his wishes, and is typically handicapped by a lack of empathy. The pacesetting leader both sets high standards and exemplifies them, exhibiting initiative and a very high drive to achieve—but to a fault, too often micromanaging or criticizing those who fail to meet her own high standards rather than helping them to improve.

The most effective leaders integrate four or more of the six styles regularly, switching to the one most appropriate in a given leadership situation. For instance, the study of school leaders found that in those schools where the heads displayed four or more leadership styles, students had superior academic performance relative to students in comparison schools. In schools where the heads displayed just one or two styles, academic performance was poorest; often the styles here were the pacesetting or coercive ones, which tended to undermine teacher morale and enthusiasm (Hay/McBer, 2000).

Among life insurance company CEOs, the very best in terms of corporate growth and profit were those who drew upon a wide range of leadership styles (Williams, 1994). They were adept at all four of the styles that have a positive impact on climate—visionary, democratic, affiliative, and coaching—matching them with the appropriate circumstances. They rarely exhibited the coercive or pacesetting styles.

Granted, the factors influencing organizational performance are diverse and complex. But the EI theory of performance at the collective level predicts positive links between EI leadership, organizational climate, and subsequent performance. Hay/McBer data indicate not only that EI-based leadership may be the most important driver of climate but also that climate in turn may account for 20 to 30 percent of organizational performance (Goleman, 2000b). If these data are borne out, the implications are greatly supportive of employing EI as a criterion for selection, promotion, and development: such an application becomes a competitive strategy.

Implications for the Future: EI and Higher Education

Given the value of the personal and organizational effectiveness of EI-based capabilities, there is a clear need to integrate that valuation into our organizations' functions. Organizations need to hire for emotional intelligence along with whatever other technical skills or business expertise they are seeking. When it comes to promotions and succession planning, EI should be a major criterion, particularly to the extent that a position requires leadership. When those with high potential are being selected and groomed, EI should be central. And in training and development, EI should again be a major focus.

However, because EI competencies entail emotional capacities in addition to purely cognitive abilities, modes of learning that work well for academic subjects or technical skills are not necessarily well suited for helping people improve an emotional competence (Goleman, 1998b). For this reason the Consortium for Research on Emotional Intelligence in Organizations has summarized empirical findings on the mode of learning best for emotional competencies and formulated guidelines for their effective development. The consortium has posted a technical report on its Web site (www.eiconsortium.org) and has fostered a book for HR professionals on how to make training in EI skills most effective (Cherniss & Adler, 2000).

Given our new understanding of the crucial role emotional competence plays in individual, group, and organizational success, the implication for education is clear: We should be helping young people master these competencies as essential life skills. There are already numerous school-based programs in the basics of EI, programs that deliver *social and emotional learning* (SEL). The Collaborative for Social and Emotional Learning has vetted the best models, and acts as a clearinghouse for these programs through its Web site (www.casel.org).

But as of this writing, when it comes to preparing young people in the essential emotional intelligence skills that matter most for their success in the workplace, for piloting their careers, and for leadership, we face a serious gap. The SEL programs cover the early school years but not higher education. Only a scattered handful of pioneering SEL courses exist at the college or professional level. And yet the data showing the crucial role EI skills play in career success make a compelling case for reenvisioning higher education in order to give these capabilities their place in a well-rounded curriculum.

Given that employers themselves are looking for EI capacities in those they hire, colleges and professional schools that offered appropriate SEL training would benefit both their graduates and the organizations they work for. The most forward-thinking educators will, I hope, recognize the importance of emotional intelligence in higher education, not just for the students, not just for the students' employers, but for the vitality of an economy—and society—as a whole. As Erasmus, the great humanist writer, tells us, "The best hope of a nation lies in the proper education of its youth."

CHAPTER FOUR

THE ECONOMIC VALUE OF EMOTIONAL INTELLIGENCE COMPETENCIES AND EIC-BASED HR PROGRAMS

Lyle M. Spencer

Acceptance of emotional intelligence competency (EIC) concepts and programs by academics, professionals, and organizations will ultimately depend on their demonstrated validity and utility. This chapter reviews the rationale and methods for evaluating EIC-based human resource programs in monetary terms, and it also presents preliminary meta-analytic estimates of the economic value added by these interventions.

Rationale

Reasons for evaluating EIC projects in economic terms include satisfying professional ethics and acceptance criteria, satisfying legal requirements, and demonstrating economic utility.

Professional Ethics and Acceptance

The Standards for Educational and Psychological Testing, prepared by a committee of the American Educational Research Association, American Psychological Association, and National Council on Measurement in Education (1999), require measures (and by inference, human resource programs based on these measures) to be reliable and valid (that is, to statistically predict) outcomes of (economic) value to individuals or organizations.

EIC researchers and practitioners are regularly savaged by critics for failing to publish reliability and validity data: for example, Barrett (2000) denounces EIC as "slickly packaged junk science perpetrated by unscrupulous consultants on ignorant customers." Published data about the efficacy of EIC programs exist (see Chapter Nine), but EIC advocates have largely failed to bring these data to human resource (HR) professionals' attention.

Legal Requirements

U.S. and Canadian courts, under civil rights and (in Canada) pay equity laws, have ruled that "any [HR] decision-making processes, from background checks to supervisory performance ratings, that affect an employee's status in an organization, are tests, and thus subject to scrutiny for adverse impact" (Latham & Wexley, 1981). These rulings effectively extend requirements for statistical reliability and validity to any assessment for selection or promotion, any development opportunity, and any performance appraisal affecting pay or career opportunities.

Legal requirements for scientific reliability have been expanded by U.S. Supreme Court Associate Justice Stephen Breyer's decision for the majority in *Kumho Tire, Inc.* v. *Carmichael* (119 Sup. Ct. 1167 [1999]), which extends an earlier U.S. Supreme Court ruling in *Daubert* v. *Merrell Dow Pharmaceuticals, Inc.* (509 U.S. 579 [1993]). Daubert required expert witness testimony to be based on "tested scientific knowledge, demonstrate reasonable reliability criteria, have been subjected to peer review, report the size of the known error rate for findings . . . [and] establish whether the knowledge enjoys widespread acceptance in the scientific community" (Daubert, cited in Wiener, 1999).

Valid development opportunities, for example, can clearly make a difference in an employee's status, and for this reason they have been the subject of many legal battles (such as the 1978 *Bakke* v. *Regents of the University of California*). Access to (quality) EIC education and training opportunities almost certainly falls under these laws. An employee can complain: "You sent me to the 'feel-good' course when my colleagues got to go to *validated* training which helped them show improved business results and get promoted? Discrimination!" And lawsuit?

The legal status of psychological tests and programs in European Community countries under EC and individual country labor laws and union and worker council agreements is less clear, but many observers believe scientific validity requirements for HR practices will become law in Europe. Multinational HRIS vendors (for example, PeopleSoft and SAP) are designing their systems to provide data on whether EIC programs pass legal tests of reliability and validity.

Economic Utility

Evaluation methods that look at the economics of human resource programs are premised on the same survival-of-the-fittest concept that governs all businesses: that is, the goal is to help investments flow from less valuable uses to uses where they generate the highest returns.

Economic value-added (EVA), cost-benefit, and return on investment (ROI) analyses lead HR staff to improve practices by helping them to

- Focus on the *right* problems or opportunities—those with the greatest cost or value, respectively, to the firm.
- Focus on *interventions* that will have the maximum impact on costly problems and valuable opportunities.

Demonstrating the economic value of outcomes also enhances the professional longevity, credibility, and satisfaction of EIC researchers and practitioners in several ways.

First, the HR function competes with every other organizational function for capital investment funds. HR professionals are more likely to be able to convince their customers to adopt programs when they can describe program benefits in economic terms. Investment proposals with business cases showing compelling ROI projections are more likely to be funded. "Soft" programs and staff (that is, those lacking economic justification) are more likely to be cut. Second, HR programs are increasingly emphasized in making ISO 9000, JACHO, Deming, and Baldrige audits and awards. Most of these assessments are qualitative. Economic value-added data can provide powerful measures of HR programs' quality. Hard data showing that HR interventions made a meaningful business contribution to an organization are more likely than other evaluations to find their way into management reports and personnel folders and to enhance HR staff careers.

The Economic Value of EIC-Based Programs

An *emotional intelligence competency* may be defined as "an *underlying* characteristic of an individual which is *causally* related to *effective* or *superior* (one standard deviation above the mean) performance in a job" (Boyatzis, 1982). This definition may be stated more generally as an EIC is *any individual characteristic (or combination of characteristics) that can be measured reliably* and that *distinguishes superior from average performers, or effective from ineffective performers, at levels of statistical significance.* This *superior performance* definition of competence—specifically, performance one standard deviation above the mean (or the top 14 percent, roughly the top one out of ten performers in a job)—is preferred for two reasons: first, the economic value of EIC programs is easily calculated, and second, like any best practice benchmark, EIC programs that predict the *best* level at which a job can be done drive human resource applications to *add* value—that is, to do *better* than individuals' or firms' present *average* level of performance.

The EVA added by EIC-based interventions is found by (1) determining the EVA of performance one standard deviation above the mean (+1 SD), and (2) determining the percentage of this increased productivity attributable to EIC as opposed to other competency and exogenous variables. Therefore the economic value added by EIC-based intervention = EVA +1 SD × % EVA attributable to EIC variables.

Finding the EVA of Performance +1 SD

As illustrated in Figure 4.1, Hunter, Schmidt, and Judiesch (1990) found that, depending on the complexity of the job, performance one standard deviation above the mean is worth between 19 percent and 48 percent of economic value added in nonsales jobs and that it results in a 48 to 120 percent increase in productivity in sales jobs. These percentages are *actual* productivity or economic value-added "performance distribution" figures—not merely "global estimation" guesstimates by employees, managers, or HR staff. Real performance distribution figures from

FIGURE 4.1. EVA ADDED BY SUPERIOR PERFORMANCE.

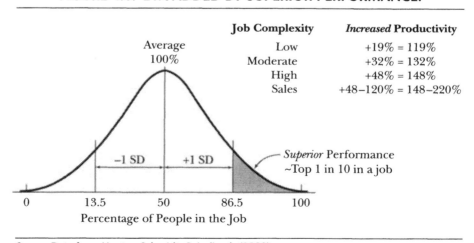

Job Complexity	*Increased* Productivity
Low	+19% = 119%
Moderate	+32% = 132%
High	+48% = 148%
Sales	+48–120% = 148–220%

Source: Data from Hunter, Schmidt, & Judiesch (1990).

organizational records are of course preferable to global estimates of the incremental value of performance that is one standard deviation above the mean.

The simplest means of valuing superior performance (that which is one standard deviation above the mean) for any job is to multiply the average salary for the job (for example, $100,000) by 100 percent plus the additional percentage of productivity contributed by superior workers. If a superior worker in a complex job is 148 percent more productive than an average worker, he or she has a productivity salary value of $148,000, even if he or she is paid an average of only $100,000. Conversely, a poor performer one standard deviation below the mean may be paid $100,000 but has a salary value of only $52,000.

Most studies of economic value added by superior performers suggest that such global estimation by salary value is very conservative. First, using the full cost of employment (salary plus benefits plus overhead, usually totaling three times base salary) as the economic value an employee must attain for the organization simply to break even is a better method of estimating. Second, most employees in valuable jobs can leverage economic benefits that are vastly greater than their salary or employment costs alone might suggest.

Figures 4.2 through 4.5 present performance distributions for computer programmers, salespeople, project managers, and account managers, respectively. Figure 4.2 shows that average programmers produce five Albrecht function points (AFPs) of debugged code per person per month. An AFP, named for inventor and IBM software engineer Alan Albrecht, is a measure of programming productivity equal to five inputs, five calculations, or data queries producing five screen or print outputs, plus a complexity factor adjustment for interfacing dissimilar programming languages. AFPs replaced lines of code as the preferred measure of programming productivity when software engineers found that poor programmers wrote too many lines of code, resulting in slower program execution and greater numbers of defects: the number of bugs varies directly with the number of lines of code written (Martin, 1990; Jones, 1986, 1991). As Figure 4.2 illustrates, superior programmers (those one standard deviation above the mean—the top 14.6 percent) produce sixteen AFPs (320 percent more than average), whereas "superstar" programmers (those two standard deviations above the mean) produce sixty-four AFPs (1,272 percent more than average). If the average programmer earns $60,000 per year, a star who does the work of 3.2 programmers is worth $192,000; thus he or she adds $132,000 in economic value. This represents a salary multiplier of 220 percent, far above the added 48 percent incremental productivity expected from the Hunter et al. (1990) data.

Figure 4.3 illustrates the finding that average salespeople in forty-four Fortune 500 firms, earning about $42,000 in direct salary, sell $3 million worth of goods or services, but superior salespeople who are one standard deviation above the

FIGURE 4.2. PERFORMANCE DISTRIBUTION FOR COMPUTER PROGRAMMERS.

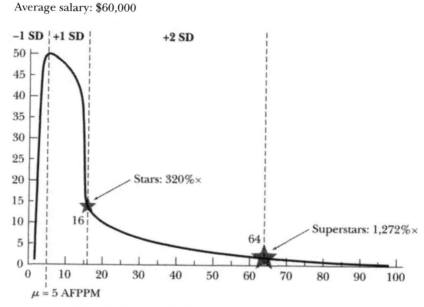

Average salary: $60,000

Albrecht Function Points per Programmer per Month

	+1 SD	+2 SD
Increased productivity	320%	1,272%
Value added	$132K	$703.2K
Multiplier effect × salary	2.2×	11.7×

Source: Data from Martin, 1990; Jones, 1986, 1991.

mean sell 123 percent more—that is, goods and services worth $6.7 million (Sloan & Spencer, 1991). This 123 percent difference between superior and average sales-people is at the top end of the 48 to 120 percent range found by Hunter et al. (1990). Note that the $3.7 million in economic value added is not 123 percent of salary, but 8,800 percent, or eighty-eight times, salary.

Figure 4.4 reflects data showing that average engineering construction managers earning $87,000 in direct salary managed projects worth $57 million (Spencer, 1997). Superior project managers had 47 percent more economic value, worth an *additional* $27 million (through avoiding costs and time overruns and

FIGURE 4.3. PERFORMANCE
DISTRIBUTION FOR SALESPEOPLE IN U.S. FIRMS.

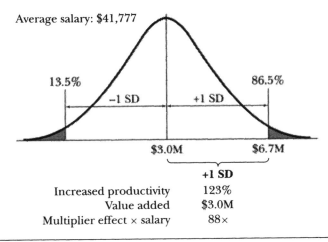

	+1 SD
Increased productivity	123%
Value added	$3.0M
Multiplier effect × salary	88×

Note: N of firms = 44.

Source: Data from Sloan & Spencer, 1991.

FIGURE 4.4. PERFORMANCE
DISTRIBUTION FOR CONSTRUCTION PROJECT MANAGERS.

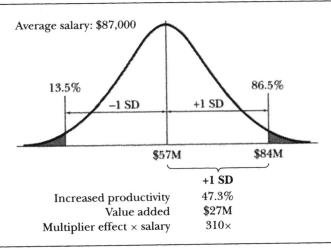

	+1 SD
Increased productivity	47.3%
Value added	$27M
Multiplier effect × salary	310×

Note: N of managers = 28.

Source: Data from Spencer, 1991.

FIGURE 4.5. PERFORMANCE DISTRIBUTION FOR ACCOUNT MANAGERS.

	Average Managers	+1 SD Managers	Increase
Defense electronics	$ 50K	$ 250K	500%
Consulting	300K	2000K	667%
Bond placement	50M	300M	600%

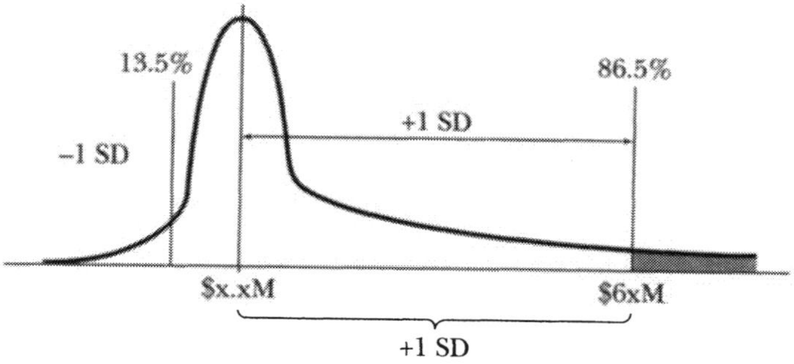

Source: Data from Hay/McBer, 1997.

selling additional engineering change orders). This 47 percent difference between superior and average managers is almost exactly the 48 percent predicted by Hunter et al. (1990). Note that the $27 million in economic value added represents not 47 percent of salary, but 31,000 percent, or 310 times, salary.

Figure 4.5 represents the finding that superior account managers generate six times the revenue produced by average account managers (salaries are not comparable, so multipliers have not been calculated) (Hay/McBer, 1997).

Performance distribution methods can also be applied to groups and organizations. For example, Figure 4.6 shows the distribution of production of pounds of polyester fiber by self-managing work group teams in Hoescht Celanese U.S. plants. Superior teams—those one standard deviation above the mean in production—outperformed average teams by 30 percent. Salary costs for these workers at $13 per hour were $270,400. The actual economic value added was an additional seven million pounds of fiber worth $1.40 per pound, which equals $9.8 million. The ratio of an additional 30 percent incremental salary value to actual economic value added is 1 to 121. Interestingly, the additional 30 percent

FIGURE 4.6. DISTRIBUTION OF PRODUCTION OF POUNDS OF POLYESTER FIBER BY SELF-MANAGING WORK GROUP TEAMS.

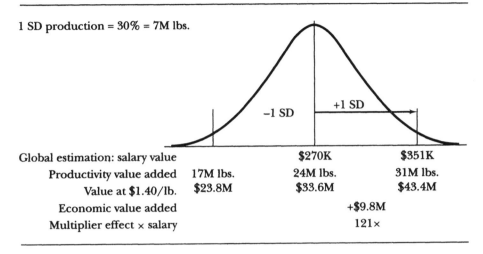

1 SD production = 30% = 7M lbs.

	−1 SD		+1 SD
Global estimation: salary value		$270K	$351K
Productivity value added	17M lbs.	24M lbs.	31M lbs.
Value at $1.40/lb.	$23.8M	$33.6M	$43.4M
Economic value added		+$9.8M	
Multiplier effect × salary		121×	

incremental productivity Hunter et al. (1990) found for individuals in moderately complex jobs appears to hold for teams as well. Teams, however, greatly leverage economic outcomes. The value of team EICs—Team Achievement Motivation, Empathy, Organizational Awareness, Collaboration, Peer Team Leadership—all of which can be affected by EIC-based selection and team-building training— can be calculated for groups in the same way it is for individuals. Even a 1 percent shift in team performance in this case was worth $98,000—which provides an economic justification for a lot of team building.

Finding the Percentage of EVA of Performance +1 SD Attributable to EIC Competencies

In finding the percentage of EVA of performing one standard deviation above the mean attributable to EIC competencies, EICs—as opposed to other individual characteristics (IQ or reaction time) and exogenous variables (for example, technology, managers, or local economies)—must first be defined. Reasonable consensus exists among researchers about the definitions of EIC competencies; Table 4.1 lists the generally accepted emotional intelligence competencies.

The question is whether any operant cognitive competencies are more closely related to IQ than to EQ (emotional quotient) (one might query Technical Expertise, Analytic Thinking, and Conceptual Thinking, for example). And if they

TABLE 4.1. EIC DICTIONARIES.

EIC Cluster	Boyatzis[a]	Spencer[b]	McClelland[c]	Fetzer Consortium[d]
Achievement	Efficiency Orientation	Achievement Orientation	Achievement Orientation	Achievement Motivation Innovativeness
	Initiative	Initiative	Initiative	Initiative (Self-Direction, Self-Motivation)
	Attention to Detail	Concern for Order and Quality		Conscientiousness
Affiliation	Empathy	Interpersonal Understanding	Interpersonal Understanding	Empathy
		Customer Service Orientation	Customer Service Orientation	Customer Service Orientation
		Teamwork and Cooperation	Teamwork and Cooperation	Team Building/Teamwork Collaboration and Cooperation
Power	Persuasiveness	Impact and Influence	Impact and Influence	Influence
	Written Communication			
	Oral Communication			Effective (Oral) Communication
	Organization Awareness			Organization Awareness
	Networking	Relationship Building	Relationship Building	Building Bonds Handling Relationships
	Negotiating			Conflict Management/ Negotiation

Cluster	[a]	[b]	[c]	[d]
Management	Developing Others	Directiveness Developing Others	Directiveness Developing Others	Coaching and Developing Teaching Others
	Group Management	Team Leadership	Team Leadership	Leadership Change Catalyst Managing Diverse Workforce Leveraging Diversity Managing Human Resources
	Cognitive	Quantitative Analysis Planning Using Technology	Analytic Thinking Technical Expertise	Analytic Thinking
Personal Effectiveness	Self-Confidence	Self-Confidence	Self-Confidence	Self-Confidence (Self-Esteem) Optimism and Hope
	Self-Control	Self-Control		Self-Control (Self-Management, Managing Emotions, Stress Tolerance)
	Flexibility	Flexibility	Flexibility	Flexibility Adaptability
	Social Objectivity	Organizational Commitment	Organizational Commitment New: Integrity	Honesty/Integrity Trustworthiness Managing Diverse Workforce Leveraging Diversity Managing Human Resources Emotional Self-Awareness

Accurate Self-Assessment

[a]Boyatzis, 1982; Boyatzis, Cowen, & Kolb, 1995.
[b]Spencer & Spencer, 1993.
[c]McClelland, 1996.
[d]Goleman, 1998b.

are more closely related, should they be included or excluded? Neuroscience studies by Damasio (1994) suggest that cognitive competence is indivisible from and influenced by emotional competence. In a classic experimental study, Damasio had orbital-cortex-damaged and normal subjects play a business game subtly rigged to ensure players always lost. Normal subjects soon refused to play the game. When asked why, they could not give rational (calculation of odds) reasons but simply said, "It just didn't feel right." The subjects' emotional sensors (the amygdala and related limbic system structures) seem to have detected the negative bias of the game before their "pure reason" prefrontal cortices had figured out that something was "wrong" and why it was wrong.

Frequently, cognitive competencies, which represent approximately 20 percent of the variables measured in most studies, do not explain any of the variance in superior job performance. Figures 4.7 and 4.8—structured equation models of independent variables that predict superior performance in two samples of executives—show an example of and an exception to this rule. (The numbers on the lines running from the dependent variables on the left side of each figure to the dependent criterion variable on the right are standardized partial regression coefficients, or beta weights. They indicate the approximate influence each independent variable has on the nonresidual variance in the dependent variable ($R^2 = .34-.35$, or 34 to 35 percent, in both cases).

Exogenous variables are either controlled for by stratified or random sampling designs or tested by entering them as separate variables in regression analyses. For example, in a study of branch managers, all subjects had the same products, promotion, technology (computers, network support, and so forth), and boss. Superior and average performers were selected as subjects randomly, on the basis of their percentage of growth in profits, in order to control for the size and history of different branch districts and the variation in the relative strength of local economies. Figure 4.7 shows the impact of the previous year's branch revenues tested in a regression equation. This variable accounted for $.10 \times .34 = 3.4\%$ of the explained variance in a branch manager's performance. EICs accounted for $.80 \times .34 = 27\%$ of the performance variance.

Published concurrent criterion and predictive validities of EICs against economic outcome variables range from $r = .10$ to $r = .90$, with r's = .40 to .60 ($R^2 = .15 -.35$) (McClelland, 1998; Spencer & Spencer, 1993). These results are usually attainable when EIC research is done in accordance with rigorous standards using behavioral event interviews and analysts trained to $r > .80$ interrater reliability.

These examples illustrate several important points about the global estimation method. First, many employees leverage incremental economic values much greater than their salaries. For this reason the actual economic contributions of superior performers who are one standard deviation above the mean should be used rather than the Hunter et al. (1990) method employing percentages of salary

FIGURE 4.7. EICS PREDICTING +1 SD SUPERIOR ECONOMIC PERFORMANCE AMONG U.S. INDUSTRIAL CONTROL FIRM BRANCH MANAGERS.

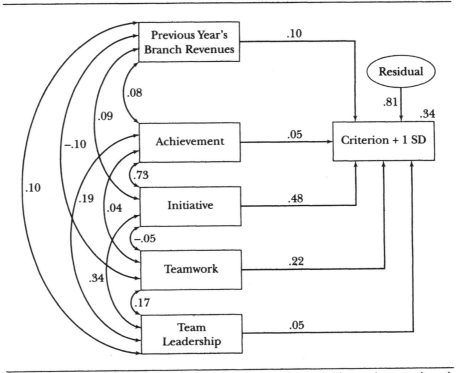

Note: N = 98 branch managers, in two samples. An exogenous variable, previous year branch revenues, accounts for ~10% of variance (R^2 = .34), EICs account for 80%; no cognitive competencies enter the regression analysis.

or cost of employment. Second, the more complex the job and the more economic value it leverages, the more a superior performance is worth. Identifying EICs for these jobs and developing HR programs that can improve them add the greatest economic value. Third, "pure" emotional and cognitive competencies, in addition to exogenous variables, predict superior performance. The definition of EIC used in this chapter—*any individual characteristic (or combination of characteristics) that can be measured reliably* and that *distinguishes superior from average performers, or effective from ineffective performers, at levels of statistical significance*—is deliberately broad. All independent variables should be controlled for or measured and analyzed to determine the percentage of variance they account for.

FIGURE 4.8. EICS PREDICTING +1 SD SUPERIOR ECONOMIC PERFORMANCE AMONG EUROPEAN FOOD AND BEVERAGE SENIOR MANAGERS.

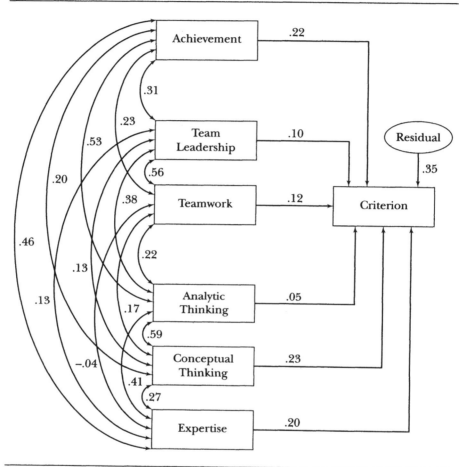

Note: N = 75 managers. Cognitive competencies account for ~48% of variance (R^2 = .35), EICs account for ~44%.

Fourth, *differentiating* EICs distinguish superior from average performers. *Threshold*, or *essential*, EICs are required for minimally adequate or average performance. Differentiating EICs add value, and for any given job they can serve as a template for personnel selection, succession planning, performance appraisal, and development. Any human resource approach that does not use an explicit benchmark *superior* to its present performance risks staffing, training, and managing to mediocrity—such an approach will be unlikely to improve upon the existing (average) performance level. Finally, the performance distributions, global estimation methodology, and findings of Hunter et al. (1990) provide powerful tools for estimating and evaluating the economic value of EIC-based HR applications. The Appendix to this chapter contains a survey form and spreadsheet template for calculating the value of performing one standard deviation above the mean in a job and for calculating the potential economic value added from staffing, training, and performance management applications.

How Much Value Can EIC-Based HR Interventions Add?

As illustrated in Figure 4.9, human resource interventions add value by shifting employees' performance curves toward greater average economic value added per employee (a shift to the right on the figure). Once the economic value of performing one standard deviation above the mean is known, this value can be used as a yardstick, called an *effect size* (es) to measure how much value an HR application can add. One effect size equals one standard deviation; intervention impacts are then measured in percentages or multiples of effect sizes. Figure 4.9 illustrates that selection effect sizes average 0.20 SD (range = 0.12–0.36, SD = 0.08); and training and performance management effect sizes average 0.46 to 0.64 (range = < 0.00 – > 1.00 [−0.07–1.07], SD = 0.37).

The economic value added by an intervention equals the economic value added by performance +1 SD × effect size × the number of people (or teams) affected. Figure 4.10 summarizes algorithms used and provides a template to calculate EVA. The steps in this algorithm are

I. Choose how you will calculate the economic value of +1 SD above the mean. Choices are
A. "Global estimation" from
   1. INPUT value of employee time per year:
      a. Salary/Year

or

FIGURE 4.9. EFFECT SIZE SHIFTS PRODUCED BY SELECTION AND BY TRAINING AND PERFORMANCE MANAGEMENT.

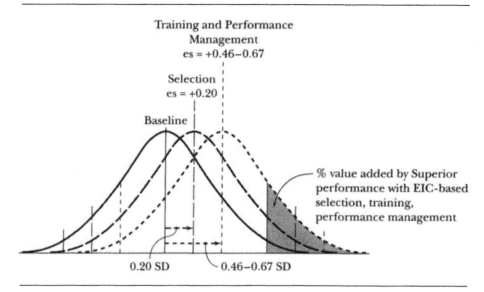

b. Full Cost of Employment/Year (usually about three times salary—get this figure from your financial analyst, or calculate it using the Economic Value of EIC in Appendix A.)

or

2. OUTPUT value—the values of economic resources (revenues, costs, capital budget) a person in the job can control, that is, can increase or save depending on his or her competence.

Choose a value calculated by one of these three methods and enter this value in spreadsheet cell B16.

B. Choose how you will estimate the economic value of +1 SD above the mean. Choices are

1. Choose findings from meta-analytic research in spreadsheet column D:
   a. 19%, for low,
   b. 32%, for moderate,
   c. 48%, for high, or
   d. 100%, for sales jobs

or

   e. Use the mean global estimate (collected using the Economic Value of EIC in Appendix A) of managers or other knowledgeable experts in your own organization. Enter this value in cell D16. Multiply B16 by D16 and enter this value in cell F16.

or

2. Use the actual measured economic value (increased revenues or profits, cost savings, and so on) at performance +1 SD above the mean. Actual economic value is preferable by far if these data are available from organization records. Enter this value in spreadsheet cells F16 and F17.

II. Estimate the percentage of job tasks or independent variables impacting EVA addressed by HR intervention.

Note: early meta-analytic studies assumed this percentage to be 100%, and report only the observed effect size shift from interventions. Later studies attempted to value intervention effects by multiplying the total value of time on the job by the percentage of time spent on tasks or EICs addressed by the intervention. For example, if managers with a total employment cost of $200,000 per year spend 50% of their time in meetings, a meeting management seminar would impact 50% × $200,000 = $100,000 economic value. This approach assumes time spent on a task equals its economic value added (a dubious assumption for most meetings!).

A more scientific—and conservative—estimate can be made by multiplying the percentage of independent variables addressed by an intervention by the statistical variance these variables make in business results (EVA dependent variables). The Figure 4.10 example uses this value from Figure 4.7, .27, entered in cell H19. All four competencies shown in Figure 4.7 to predict EVA were addressed by the Incon case intervention discussed at the end of this chapter.

If only some independent variables are addressed by an intervention, a third alternative is to multiply intervention time spent on independent variables by the variance these variables cause in business results outcomes. Figure 4.8 shows Teamwork and Team Leadership competencies account for 25% of .34 = 8.5% of explainable variance in Branch Manager profits, so training in these team competencies could impact 8.5% of EVA.

A. Choose Intervention

1. Time on Task,
2. Variance Impacted, or
3. The product of Time on Task and Variance Impacted and enter this value in cell H19.

III. Choose the most likely effect size shift for your application.

A. From meta-analytic data:

1. .10 for EIC data feedback and goal setting

    2. .19 for business results goal setting

    3. .20 for selection

    4. .46 to .67 for training

    5. .60 for performance management

or

    B. From estimates by knowledgeable experts, or (best) from measured results in your organization.

        Enter this value in cell J19. Multiply the economic value of +1 SD in cell F19 by percentage of independent variables causing EVA outcomes in cell H19 by effect size shift in Cell J19 to find the EVA per full time equivalent employee, and enter this value in cell L19.

  IV. Multiply EVA per FTE value in cell L19 by the number of people (or teams) per year impacted (selected, trained, performance managed) per year in cell N17. This product, in cell P17, is the total economic value added your EIC application can add to your organization per year.

Staffing

Staffing adds value by (1) hiring, placing, or promoting greater numbers of superior performers (that is, persons better matched to specific jobs, which increases both performance and satisfaction); (2) deselecting marginal performers (General Electric CEO Jack Welch ruthlessly outplaces the bottom 15 percent of GE managers each year); and (3) reducing turnover (by making better job-person matches so employees selected perform better and are not fired, are more satisfied and don't quit). The costs of turnover include

- Lost productivity during the time of acquiring new staff (fifty-five to fifty-seven days—or approximately two months of sales or production costs totaling roughly one third of an employee's first-year salary).

- Lower productivity during a new hire's learning curve period—the time from day she is hired to the day she is 100 percent productive (that is, has the average productivity of average experienced people in the job). Learning curve time averages twelve months for technical and professional personnel.

- Out-of-pocket direct costs for relocation and training. The *minimum* cost of replacing a technical or professional person is his direct salary for a year (Spencer, 1986); the actual cost is probably two to three times his direct salary if the full cost of employment, including benefits and overhead, is added to the salary and if lost productivity (from, for example, lost sales, the loss of a major contract, or a delay in time to market of a new product during those fifty-five to fifty-seven

FIGURE 4.10. ALGORITHM FOR CALCULATING EVA FROM PERFORMANCE DISTRIBUTION AND EFFECT SIZE SHIFT DATA.

	A	B	C	D	E	F	G	H	I	J	K	L	M	N	O	P
2	ECONOMIC VALUE OF COMPETENCY/BASED HR APPLICATIONS															
3	Input data =		Calculated data =				*100* (numbers in italics) = example data		19% (numbers not in italics) = mean meta-analytic study findings		$ = 000s					
4			1. $Economic Value Added by +1 SD		1.2 Measured $ EVA at +1SD *Choose:*		2. % Tasks or independent variables impacting EVA addressed by HR Intervention *Choose:*		3. Economic Value Added by EIC HR Intervention	Effect Size Shift (SD) *Choose:*		4. $Value Added per FTE		4. #Staff Impacted/Year		5. Total $ Value Added by HR Application/Year
			%Value Added by +1SD Performance						EIC HR Application							
5	1.1 Job Value	*Choose:*	A. $Salary/Year	$	*100*	Complexity	% *Choose:*		A. % Job Tasks addressed by intervention		A. EIC Feedback & Goal Setting					
6						A. Low	19%	1.00	*or*	0.1						
7			B. $Full Cost of employment/year (~2-7.5.0 x Salary)	$	*300*	B. Medium	32%		B. % Variance explained by independent variables addressed by training		B. Business Results Goal Setting					
8			*or*			*or*			0.27	*or*						
9	C. $Economic resources (revenues, costs, capital budget) person in the job can control								C. = A (% intervention time spent on independent variables which predict EVA) x B (%variance these variables cause in EVA)	0.19	C. Selection					
10			C. High	48%												
11			*or*							0.2						
12			D. Sales	100%					D. Training	0.44.67						
13			*or*						*or*							
14									E. Perf. Mgmt	0.6						
15			E. Other ___ Mgmt Estimate				D. Other ___ Mgmt Estimate		F. Other ___ Mgmt Estimate							
16			CHOICE	$	*300*	x	48%		= A.	$	*144*					
17				$ Value Added/Year	B.	$	*1,690*									
						$	*1,690*									
19			CHOICE					0.27	x	0.125	=	$ 37	x	28	x	1,597
20			Investment	$	224											
21			Return	$	1,597											
22			ROI (1 Year)	613%												

days it takes to replace an employee) is taken into account (McClelland, 1998; Spencer & Spencer, 1993).

Increased revenues and productivity come from better performers—as the averaged data in Figure 4.2 show, superior performers produce 19 percent, 32 percent, 48 percent, and 48 to 120 percent more in low, moderate, and high complexity jobs and sales jobs, respectively. A median 24 percent productivity increase from competency-based selection means the same amount of work can be done with $\{100\% - [100\%/(100\% + 24\%\ \text{productivity improvement})]\} = 20.5\%$ fewer staff.

Table 4.2 shows a meta-analysis of eight ECI-based selection systems. The median productivity increase was 19 percent, the median turnover decrease was 63 percent, the median economic value added was $1.6 million, and the median return on investment was greater than 1,000 percent. These figures appear incredible until one recalls how much even one additional superior performer can contribute (for example, one superior salesperson generates $3.7 million in additional revenues). A bad hire in an executive position was calculated by PepsiCo to cost $250,000 (McClelland, 1998); a bad placement to the Middle East costs

TABLE 4.2. META-ANALYSIS OF EFFECTS OF EIGHT COMPETENCY-BASED SELECTION SYSTEMS.

Industry (Job Family)	N	Design	Productivity Increase	Turnover Decrease	Economic Value Added	Return on Investment
Retail (sales)	60	Control	19%	50%	$720K	2,300%
Wholesale (sales)	80	Control	16%	50%		
Computer (sales trainees)	700	Longitudinal	—	90%	>$3.15M	>1,000%
Food and beverage (executives)	47	Longitudinal	10%	87%	$3.75M	>1,000%
Cosmetics (sales)	74	Control	33%	63%	$2.56M	>1,000%
Computer (programmers)	100	Longitudinal	—	99%	$1.43M	>1,000%
Retail/ customer service (telemarketers)	320	Longitudinal	24%	99%	>$1.6M	>1,000%
Financial services	120	Control	24%	—	$750K	525%
Median			19%	63%	$1.6M	>1,000%

Mobil $375,000. An EIC intervention program costs $80,000 to $120,000. A single superior hire or avoided hiring mistake usually justifies the cost of the investment in EIC-based staffing programs.

Consider some of the examples in Table 4.2 more closely.

Retail (sales). Fifty percent of sixty new hires were selected on the basis of competencies assessed using a behavioral event interview (BEI), and the other 50 percent were selected using traditional biodata criteria (one requirement was "ten years of sales experience," which meant mostly middle-aged white males were hired, an affirmative action concern). In the year following selection, turnover in the competency-selected group was 20 percent (six people) and average sales were $5,000 per week compared to 40 percent turnover (twelve people) and average sales of $4,200 per week in the traditional group. Benefits of the competency-based selection system were

- Avoidance of turnover costs: six salespeople retained at a saving of $20,000 per person in costs to replace them translates into saved costs of $120,000.
- Increased revenues: thirty salespeople producing $40,000 in extra sales per year with a 50 percent gross margin equals a $600,000 per year net increased contribution.

The total one-year benefit from a $720,000 return on $30,000 invested in the competency study and selection training was 2,300 percent (Spencer, 1986, pp. 95–96). In addition, the competency-based selection system resulted in the hiring of more female and minority salespeople (without prior sales experience), thereby lessening the likelihood of an affirmative action problem.

Computer (programmers). A reduction in turnover among competency-selected programmers saved the company the cost of replacing twenty-two professionals at $65,000 each, a $1.43 million return on an $120,000 investment in competency research and selection training.

Food and beverage (executives). An 87 percent reduction in the turnover of executives costing $250,000 each to replace saved the firm (PepsiCo) $4 million (McClelland, 1998).

Cosmetics (sales). Thirty-three people were hired using the BEI and a competency model; a control group of forty-one was selected without behavioral interviews. In the following three years, five of the competency-selected group quit or were fired, compared with seventeen in the control group. Competency-selected people increased their sales an average of 18.7 percent per quarter, compared to a 10.5 percent average increase for salespeople in the control group. On an annual basis, competency-selected people each sold $91,370 more than control-group salespeople, a net revenue increase of $2,558,360 ($91,370 × 28 salespeople).

Computer (sales). A large computer firm decided to transform several thousand senior staff—"overhead people who cost money," with an average yearly compensation of $57,000 per person—into "salespeople who make money." Not all the staff "bureaucrats" had the competencies to be effective in sales: the initial attrition rate from the sales training was 30 percent, or 210 of the 700 staff sent for sales training each year. (Sales trainees were terminated after four months if they had failed three consecutive month-end tests.) Each failure cost the firm $16,667 in salary costs alone, which totaled $3.5 million per year for the 210 failures (this figure is conservative because costs of trainee benefits and other costs of training—instructors, materials, and overhead—were also lost). Using an EIC model developed by studying its successful salespeople, the firm cut program attrition to 3 percent (twenty-one dropouts), a 90 percent reduction worth $3.15 million (Rondina, 1988).

Training and Performance Management

Training, development activities, and performance management add value by (1) shortening the time it takes employees to reach 100 percent productivity (defined as the average productivity of average experience workers in the job) and (2) increasing productivity by shifting average employees' performance toward that of superior performers.

Figure 4.11 shows the economic value of shortening a learning curve by 33 percent by teaching new hires the EICs and best practices of superior performers (Spencer, 1986). The learning curve time to reach 100 percent productivity is divided into three equal periods, each costing one-third of the total employment costs for the entire learning curve period (in this case $100,000/3 = new hires' productivity, where 100 percent equals the average productivity of an average experienced employee without training—the control condition) after they have the EIC-based training. Economic value added for trained and control subjects equals the estimated percentage increase in productivity times the value of time during each subperiod. The total productivity value for untrained subjects is $50,000, whereas it is $88,000 for trained subjects; hence training adds $38,000 per trainee.

Productivity improvements from training are estimated from manager approximations of trainees' productivity before and after training as shown in Figure 4.12 (Spencer, 1986). Assuming the full cost of employee time per year is three times salary ($33,333), or $100,000, and time on tasks addressed by training is 50 percent of total time, training affects 50% × $100,000 = $50,000 of employees' economic time value. Managers (or 360-degree raters: bosses, peers, subordinates, and customers surrounding the person being rated) estimate employees' produc-

FIGURE 4.11. VALUE OF SHORTENING LEARNING CURVE TIME FOR EMPLOYEES WITH EMPLOYMENT COST OF $100,000 PER YEAR.

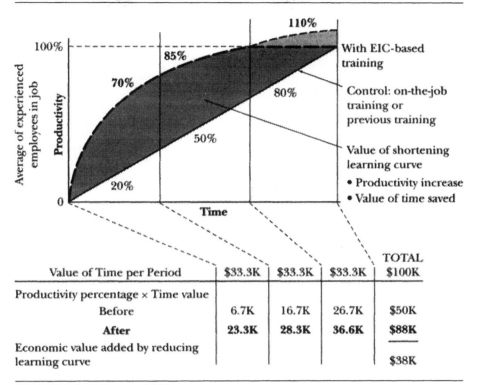

Value of Time per Period	$33.3K	$33.3K	$33.3K	TOTAL $100K
Productivity percentage × Time value				
Before	6.7K	16.7K	26.7K	$50K
After	23.3K	28.3K	36.6K	$88K
Economic value added by reducing learning curve				$38K

Source: Data from Spencer, 1986.

tivity before training and three months after training. Productivity before training is multiplied by the economic value of time on tasks addressed by training, in this case 80% × $50,000 = $40,000. This baseline value is subtracted from productivity value of time after training, in this case 120% × $50,000 = $60,000, showing a gain of $20,000 per trainee.

Economic value added from training and performance management can also be estimated directly by calculating the following: Effect size shift + Known economic value of performing +1 SD. Table 4.3 shows a meta-analysis of effect sizes and returns on investment (ROIs) in four studies. With outliers below the 10th and above the 90th percentile eliminated, the mean effect size shift for training in these studies was 0.44, with a standard deviation of 0.27, and ROI was 116 percent, with

FIGURE 4.12. MANAGER RATINGS OF TRAINEES' PRODUCTIVITY ON TASKS BEFORE AND AFTER TRAINING.

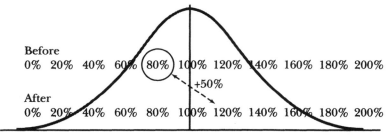

Productivity gain = 120% − 80% = 40%/80% baseline = 50% gain

Economic value added per trainee before training = 80% × $50K = $40K

Economic value added per trainee after training = 120% × $50K = $60K

Gain in economic value per trainee = $60K − $40K = $20K

Source: Data from Spencer, 1986.

a standard deviation of 154 percent. Effect size findings in Table 4.3 are 28 percent more conservative than the mean 0.64 to 0.67 effect size shifts for both training and performance management reported by Burke and Day (1986) and by Falcone, Edwards, and Day (1986). ROIs varied significantly with the complexity of jobs, whether researchers used salary (as most did), cost of employment, or actual economic value added by superior performance, as demonstrated in Figures 4.2 through 4.5.

The identical effect size shift for training and performance management reported by Burke and Day (1986) and Falcone et al. (1986) is in itself an interesting finding. One hypothesis is that good performance management *is* training—that is, rather than simply forcing employees towards goal accomplishment, performance management that involves coaching teaches EICs and best practices that help employees improve performance. For example, Latham and Locke's meta-analysis (1979) of the effects of goal-setting (which showed a mean 19 percent productivity increase for jobs of varying complexity) supports findings of effect size shifts from performance management. Using the *rule of 40* (that is, performing one standard deviation above the mean equals 40 percent increased productivity), goal-setting has an effect size of 0.475 (19 percent/40 percent).

TABLE 4.3. ES SHIFTS AND ROI FOR A PORTFOLIO OF TRAINING PROGRAMS.

Program	Executive Leadership Performance Shift	ROI	Management Performance Shift	ROI	Communication Performance Shift	ROI	Sales Performance Shift	ROI	Technical Performance Shift	ROI	All Performance Shift	ROI	All (Conservative) Performance Shift	ROI	+1 SD Performance Shift	ROI	−1 SD Performance Shift	ROI
*Executive-2**	−0.05	−105%									−0.05	−105%	−0.05	−105%			−0.05	−105%
*Leadership skills**	0.12	−36%									0.12	−36%	0.12	−36%				
Managers-1			0.76	126%							0.76	126%	0.76	126%				
Managers-2			1.11	492%							1.11	492%	1.11	492%	1.11	492%		
Lab managers-1			−0.09	−129%							−0.09	−129%	−0.09	−129%			−0.09	−129%
*Project management**			0.37	60%							0.37	60%	0.37	60%				
Supervisors-1			0.23	−39%							0.23	−39%	0.23	−39%				
Supervisors-2			0.38	125%							0.38	125%	0.38	125%				
Team building			0.12	−86%							0.12	−86%	0.12	−86%				
*In-house time management**			0.89	1,989%							0.89	1,989%	0.89	1,989%	0.89			
Off-the-shelf time management			0.28	106%							0.28	106%	0.28	106%				
Oral presentations					0.26	69%					0.26	69%	0.26	69%				
Written communication					1.07	275%					1.07	275%	1.07	275%	1.07	275%		
*Territory management**							0.54	85%			0.54	85%	0.54	85%				
Product sales							0.67	3,931%			0.67	3,931%	0.67	3,931%				
*Problem solving**									0.31	16%	0.31	16%	0.31	16%				
*Hazard energy**									0.90	306%	0.90	306%	0.90	306%	0.90	306%		
*Specialty valves**									0.37	130%	0.37	130%	0.37	130%				
Median	0.04	−71%	0.37	106%	0.67	172%	0.61	2,008%	0.37	130%	0.37	96%	0.37	77%	0.99	306%	(0.07)	−117%
Mean	0.04	−71%	0.45	294%	0.67	172%	0.61	2,008%	0.53	151%	0.46	406%	0.46	87%	0.99	358%	(0.07)	−117%
SD	0.12	49%	0.39	661%	0.57	146%	0.09	2720%	0.32	146%	0.37	999%	0.37	164%	0.11	117%	0.03	17%

Note: Outliers are shown in italics.

Source: Data from Burke & Day (1986); Falcone, Edwards, & Day (1986); Morrow, Jarrett, & Rupinski (1997); Spencer & Morrow (1996).

Meta-analytic studies consistently find that training programs that generate performance one standard deviation *below* the mean have zero or negative effect sizes and negative returns on investment. Table 4.3 shows that most training has a positive effect size and return on investment. The exception is top executive training. Although hypotheses advanced to explain this finding include that you can't teach old dogs new tricks, these top executive sessions are usually not really training but rather vacations or perks, held in lush surroundings with ample time off to play golf or ski, and such "training" is rarely EIC-based.

Most meta-analytic studies do not report the percentage of variance in effect size that can be attributed to EIC training versus training in cognitive abilities, technical knowledge, or other skills. An exception is Miron and McClelland's meta-analysis (1979) of the effects of Achievement Motivation training on small business entrepreneurs, which used a modified Solomon four-group design in which some entrepreneurs were trained in Achievement Motivation, a comparison group was trained in business knowledge and skills (accounting, finance, manufacturing, marketing and sales, and human resources), and a third group was trained in both Achievement Motivation and business skills. Standard Metropolitan Statistical Area (SMSA) means for dependent variables in comparable small businesses were used as a control. Only Achievement Motivation training made a difference (effect size = 0.50) in the independent variables: the number of jobs created (an increase of 32 percent) and the reported income and taxes of businesses, proprietors, and the incremental employees hired (see Figure 4.13). Achievement Motivation combined with business skills training had no significant impact. Business skills training alone actually decreased the entrepreneurs' business activity and results. The researchers hypothesized that business skills training diminished trainees' efficacy and self-confidence by making success in business ventures seem too complex and difficult to achieve.

A reanalysis of the data reported in Table 4.3 attempted to classify training programs into EIC and non-EIC groups to estimate the value added by EIC inputs (Spencer & Morrow, 1996). Training programs were classified as EIC-based if they (1) explicitly taught at least one EIC (for example, Achievement Motivation), and (2) used experiential adult learning methods that required trainees to practice and demonstrate EICs. EIC-based training programs positively shifted performance an average of 0.70 SD and returned a mean ROI of 700 percent. Content knowledge and other training shifted performance 0.41 SD and returned an average 87 percent ROI. These data suggest that EIC-based training can produce as much as 1.7 times the effect size shift and 8 times the ROI of non-EIC-based training. These findings, however, are not conclusive because (1) the criteria for classifying training as EIC or non-EIC were not tested for interreliability; (2) the sample size was too small to report statistical significance; and (3) EIC-based training results were biased by a large outlier of 3,971 percent ROI for one sales training program.

FIGURE 4.13. EFFECTS OF ACHIEVEMENT MOTIVATION TRAINING ON SMALL BUSINESS.

Cost for 100 trainees: $287,500 (funded by the U.S. Small Business Administration)

Benefits: Compared to a control group, achievement motivation trainees generated

- Increased jobs: 32% more (227 total, or 2.3 per business)
- Increased income:

	Reported Income Year 1	Tax Rate	Tax Revenues
Businesses	$615,000	22.0%	$189,900
Proprietors	484,000	20.0	97,400
Employees	651,000	11.5	75,000
Total year 1			362,300
Total year 2			705,000
Total years 1 and 2			$1,067,300

- Effect size shift: ~0.5 SD
- Time to recover training cost: 9.5 months
- ROI: 1 year 26%; 2 years 271%

Source: Data from Miron & McClelland, 1979.

Figure 4.14 shows a normalized plot of training ROIs against effect size shifts and the extrapolated effect size and ROI of U.S. training programs. Training effect size shifts closely predict returns on investment. Meta-analytic estimates of effect size shifts and potential returns from training are very useful in developing business cases for development and performance management HR interventions. For example, the Consortium for Research on Emotional Intelligence in Organizations has published guidelines for the design and delivery of development programs based on fourteen model programs that significantly improved EICs or performance results (Cherniss & Adler, 2000). The potential economic value added by the consortium's guidelines can be straightforwardly calculated. As illustrated in Figure 4.14, the bottom quartile (23 percent) of training programs produces a negative return on investment of 80 to 90 percent. If U.S. organizations invest $60 billion in training per year, the training efforts in the bottom quartile cost $12.6 billion and have a negative ROI of greater than $10 billion. The next quartile (27 percent) costs $17.4 billion and produces an average ROI of 44% ($7.7 billion). Net return on investment for training programs in the bottom half of the distribution is therefore −$10 billion + $7.7 billion = −$2.3 billion.

A conservative assumption is that application of the guidelines could raise the bottom half of the distribution—those training programs costing $30 billion and returning −$2.3 billion—to the average 116 percent ROI. This application would

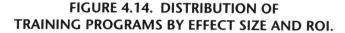

**FIGURE 4.14. DISTRIBUTION OF
TRAINING PROGRAMS BY EFFECT SIZE AND ROI.**

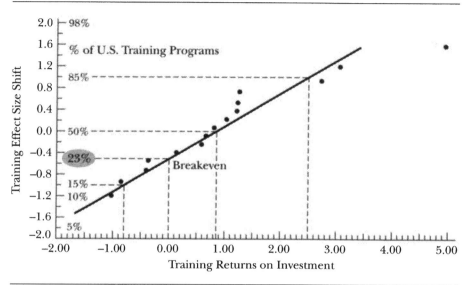

Note: r = .94, R² = 0.86, p < .001).

produce $30 billion × 1.16 = $34.8 billion, versus the current loss of $2.3 billion, a net gain of $37.1 billion. This estimate assumes only a single year's benefit rather than a stream of benefits over two or more years, on the basis that data reported in the meta-analytic studies are for only one year and that the Ebbinghaus curve suggests that few training programs have multiyear benefits.

Recommended Economic Value Analysis Protocol

A five-step protocol for developing business cases for, as well as evaluating, EIC-based HR interventions is shown in the following pages, using a recent case study example. "Incon" is a $2 billion U.S. industrial controls firm with four hundred branch managers (BMs) in fifty-six countries. In 1997, Incon developed a BM competency model and training program that was used to train a pilot group of twenty-six U.S. BMs. At the end of 1999, management asked for a business case and preliminary evaluation of this effort. In order to achieve this, the steps detailed here were taken.

Step 1: Define Performance Criterion

The initial step of defining the performance criterion appears obvious, but in many organizations, managers lack consensus about measures of output performance. Most firms have explicit or de facto *balanced scorecard* variables, but these need to be probed to determine what management really values.

CASE EXAMPLE

Incon's balanced scorecard for sales managers included growth in revenues, return on sales, cost reduction, customer satisfaction, improvement in productivity and operational efficiency, sales of new products and services, organizational climate, and qualified turnover of subordinate managers and salespeople. When pressed, finance told HR that the only performance measures that mattered were increased profits: growth in revenues × return on sales. This measure was used as the dependent variable in developing the business case and evaluating the competency-based training program.

Step 2: Develop a Business Case

The first question in developing a business case should always be: is there enough variance in the value of dependent variable to make investment in an intervention worthwhile. This question can be answered in a number of ways.

A. Calculating the Economic Value. Calculating the economic value of the problem or opportunity the HR program will address involves several operations:

- Valuing the problem (cost per incident × # incidents)
- Valuing the opportunity: the economic value added (EVA) per employee (team or firm) per year at the benchmark or desired level of performance—for example, a criterion sample of employees (teams, firms) +1 SD above the mean (EVA/employee/year × # employees).

CASE EXAMPLE

Data for the business case were easily developed from firm financial records with basic descriptive statistics. Sales for branch managers ranged from $4 million to $90 million, with a mean of $17.0 million. As shown in Table 4.4, BMs one standard deviation above the mean had 5.66 percent higher return on $12.8 million more sales, worth $2.94 million, 134 percent more than average performance. Variance in BM performance is very large, hence offers a large opportunity for an HR intervention that improves average BM performance.

**TABLE 4.4. CRITERION SAMPLE: AVERAGE V. STAR (+1 SD)
VARIANCE AND ECONOMIC VALUE ADDED.**

	Revenue	Operating Income	Profit
Mean	$17.02M	5.33%	$1.26M
SD	$12.82M	5.66%	$1.69M
EVA of superior performer (+1 SD)	$29.84M	10.99%	$2.94M

The second business case question is how much impact is the HR intervention likely to have on business results dependent variable(s), i.e. its probable EVA in problem cost savings or opportunity increased profits.

B. Estimating the Percentage of EVA Variance. HR intervention can influence the amount of variance in superior performance +1 SD due to competencies impacted by training. This can be estimated from meta-analytic studies, or better, by an empirical competency study of superior versus average performers. This step identifies independent variables with the greatest impact on dependent result variables, hence priorities for training.

CASE EXAMPLE

Incon completed a competency study of Branch Managers. Behavioral event interview (BEI) and other assessment data identified competencies that differentiate superior performers from averages, and predict outcome results, and best practices: work processes, technology, organization/team/job design, staffing, development, performance management, rewards, climate and culture interventions used by superior performers to get significantly better results.

As shown in Figure 4.7, competencies that differentiated superior performers included Achievement (ACH), Initiative (INT), Teamwork (TW), and Team Leadership (TL). BM competencies accounted for 27 percent of variance in performance, worth .27 × $1.69 million = $456,300.

C. Estimating the Percentage Change HR Intervention Can Make. HR intervention can affect specific results variables. The percentage change or "effect size shift" can be estimated from published meta-analytic studies—or better, from evaluation of pilot interventions using random samples of firm employees.

CASE EXAMPLE

Incon used conservative estimates of training effect size shifts (ES = .44, SD = .27).

D. Calculate Expected EVA and ROI. It's then necessary to calculate the EVA and ROI expected from the HR intervention. If training can achieve a .44 expected effect size shift in average trainee performance, the expected value added (EVA) per trainee would be .44 × 456,300 = $200,772, and total return from training 28 BMs at a cost of $8,000 per trainee $5,621,616, a potential 2,410 percent ROI, as shown in Table 4.5.

E. Calculate a Sensitivity Analysis. Calculate a "sensitivity analysis" for the minimum effect size shift needed to justify the investment in training and the probability of achieving this effect size shift and return.

CASE EXAMPLE

If the firm's cost of capital is 8.5 percent, and the standard deviation of effect size shifts from training is .27, the effect size shift needed to achieve an adequate return, and the probability of successfully achieving this return, can be calculated as follows:

$$es_{ROI} = \frac{I(1+\%CC)}{VA_{es}N} = \frac{\$224,000*(1+.085)}{\$200,772*28} = .04$$

where
es_{ROI} is the effect size needed to achieve the required ROI when
I = investment in training ($224,000),
%CC is the firm's cost of capital (8.5%)
VA_{es} = value added ($456,300) by the expected es (.44) per trainee = $200,772, and
N = number of persons trained (28).

$$\text{Probability of success} = p @ z = \frac{\mu es(.44) - es_{ROI}(.04)}{SD_{es}(.27)} = 93\%$$

where
p is the probability at the calculated z value (available from any statistics text).
In this case, an effect shift of 4 percent justifies the investment in training, and the probability of achieving an acceptable return is 93 percent, as shown in Table 4.6. The business case for training is reasonable.

TABLE 4.5. BUSINESS CASE FOR TRAINING.

ES shift from training	0.44
EVA of training per person	$456,300
N trained in U.S.	28
Total EVA	$5,621,616
Investment per trainee	$8,000
Investment in U.S. training	$224,000
ROI	2,410%

TABLE 4.6. SENSITIVITY AND PROBABILITY OF SUCCESS ANALYSIS.

ROI required	8.50%
ES required for desired ROI	0.04
z @ ES shift required	1.481
p success	93%

Step 3: Design Course and Evaluation

This process involves two phases:

A. Course Design. Ideally, competency-based training uses experiential adult learning methods to develop individual competencies, gives trainees opportunities to practice using competencies, and follows training with on-the-job action learning projects in which trainees apply competencies (with coaching, feedback, and technical assistance from instructor-consultants) to implement best practices used by superior performers to improve results.

B. Evaluation Design. Ideally, a randomized treatment and training versus control group, usually a "wave" or "waiting list" design in which participants trained in later periods serve as a control groups for those trained earlier.

CASE EXAMPLE

In this case, business pressures limited training to a two-day seminar in which twenty-eight United States branch managers learned *about* (the definitions of) EICs, received feedback on their EICs as compared with superior performers, and set goals to improve their EICs and business performance. A post-hoc quasi-experimental "wave" evaluation design compared twenty-eight trainees with fourteen matched sales managers who did not receive the training as controls.

Step 4: Train, Monitor, and Coach

In this step the training is actually conducted, and follow-up activities such as monitoring and coaching are begun.

CASE EXAMPLE

Follow-up, monitoring, coaching, and goal progress review meetings with trainees are in progress in the company.

Step 5: Evaluate Effects of Training

The final step in EIC-based training is to evaluate the change in trainees' competence and calculate the economic value added in comparison with the competence and EVA of the control group.

CASE EXAMPLE

As shown in Table 4.7, the EIC definition training, feedback, and goal-setting intervention at Incon appears to have significantly increased participant branch managers' sales and profits, producing a 13 percent ROI. Trainees' return on sales decreased (insignificantly) compared to that of the control group—perhaps because trained managers were investing in revenue—increasing marketing and area expansion efforts. However, trainees' increased revenues more than made up for this decline. The 0.04 effect size shift achieved by training was only 10 percent of the expected 0.46. This shows that even a very small shift in performance can result in significant statistical and economic results when the economic value of the problem or opportunity in the business case is large.

- Es shift from training: $57K/$456K ~.125
- Investment: $8,000/BM trained × 28 BMs trained = $224K
- Return: +$57K Profit/BM trained × 28 BMs trained = $1596K additional profit
- ROI = 613 percent

TABLE 4.7. TREATMENT GROUP VERSUS CONTROL GROUP PERFORMANCE OVER ONE YEAR, AFTER TRAINING.

	Revenue	Operating Income	Profit
Trained group (N = 23)	$3.117M	0.3%	$249,000
Control group (N = 7)	$1.660M	7.0%	$192,000
EVA from training	$1.457M	−0.4%	$57,000
p (t test)	< .04	—	< .02

Trainees increased revenues and profits significantly more than the control group. Trainee versus control return on sales did not differ significantly. The .125 effect size shift achieved by training and feedback is similar to that reported by McClelland for EIC assessment feedback to executives. That the .125 effect size is 28 percent of the .44 meta-analytic mean for all training programs suggests that more in-depth training involving action learning projects could increase return on training investments.

Did the training actually *cause* the economic value added? Probably, through feedback and goal-setting, but the case for competency-based training remains incomplete. A complete evaluation protocol would include a design (see Figure 4.15) that measures (1) the change in trainees' competence, (2) the change in results, (3) the predictive link between changed competence and changed results, and (4) additional analyses to refute alternative hypotheses for the changed results (looking at the effects of selection processes and at differences in local economies, budgets, management, climate, and so forth), if these alternative explanations have not been eliminated by stratification or randomization.

Path A is the current criterion validity between competencies and economic performance before training; path B is posttest concurrent validity. Path C is the predicted validity of competence before training compared to competence after training. Do the smart get smarter? That is, are there competencies that predict gaining from training? Such findings are useful in selecting individuals to send to training programs and for verifying hypotheses about *learning environments.* (In the case example, the competencies of Achievement Motivation, Influence, Flexibility, and Developing Others predicted significant gains from training.) Path D is the predictive validity of economic performance before training for economic performance after training (do the rich get richer?). In the case example the trained BMs' branch sales were significantly larger at time #1—data that should be partialed out.

FIGURE 4.15. EVALUATION DESIGN FOR EIC INTERVENTIONS.

	O_1	X	O_2	$Time_2-Time_1$	Trained–Control $(Time_2-time_1)$
Trained group A	$comp_1$ B		$comp_2$	$comp_2-comp_1$	
	ec $perf_1$	C	ec $perf_2$	(ec $perf_2-$ ec $perf_1$)	
			D		T ($comp_2-comp_1$)– C ($comp_2-comp_1$)
Control group	$comp_1$		$comp_2$	$comp_2-comp_1$	E
	ec $perf_1$		ec $perf_2$	(ec $perf_2-$ ec $perf_1$)	T (ec $perf_2-$ec $perf_1$)– C (ec $perf_2-$ec $perf_1$)

Note: Comp$_1$ = competencies before training; comp$_2$ = competencies after training; ec perf$_1$ = economic performance before training; ec perf$_2$ = economic performance after training; T = trained group; C = control group.

Path E is critical for proving the case for competency-based training. Statistically significant findings suggest that competence changed by training predicts or causes economic gains significantly different from the gains manifested by the control group(s). In the case example, researchers are conducting a posttraining assessment of trainees' competencies to measure the difference made by training and to see whether economic gains can be attributed to changed competence resulting from training. An additional 250 BMs have been trained, mostly in Europe, which will provide cross-validation samples.

Lessons from this case include the following:

1. Economic analysis, business case development, and evaluation and data collection design should *always* precede *every* EIC intervention. An axiom of behavioral science is "It never gets better than your dependent variable—it only gets worse."
2. Intervene only when intervention is justified by a business case. Go for large-value problems and opportunities (follow Nobel Laureate Peter Medewar's advice: "the way to win a Nobel prize is to have an instinct for a jugular problem"). Even a small difference in a *big* value problem or opportunity can

produce significant results; even a *big* difference in a trivial problem can yield only trivial results. Do sensitivity analyses, and calculate the probability of achieving a significant ROI.

3. EICs should be taught in the context of planning for and practicing best practices. Numerous *tricks of the masters* for expanding sales territories; introducing new products and services; reengineering customer service (for example, having one rather than multiple points of contact) and internal operations (for example, using estimating software or consolidating duplicate cost centers); designing, organizing, and leading teams (for example, creating sales teams of salespeople and engineers); staffing (for example, using explicit strategies for hiring competitors' top salespeople to capture market share in new territories and launch new products and services); rewarding; and so forth, will be mentioned by superior performers in their interviews. These should be taught to others in order to illustrate *how* superior performers demonstrate EICs.

4. Action learning projects in which trainees use EICs to implement best practices to improve economic performance should be required, in addition to standard goal-setting.

5. Follow-up monitoring, technical assistance and coaching, and goal progress review meetings (to share learning and collect posttest data) should be integral parts of every EIC program (see Chapters Seven, Nine, and Ten for more on how to design effective training and development interventions).

Summary

Professional standards and ethics, acceptance of the concept of emotional intelligence competencies and practice improvement, legal rulings, and clients' desire for value for their money will all increasingly require EIC researchers and practitioners to report reliability and EVA validity statistics for their interventions.

Global estimation or performance distribution methods (see the Appendix) make collection of these data quick, cheap, and easy—no more onerous than the "reactions" smile-sheet exercises that follow most training programs. Fifteen years of published meta-analytic data show that EIC-based staffing, training, and performance management interventions can add economic value, although the effect size shifts produced by EIC inputs, rather than by knowledge content inputs, have not been conclusively established. All EIC research and practice should report the value and change in EVA for business case dependent variables attributable to EIC inputs. The alternative is that EIC methods and variables will continue to be viewed as a "junk science" fad by many who could benefit from them.

APPENDIX: ECONOMIC VALUE OF COMPETENCE SURVEY.

This survey collects data you can use to cost-justify competency-based human resources applications in your organization.

Please answer the following questions in the highlighted boxes for an economically valuable job you want to analyze (a sales job is ideal).

A. **Your firm's INDUSTRY (product/service)?** _____

B. **The JOB or ROLE you are analyzing?** _____

1a. The average annual **SALARY** for this job? _____
OR
1b. The **FULL COST OF EMPLOYMENT** (salary + benefits + overhead) for this job? _____

2. The **FINANCIAL RESOURCES—annual revenues, expense budget** or payroll,
and/or **capital assets** a person in this job controls? _____

C. **PRODUCTIVITY of average and superior (defined as the top 1 out of 10) employee in this job.**

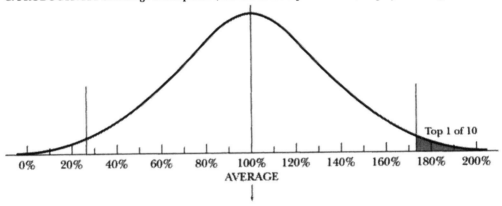

3. **The PRODUCTIVITY PERCENTAGE of a superior performer,** compared to that of an experienced average employee, in the job, where average employee productivity is defined as 100%? In estimating this percentage, if you do not know the actual value, it may help to think in

100%		
Average Employee		**Superior** Employee (top 1 out of 10)

4. **DOLLAR or other currency figures** for yearly sales or other economic outcomes?

Average Employee		**Superior** Employee (top 1 out of 10)

D. **STAFFING**

5. **NUMBER** of **EMPLOYEES** in this job/role? _____

6. **ANNUAL TURNOVER (quit or fire) RATE (%)** of employees in this job? _____

APPENDIX: ECONOMIC VALUE OF COMPETENCE SURVEY, Cont'd.

E. TRAINING, DEVELOPMENT, PERFORMANCE MANAGEMENT

7. Number of EMPLOYEES in job **TRAINED** per/year? _____

8. PERCENTAGE OF TOTAL JOB tasks addressed by training? _____

9. Please fill in the **RELATIVE PERCENTAGES OF TRAINING TIME** (adding to 100%) spent
a. Learning facts, theories, or ideas? _____
b. Practicing motivation or behavioral skills? _____

                                                                                     100%

10. **LEARNING CURVE:** How many **MONTHS does it take for a new hire to become fully productive**
(equal to the average productivity of an experienced person in the job)?
a. **BASELINE: Without training** (or with current less effective training)? _____
b. **With training** (or new competency-based training)? _____

11. The **PRODUCTIVITY PERCENTAGE** of the average trainee **BEFORE** training,
on the bell curve 0% — 200% scale shown above where 100% = the average performance
of an experienced person in the job? _____

12. The **PRODUCTIVITY PERCENTAGE** of the average trainee **AFTER** training,
on the scale below the curve, where 100% = the average performance of an experienced
person in the job (fill in a % productivity if greater than 200% after training)? _____

13. For how many **MONTHS** after training is this **INCREASED PRODUCTIVITY MAINTAINED?** _____

Note: Spreadsheets showing how to use this survey are available from the author via e-mail at
lyle_spencer@hotmail.com.

CHAPTER FIVE

MEASUREMENT OF INDIVIDUAL EMOTIONAL COMPETENCE

Marilyn K. Gowing

In his book *Working with Emotional Intelligence,* Daniel Goleman (1998b) states that "today's workforce is being judged by a new yardstick." He notes that "we are being judged . . . not just by how smart we are, or by our training and expertise, but also by how well we handle ourselves and each other" (p. 1). Goleman refers to these "human talents" as "emotional intelligence" (EI).

But is this yardstick really new? Goleman himself acknowledges that the roots of emotional intelligence, as he defines it, are in classic management theory. For example, in 1955, Robert L. Katz argued that the performance of an effective administrator depended on three sets of fundamental skills—technical skill, conceptual skill, and human skill, or "the way the individual perceives (and recognizes the perceptions of) his superiors, equals, and subordinates, and in the way he behaves subsequently" (p. 34). Even prior to that time, as early as the 1940s, theorists involved in the Ohio State Leadership Studies, under the direction of Hemphill (1959), developed the constructs of Structure and Consideration, with the latter representing the effectiveness of the leader in establishing "mutual trust, respect and a certain warmth and rapport between supervisor and his/her group" (Fleishman & Harris, 1962, p. 43).

Similarly, the U.S. Office of Strategic Services (1948) during World War II developed a process for whole person assessment based on the earlier work of Murray (1938) that included the evaluation of cognitive and noncognitive abilities. This process later evolved into the *assessment center,* which was first used operationally in the private sector at AT&T in 1956 (Bray, 1964; Bray, Campbell, & Grant, 1974) and in the government, over ten years later, at the Internal Revenue Service. Assessment centers have also been used to evaluate academic performance. Alverno College in Milwaukee, Wisconsin, has a criterion-referenced educational program. Rather than taking traditional kinds of tests, students must pass competency examinations, many of which are based on the assessment center method (Byham, 1977). Several graduate school business programs have incorporated the assessment center process for career counseling (programs at Stanford University, Brigham Young, and Baylor, for example; see Byham, 1977). More recently, Richard Boyatzis at Case Western Reserve University has incorporated a management assessment center course into the graduate business program as a way of supporting self-directed change (Boyatzis, 1994).

The assessment center process employs multiple assessment techniques (with at least one being a work simulation), multiple assessors, pooling of information from assessors, and techniques to evaluate behaviors associated with individuals' cognitive and noncognitive dimensions. Many of the dimensions traditionally evaluated by managerial assessment centers—for example, Oral Communication, Development of Subordinates, Sensitivity, Organizational Sensitivity, and Extraorganizational Sensitivity (Thornton & Byham, 1982)—parallel the emotional competencies in Goleman's *emotional competence framework,* such as Communication, Developing Others, Understanding Others, and Political Awareness (see Chapters Two and Three). These competencies have been found to be predictive of successful performance in managerial positions in many corporations, with the most convincing evidence coming from the Management Progress Study at AT&T. In this study, assessment center results were withheld from management. Thus promotion decisions were not influenced by these results. Nonetheless, those who had progressed the greatest number of levels upward in AT&T were later found to be the people with, on average, the strongest assessment center performance. Assessment centers have been widely employed by organizations in both the private and public sectors for many occupations at various levels (Moses & Byham, 1977; Thornton & Byham, 1982). Similarly, other approaches, such as the behavioral event interview and targeted selection interviews, have built on the same concepts that underlie the assessment center methodology to ensure objective assessment of the competencies needed by superior workers (see Chapter Seven). Thus the employer community has recognized the critical role of emotional competence in the world of work for some time and has had considerable experience in measuring many of the components of emotional competence. What is new is the attempt to measure emotional intelligence as a type of intelligence similar to cognitive intelligence (see Mayer & Salovey, 1997). The roots of this definition of emotional intelligence are in the arena of intelligence research in the field of psychology.

With today's burgeoning economic expansion coupled with an aging baby boomer workforce, Corporate America is confronting management succession challenges in the context of a war over talent. Each selection and promotion decision becomes increasingly critical to the future economic viability of the company, including its ability to compete in the fast-paced dot-com society. The evidence is mounting that our most effective corporate leaders are those who engage the hearts as well as the minds of employees (Goleman, 1998b; Kouzes & Posner, 1999; Rosen, 1998). In an ideal world, key corporate positions would be filled by individuals who have not only the intellectual abilities to meet the cognitive challenges of leadership but also the emotional capabilities to inspire and empathize with others.

In this chapter, I present an update on the latest measures of emotional intelligence and describe their intended purposes and the scientific literature supporting these instruments. I describe some encouraging applications of these measures and relate the diverse approaches to one another, setting the conceptual stage for future research initiatives. Finally, I forecast some new directions for measures of emotional intelligence.

Conceptual Underpinnings and Distinctions

It is important to distinguish between two terms—emotional intelligence and emotional competence. *Emotional intelligence* refers to a person's basic underlying capability to recognize and use emotion. Mayer and Salovey, who coined the term, have stated further that emotional intelligence is "the ability to perceive and express emotion, assimilate emotion in thought, understand and reason with emotion, and regulate emotion in the self and others" (Mayer, Salovey, & Caruso, 2000, p. 1; see also Mayer & Salovey, 1997). These authors have also attempted to measure emotional intelligence itself, examining the construct at the ability level. Goleman, Bar-On (1997b), Cooper and Sawaf (1997), and others have preferred to examine emotional intelligence through the exploration of emotional competence. *Emotional competence* describes the personal and social skills that lead to superior performance in the world of work. It was David McClelland (1973) who really first focused attention on the word *competencies* and recommended that the competencies and associated habits of star performers be studied as they clearly added economic value to the organization.

In essence, Mayer and his colleagues built on the foundation of personality theory in developing their emotional intelligence assessments. Boyatzis and Goleman began with a theory of performance in the world of work. Reuven Bar-On has seemed to draw on both personality theory and the theory of performance in the workplace, and Esther Orioli, working with Robert Cooper, has taken a broader perspective still in mapping the environment, competencies for performance, and outcome measures. The different theories underlying each of the measures of these researchers have resulted in very different assessment tools, all dedicated to measuring aspects of emotional intelligence.

Historically, there have been a number of models of what we might call *social intelligence* (Thorndike & Stern, 1937; Gardner, 1993; Sternberg, 1996, 1997). To help us gain a better understanding of the contemporary models of emotional intelligence and emotional competence, I have prepared a crosswalk that illustrates the relationship between the emotional competence framework developed by Goleman (1998b) and other current EI measures.

Goleman and his colleague, Richard Boyatzis, designed a measure to closely parallel the Goleman framework. That measure, the Emotional Competence Inventory (Boyatzis, Goleman, & Rhee, 2000), has a nearly one-to-one relationship with the framework. The three other models discussed in this chapter have some degree of overlap but also interesting differences. The latter comparisons will be presented as part of the discussion of the construct validity of the various measures of emotional intelligence or emotional competence. The new *Standards for Educational and Psychological Testing,* prepared by the American Educational Research Association, American Psychological Association, and National Council on Measurement in Education (American Educational Research Association, 1999), define *construct* as "a theoretical variable inferred from multiple types of evidence, which might include the interrelations of the test scores with other variables, internal test structure, observations of response processes, as well as the content of the test" (p. 174). *Construct validity* is defined as "a term used to indicate that the test scores are to be interpreted as indicating the test-taker's standing on the psychological construct measured by the test" (p. 174).

This chapter explores a number of the currently available measures of emotional intelligence and emotional competence. (For a comprehensive historical review of some of the measures leading up to the development of these measures, see Mayer, Salovey, & Caruso, 2000.) It describes the constructs being measured and the method being employed to assess those constructs and analyzes the evidence for the reliability and validity of those measures, including a summary of the content, construct, and criterion-related validity studies undertaken to date. It also provides contact information for the test publishers and, where available, for technical manuals and the like.

The Emotional Competence Inventory

Table 5.1 shows the emotional competence framework developed by Daniel Goleman (1995a, 1998b) after his research into hundreds of competency models from private and public sector organizations employing over two million members of our nation's workforce. The Emotional Competence Inventory (ECI) was originally designed to measure all the competencies in this framework. Boyatzis and Goleman have stated that "emotional intelligence is observed when a person demonstrates the competencies that constitute self-awareness, self-management, social awareness, and social skills at appropriate times and ways in sufficient frequency to be effective in the situation" (Boyatzis, Goleman, & Rhee, 2000, p. 3). The differences between the constructs in the framework and the constructs in the ECI resulted from an early pilot test of the instrument. After analyzing data on the first version of the ECI, Boyatzis and Goleman integrated Innovation behaviors into the Initiative scale. The Optimism scale was integrated into the newly named Achievement Orientation scale, because the Optimism scale and the Achievement Drive scale were highly correlated. The Leveraging Diversity items were highly correlated with the Understanding Others scale and so they were integrated into the newly named Empathy scale. The Commitment items were highly correlated with the Leadership scale and so they were integrated with that scale. The Collaboration items were highly correlated with the Team Capabilities scale and so they were integrated into the newly named Teamwork and Collaboration scale. Finally, two other minor name changes were made. Political Awareness was changed to Organizational Awareness and Emotional Awareness was altered to Emotional Self-Awareness.

Boyatzis and Goleman define *clusters* as behavioral groups of the desired competencies (Boyatzis, Goleman, & Rhee, 2000). Although Goleman (1998b) originally hypothesized five competency clusters, the Emotional Competence Inventory assesses only four. The clusters were consolidated in the light of the results of the pilot test of the first version of the ECI and discussions with research staff of Hay/McBer that drew on the Hay/McBer database of competency assessment information from hundreds of companies.

Method of Assessment

The ECI is a 360-degree assessment that gathers self, subordinate, peer, and supervisory ratings on twenty social and emotional competencies. Survey respondents use a 6-point scale to describe themselves or another person on each competence. Each step on the scale is progressively labeled, starting from "the

TABLE 5.1. COMPARISON OF THE EMOTIONAL COMPETENCE INVENTORY AND GOLEMAN'S EMOTIONAL COMPETENCE FRAMEWORK.

The Emotional Competence Framework (Goleman 1998b)	The Emotional Competence Inventory (Boyatzis, Goleman, and Rhee, 2000)
Personal Competence. How we manage ourselves.	
A. **Self-Awareness.** Knowing one's internal states, preferences, resources, and intuitions.	A. **Self-Awareness.**
A1. **Emotional Awareness.** Recognizing one's emotions and their effects.	A1. **Emotional Self-Awareness.** Recognizing one's emotions and their effects.
A2. **Accurate Self-Assessment.** Knowing one's strengths and limits.	A2. **Accurate Self-Assessment.** Knowing one's strengths and limits.
A3. **Self-Confidence.** A strong sense of one's self-worth and capabilities.	A3. **Self-Confidence.** A strong sense of one's self-worth and capabilities.
B. **Self-Regulation.** Managing one's internal states, impulses, and resources.	B. **Self-Management.**
B1. **Self-Control.** Keeping disruptive emotions and impulses in check.	B1. **Self-Control.** Keeping disruptive emotions and impulses under control.
B2. **Trustworthiness.** Maintaining standards of honesty and integrity.	B2. **Trustworthiness.** Displaying honesty and integrity.
B3. **Conscientiousness.** Taking responsibility for personal performance.	B3. **Conscientiousness.** Demonstrating responsibility in managing oneself.
B4. **Adaptability.** Flexibility in handling change.	B4. **Adaptability.** Flexibility in adapting to changing situations or obstacles.
B5. **Innovation.** Being comfortable with novel ideas, approaches, and new information.	
C. **Motivation.** Emotional tendencies that guide or facilitate reaching goals.	
C1. **Achievement Drive.** Striving to improve or meet a standard of excellence.	B5. **Achievement Orientation.** The guiding drive to meet an internal standard of excellence.
C2. **Commitment.** Aligning with the goals of the group or organization.	
C3. **Initiative.** Readiness to act on opportunities.	B6. **Initiative.** Readiness to act.
C4. **Optimism.** Persistence in pursuing goals despite obstacles and setbacks.	
Social Competence. How we handle relationships.	C. **Social Awareness.**
D. **Empathy.** Awareness of others' feelings, needs, and concerns.	C1. **Empathy.** Understanding others, and taking an active interest in their concerns.

TABLE 5.1. COMPARISON OF THE EMOTIONAL COMPETENCE INVENTORY AND GOLEMAN'S EMOTIONAL COMPETENCE FRAMEWORK, Cont'd.

The Emotional Competence Framework (Goleman 1998b)	The Emotional Competence Inventory (Boyatzis, Goleman, and Rhee, 2000)
D1. **Understanding Others.** Sensing others' feelings and perspectives, and taking an active interest in their concerns.	C1. **Empathy.** Understanding others, and taking an active interest in their concerns.
D2. **Developing Others.** Sensing others' development needs, and bolstering their abilities.	D1. **Developing Others.** Sensing others' development needs, and bolstering their abilities.
D3. **Service Orientation.** Anticipating, recognizing, and meeting customers' needs.	D2. **Service Orientation.** Recognizing and meeting customers' needs.
D4. **Leveraging Diversity.** Cultivating opportunities through different kinds of people.	
D5. **Political Awareness.** Reading a group's emotional currents and power relationships.	C2. **Organizational Awareness.** Empathizing at the organizational level.
E. **Social Skills.** Adeptness at inducing desirable responses in others.	D. **Social Skills.**
E1. **Influence.** Wielding effective tactics for persuasion.	D4. **Influence.** Wielding interpersonal influence tactics.
E2. **Communication.** Listening openly, and sending convincing messages.	D5. **Communication.** Sending clear and convincing messages.
E3. **Conflict Management.** Negotiating and resolving disagreements.	D7. **Conflict Management.** Resolving disagreements.
E4. **Leadership.** Inspiring and guiding individuals and groups.	D3. **Leadership.** Inspiring and guiding groups of people.
E5. **Change Catalyst.** Initiating or managing change.	D6. **Change Catalyst.** Initiating or managing change.
E6. **Building Bonds.** Nurturing instrumental relationships.	D8. **Building Bonds.** Nurturing instrumental relationships.
E7. **Collaboration and Cooperation.** Working with others toward shared goals.	D9. **Teamwork and Collaboration.** Creating a shared vision and synergy in teamwork, working with others toward shared goals.
E8. **Team Capabilities.** Creating group synergy in pursuing collective goals.	D9. **Teamwork and Collaboration.** Creating a shared vision and synergy in teamwork, working with others toward shared goals.

behavior is only slightly characteristic of the individual (i.e., he/she behaves this way only sporadically)" and ending with "the behavior is very characteristic of this individual (i.e., he/she behaves this way in most or all situations where it is appropriate." In addition to the 6-point scale, answer options also include "I don't know" or "I have not had the opportunity to observe the person in an appropriate setting." The instrument contains 110 items and takes approximately thirty-five minutes to complete. The ECI is designed for use only as a development tool, not for making hiring, promotion, or compensation decisions.

About 40 percent of the ECI is taken from the Self-Assessment Questionnaire (SAQ) developed by Boyatzis and his colleagues (Boyatzis, 1994; Boyatzis, Cowen, & Kolb, 1995). The SAQ was developed from competencies that had been validated against performance in hundreds of competency studies of managers, executives, and leaders in North America. The SAQ had also been validated against performance for a variety of job families in dozens of industrial organizations in Italy and in one large financial institution in Brazil. Reliability and construct validation had been established against other questionnaire measures as well as against behavioral measures coded from videotapes and audiotapes of candidates' behavior in exercises and numerous longitudinal studies of competency development (Boyatzis, Wheeler, & Wright, 1997).

The first version of the ECI was pilot tested in the fall of 1998 with 596 people, including samples of managers and salespeople from several industrial corporations and graduate students in master's degree programs in management, engineering, and social work. After analysis of the reliabilities and the intercorrelation of the items, the ECI was revised in December of 1998. Subsequently the instrument underwent another revision as a result of the previously mentioned discussions with the research team at Hay/McBer. Basically those discussions involved arranging and constructing items to reflect the developmental scaling characteristic of the current McBer instruments. Although the developmental scaling will ultimately be empirically determined, the initial developmental scaling assumptions are based on expert opinion from previous studies (Spencer & Spencer, 1993; McClelland, 1998).

For scoring purposes, *tipping points* are identified. A tipping point, determined by prior studies, is the score at which the individual is expected to be tipped over into superior performance on the competency on the job. Future studies will help to determine the validity of these tipping points.

Reliability Evidence

The *Standards for Educational and Psychological Testing* (American Educational Research Association, 1999) define *reliability* as "the degree to which scores are free of errors of measurement for a given group" (p. 180). The more evidence of reliability can be documented, the more confidence one can have of finding evidence of validity. One measure of a scale's reliability is its *internal consistency*. The *Standards for Educational and Psychological Testing* define an *internal consistency coefficient* as "an index of the reliability of test scores derived from the statistical interrelationships among item responses or scores on separate parts of a test" (p. 176). Cronbach's alpha is one such measure of internal consistency. Table 5.2 provides the Cronbach's alpha estimates for reliability of the self-assessment and the composite others' assessment average item scores on the ECI (Boyatzis, Goleman, & Rhee, 2000). The scale reliabilities for the self-assessments range from .618 for Adaptability to .866 for Change Catalyst. The reliabilities for composite others' assessment ranged from .798 for Emotional Self-Awareness to .948 for Empathy. These levels for others' assessment are encouraging as reliabilities in the .8 and .9 range are desired when the instrument will be used to make distinctions at the individual level.

TABLE 5.2. CRONBACH'S ALPHA RELIABILITY ESTIMATES FOR THE ECI.

Scale Reliabilities in Terms of Cronbach's Alpha for Average Item Scores

	Self-Assessment Form	Composite Others' Assessment Form
Emotional Self-Awareness	.629 (668)	.798 (427)
Accurate Self-Assessment	.715 (663)	.886 (427)
Self-Confidence	.825 (660)	.909 (428)
Self-Control	.808 (668)	.906 (427)
Trustworthiness	.667 (667)	.814 (427)
Conscientiousness	.816 (664)	.911 (428)
Adaptability	.618 (664)	.834 (428)
Achievement Orientation	.835 (660)	.921 (428)
Initiative	.754 (663)	.897 (427)
Empathy	.837 (657)	.948 (425)
Organizational Awareness	.786 (660)	.913 (426)
Developing Others	.818 (653)	.927 (426)
Service Orientation	.854 (628)	.938 (426)
Leadership	.658 (649)	.824 (427)
Influence	.767 (637)	.881 (425)
Communication	.789 (654)	.910 (427)
Change Catalyst	.866 (637)	.935 (426)
Conflict Management	.778 (660)	.894 (426)
Building Bonds	.773 (670)	.882 (427)
Teamwork and Collaboration	.842 (645)	.943 (426)

Note: Sample size is shown in parentheses following each coefficient alpha.

Source: Boyatzis, R. E., Goleman, D., & Rhee, K. "Clustering Competence in Emotional Intelligence," p. 347. In R. Bar-On and J.D.A. Parker (Eds.), *The Handbook of Emotional Intelligence.* Copyright © 2000. Reprinted by permission of Jossey-Bass, Inc., a division of John Wiley & Sons, Inc.

Validity Evidence

The *Standards for Educational and Psychological Testing* state that *validity* refers to "the degree to which evidence and theory support the interpretations of test scores entailed by proposed uses of tests. The process of validation involves accumulating evidence to provide a sound scientific basis for the proposed score interpretations" (p. 9). Further, "a few lines of solid evidence regarding a particular proposition are better than numerous lines of evidence of questionable validity" (p. 11). Historically, validity was compartmentalized into content, construct, and criterion-related validity (predictive and concurrent). Currently the *Standards* treat validity as a "unitary concept," suggesting that "it is the degree to which all the accumulated evidence supports the intended interpretation of test scores for the proposed purpose" (p. 11). The *Standards* present several sources of validity evidence: *evidence based on test content,* that is, the relationship between the test's content and the construct it is intended to measure; *evidence based on response processes,* that is, evidence concerning the detailed fit between the construct and the performance or response actually engaged in by the people taking the test; *evidence based on internal structure,* that is, the degree to which relationships among test items and test components conform to the construct on which the proposed test score interpretations are based; and *evidence based on relations to other variables,* that is, convergent and discriminant evidence (relationships between test scores and other measures intended to assess similar constructs provide convergent evidence, whereas relationships between test scores and measures of different constructs provide discriminant evidence), test-criterion relationships, and validity generalization—statistical summaries or meta-analyses of past validation studies in similar situations may be useful in estimating test-criterion relationships in a new situation.

The Emotional Competence Inventory is supported by construct validity evidence, content validity evidence, and validity generalization evidence from its predecessor instrument, the Self-Assessment Questionnaire. At present, there is no evidence of convergent or discriminant validity with measures of similar and different constructs.

The ECI authors have undertaken some work to understand the inventory's internal structure. On the basis of preliminary factor analysis and cluster analysis, three clusters emerged—Self-Awareness, Self-Management, and Social Skills. The authors plan to undertake additional cluster analyses with larger samples to see if their fourth hypothesized cluster—Social Awareness—finds empirical support. Future research should also address test-criterion relationships as well as evidence of convergent and discriminant validity with other measures of emotional intelligence and emotional competence and with measures of other types of intelligence.

Test Publisher

The Emotional Competence Inventory is published by Hay/McBer Emotional Intelligence Services: Web site: www.eisglobal.com

Ability Scales of Emotional Intelligence: The Multifactor Emotional Intelligence Scale

Mayer, Caruso, and Salovey have developed multiple-task ability scales to measure emotional intelligence, as opposed to emotional competence. The first scale was the Multifactor Emotional Intelligence Scale (MEIS). Mayer and Salovey (1997; see also Salovey & Mayer, 1990) have proposed an interesting theoretical framework for understanding emotional intelligence and its associated abilities. They have also found some encouraging preliminary empirical evidence to support their theory and the marker tests that they have designed to measure those abilities. Their framework is presented in Table 5.3. Mayer and Salovey (1997) are explicitly focused on an internal concept of emotional intelligence—the perception, use, understanding, and management of emotion. They predict, with empirical justification, that these internal abilities have external consequences. Their measure contrasts with the Boyatzis and Goleman measure in that the latter is a more directly behavioral measure, providing sample behaviors that may occur.

Basically, Mayer and Salovey (1997) define *emotional intelligence* as involving "the ability to perceive accurately, appraise, and express emotion; the ability to access and/or generate feelings when they facilitate thought; the ability to understand emotion and emotional knowledge; and the ability to regulate emotions to promote emotional and intellectual growth" (p. 10). In Table 5.3, the four branches are arranged from the more basic psychological processes at the top to the higher, more psychologically integrated processes at the bottom, with Perception, Appraisal, and Expression of Emotion at the lowest level. I have labeled the abilities and their subcomponents in Table 5.3 to facilitate their comparison with the Goleman model of emotional competence in Table 5.4. The MEIS, which is based upon the Mayer and Salovey four-branch model of emotional intelligence, is the only measure designed as a true ability measure, tapping intellectual abilities relating to feelings and emotion.

In some cases the competencies in the emotional competence framework overlap with the emotional intelligence abilities identified by Mayer and Salovey (1997). As an example, the "ability to manage emotion in oneself" certainly seems comparable to Self-Control defined as "keeping disruptive emotions and impulses in check" (later revised to "keeping disruptive emotions and impulses under

TABLE 5.3. MAYER AND SALOVEY'S EMOTIONAL INTELLIGENCE FRAMEWORK.

D.

D1. Ability to stay open to feelings, both those that are pleasant and those that are unpleasant.	D2. Ability to reflectively engage or detach from an emotion depending on its judged informativeness or utility.	D3. Ability to reflectively monitor emotions in relation to oneself and others, such as recognizing how clear, typical, influential, or reasonable they are.	D4. Ability to manage emotion in oneself and others by moderating negative emotions and enhancing pleasant ones, without repressing or exaggerating information they may convey.

C. Understanding and Analyzing Emotions; Employing Emotional Knowledge

C1. Ability to label emotions and recognize relations among the words and the emotions themselves, such as the relation between liking and loving.	C2. Ability to interpret the meanings that emotions convey regarding relationships, such as that sadness often accompanies a loss.	C3. Ability to understand complex feelings such as simultaneous feelings of love and hate or blends such as awe as a combination of fear and surprise.	C4. Ability to recognize likely transitions among emotions, such as the transition from anger to satisfaction or from anger to shame.

B. Emotional Facilitation of Thinking

B1. Emotions prioritize thinking by directing attention to important information.	B2. Emotions are sufficiently vivid and available that they can be generated as aids to judgments and memory concerning feelings.	B3. Emotional mood swings change the individual's perspective from optimistic to pessimistic, encouraging consideration of multiple points of view.	B4. Emotional states differentially encourage specific problem approaches: for instance, happiness can facilitate inductive reasoning and creativity.

A. Perception, Appraisal, and Expression of Emotion

A1. Ability to identify emotion in one's physical states, feelings, and thoughts.	A2. Ability to identify emotions in other people, designs, artwork, and so forth, through language, sound, appearance, and behavior.	A3. Ability to express emotions accurately and to express needs related to those feelings.	A4. Ability to discriminate between accurate and inaccurate or honest and dishonest expressions of feelings.

Source: From *Emotional Development and Emotional Intelligence* by Peter Salovey and David Sluyter, p. 11. Copyright © 1997 by Peter Salovey and David Sluyter. Reprinted by permission of Basic Books, a member of Perseus Books, L.L.C.

TABLE 5.4. COMPARISON OF THE MULTIFACTOR INTELLIGENCE SCALE AND GOLEMAN'S EMOTIONAL COMPETENCE FRAMEWORK.

The Emotional Competence Framework (Goleman, 1998b)	Multifactor Emotional Intelligence Scale (MEIS) (Mayer & Salovey, 1997)
Personal Competence. How we manage ourselves.	D. **Reflectively Regulating Emotions.** Reflective regulation of emotions to promote emotional and intellectual growth.
A. **Self-Awareness.** Knowing one's internal states, preferences, resources, and intuitions.	A. **Perceiving and Expressing Emotion.** Perception, appraisal, and expression of emotion.
A1. **Emotional Awareness.** Recognizing one's emotions and their effects.	A1. Ability to identify emotion in one's physical states, feelings, and thoughts. C1. Ability to label emotions and recognize relations among words and the emotions themselves, such as the relation between liking and loving. D1. Ability to stay open to feelings, both those that are pleasant and those that are unpleasant.
A2. **Accurate Self-Assessment.** Knowing one's strengths and limits. A3. **Self-Confidence.** A strong sense of one's self-worth and capabilities.	
B. **Self-Regulation.** Managing one's internal states, impulses, and resources.	D4. Ability to manage emotion in oneself and others by moderating negative emotions and enhancing pleasant ones, without repressing or exaggerating information they may convey.
B1. **Self-Control.** Keeping disruptive emotions and impulses in check.	D4. Ability to manage emotion in oneself and others by moderating negative emotions and enhancing pleasant ones, without re-pressing or exaggerating information they may convey.
B2. **Trustworthiness.** Maintaining standards of honesty and integrity. B3. **Conscientiousness.** Taking responsibility for personal performance. B4. **Adaptability.** Flexibility in handling change. B5. **Innovation.** Being comfortable with novel ideas, approaches, and new information.	B4. Emotional states differentially encourage specific problem approaches: for instance, happiness can facilitate inductive reasoning and creativity.
C. **Motivation.** Emotional tendencies that guide or facilitate reaching goals. C1. **Achievement Drive.** Striving to improve or meet a standard of excellence. C2. **Commitment.** Aligning with the goals of the group or organization.	

TABLE 5.4. COMPARISON OF THE MULTIFACTOR INTELLIGENCE SCALE AND GOLEMAN'S EMOTIONAL COMPETENCE FRAMEWORK, Cont'd.

The Emotional Competence Framework (Goleman, 1998b)	Multifactor Emotional Intelligence Scale (MEIS) (Mayer & Salovey, 1997)
C3. **Initiative.** Readiness to act on opportunities.	
C4. **Optimism.** Persistence in pursuing goals despite obstacles and setbacks.	B3. Emotional mood swings change the individual's perspective from optimistic to pessimistic, encouraging consideration of multiple points of view. (Not a good match.)
Social Competence. How we handle relationships.	D. **Reflectively Regulating Emotions.** Reflective regulation of emotions to promote emotional and intellectual growth.
	D4. Ability to manage emotion in oneself and others by moderating negative emotions and enhancing pleasant ones, without repressing or exaggerating information they may convey.
D. **Empathy.** Awareness of others' feelings, needs, and concerns.	A2. Ability to identify emotions in other people, designs, artwork, and so forth, through language, sound, appearance, and behavior.
	C1. Ability to label emotions and recognize relations among the words and the emotions themselves, such as the relation between liking and loving.
	D1. Ability to stay open to feelings, both those that are pleasant and those that are unpleasant.
D1. **Understanding Others.** Sensing others' feelings and perspectives, and taking an active interest in their concerns.	D1. Ability to stay open to feelings, both those that are pleasant and those that are unpleasant.
D2. **Developing Others.** Sensing others' development needs, and bolstering their abilities.	
D3. **Service Orientation.** Anticipating, recognizing, and meeting customers' needs.	
D4. **Leveraging Diversity.** Cultivating opportunities through different kinds of people.	
D5. **Political Awareness.** Reading a group's emotional currents and power relationships.	
E. **Social Skills.** Adeptness at inducing desirable responses in others.	
E1. **Influence.** Wielding effective tactics for persuasion.	
E2. **Communication.** Listening openly and sending convincing messages.	A3. Ability to express emotions accurately, and to express needs related to those feelings.

TABLE 5.4. COMPARISON OF THE MULTIFACTOR INTELLIGENCE SCALE AND GOLEMAN'S EMOTIONAL COMPETENCE FRAMEWORK, Cont'd.

The Emotional Competence Framework (Goleman, 1998b)	Multifactor Emotional Intelligence Scale (MEIS) (Mayer & Salovey, 1997)
E3. **Conflict Management.** Negotiating and resolving disagreements.	D1. Ability to stay open to feelings, both those that are pleasant and those that are unpleasant.
	D3. Ability to reflectively monitor emotions in relation to oneself and others, such as recognizing how clear, typical, influential, or reasonable they are.
E4. **Leadership.** Inspiring and guiding individuals and groups.	
E5. **Change Catalyst.** Initiating or managing change.	
E6. **Building Bonds.** Nurturing instrumental relationships.	
E7. **Collaboration and Cooperation.** Working with others toward shared goals.	
E8. **Team Capabilities.** Creating group synergy in pursuing collective goals.	
	B. **Assimilating Emotion in Thought.** Emotional facilitation of thinking.
	C. **Understanding Emotions.** Understanding and analyzing emotions; employing emotional knowledge.
	A4. Ability to discriminate between accurate and inaccurate or honest and dishonest expressions of feeling.
	B1. Emotions prioritize thinking by directing attention to important information.
	B2. Emotions are sufficiently vivid and available that they can be generated as aids to judgment and memory concerning feelings.
	C2. Ability to interpret the meanings that emotions convey regarding relationships, such as that sadness often accompanies a loss.
	C3. Ability to understand complex feelings such as simultaneous feelings of love and hate or blends such as awe as a combination of fear and surprise.
	C4. Ability to recognize likely transitions among emotions, such as the transition from anger to satisfaction or from anger to shame.
	D2. Ability to reflectively engage or detach from an emotion depending upon its judged informativeness or utility.

control"). In other cases the Mayer and Salovey abilities appear to be the foundation of the Goleman competencies. For example, the "ability to stay open to feelings" and the "ability to reflectively monitor emotions in relation to oneself and others" seem to be the foundation of the competence of Conflict Management defined as "negotiating and resolving disagreements" (later revised to "resolving disagreements"). In many cases there is no direct link between the emotional competencies and the emotional abilities. For example, there is no direct counterpart in the Goleman model to Mayer and Salovey's Assimilating Emotion in Thought or Understanding Emotion. Specific abilities that do not appear in the Goleman framework of competencies include the "ability to discriminate between accurate and inaccurate or honest and dishonest expressions of feeling," "ability to interpret the meanings that emotions convey regarding relationships," "ability to understand complex feelings," "ability to recognize likely transitions among emotions," and "ability to reflectively engage or detach from an emotion depending upon its judged informativeness or utility." It may well be that the emotional intelligence constructs defined by Mayer and his colleagues are at a more micro or basic level and the emotional competencies are at a more macro level of performance. These differences should result in some interesting research studies using measures of both emotional competence and emotional intelligence to further clarify our understanding of the underlying constructs.

Method of Assessment

The MEIS contains twelve subscales to correspond to the twelve hypothesized abilities shown in Table 5.3. The tests are as follows:

Branch 1: Perceiving and Expressing Emotion

1. Faces (eight stimuli, forty-eight items). Eight faces representing a variety of emotions are presented and the test-taker answers on a 5-point scale whether a given emotion was "Definitely Not Present" (1) or "Definitely Present" (5) or somewhere in between.

2. Music (eight stimuli, forty-eight items). Eight brief, original pieces of music are presented to the test-takers, who rate the emotional content of the music on the same scale used for Faces.

3. Designs (eight stimuli, forty-eight items). Eight original, computer-generated graphic designs portraying a variety of feelings are given to the test-takers, who rate them by faces expressing various degrees of emotion.

4. Stories (six stimuli, forty-two items). Six stories are presented to the test-takers, who rate the emotional content by selecting the applicable emotional adjectives. The adjectives vary by story.

Branch 2: Assimilating Emotion in Thought

5. Synesthesia (six stimuli, sixty items). Test-takers imagine an event that could make them feel a particular feeling, which they then describe on ten semantic differential scales. For example, one item asks, "Imagine an event that could make you feel both surprised and somewhat displeased. Now describe your feelings on" each of ten 5-point scales, where 1 is "warm" and 5 is "cold."

6. Feeling Biases (four stimuli, twenty-eight items). Four passages ask the test-takers to assimilate their present mood into judgments of how they feel toward a fictional person in each passage. The test-takers then rate several traits. The traits vary for the different passages.

Branch 3: Understanding Emotions

7. Blends (eight stimuli, eight items). The items concern the ability to analyze blended or complex emotions. As an example, test-takers are asked to select the two emotions that most closely combine to form optimism. The eight items address blends of two emotions, three emotions, and four emotions.

8. Progressions (eight stimuli, eight items). The items tap the ways emotional reactions proceed over time, focusing on the intensification of feelings. As an example, test-takers are asked to complete this thought: "If you feel angrier and angrier toward someone so that you are losing control, it would result in . . ." Standardized multiple-choice responses are provided for these items.

9. Transitions (four stimuli, twenty-four items). The items measure how emotions follow upon one another. One item states, for example: "A person is afraid and later is calm. In between, what are the likely ways the person might feel?" Each item is followed by six alternative feelings, and test-takers rate each feeling from "Extremely Unlikely" (1) to "Extremely Likely" (5). The alternatives differ for each item.

10. Relativity (four stimuli, forty items). The items depict social encounters involving conflict between two characters. The test-taker has to estimate the feelings of both characters and to rate the feeling reactions on the same scale used to rate Transitions.

Branch 4: Reflectively Regulating Emotions

11. Managing Feelings of Others (six stimuli, twenty-four items). Test-takers are asked to evaluate plans of action in response to fictional people who need assistance who are described in brief vignettes. Test-takers rate four possible courses of action on a 5-point scale from "Extremely Ineffective" to "Extremely Effective."

12. Managing Feelings of the Self (six stimuli, twenty-four items). The test-taker is presented with six vignettes, each one describing a particular emotional

problem. Test-takers rate their given response on the same 5-point scale used in Managing Feelings of Others.

The tests were initially scored by group consensus (reflecting the consensus of the test-takers about the emotional content of the stimuli), expert judgment (reflecting the judgment of experts about the emotional content of the test), and/or target scoring (the test-taker reported the emotion he or she was feeling or expressing at the time). After preliminary research, it became clear that the best approach to scoring the tests was the consensus approach. Once this approach has been adopted, it raises questions about those who take the tests and provide the consensus: Are the samples truly representative? Were stratified, random samples used to select the test-taking population?

Reliability Evidence

Table 5.5 presents the Cronbach's alpha reliabilities for each of the twelve scale scores. The alphas for consensus scoring, the method recommended by the authors, range from .49 to .94. The lowest reliabilities are for the scales with the fewest items. It is to be hoped that the authors will add items to the branch scales in the future to bring the alphas up to a higher level. Reliabilities for Feeling Biases, Managing Others, and Managing Self are barely in the .70s. If the alternative responses for the vignettes in these three scales were standardized rather than varied by vignette, these reliability estimates might be higher. Of course the current response alternatives for any given vignette might not apply to another vignette, and this issue would have to be resolved prior to standardization. At the branch level, which is the level at which feedback is given to test-takers, the alphas are, branch 1, .96; branch 2, .86; branch 3, .89; branch 4, .81; and the full scale score is .96. Many of these branch-level reliability estimates are excellent.

Validity Evidence

The MEIS has evidence of construct validity and content validity and also validity evidence based on relations to other variables. Interestingly, the authors also provide evidence based on the internal structure of the MEIS and evidence based on the response process. The evidence of internal structure is also presented in Table 5.5 in the intercorrelations among the scales within each of the four branches. For branch 1, Emotional Identification, the intercorrelations are all above .40. Mayer, Caruso, and Salovey (2000a) note that some of the verbal intelligence subscales correlate at the .40 level. The two scales for branch 2 correlate at .39. Blends, Progressions, and Relativity have intercorrelations of .30 or higher in branch 3; however, the intercorrelations for Transitions are disappointing. Finally, Managing Others

TABLE 5.5. INTERCORRELATIONS OF THE CONSENSUS-SCORED TASKS OF THE MEIS, WITH RELIABILITIES (COEFFICIENT ALPHA) ON THE DIAGONAL.

Branch and Task	Branch 1 Subscales				Branch 2 Subscales		Branch 3 Subscales				Branch 4 Subscales	
	Fa	Mu	De	St	Sy	Fe	Bl	Pr	Tr	Re	Mo	Ms
1. Emotional Identification												
Faces	**0.89**											
Music	0.61	**0.94**										
Designs	0.68	0.60	**0.90**									
Stories	0.54	0.47	0.54	**0.85**								
2. Assimilating Emotions												
Synesthesia	0.24	0.24	0.26	0.38	**0.86**							
Feeling Biases	0.30	0.24	0.35	0.47	0.39	**0.71**						
3. Understanding Emotions												
Blends	0.07	0.13	0.09	0.24	0.22	0.26	**0.49**					
Progressions	0.10	0.15	0.14	0.25	0.34	0.35	0.41	**0.51**				
Transitions	0.25	0.29	0.29	0.37	0.26	0.34	0.19	0.17	**0.94**			
Relativity	0.30	0.35	0.32	0.41	0.32	0.38	0.30	0.34	0.43	**0.78**		
4. Managing Emotions												
Managing Others	0.20	0.21	0.20	0.28	0.25	0.24	0.16	0.22	0.18	0.37	**0.72**	
Managing Self	0.19	0.15	0.14	0.30	0.27	0.22	0.20	0.23	0.17	0.25	0.54	**0.70**

Note: N = 500. Correlations above r = .08 are significant beyond p < .01.

Source: Reprinted from *Intelligence, volume 24.* Mayer, J. D., Caruso, D. R., & Salovey, P., "Emotional Intelligence Meets Traditional Standards for an Intelligence," p. 282. Copyright 2000, with permission from Elsevier Science.

and Managing Self have a respectable level of intercorrelation at .54. Further support for the internal structure of the MEIS comes from two factor analyses conducted by the authors (Mayer, Caruso, & Salovey, 2000a). Table 5.6 shows the results of these analyses. Basically, three factors emerged from the unrotated solution: Emotional Intelligence (a general emotional intelligence factor) (I on Table 5.6), Managing Versus Perceiving Emotions (II), and Managing Emotions (III).

The rotated version also resulted in a three-factor solution: Emotional Understanding (I), Emotional Perception (II), and Managing Emotion (III). The authors also investigated a four-factor solution using covariance structural modeling and found that it was viable. However, because two of the four factors, Assimilating Emotions and Understanding Emotions, intercorrelated at .87, they decided to proceed with the three-factor solution. Preliminary evidence from the Mayer-

TABLE 5.6. THREE-FACTOR SOLUTIONS FOR THE EMOTIONAL INTELLIGENCE TEST SCORED ACCORDING TO CONSENSUS AND ACCORDING TO EXPERT CRITERIA, IN UNROTATED AND ROTATED SOLUTIONS: PRINCIPAL COMPONENTS FACTORING.

Branch and Task	Unrotated			Oblique Rotated (Pattern Matrix)*		
	I	II	III	I	II	III
1. Emotional Identification						
Faces	0.67	−0.48	−0.11	−0.10	0.86	0.04
Music	0.63	−0.34	−0.04	0.02	0.70	0.02
Design	0.69	−0.44	−0.02	0.01	0.82	−0.03
Stories	0.73	−0.09	0.05	0.30	0.52	0.08
2. Assimilating Emotions						
Synesthesia	0.51	0.19	0.10	0.43	−0.12	0.10
Feeling Biases	0.59	0.13	0.21	0.53	−0.20	−0.00
3. Understanding Emotions						
Blends	0.35	0.32	0.24	0.57	−0.10	−0.01
Progressions	0.43	0.38	0.25	0.64	−0.11	0.02
Transitions	0.48	0.04	0.12	0.35	0.23	0.00
Relativity	0.61	0.18	0.09	0.45	0.20	0.14
4. Managing Emotions						
Managing Others	0.49	0.36	−0.49	−0.05	0.00	0.81
Managing Self	0.44	0.36	−0.38	0.03	−0.03	0.68

Note: Loadings above ±0.25 are in bold typeface for clarity.

*Loading indicated that all three factors were unipolar (that is, loadings on a factor above +0.25 all shared the same sign). Rotated factors II and III, however, were negative. To clarify results and facilitate discussion, loadings on rotated factors II and III were reversed in sign here and in subsequent analyses.

Source: Reprinted from *Intelligence, volume 24.* Mayer, J. D., Caruso, D. R., & Salovey, P., "Emotional Intelligence Meets Traditional Standards for an Intelligence," p. 284. Copyright 2000, with permission from Elsevier Science.

Salovey-Caruso Emotional Intelligence Test (the MSCEIT) indicates a four-factor solution supportive of the Mayer and Salovey model.

In the development of their MEIS items, Mayer, Caruso, and Salovey (2000a) are attempting to capture both the content of emotional situations and the response processes that people go through in responding to those situations. This replication of emotional experiences and reactions provides evidence of content validity as well as evidence of validity based on response process. As these authors use the results of their research to refine their measures to capture fully the realm of emotional intelligence, the research community will benefit from the establishment of these content and response process marker measures.

Mayer, Caruso, and Salovey (2000a) also summarize evidence regarding the relationship of the MEIS to other variables, including a measure of Verbal IQ (a short version of Army Alpha; Cronbach's alpha of .88) and a measure of Empathy (designed by the authors; Cronbach's alpha, .86). Mayer et al. have also correlated scores on the MEIS with scores on a variety of secondary criteria including Life Satisfaction, Artistic Skills, Parental Warmth, Psychotherapy, and Leisure (Life Space). Table 5.7 presents the results for a sample of 503 adults (full- and part-time college students, corporate employees, career workshop attendees, and executives in outplacement settings).

TABLE 5.7. CORRELATIONS BETWEEN INDIVIDUAL TASKS ON THE MEIS AND SELECTED CRITERION VARIABLES.

Criterion Variables	Overall Score g_{ei}	Subfactor Scores Perception	Understanding	Management
Primary criteria				
Ability				
Verbal IQ	0.36**	0.16**	0.40**	0.20**
Empathy				
Overall	0.33**	0.20**	0.25**	0.34**
Secondary criteria				
Life Satisfaction	0.11*	0.01	0.11*	0.13**
Artistic Skills	0.05	0.03	0.07	0.00
Parental Warmth	0.23**	0.20**	0.18**	0.15**
Psychotherapy	0.03	0.04	0.14*	0.02
Leisure (Life Space)				
Culture-Seeking	0.00	−0.07	0.01	0.03
Self-Improvement	−0.16**	−0.07	−0.22**	−0.05
Entertainment	−0.02	0.09*	−0.04	0.05

*$p < 0.05$, **$p < 0.01$, two-tailed tests.

Source: Reprinted from *Intelligence, volume 24.* Mayer, J. D., Caruso, D. R., & Salovey, P., "Emotional Intelligence Meets Traditional Standards for an Intelligence," p. 287. Copyright 2000, with permission from Elsevier Science.

As expected, the MEIS correlates with verbal intelligence as it too is a measure of intelligence. Although the overall emotional intelligence score correlates fairly highly with verbal intelligence (.36), the explanation appears to be the strong interrelationship (.40) between Understanding Emotions (something that clearly has a cognitive component) and Verbal IQ. Perception correlates only .16 and Management of Emotions correlates .20. The overall Empathy score correlates .33 with the overall emotional intelligence score. This relationship is modest and suggests that two different constructs are being measured. The correlations with secondary criteria are not particularly strong, but the significant, positive relationships between Life Satisfaction and Parental Warmth and Emotional Intelligence do make sense. Mayer, Caruso, and Salovey (2000b) report that in their studies the MEIS is relatively independent of many of the self-report trait scales of personality as measured by the 16 PF (Sixteen Personality Factor Inventory). Some significant correlations were found between the MEIS and the FIRO-B (Fundamental Interpersonal Relations Orientation-Behavior Inventory), including $r = .22$, $p < .01$ for wanted inclusion (how much a subject desires to be with people) and $r = .19$, $p < .01$ with wanted affection (how much closeness a subject desires with others).

Mayer, Salovey, and Caruso (2000b) also reported that the greater the emotional intelligence as reflected in the MEIS, the lower the violent and trouble-prone behavior among college students. In addition, Rice (1999) found that the MEIS scores of eleven team leaders correlated .51 with the department manager's ranking of those leaders' effectiveness. The MEIS scores of the team members were also significantly related to the department manager's ratings of the team's performance on customer service, $r = .46$. Although these findings are encouraging, they are from an unpublished study with a fairly small sample (164 employees) and so need to be replicated.

Test Publisher

The Multifactor Emotional Intelligence Scale is published by Multi-Health Systems, Inc., 908 Niagara Falls Blvd., North Tonawanda, NY 14120-2060; e-mail: oeg@mhs.com; telephone: 800-456-3003.

The Mayer-Salovey-Caruso Emotional Intelligence Test

Closely related to the MEIS is a newer test, the Mayer-Salovey-Caruso Emotional Intelligence Test (MSCEIT). Like the MEIS, the MSCEIT is an ability measure of emotional intelligence designed to yield an overall emotional intelligence score as well as subscale scores for perception, facilitation, understanding, and management of emotions. Each of these four branches has several subtests. The constructs in the MSCEIT parallel those assessed by the MEIS.

The structure of emotional intelligence can be inferred from a study of the intercorrelations among the twelve MEIS and MSCEIT tasks (preliminary results from the MSCEIT provide a similar picture). Factor analyses indicate that emotional intelligence can be represented as a two-level hierarchy. At the top of the hierarchy is Emotional Intelligence, an overall emotional intelligence factor that represents a fairly cohesive group of skills. The Emotional Intelligence factor can be broken down further into four subsidiary factors representing emotional perception, emotional facilitation, emotional understanding, and emotional management. Mayer, Salovey, and Caruso rely largely on the factor analyses done for the MEIS to support this factorial structure.

Method of Assessment

The branch labels and subtests for the MSCEIT vary somewhat from those for the MEIS, as follows (see Mayer, Caruso, & Salovey, 2000b):

Branch 1: Perception of Emotion. Three subtests are included in this branch—perception of emotion in faces, in landscapes, and in abstract designs. Typically the test-taker views the face, landscape, or design and must then report the amount of emotional content in it, judging, for example, how much happiness is in it, how much sadness, how much fear, and so on. The participant indicates on a 5-point scale the degree to which each emotion is present. Branch 1 tasks are designed to be uncontaminated by verbal content. For that reason the response alternatives for each item in the landscape and abstract design tasks are anchored by faces expressing varying degrees of emotion. However, in the faces task a numerical scale is used, to prevent interference between the stimulus faces and faces on a response scale. The different anchors for the three subtests (face anchors for two and numerical anchors for the third) may result in methodological effects.

Branch 2: Emotional Facilitation. Several subscales are used to assess whether people use emotion to facilitate cognitive activities. One such subtest is the Synesthesia scale (used also in the MEIS). This task asks participants to judge the similarity between an emotional feeling such as love and other internal experiences such as temperatures and tastes. The idea is that such internal comparisons indicate that emotions are not only being sensed and perceived but also processed in some meaningful way.

Branch 3: Understanding Emotion. Sample tasks for this branch are similar to branch 3 tasks for the MEIS in that they measure Blends, Progressions, and Transitions. In the Blends subtest the test-taker tries to match a set of emotions, such as joy and acceptance, to a single emotion that is the closest to the blend of emotions. Responses are in a multiple-choice format. One item might ask which alternative combines "joy and acceptance": (a) guilt, (b) challenge, (c) mania, (d) love, or (e) desire. The Transitions task focuses on what happens as an emotion intensifies or changes. A test-taker might be asked to respond to this item: "Jamie felt happier and happier, joyful and excited; if this feeling intensified it would be closest to: (a) challenge, (b) admiration, (c) pride, (d) peacefulness, (e) ecstasy." In Progressions the task asks the participant to identify a change of relationship that might bring about a specific mood change. For example, a test-taker might choose an alternative such as "a piece of music he liked came on the radio" to explain why a person's happiness might rise slightly.

Branch 4: Managing Emotion. Like the MEIS, the MSCEIT includes tasks concerned with the best way to regulate emotions in oneself and in other people to assess the Managing Emotion ability. For example, if a sad person wanted to cheer up, the alternatives might be "talking to some friends," "seeing a violent movie," "eating a big meal," and "taking a walk alone." The scoring of the alternatives is based on a consensus about which alternatives are more likely to lead to cheering a person up. There is also a scale that asks about managing emotions in situations in order to evaluate the ability to manage emotion in others.

Reliability Evidence

Currently there appears to be no reliability evidence for the tasks constituting the MSCEIT. The coefficient alphas that are cited are for the similar tasks in the MEIS.

Validity Evidence

Currently there appears to be little convergent and divergent validity evidence for the tasks constituting the MSCEIT. Most of the evidence involves the MEIS. In one study, however, the MSCEIT scores were compared with those for the Bar-On Emotional Quotient Inventory (EQ-i) (Bar-On, 1997b). The overall intertest correlation was .36 for a sample of 137, which indicates that the two tests are measuring some related aspects (10 percent of the variance is in common) but also measuring different aspects of emotional intelligence or competence. The scales of the MSCEIT are almost entirely unrelated to the Positive Impression scale of the EQ-i ($r = .16$, which is not significant).

There is also little evidence of relationships between the MSCEIT task scores and outcome measures of performance. The relationships that do exist appear to be for the MEIS. Although Mayer, Salovey, and Caruso seem to rely on the reliability and validity information provided for the MEIS to support the MSCEIT, there appear to be sufficient differences across the ability tasks to suggest that independent reliability and validity evidence should be established for the MSCEIT.

Test Publisher

The Mayer-Salovey-Caruso Emotional Intelligence Test is published by Multi-Health Systems, Inc., 908 Niagara Falls Blvd., North Tonawanda, NY 14120-2060; e-mail: oeg@mhs.com; telephone: 800-456-3003.

The Emotional Quotient Inventory

One of the pioneers in the measurement of emotional intelligence is Reuven Bar-On. Since the early 1980s, Bar-On has been interested in measuring what he calls *emotional and social intelligence,* which he defines as a multi-factorial array of inter-related emotional, personal and social abilities that influence our overall ability to actively and effectively cope (Bar-On, 2000a). Bar-On adds that this noncognitive intelligence is an important factor in determining one's ability to succeed in life, to cope with daily situations, and to get along in the world. The abilities that make up emotional and social intelligence directly influence one's general emotional well-being (i.e., one's present psychological condition or overall degree of emotional health (Bar-On, 1997a, 1997b). Bar-On coined the term *emotional quotient* (EQ) for his measure, as a parallel to the term *intelligence quotient* (IQ) used with cognitive measures. His interest is in learning more about emotionally and socially competent behavior and eventually about the underlying construct of emotional and social intelligence (Bar-On, 2000a).

Over the past twenty years, Bar-On has developed a theoretical framework for emotional and social intelligence consisting of five meta-factors (major conceptual components) and fifteen factors. These fifteen factors are presented in Table 5.8. Later a series of factor analyses led to a clarification of the roles of these factors. However, as these are the scales and subscales of the Emotional Quotient Inventory (EQ-i), these are the factors that are compared to the Goleman emotional competence framework in Table 5.9. This crosswalk between the emotional competence framework and Bar-On's EQ-i scales and subscales shows similarities across the two models. Specifically, Bar-On's Intrapersonal scales seem

TABLE 5.8. THE FIVE META-FACTORS AND FIFTEEN FACTORS OF EMOTIONAL AND SOCIAL INTELLIGENCE MEASURED BY THE BAR-ON EQ-I.

A. Intrapersonal EQ

    A1. Emotional Self-Awareness
    A2. Assertiveness
    A3. Self-Regard
    A4. Self-Actualization
    A5. Independence

B. Interpersonal EQ

    B1. Empathy
    B2. Social Responsibility
    B3. Interpersonal Relationship

C. Adaptability EQ

    C1. Reality Testing
    C2. Flexibility
    C3. Problem Solving

D. Stress Management EQ

    D1. Stress Tolerance
    D2. Impulse Control

E. General Mood EQ

    E1. Optimism
    E2. Happiness

to parallel Goleman's Personal Competence. Emotional Self-Awareness is similar to Emotional Awareness; Self-Regard is related to Accurate Self-Assessment and Self-Confidence; Impulse Control is related to Self-Regulation and Self-Control; Social Responsibility is related to Trustworthiness, Conscientiousness, and Collaboration and Cooperation; Flexibility is related to Adaptability; Problem Solving is related to Innovation; Self-Actualization is similar to Achievement Drive; and Optimism is a good match to Optimism. The Interpersonal Skills map to Social Competence. Empathy is a match to Empathy; Interpersonal Relationship is similar to Building Bonds. Some of Bar-On's competencies are not included in the Goleman framework—Reality Testing, Stress Tolerance, and Happiness.

Method of Assessment

Bar-On (2000a) describes the Emotional Quotient Inventory as a self-report measure of emotionally and socially competent behavior which provides an estimate of one's emotional and social intelligence. Although the instrument was initiated in the early 1980s as an experimental tool, it has now been translated into twenty-two languages and has normative data from fifteen countries. Bar-On refined the EQ-i over the years in light of the results of the normative studies and published

TABLE 5.9. COMPARISON OF THE EMOTIONAL QUOTIENT INVENTORY AND GOLEMAN'S EMOTIONAL COMPETENCE FRAMEWORK.

The Emotional Competence Framework (Goleman, 1998b)	Bar-On EQ-i (Emotional Quotient Inventory) (Bar-On, 1997b)
Personal Competence. How we manage ourselves.	**A. Intrapersonal Scales.** Managing ourselves.
A. **Self-Awareness.** Knowing one's internal states, preferences, resources, and intuitions.	A. **Intrapersonal EQ.** The ability to know oneself and one's emotions as well as to accept and express oneself.
A1. **Emotional Awareness.** Recognizing one's emotions and their effects.	A1. **Emotional Self-Awareness.** The ability to be aware of, recognize, and understand one's emotions.
A2. **Accurate Self-Assessment.** Knowing one's strengths and limits.	A3. **Self-Regard.** The ability to be aware of, understand, accept, and respect oneself.
A3. **Self-Confidence.** A strong sense of one's self-worth and capabilities.	A3. **Self-Regard.** The ability to be aware of, understand, accept, and respect oneself.
B. **Self-Regulation.** Managing one's internal states, impulses, and resources.	D2. **Impulse Control.** The ability to control one's emotions and resist or delay an impulse, drive, or temptation to act.
B1. **Self-Control.** Keeping disruptive emotions and impulses in check.	D2. **Impulse Control.** The ability to control one's emotions and resist or delay an impulse, drive, or temptation to act.
B2. **Trustworthiness.** Maintaining standards of honesty and integrity.	B2. **Social Responsibility.** The ability to demonstrate oneself as a cooperative, contributing, and constructive member of one's social group.
B3. **Conscientiousness.** Taking responsibility for personal performance.	B2. **Social Responsibility.** The ability to demonstrate oneself as a cooperative, contributing, and constructive member of one's social group.
B4. **Adaptability.** Flexibility in handling change.	C. **Adaptability EQ.** The ability to realistically and flexibly adjust to change and to effectively solve problems as they arise.
	C2. **Flexibility.** The ability to adjust one's feelings, thoughts, and behavior to changing situations and conditions.
B5. **Innovation.** Being comfortable with novel ideas, approaches, and new information.	C3. **Problem Solving.** The ability to effectively and constructively solve problems of a personal and social nature.
C. **Motivation.** Emotional tendencies that guide or facilitate reaching goals.	E. **General Mood EQ.** The ability to be optimistic and positive as well as to enjoy life; this contributes to the emotional energy and self-motivation required to cope with daily environmental demands and pressures.
C1. **Achievement Drive.** Striving to improve or meet a standard of excellence.	A4. **Self-Actualization.** The ability to realize one's potential and to do what one wants to do, enjoys doing, and can do.

TABLE 5.9. COMPARISON OF THE EMOTIONAL QUOTIENT INVENTORY AND GOLEMAN'S EMOTIONAL COMPETENCE FRAMEWORK, Cont'd.

The Emotional Competence Framework (Goleman, 1998b)	Bar-On EQ-i (Emotional Quotient Inventory) (Bar-On, 1997b)
C2. **Commitment.** Aligning with the goals of the group or organization.	B2. **Social Responsibility.** The ability to demonstrate oneself as a cooperative, contributing, and constructive member of one's social group.
C3. **Initiative.** Readiness to act on opportunities.	A5. **Independence.** The ability to be self-directed and self-reliant in one's thinking and actions and to be free of emotional dependency.
C4. **Optimism.** Persistence in pursuing goals despite obstacles and setbacks.	E1. **Optimism.** The ability to look at the brighter side of life and to maintain a positive attitude, even in the face of adversity.
Social Competence. How we handle relationships.	B. **Interpersonal Scales.** Managing our relationships.
D. **Empathy.** Awareness of others' feelings, needs, and concerns.	B1. **Empathy.** The ability to be aware of, understand, and appreciate the feelings of others.
D1. **Understanding Others.** Sensing others' feelings and perspectives, and taking an active interest in their concerns.	B1. **Empathy.** The ability to be aware of, understand, and appreciate the feelings of others.
D2. **Developing Others.** Sensing others' development needs, and bolstering their abilities.	
D3. **Service Orientation.** Anticipating, recognizing, and meeting customers' needs.	B1. **Empathy.** The ability to be aware of, understand, and appreciate the feelings of others.
D4. **Leveraging Diversity.** Cultivating opportunities through different kinds of people.	
D5. **Political Awareness.** Reading a group's emotional currents and power relationships.	
E. **Social Skills.** Adeptness at inducing desirable responses in others.	B. **Interpersonal EQ.** The ability to understand and appreciate the feelings of others as well as to establish and maintain mutually satisfying interpersonal relations.
E1. **Influence.** Wielding effective tactics for persuasion.	A2. **Assertiveness.** The ability to express one's feelings, beliefs, and thoughts and to defend one's rights in a nondestructive manner.
E2. **Communication.** Listening openly, and sending convincing messages.	B1. **Empathy.** The ability to be aware of, understand, and appreciate the feelings of others.

TABLE 5.9. COMPARISON OF THE EMOTIONAL QUOTIENT INVENTORY AND GOLEMAN'S EMOTIONAL COMPETENCE FRAMEWORK, Cont'd.

The Emotional Competence Framework (Goleman, 1998b)	Bar-On EQ-i (Emotional Quotient Inventory) (Bar-On, 1997b)
	A2. **Assertiveness.** The ability to express one's feelings, beliefs, and thoughts and to defend one's rights in a nondestructive manner.
E3. **Conflict Management.** Negotiating and resolving disagreements.	
E4. **Leadership.** Inspiring and guiding individuals and groups.	
E5. **Change Catalyst.** Initiating or managing change.	C. **Adaptability EQ.** The ability to realistically and flexibly adjust to change and to effectively solve problems as they arise.
	C2. **Flexibility.** The ability to adjust one's feelings, thoughts, and behavior to changing situations and conditions.
E6. **Building Bonds.** Nurturing instrumental relationships.	B3. **Interpersonal Relationship.** The ability to establish and maintain mutually satisfying relationships that are characterized by emotional closeness and intimacy and by giving and receiving affection.
E7. **Collaboration and Cooperation.** Working with others toward shared goals.	B2. **Social Responsibility.** The ability to demonstrate oneself as a cooperative, contributing, and constructive member of one's social group.
E8. **Team Capabilities.** Creating group synergy in pursuing collective goals.	
	C1. **Reality Testing.** The ability to validate one's feelings and thoughts by assessing the correspondence between what is internally and subjectively experienced and what externally and objectively exists.
	D. **Stress Management EQ.**
	D1. **Stress Tolerance.** The ability to manage strong emotions, adverse events, and stressful conditions without "falling apart" by actively and positively coping with the immediate situation.
	E2. **Happiness.** The ability to feel satisfied with one's life, to enjoy oneself and others, and to have fun and express positive emotions.

a new version of the EQ-i specifically for adults (people seventeen and older) in 1997. There is also a youth version of the EQ-i (EQ-i:YV) for children from six to twelve years of age and for adolescents from thirteen to seventeen, which has been normed on 9,500 individuals in North America. A semistructured EQ-interview and a 360-degree assessment (EQ-360) are presently being normed and validated.

The preliminary pilot testing of the EQ-i was especially important for item selection and alteration, continued scale development and validation, and the establishment of the final form of the response format prior to publication. The pilot test also provided cross-cultural data and information regarding interactions of age and of gender.

The published version of the EQ-i contains 133 items, however, 15 of these are associated with scales intended to assess response validity. These scales are the Omission Rate, Inconsistency Index, Positive Impression, and Negative Impression scales. The EQ-i scale scores are automatically corrected in relation to the scores on the Positive and Negative Impression scales in order to reduce the effects of socially desirable response bias. Fortunately, the overall EQ score correlates only .19 with Positive Impression, suggesting that the scales are not strongly biased by socially acceptable responses.

The inventory takes approximately forty minutes to complete. Item responses are captured on a 5-point Likert scale ranging from "Very seldom or Not true of me" to "Very often or True of me." Application of the Flesch formula for readability puts the inventory at the sixth-grade reading level. The respondent receives a total EQ score, scores on the five composite scales, and scores on the fifteen subscales. The scores are computer generated, and the results are displayed numerically, verbally, and graphically and are followed by a textual report. Raw scores are automatically tabulated and converted to standard scores based on a mean of 100 and a standard deviation of 15. As mentioned, this scoring structure resembles that of various cognitive intelligence (IQ) measures, hence the term EQ.

As a result of normative studies conducted with nearly four thousand people in the United States and Canada, Bar-On concluded that there are (1) significant differences on the EQ-i based on age, with older groups scoring higher and with the highest scores for those in their forties and fifties; (2) no significant differences for racial or ethnic groups, and (3) no significant differences overall for sex groups but some differences in the subscales (with women scoring higher on interpersonal skills and men scoring higher on Stress Management and Adaptability).

Reliability Evidence

Table 5.10 presents Cronbach's alphas for the fifteen subscales of the EQ-i. For the largest North American sample ($N = 3,831$), they range from .70 for Social Responsibility to .89 for Self-Regard. Additional reliability studies have produced

TABLE 5.10. INTERNAL CONSISTENCY COEFFICIENTS FOR THE EQ-I SUBSCALES EXAMINED WITH CRONBACH'S ALPHA ON NORTH AMERICAN SAMPLES AND ARGENTINEAN, GERMAN, SOUTH AFRICAN, NIGERIAN, ISRAELI, AND INDIAN SAMPLES.

EQ-i	NA1	NA2	NA3	AR	GE	SA	NI	IS	IN	AVE
Emotional Self-Awareness	.80	.78	.80	—	—	.76	—	—	—	.79
Assertiveness	.81	.77	.65	.77	.81	.78	.69	.80	.75	.76
Self-Regard	.89	.87	.85	.90	.87	.89	.89	.84	.81	.86
Self-Actualization	.80	.80	.68	.85	.75	.75	.76	.76	.71	.76
Independence	.79	.77	.74	.73	.75	.65	.68	.64	.73	.72
Empathy	.75	.77	.75	—	—	.69	—	—	—	.74
Interpersonal Relationship	.77	.83	.78	.74	.75	.74	.75	.74	.71	.76
Social Responsibility	.70	.83	.75	.68	.68	.62	.68	.64	.62	.69
Problem Solving	.80	.84	.78	.81	.75	.74	.76	.76	.69	.77
Reality Testing	.75	.80	.74	.80	.78	.69	.59	.75	.69	.73
Flexibility	.77	.74	.74	.79	.66	.69	.61	.62	.68	.70
Stress Tolerance	.84	.81	.74	.86	.85	.77	.67	.81	.83	.80
Impulse Control	.79	.80	.88	.88	.83	.77	.73	.80	.77	.80
Happiness	.81	.83	.74	.86	.82	.75	.71	.80	.76	.79
Optimism	.82	.82	.77	—	—	.72	—	—	—	.79

Note: NA1 = North American Normative Sample (*N* = 3,831); NA2 = North American Military Sample (*N* = 1,419); NA3 = North American Military Sample (*N* = 1,146); AR = Argentinean (*N* = 446); GE = German (*N* = 168); SA = South African (*N* = 448); NI = Nigerian (*N* = 267); IS = Israeli (*N* = 418); IN = Indian (*N* = 235); AVE = Average.

Source: Reprinted with permission from Bar-On, 1997b, p. 96. Copyright © 1997, Multi-Health Systems Inc. All rights reserved. In the U.S.A., 908 Niagara Falls Blvd., N. Tonawanda, NY 14120-2060, 800-456-3003. Internationally, +1-416-492-2627; Fax, +1-416-492-6640. Reproduced by permission.

similar internal consistency results for large samples (for example, 9,500 children and adolescents in the United States and Canada, 5,000 late adolescents and young adults in Israel, and 1,700 adults in the Netherlands) (Bar-On, 1997b). For some normative samples the alphas drop into the .60s. This is problematic in light of the fact that the inventory is used to distinguish differences between people, but could probably be fixed by adding items to the scales in question. Bar-On also describes two instances of test-retest reliability. In the first, forty adults in an Israeli sample were retested with the EQ-i after a period of three months. The reliability coefficient was .66. In a second study of thirty-nine adults in South Africa retaking the EQ-i after four months, the coefficient was .73. These are encouraging results, but they need to be replicated with much larger samples.

Validity Evidence

The EQ-i is supported by content validity and construct validity evidence based on internal structure and evidence based on other variables. The EQ-i was constructed by first identifying key factors related to effective emotional and social functioning and then developing items to assess those factors. Bar-On (2000a) cogently summarizes the results of a comprehensive program of research involving a multimethod, multitrait approach intended to further support the evidence of construct validity through convergent and divergent correlations. The findings that are most interesting involve extremely small correlations with traditional measures of IQ (ranging from .01 to .12). As the U.S. sample is only forty, future studies should concentrate on increasing that sample.

Factor analysis was performed to clarify the internal structure of the EQ-i. These analyses were performed on data from the normative sample ($N = 3,831$), progressing from exploratory to confirmatory factor analysis. A thirteen-factor solution with a varimax rotation initially afforded the most meaningful interpretation theoretically. (That is, the results of this exploratory factor analysis provided a reasonable match with the scale structure of the EQ-i.) An initial confirmatory factor analysis was then applied to resolve the difference between the fifteen-factor structure of the EQ-i and the thirteen factors that initially emerged from exploratory factor analysis. Although the confirmatory factor analysis clearly indicated a fifteen-factor structure that fits the theoretical basis of the EQ-i, an additional confirmatory factor analysis was applied to the same population in an attempt to explain an alternative factorial structure that appears to be equally acceptable. The items from five subscales (Independence, Self-Actualization, Optimism, Happiness, and Social Responsibility) were excluded from the second confirmatory factor analysis. Self-Actualization, Optimism, and Happiness were excluded because a number of their items originally loaded on a single factor together with Self-Regard and others loaded on a second factor; moreover, these three factors appear in the literature more as facilitators of emotional and social intelligence than as actual components of the construct. David Wechsler (1940, 1943) referred to them as "conative factors." Independence was excluded from the analysis because its items loaded heavily on Assertiveness and also because it does not appear in the literature as a component of emotional and social intelligence. However, Assertiveness, or Self-Expression, does appear in the literature as part of the construct. For similar empirical and theoretical reasons, Bar-On decided to exclude Social Responsibility and retain Empathy. Moreover, at .80, these two subscales proved to be the highest correlating components of the EQ-i, meaning that they are tapping very similar constructs. The end result of the confirmatory factor analysis is shown in Table 5.11, a ten-factor solution. Bar-On concludes that these ten factors appear to be the key components of emotional and social intelligence, with the remaining five factors serving as important correlates and facilitators of the construct. Bar-On (2000a) also suggests that the ten key components and five facilitators together describe and predict emotionally and socially competent behavior. The average intercorrelation of the fifteen subscales is .50. This is similar to the correlations among the various components of IQ tests.

The EQ-i's construct validity was assessed by examining the degree of correlation between its scales and the scales of more than twenty other psychological tests dating from 1983 on. These concomitantly administered tests included a number of measures thought to directly tap emotional intelligence or closely related aspects of it: for example, the Mayer-Salovey-Caruso Emotional Intelligence Test, Multifactor Emotional Intelligence Scale, Toronto Alexithymia Scale, Trait Meta-Mood Scale, and measures including physiological indicators of emotional awareness and expression.

The Bar-On EQ-i *Technical Manual* (Bar-On, 1997b) contains detailed information from seven other types of validity studies conducted on the EQ-i from 1983 to 1997, summarizing approximately fifty research findings. Given these findings, Bar-On concludes that the EQ-i has been shown to predict academic performance, occupational performance, job satisfaction, the ability to cope with work-related stress, marital satisfaction, the acculturation of new immigrants, the ability to cope with physical and emotional health, and various aspects of criminal behavior.

Scores on the EQ-i have been shown to be predictive of occupational success for U.S. Air Force recruiters. Table 5.12 shows the EQ-i scores for successful and unsuccessful recruiters. Successful recruiters filled their recruitment quotas. Unsuccessful recruiters filled 70 percent or less of their quotas. The ability to identify and select successful recruiters saved the U.S. Air Force nearly $3 million annually by significantly reducing mismatches (hiring the wrong people for the job, training them, and paying their salaries for an average of seven months before firing them). The U.S. General Accounting Office in a January 1998 report recommended that given the successful experience of the Air Force, the entire Department of Defense develop or procure personality screening tests that can aid in the selection of recruiters. As a result of this recommendation the EQ-i is currently being used for recruitment and selection in the Army, Navy, and Marines as well as in the Air Force. The EQ-i also appears to be of value in predicting academic success in the military. Other studies suggest that the EQ-i may have some value in predicting an individual's ability to adjust to a new country or to benefit

TABLE 5.11. THE FACTORIAL STRUCTURE OF
KEY COMPONENTS OF EMOTIONAL INTELLIGENCE.

Factor	Item	Loading	Factor	Item	Loading
1. Self-Regard	11	.37	6. Flexibility	14	.40
	24	.48		28	.52
	40	.53		43	.58
	56	.64		59	.46
	70	.64		74	.53
	85	.62		87	.57
	100	.74		103	.70
	114	.75		131	.43
	129	.61			
			7. Reality Testing	8	.39
2. Interpersonal				38	.65
Relationship	31	.54		53	.46
	39	.69		68	.52
	62	.63		83	.68
	69	.48		97	.42
	99	.42			
	113	.67	8. Stress Tolerance	4	.58
	128	.38		20	.57
				33	.64
3. Impulse Control	13	.73		49	.59
	73	.51		64	.42
	86	.35		78	.52
	117	.76		108	.54
	130	.75		122	.35
4. Problem Solving	1	.58	9. Assertiveness	37	.57
	15	.72		67	.67
	29	.66		82	.57
	45	.63		96	.54
	60	.73		111	.54
	89	.67		126	.59
5. Emotional			10. Empathy	61	.50
Self-Awareness	7	.76		72	.68
	9	.58		98	.64
	23	.76		119	.68
	35	.35		124	.59
	52	.74			
	116	.64			

TABLE 5.12. EQ-I MEAN SCORES FOR SUCCESSFUL AND UNSUCCESSFUL RECRUITERS IN THE U.S. AIR FORCE.

EQ-i	Successful	Unsuccessful	t	p
Total EQ	104.4	101.7	2.8	.01
Emotional Self-Awareness	100.6	98.2	1.8	.07
Assertiveness	106.4	100.4	4.0	.00
Self-Regard	108.8	106.0	2.3	.02
Self-Actualization	100.7	96.6	2.9	.00
Independence	108.0	105.3	2.1	.04
Empathy	100.9	99.4	1.1	.26
Interpersonal Relationship	99.3	97.8	0.9	.37
Social Responsibility	106.7	107.8	−0.8	.41
Problem Solving	106.5	101.8	3.4	.00
Reality Testing	108.2	108.0	0.2	.84
Flexibility	107.5	103.3	3.2	.00
Stress Tolerance	106.7	102.5	3.4	.00
Impulse Control	102.5	102.2	0.2	.82
Happiness	102.3	97.8	3.1	.00
Optimism	101.4	97.7	2.7	.01

Note: N of successful recruiters = 461; *N* of unsuccessful recruiters = 149.

Source: Reprinted with permission from Bar-On, 1997b, p. 143. Copyright © 1997, Multi-Health Systems Inc. All rights reserved. In the U.S.A., 908 Niagara Falls Blvd., N. Tonawanda, NY 14120-2060, 800-456-3003. Internationally, +1-416-492-2627; Fax, +1-416-492-6640. Reproduced by permission.

from a rehabilitation program. However, these latter two studies need to be replicated with larger sample sizes before definitive conclusions can be drawn.

Reuven Bar-On is currently developing a comprehensive list of EQ profiles, based on the EQ-i and drawing from a database of over fifty thousand subjects, for approximately seventy different occupational and professional groups. For example, there will be profiles for successful insurance people, firefighters, and senior managers. This information will be particularly beneficial for career development programs.

The EQ-i was the first test of emotional intelligence to be published by a psychological test publisher. The EQ-i was also the first test of emotional intelligence to be described and reviewed by the *Buros Mental Measurement Yearbook*.

Test Publisher

The Emotional Quotient Inventory is published by Multi-Health Systems, Inc., 908 Niagara Falls Blvd., North Tonawanda, NY 14120-2060; e-mail: oeg@mhs.com; telephone: 800-456-3003.

The EQ Map

Esther M. Orioli, cofounder, president, and CEO of Q-Metrics, and Robert K. Cooper, cofounder and chair of the board of Q-Metrics and author of *Executive EQ: Emotional Intelligence in Leadership and Organizations,* jointly developed the EQ Map. EQ is defined as "the ability to sense, understand and effectively apply the power and acumen of emotions as a source of human energy, information, trust, creativity, and influence" (Q-Metrics, 1996/1997, p. 1). Mapping is defined as "a unique, non-judgmental, interactive approach to assessing many areas including emotional intelligence, stress, self-esteem, resiliency, creativity and others. While tests typically provide a numeric score indicating one's skills or knowledge, maps provide a bird's eye approach to surveying the landscape, identifying strengths and pinpointing vulnerabilities and targeting specific actions to be taken. The goal of mapping is personal discovery and self-learning" (Orioli, Trocki, & Jones, 2000, p. 4).

The EQ Map is described as a multidimensional guide that helps respondents to discover the many facets that make up their personal emotional intelligence and to learn the relationship of emotional intelligence to performance, creativity, and success. Unlike the previously described measures of emotional intelligence, the EQ Map attempts to capture information on the current environment of the respondent, in terms of Life Pressures and Life Satisfaction, as well as the effects of the EQ profile on a variety of outcomes including General Health, Quality of Life, Relationship Quotient, and Optimal Performance. The organizational structure of the EQ Map, including the constructs measured by its twenty scales, is presented in Table 5.13.

The EQ Map is divided into five parts. Part 1 is the Current Environment, addressing one's current life circumstances including pressures, changes, and satisfactions both at work and at home. These areas reflect the context. Part 2 is Emotional Awareness, looking at the basics of emotional literacy, the core of emotional intelligence—one's ability to be self-aware, aware of others, and to express such awareness. Part 3, EQ Competencies, concerns fundamental skills and behavioral patterns developed over time to respond to the people, events, and circumstances of life. Part 4, EQ Values and Attitudes, examines how one views the world and what one values within it, which determines the choices one makes and the ways one behaves in the world. Part 5 describes Outcomes—the effects of EQ on the quality of life, level of work performance, general health, and relationships. Table 5.14 presents these constructs in relation to the Goleman emotional competence framework. Nine of the EQ Map scales match fairly closely to the Goleman competencies. It is interesting that several of these scales are taken from

TABLE 5.13. THE EQ MAP FRAMEWORK.

A. Part 1: Current Environment
    A1. Scale 1   Life Pressures
    A2. Scale 2   Life Satisfactions

B. Part 2: Emotional Awareness
    B1. Scale 3   Emotional Self-Awareness
    B2. Scale 4   Emotional Expression
    B3. Scale 5   Emotional Awareness of Others

C. Part 3: EQ Competencies
    C1. Scale 6   Intentionality
    C2. Scale 7   Creativity
    C3. Scale 8   Resilience
    C4. Scale 9   Interpersonal Connections
    C5. Scale 10   Constructive Discontent

D. Part 4: EQ Values and Attitudes
    D1. Scale 11   Outlook
    D2. Scale 12   Compassion
    D3. Scale 13   Intuition
    D4. Scale 14   Trust Radius
    D5. Scale 15   Personal Power
    D6. Scale 16   Integrated Self

E. Part 5: Outcomes
    E1. Scale 17   General Health
    E2. Scale 18   Quality of Life
    E3. Scale 19   Relationship Quotient
    E4. Scale 20   Optimal Performance

Source: Adapted from Orioli, Jones, & Trocki, 1999.

each of the map's three emotional dimensions—Emotional Awareness (specifically, Emotional Self-Awareness and Emotional Awareness of Others), EQ Competencies (Constructive Discontent, Creativity, Resilience, Interpersonal Connections), and EQ Values and Attitudes (Personal Power, Compassion).

Orioli, Trocki, and Jones (2000) summarize the research literature underlying the major sections of the EQ Map in the *EQ Map Technical Manual*. The linkage with the relevant literature is made at both the section level (describing, for example, what studies were considered in the development of the constructs assessing Current Environment) and the scale level (looking at material relevant to, for example, Life Pressures and Life Satisfactions). Even though many studies are cited, it is not clear exactly how those studies influenced the development of the items in the EQ Map. For a full appreciation of the content and construct validity

TABLE 5.14. COMPARISON OF THE EQ MAP AND GOLEMAN'S EMOTIONAL COMPETENCE FRAMEWORK.

The Emotional Competence Framework (Goleman, 1998b)	E. M. Orioli's EQ Map (Published by Q-Metrics)
Personal Competence. How we manage ourselves.	
A. **Self-Awareness.** Knowing one's internal states, preferences, resources, and intuitions.	
A1. **Emotional Awareness.** Recognizing one's emotions and their effects.	B1. **Emotional Self-Awareness.** The degree to which you are able to notice your feelings, label them, and connect to their source.
A2. **Accurate Self-Assessment.** Knowing one's strengths and limits.	
A3. **Self-Confidence.** A strong sense of one's self-worth and capabilities.	D5. **Personal Power.** The degree to which you believe that you can meet challenges and live the life you choose.
B. **Self Regulation.** Managing one's internal states, impulses, and resources.	
B1. **Self-Control.** Keeping disruptive emotions and impulses in check.	C5. **Constructive Discontent.** Your ability to stay calm, focused, and emotionally grounded, even in the face of disagreement or conflict.
B2. **Trustworthiness.** Maintaining standards of honesty and integrity.	D4. **Trust Radius.** The degree to which you expect other people to be trustworthy, to treat you fairly, to be inherently good.
B3. **Conscientiousness.** Taking responsibility for personal performance.	
B4. **Adaptability.** Flexibility in handling change.	
B5. **Innovation.** Being comfortable with novel ideas, approaches, and new information.	C2. **Creativity.** Your ability to tap multiple non-cognitive resources that allow you to envision powerful new ideas, frame alternative solutions, and find effective new ways of doing things.
C. **Motivation.** Emotional tendencies that guide or facilitate reaching goals.	C1. **Intentionality.** This is your ability to act deliberately, to say what you mean and mean what you say. The scale explores how consciously you are able to make decisions consistent with your personal and professional goals and values.
C1. **Achievement Drive.** Striving to improve or meet a standard of excellence.	
C2. **Commitment.** Aligning with the goals of the group or organization.	

TABLE 5.14. COMPARISON OF THE EQ MAP AND GOLEMAN'S EMOTIONAL COMPETENCE FRAMEWORK, Cont'd.

The Emotional Competence Framework (Goleman, 1998b)	E. M. Orioli's EQ Map (Published by Q-Metrics)
C3. **Initiative.** Readiness to act on opportunities.	
C4. **Optimism.** Persistence in pursuing goals despite obstacles and setbacks.	C3. **Resilience.** Your ability to bounce back, to be flexible, to retain a sense of curiosity and hopefulness about the future, even in the face of adversity.
	D1. **Outlook.** The way you view the world and your place within it; how positively or negatively you interpret life events and experiences.
Social Competence. How we handle relationships.	
D. **Empathy.** Awareness of others' feelings, needs, and concerns.	D2. **Compassion.** Your ability to be exceptionally empathic, to appreciate and honor another person's feelings and point of view. Compassion also consists of your ability to be forgiving of yourself and of others.
D1. **Understanding Others.** Sensing others' feelings and perspectives, and taking an active interest in their concerns.	B3. **Emotional Awareness of Others.** The ability to hear, sense, or intuit what other people may be feeling, from their words, their body language, or other direct or indirect cues.
D2. **Developing Others.** Sensing others' development needs and bolstering their abilities.	
D3. **Service Orientation.** Anticipating, recognizing, and meeting customers' needs.	
D4. **Leveraging Diversity.** Cultivating opportunities through different kinds of people.	
D5. **Political Awareness.** Reading a group's emotional currents and power relationships.	
E. **Social Skills.** Adeptness at inducing desirable responses in others.	
E1. **Influence.** Wielding effective tactics for persuasion.	
E2. **Communication.** Listening openly and sending convincing messages.	B2. **Emotional Expression.** The degree to which you can express your feelings and gut-level instincts, allowing them to be used as integral part of your daily actions and interactions.

TABLE 5.14. COMPARISON OF THE EQ MAP AND GOLEMAN'S EMOTIONAL COMPETENCE FRAMEWORK, Cont'd.

The Emotional Competence Framework (Goleman, 1998b)	E. M. Orioli's EQ Map (Published by Q-Metrics)
E3. **Conflict Management.** Negotiating and resolving disagreements.	
E4. **Leadership.** Inspiring and guiding individuals and groups.	
E5. **Change Catalyst.** Initiating or managing change.	
E6. **Building Bonds.** Nurturing instrumental relationships.	C4. **Interpersonal Connections.** This explores your ability to create and sustain a network of people with whom you are your real and whole self; to whom you can express caring and appreciation; with whom you can share your vulnerabilities and hopes.
E7. **Collaboration and Cooperation.** Working with others toward shared goals.	
E8. **Team Capabilities.** Creating group synergy in pursuing collective goals.	
	A1. **Life Pressures.** Life pressures are the stressors and strains in your life, both at work and at home, that you experience as constraining, difficult, or draining.
	D6. **Integrated Self.** The degree to which your intellectual, emotional, spiritual, and creative selves fit together in a consistent, synchronized whole.
	E1. **General Health.** The effect of your EQ profile on your physical, behavioral, and emotional health.
	E2. **Quality of Life.** The effect of your EQ profile on your sense of self-acceptance and your general satisfaction with life.
	E3. **Relationship Quotient.** The effect your EQ profile has on the quality and depth of your interpersonal connections with others.
	E4. **Optimal Performance.** The effect of your EQ profile on your day-to-day performance.
	A2. **Life Satisfactions.** Life Satisfactions are those interpersonal relationships, situations, or life circumstances that you experience as pleasurable, fulfilling, or rewarding, both at work and at home.

evidence for the EQ Map, the reader has to return to the original studies cited in the technical manual.

The results of a principal components factor analysis of the twenty scales are shown in Table 5.15. The three factors in this table, Increasing Energy and Effectiveness Under Pressure, Building Trusting Relationships, and Creating the Future, have been incorporated into *the Q-Metrics approach*. This approach helps respondents to determine how well they cope with pressures, how much they trust themselves and others, and how well they think creatively. The Q-Metrics approach, pictured graphically in Figure 5.1, is an interesting way to reassemble the data provided from the twenty scales of the EQ Map. Specifically, this approach provides an alternative way for respondents to interpret their individual

TABLE 5.15. FACTOR ANALYSIS FOR THE EQ MAP— EXTRACTION METHOD: PRINCIPAL COMPONENT ANALYSIS.

	Factor Extraction
Increasing Energy and Effectiveness Under Pressure	
Life Pressures	.74
Life Satisfactions	.59
Emotional Self-Awareness	.67
Emotional Expression	.70
Resilience	.62
General Health	.67
Optimal Performance	.54
Building Trusting Relationships	
Emotional Awareness of Others	.73
Interpersonal Connection	.80
Compassion	.84
Trust Radius	.77
Integrated Self	.70
Relationship Quotient	.78
Creating the Future	
Intentionality	.77
Creativity	.69
Constructive Discontent	.83
Outlook	.86
Intuition	.77
Personal Power	.88
Quality of Life	.81

Source: Reprinted with permission from Orioli, Trocki, & Jones, 2000, p. 16.

FIGURE 5.1. THE Q-METRICS APPROACH.

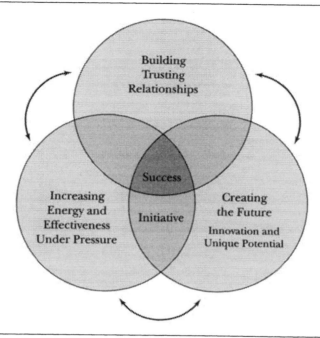

results in relation to three broad categories of behaviors. Those categories are defined as follows:

Increasing Energy and Effectiveness Under Pressure. Increasing Energy and Effectiveness Under Pressure is a cluster of abilities for managing one's energy level throughout the day and optimizing interactions with others. This factor concerns capacities that tend to decline when we are under pressure. Maintaining them helps us sustain exceptional attentiveness and a high level of effectiveness in our performance.

Building Trusting Relationships. Building Trusting Relationships is a cluster that addresses our abilities to trust ourselves, trust others, and allow the creative discord that results in sound, effective solutions. These abilities can enhance interactions with customers, clients, and work teams. They can also save time and help us get things done at a more substantive, meaningful level.

Creating the Future. Creating the Future deals with the ability to think beyond the conventional, come up with unorthodox solutions, and serve colleagues, clients, and others in one's life with truly creative results. Creating the Future develops uncommon yet highly practical ways to identify the most promising opportunities for personal and professional breakthroughs. This cluster capitalizes on the individual's unique potential—core talents and strengths—and the ability to recognize and help activate the unique potential of others (Cooper, 1997).

Method of Assessment

In 1996, the EQ Map was constructed using a variety of existing scales, measures, and questions from a library of assessment devices available at Essi Systems, Inc. Essi partnered with Advanced Intelligence Technologies to test the first of many versions of what would later become the EQ Map. From a review of the literature, it became clear that the EQ Map would have to contain a section on competencies. It was recognized that knowing how to do something does not dictate whether someone would do something. Deciding what is important and how to act on that importance is a matter of one's value system and guiding beliefs. Thus the EQ Map was modified to include values and attitudes. In order to capture the context or the whole person perspective, integrating as many components of real life as possible in as comprehensive a manner as possible, the context scales capturing the current environment were added. Finally, the outcomes were added to deal with the role EQ plays in life.

The EQ Map is written at an eighth-grade reading level. It is a self-administered, self-report measure that takes approximately forty minutes to complete. The EQ Map is designed strictly for developmental purposes, not for employment selection or promotion. The twenty scales are scored using a variety of approaches. For example, Life Pressures are rated on a 4-point scale. Respondents are asked to think about the past month and for each work or personal pressure listed (such as job security or financial difficulties) to indicate how much it has been a source of distress, using a scale ranging from "Great" (3) to "None/Didn't occur" (0). All the Emotional Awareness dimension scales are scored on how well the statement describes actions or intentions, from "Very Well" (3) to "Not at All" (0). In some cases the numerical values for the answer scales are reversed, offering, for example, choices from "I feel like a fraud" (0) to "Not at All" (3). The Outcome scales also have different response alternatives in some cases but still use a 4-point scale. The EQ Map is self-scored by the respondent. Responses for the twenty scales are then placed in one of four *performance zones,* which represent the varying levels being mapped. The top two zones are considered strengths, areas of capacity and skill.

The lower two zones reflect areas of vulnerability or difficulty. The four zones are defined as follows in the *EQ Map Interpretation Guide* (Q-Metrics, 1996/1997, p. 2):

> *Optimal.* Your greatest EQ strengths; in these areas you show great strength, effectiveness and creativity, even under pressure.
>
> *Proficient.* You demonstrate steady, balanced EQ effectiveness in most situations.
>
> *Vulnerable.* You demonstrate some skills and competencies, but often run into difficulty bringing EQ into your day-to-day life. Your overall EQ performance is unsteady and may fluctuate from situation to situation.
>
> *Caution.* Your EQ ability is compromised or needs enhancement and may prove difficult to use without concentrated attention.

Reliability Evidence

Table 5.16 provides the Cronbach's alpha estimates of reliability for the EQ Map scales. (In this analysis some scales are split into sections, thus the total number of scales presented in Table 5.16 is greater than twenty.) The estimates of internal homogeneity range from .53 for Behavioral Symptoms to .91 for Quality of Life. The lower reliabilities for the three components of the General Health scale might improve if the subscales were combined. The other estimates of alpha could probably be increased if more items were added to each scale. Table 5.16 also shows the test-retest reliability for the EQ Map. Although the correlations are encouraging, additional evidence is needed from larger sample sizes.

Validity Evidence

The EQ Map is supported by evidence of content validity, construct validity, and convergent and divergent validity. The content and construct validity evidence was presented earlier in the discussion. Orioli et al. (2000) present the results of the convergent and divergent studies done to date. Specifically, in a validation study with 131 subjects who completed the MBI (Maslach Burnout Inventory) General Survey, BSI (Brief Symptom Inventory) scales, an impulsivity scale, the EQ Map, and an emotional skills assessment, the authors were able to obtain convergent validity evidence for many of the EQ Map scales. Table 5.17 presents the convergent and divergent validity evidence.

Test Publisher

The EQ Map is published by Q-Metrics, 70 Otis St., San Francisco, CA 94103; telephone: 888-252-MAPS (252-6277); e-mail: qmetricseq@aol.com.

TABLE 5.16. INTERNAL RELIABILITY AND TEST-RETEST RELIABILITY FOR THE EQ MAP.

	Number of Items	Interscale Reliability ($N = 824$)	Test-Retest Reliability ($N = 88$)
Life Pressures	32	.85	.65
Work Pressures	17	.83	.64
Personal Pressures	15	.71	.70
Life Satisfactions	21	.85	.62
Work Satisfactions	13	.80	.70
Personal Satisfactions	8	.86	.51
Emotional Self-Awareness	8	.81	.73
Emotional Expression	8	.80	.72
Emotional Awareness of Others	10	.80	.64
Intentionality	9	.82	—
Creativity	10	.86	—
Resilience	14	.82	—
Interpersonal Connections	10	.78	—
Constructive Discontent	10	.77	—
Compassion	8	.74	—
Outlook	12	.85	—
Intuition	11	.78	—
Trust Radius	12	.74	—
Personal Power	11	.83	—
Integrated Self	9	.68	—
Physical Symptoms	9	.61	.74
Behavioral Symptoms	12	.53	.66
Emotional Symptoms	10	.89	.68
Quality of Life	11	.91	.76
Relationship Quotient	7	.81	—
Optimal Performance	7	.74	—

Source: Reprinted with permission from Orioli, Trocki, & Jones, 2000.

TABLE 5.17. CORRELATIONS BETWEEN EQ MAP SCALES, MBI-GENERAL SURVEY DIMENSIONS, AND BSI SYMPTOM DIMENSIONS.

Scale	Correlation with EQ Map	Scale	Correlation with EQ Map
Emotional Symptoms (EQ Map)		Work Pressures (EQ Map)	
G.S.I. (BSI)	.63	Emotional Exhaustion (MBI)	.50
P.S.T. (BSI)	.63	Cynicism (MBI)	.46
Anxiety (BSI)	.55	Professional Efficacy (MBI)	−.29
Interpersonal Sensitivity (BSI)	.56		
Obsessive Compulsive (BSI)	.63	Personal Satisfactions (EQ Map)	
Depression (BSI)	.60	Emotional Exhaustion (MBI)	−.08
Emotional Exhaustion (MBI)	.40	Professional Efficacy (MBI)	−.01
Cynicism (MBI)	.25	Cynicism (MBI)	−.05
		Impulsivity	−.17
Physical Symptoms (EQ Map)		Sensation Seeking	.01
Somatization (BSI)	.60		
Anxiety (BSI)	.43	Personal Power (EQ Map)	
Depression (BSI)	.33	Emotional Exhaustion (MBI)	−.36
Emotional Exhaustion (MBI)	.26	Professional Efficacy (MBI)	.34
		Cynicism (MBI)	−.31
Compassion (EQ Map)		Interpersonal Sensitivity (BSI)	.58
Hostility (BSI)	.60		
Interpersonal Sensitivity (BSI)	.57	Personal Pressures (EQ Map)	
		Emotional Exhaustion (MBI)	.22
Work Satisfactions (EQ Map)		Professional Efficacy (MBI)	.00
Emotional Exhaustion (MBI)	−.47	Cynicism (MBI)	.16
Professional Efficacy (MBI)	.50	Interpersonal Sensitivity (BSI)	.15
Cynicism (MBI)	−.53	Depression (BSI)	.14
		Anxiety (BSI)	.20

Note: N of subjects completing all instruments = 131.

Source: Reprinted with permission from Orioli, Trocki, & Jones, 2000, p. 16.

Other Measures

This chapter summarizes the most widely used emotional intelligence measures. Researchers have developed additional measures that show promise for future applications. Two of these are the Job Competencies Survey by Victor Dulewicz and Malcolm Higgs (1998) and a thirty-three-item measure developed by Nicola Schutte and her associates and based on the work of Salovey and Mayer (Schutte et al., 1998).

Future Directions in Assessment

The measures described in this chapter hold great promise for future research. These measures are all aimed at measuring emotional intelligence and emotional competence, although they seem to be analyzing the constructs at different levels. Mayer and Salovey and their colleagues appear to have an interest in the most micro level of analysis—the abilities of emotional intelligence. That is, Mayer and Salovey and their colleagues are most interested in internal capacities related to emotional processing and the prediction of important outcomes. However, some of these abilities do overlap with what others define as emotional competencies. Goleman and Boyatzis, Bar-On, and Orioli and Cooper all attempt to measure emotional competencies. They focus on positive social behaviors and their prediction of important outcomes. In some cases these competencies overlap, but in others they are different constructs. Finally, Orioli and Cooper go beyond competencies through their attempts to incorporate environmental and outcome variables into their measure, the EQ Map. Figure 5.2 illustrates some of the interrelationships

FIGURE 5.2. COMPARISON OF EI MEASURES.

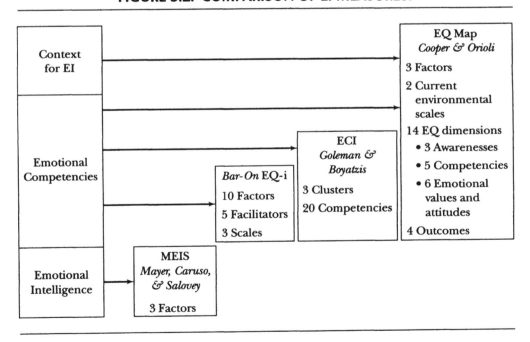

among the various measures of emotional intelligence and emotional competence. This figure can serve as a template for those searching for convergent and discriminant validity across these measures.

It is important to remember that there are also significant distinctions among the measures in terms of their response formats. Bar-On's Emotional Quotient Inventory and Orioli's EQ Map are both self-report measures with the attendant limitations associated with that type of measurement. Fortunately, Bar-On's self-report measure has already shown evidence of criterion-related validity that documents its usefulness in spite of its format. The Boyatzis and Goleman Emotional Competence Inventory used as a 360-degree assessment includes self-ratings (again with the problems of self-report measures), peer ratings (which traditionally have been shown to have greater predictive validity), and superior ratings. When the 360-degree process is used in human resource management programs other than training and development (for example, for selection or promotion or for performance management), respondents may answer items differently due to the administrative purpose for which the tool is intended. Finally, for a true measure of abilities and competencies, it is always valuable to include objective assessments of those abilities and skills as a check and balance to self-reports and to 360-degree evaluations. For example, even though an individual may claim to have good judgment (self-report) and even though that individual may be considered by peers and superiors to have good judgment, as reflected in 360-degree ratings, the score on an independent situational judgment test or a measure of cognitive ability will provide more confidence about that individual's true level of ability. Fortunately, in the area of emotional intelligence, Mayer, Salovey, and Caruso have provided a measure of the internal abilities supporting the emotional competence measures. Future studies using all three types of assessment—self-reports, 360-degree assessments, and ability tasks—will contribute to our understanding of the emotional intelligence constructs.

In the beginning of this chapter, I summarized the historical involvement of the employer community in the assessment of social or emotional competencies, especially through the assessment center process. The next generation of assessment seems poised to include assessment centers on computer—in essence, virtual reality simulations that replicate experiences in the real world of work. The development of these simulations offers a wonderful opportunity for improving the evaluation of emotional competencies. With the click of a mouse, the individuals in the scenarios might be changed to show different types of emotion and greater or lesser degrees of those emotions. For example, Jerry Goleman at Northwestern University, with funding from the U.S. Department of Justice, has developed a simulation called Crime and Punishment. This simulation is intended to evaluate the fairness of judges who review court materials and watch witnesses testify in front of them. By clicking the mouse, the witness changes race, sex, degree of eye contact with the judge, type of dress (from uniform to civilian clothes), and so forth. Facial expressions can be altered to elicit different emotions in the judge. It is wonderful to have such strong marker measures of emotional intelligence and competence (the Multifactor Emotional Intelligence Scale, the Mayer-Salovey-Caruso Emotional Intelligence Test, the Emotional Competence Inventory, the Bar-On Emotional Quotient Inventory, and the EQ Map) to administer simultaneously with the virtual reality simulations to help ensure that these new simulations are in fact measuring what they say they are measuring.

Although most of the measures presented in this chapter have been designed to aid in individuals' development and not in selection or promotion (the exception being the Bar-On EQ-i, which has been successfully used in selecting Air Force recruiters), I envision a future in which measures of emotional intelligence will be used for selection and promotion in public and private sector organizations. It may well be that these new measures, including those designed as virtual reality, will have more rigorous construct validity due to the availability of the self-report and 360-degree assessments summarized here. In fact, without the measures reviewed in this chapter, the next generation of assessment tools would not be possible.

In conclusion, it is important to understand that many of the measures presented here are fairly new in design and application. Consequently, one should anticipate the body of reliability and validity evidence to be growing with each new study. The results to date are most encouraging, and these researchers will surely continue to play a major part in furthering our understanding of the role of emotional intelligence in the workplace and in our lives.

CHAPTER SIX

GROUP EMOTIONAL INTELLIGENCE AND ITS INFLUENCE ON GROUP EFFECTIVENESS

Vanessa Urch Druskat
Steven B. Wolff

The use of work groups in organizational settings has grown dramatically in the last decade as organizations have discovered that integrating diverse perspectives, skills, and knowledge enhances innovation and improves decisions (Lawler, 1998). The increased use of groups has also created keen interest in determining what makes them effective so that their success can be facilitated. A number of existing theoretical models help to answer this question by defining factors that influence a group's effectiveness. Common factors in most models include organizational context (reward systems, culture, educational systems, and so forth), group design (size, skills, and so forth), group processes, and boundary management (Cohen, 1994; Shea & Guzzo, 1987; Hackman, 1987; Sundstrom, DeMeuse, & Futrell, 1990). At its core, however, effective teamwork requires achieving cooperation and collaboration among group members. Yet no theory addresses with enough depth to be useful to those interested in building effective teams the actions and beliefs that underlie the emergence of these important interaction processes (Cannon-Bowers, Tannenbaum, Salas, & Volpe, 1995; Donnellon, 1996).

The need to understand more clearly how cooperation and collaboration develop in groups has increased over the years as work groups, once used exclusively

---

The authors contributed equally to this chapter.

on the shop floors of manufacturing organizations, are implemented among many other workers, including knowledge workers making highly complex and important decisions. Today, cross-functional groups are used throughout organizational levels to promote better informed, more innovative decisions and quicker response times. Mandates for such improved decision making place a premium on give-and-take cooperative interaction processes that facilitate information sharing, idea and knowledge integration, and collaboration among what Dougherty (1992) calls differing *thought worlds* or types of expertise.

In this chapter we argue that determining how groups develop effective interaction processes requires an understanding of the role of emotion in groups. Because many human emotions grow out of social interactions (Kemper, 1978), emotion is a pervasive influence in groups and is fundamentally linked to how group members interact and work together. We argue that the ability of a group to intelligently manage emotion plays an important role in its interaction processes and effectiveness. We also develop a model that examines in detail the emotional processes that exist at multiple levels in a group setting, and we introduce the concept of group emotional intelligence (GEI), which we argue is necessary for managing these emotional processes. We define group emotional intelligence as the ability to develop a set of norms that manage emotional processes so as to cultivate trust, group identity, and group efficacy. We argue that these collective beliefs facilitate the development of group member cooperation and collaboration.

The chapter is organized into five sections. In section one, we define the collective beliefs that facilitate member cooperation and collaboration. As the chapter proceeds, we define the emotion-focused norms required to cultivate those collective beliefs, and we outline how those group norms develop. Section two takes an in-depth look at the emotional process in groups, including the ways emotions influence and are influenced by the group. Section three describes the roles that individual emotional intelligence and group emotional intelligence play in groups and presents an applied framework of the group norms that characterize GEI. Section four describes the processes through which GEI norms develop in a group. We end with a synthesis of the ways GEI influences group effectiveness and a discussion of the implications of our model for building effective work groups.

The Desired Outcome: Building Cooperation and Collaboration

Research consistently reveals that cooperation and collaboration are fundamental interaction processes in work groups and fundamental ingredients for group effectiveness (Ancona & Caldwell, 1992; Argote, 1989; Campion, Medsker, &

Higgs, 1993; Druskat, 1996; Tjosvold & Tjosvold, 1994). Using the assumption that salient cognition predicts behavior (see Fiske & Taylor, 1991; Scheier & Carver, 1982), we reviewed the extensive literature on group dynamics and interpersonal relationships to determine the collective beliefs in groups that predict and facilitate cooperation and collaboration. Three such beliefs were identified: trust, group identity, and group efficacy. In the pages that follow we argue that group emotional intelligence is necessary for building these collective beliefs and, thus, effective interaction processes (that is, cooperation and collaboration).

Many agree that trust is an essential ingredient for developing cooperation in groups (Coleman, 1988; Jones & George, 1998; McAllister, 1995). Definitions of trust view it as growing out of affect and friendship (that is, stemming from reciprocal care and concern) and out of calculus-based cognitions (for example, I trust that you can and will do what you say) (see McAllister, 1995; Rousseau, Sitkin, Burt, & Camerer, 1998). It seems clear that trust is both affective and cognitive and involves a sense of expectation, obligation (Coleman, 1990), and reciprocity (Clarkson, 1998). Coleman (1990) asserts that the social environment also plays an important role in trust. For example, a trustworthy social environment encourages the assumption that an obligation will be fulfilled and an expectation met, thus creating a system of mutual trust. Clearly, obligations, expectations, and reciprocity are related constructs that can turn trust into a powerful group resource fostering cooperation and partnership or collaboration.

The second collective belief we consider necessary for building effective interaction processes in groups is group identity, defined as a group's collective belief that it is a unique, important, and attractive entity. Group identity "brings up a boundary" (Yan & Louis, 1999) around a group that clearly defines group membership and facilitates feelings of inclusiveness and attachment. Given these characteristics, group identity creates the sense of security that Kahn (1998) describes as necessary for task engagement during periods of organizational unpredictability. Research has found that successful managers strive to build group identity in their work groups (by using symbols such as group names, for example) in order to increase cooperation between members and commitment to the group and its task (Boyatzis, 1982). Thus group identity is a collective belief that facilitates the sense among group members that their goals and futures are positively linked. This increases members' commitment to each other and facilitates the cooperation and collaboration necessary for group success.

The final collective belief we consider necessary for building effective interaction processes is group efficacy, defined as the collective belief in a group that it can be effective (Lindsley, Brass, & Thomas, 1995). Field research has consistently found a group's sense of efficacy to be linked to its task effectiveness (Campion et al., 1993; Shea & Guzzo, 1987; Silver & Bufanio, 1996). We argue that group efficacy is a facilitator of cooperation and collaboration because it gives group members the sense that they can be more effective as a unit than individually. As such, group efficacy becomes a self-fulfilling prophecy (see Darley & Fazio, 1980).

Together these three collective beliefs are a powerful group resource that improves group decision making and group effectiveness by facilitating cooperation and collaboration (Ancona & Caldwell, 1992; Clarkson, 1998; Coleman, 1990; Dirks, 1999; Edmondson, 1999; Jones & George, 1998). In the following discussion of the role of emotions in the group context, we argue that the ways emotions are treated in a group influence the emergence of these collective beliefs. We specifically suggest that GEI norms facilitate the development of trust, group identity, and group efficacy, which subsequently facilitate effective task-focused processes including cooperation and collaboration.

Emotions in the Group Context

Many human emotions grow out of social interactions (Kemper, 1978), making emotion an inevitable and pervasive influence on group life (Barsade & Gibson, 1998). Knowing how emotions affect behavior in groups is therefore useful for understanding and predicting group behavior. In this section we detail the process through which emotions influence behavior and then describe how understanding this process provides insights about the influence of emotions in work groups.

The theoretical representation of emotion we use borrows from the anthropological literature and is based on the work of Levy (1984). An anthropological perspective is useful for understanding emotion in groups because it incorporates cultural influence into the interpretation and management of emotion. We argue that group cultural norms, like cultural norms in communities and societies, exert a powerful influence on the processing and expression of emotion by group members. Levy's perspective (1984) uses a cognitive appraisal theory of emotion (see Lazarus, 1991) that suggests the emotional process occurs in a sequence that begins with an eliciting event and proceeds as follows: (1) awareness of the eliciting event or situation, (2) interpretation of the situation such that emotional arousal or an *emotional feeling* enters into conscious awareness, and (3) selection of an action or behavior as a response to the feeling. This process is represented in Figure 6.1.

Anthropologists have long proposed that cultures have conventions and norms that influence the management of emotions (see Ekman, 1980; Lutz, 1988). That is, cultural norms or rules create commonality and predictability among individuals in their interpretation and response to emotional stimuli. As Figure 6.1 illustrates, culture has the opportunity to influence the emotional process at two points.

FIGURE 6.1. THE EMOTIONAL PROCESS.

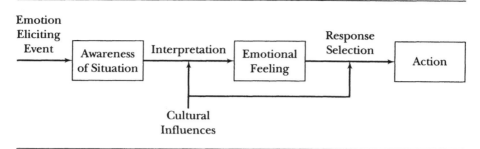

First, an individual's interpretation of an eliciting event is shaped by culture. For example, in some cultures arriving late to a meeting is interpreted as socially correct whereas in other cultures it is considered unacceptable. The difference between the two cultures in people's interpretation of lateness will therefore elicit different emotions from the individuals involved. Second, culture influences the selection of a response to emotion. Levy (1984) considers culture an internalized "system of control for producing integrated, adaptive, sane behavior" (p. 232). Thus culture provides specific "display rules" that influence the selection of a culturally acceptable response (Ekman, 1980). For example, Kleinman (1988) found that it is unacceptable to express depression in Chinese culture, thus the feeling of depression is often expressed as a physical ailment.

Three aspects of this model in particular help us understand the role of emotion in work groups. First, the model illustrates that emotions contain important information that can alert group members to issues that require the group's attention and response (Fein, 1990), for example, a feeling of tension can alert a group member to unresolved conflict in the group. Second, the model posits a connection between emotions and behavior. In so doing, it emphasizes that emotions play a role in driving group member behavior. Third, the model proposes that once emotions reach consciousness, their interpretation and expression are influenced by expectations or norms such as those that exist as part of the group's culture.

A fourth implication for work groups grows out of the emotion-behavior connection. According to Folkman and Lazarus (1988), an emotional cycle is created from this connection. Emotion leads to behavior, which leads to changes in the relationship between the individual and the environment (that is, the group and its members), which leads to emotion. Moreover, this cycle can take a positive or negative direction. It can create an upward self-reinforcing spiral of trust, group identity, and group efficacy, or it can create a downward self-reinforcing spiral of dysfunctional conflict and detachment (Hackman, 1990; Lindsley, Brass, & Thomas, 1995). We propose that emotionally intelligent responses to stimuli contribute to the development of a positive cycle. However, we also propose that in the group context, individual emotional intelligence is not enough to support the positive cycle. Such support requires both individual and group emotional intelligence.

The influence of cultural norms on the interpretation of an emotional stimulus and on the resulting behavior forms the basis of our definition of group emotional intelligence. An integral element of our definition is the group's ability to create norms (that is, group cultural influences) that channel the interpretation of emotional stimuli and subsequent behaviors in ways that have a positive impact on group effectiveness. A full definition of GEI and the process of its creation is presented later. To prepare more fully for that definition, we first discuss individual emotional intelligence and its role in the group.

Emotional Intelligence

Goleman (1998b) proposes that emotional intelligence has two overall categories of competence—both of which are related to the management of the emotional process just described. The first is *personal competence* and involves Self-Awareness, Self-Regulation, and Self-Motivation. The lightning speed with which the emotional process occurs makes the first two personal competencies important in social situations. They keep one from responding to emotional stimuli before fully contemplating the consequences of the response. Indeed, emotional intelligence involves keen awareness of the emotional process and the ability to manage it effectively (Goleman, 1995a, 1998b; Mayer & Salovey, 1997). Self-Awareness and Self-Regulation enhance the individual's ability to mobilize a culturally appropriate interpretation of emotional stimuli and to enact a situationally appropriate behavioral response. Self-Motivation, the third personal competency, is what assists an individual in controlling emotions so that they guide and facilitate reaching goals.

The second category of competence that defines emotional intelligence is *social competence* (Goleman, 1998b). This involves Social Awareness (that is, Empathy) and Social Skills. These involve the ability to label and recognize others' emotions, needs, and concerns and the ability to help others manage their emotions so as to achieve desirable responses (for example, enhancing positive and moderating negative outcomes) (Goleman, 1995a, 1998b; Mayer & Salovey, 1997). Figure 6.2 represents the inclusion of individual emotional intelligence in our model, where it influences the interpretations of a situation and the behavioral reactions to emotional arousal.

**FIGURE 6.2. EMOTIONAL INTELLIGENCE
AND THE EMOTIONAL PROCESS.**

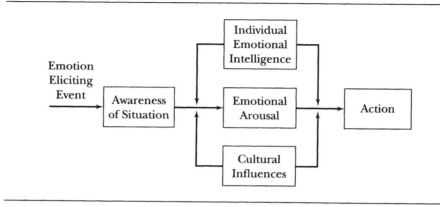

The emotion-behavior cycle we have been discussing reveals how individual emotional intelligence can have an impact in a group. When emotion is stimulated in a social situation (for example, group conflict), any response affects relationships among those involved, creating further emotion (Folkman & Lazarus, 1988). The emotion-behavior-emotion cycle can fuel a self-reinforcing spiral of positive or negative emotions that over time build a system of collective beliefs about issues such as trust, safety, and group efficacy. Emotionally intelligent responses to stimuli contribute to the development of a positive cycle. For example, Wolff (1998) found that respectful and supportive behavior among group members fuels beliefs about safety in the group, beliefs that in turn create cohesion and group satisfaction. However, we argue that creating an upward self-reinforcing spiral of trust, group identity, and group efficacy requires more than a few group members who exhibit emotionally intelligent behavior. It requires the ability to develop group norms that influence the stages in the emotional process (the awareness of emotions, interpretation of events, and behavioral responses to emotion) in constructive ways, or what we have labeled group emotional intelligence.

Group Emotional Intelligence

We define group emotional intelligence as the ability of a group to generate a shared set of norms that manage the emotional process in a way that builds trust, group identity, and group efficacy. As we have discussed, the emotion-behavior-emotion cycle can spiral positively or negatively. A group with high emotional intelligence creates a positive cycle through the norms it develops to influence the emotional process.

Group emotional intelligence operates through two mechanisms. Recall two of the main insights about the emotional process in groups: (1) group cultural norms influence the interpretation of and behavioral response to emotion, and (2) emotional awareness provides information about matters that may need the group's attention. Thus GEI can operate through norms that regulate the interpretation of and response to emotional stimuli (that is, through regulation mechanisms), and it can operate through norms that affect the degree to which the group becomes aware of emotional information (that is, through awareness mechanisms).

A distinguishing feature of the group context is that awareness and regulation mechanisms focus on three distinct arenas of interaction—interpersonal, group, and cross-boundary. Thus the group must develop norms that facilitate awareness and regulation of (1) the emotion of individual members (awareness and regulation here are similar to Empathy and Social Skills as defined in individual emotional intelligence theory), (2) the group, or shared, emotion (similar to group atmosphere, Lewin, 1948, or group mind, McDougall, 1920), and (3) the emotion inherent in relationships with groups and individuals outside the group boundary. In each arena, emotionally competent behavior builds trust, group identity, and group efficacy—beliefs that have been linked empirically to group effectiveness. Figure 6.3 adds GEI to our model and reveals the connection between the emotional process and collective beliefs. GEI replaces the more general cultural influences shown in Figure 6.2. We also add an arrow directly from GEI to emotional arousal to represent the ability of the group to develop norms that encourage awareness of the group's emotional state and its ability to use the information embedded in the emotion.

Managing Emotion in the Individual Arena

Group emotional intelligence norms that facilitate awareness of individual needs and that regulate behavior to address those needs will have a positive impact on group effectiveness. In their study of group intelligence and group performance, Williams and Sternberg (1988) found that even one overly zealous or domineering member in a group significantly inhibited the quality of that group's performance. This might be due to the *emotional contagion* described by Barsade (1998), who found that one member with strong emotion could influence the emotion of an entire group. Thus the first set of GEI norms must act to balance attending to individual member emotions and needs with influencing or regulating them so as

FIGURE 6.3. THE CONNECTION BETWEEN THE EMOTIONAL PROCESS AND COLLECTIVE BELIEFS.

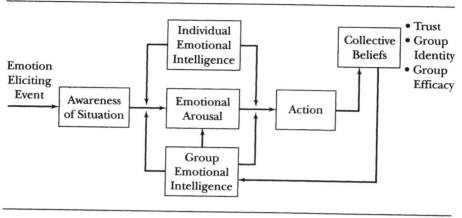

to induce desirable member behaviors and attitudes. As outlined in Figure 6.4, we propose two elements of individual-focused GEI: (1) Group Awareness of Member Emotions (feelings, needs, preferences, resources, and concerns) and (2) Group Regulation of Member Emotional Expression. The following discussions review the specific GEI norms that fall under each of these categories.

Group Awareness of Members. Theory and research suggest two interrelated GEI norms that facilitate member awareness of the feelings, needs, and concerns of other members. The first norm is *perspective taking* (Boland & Tenkasi, 1995; Schober, 1998). Perspective taking occurs in conversation and is exhibited as the willingness to consider matters from the other person's point of view. Successful conversation (Schober, 1998) and successful problem solving (Boland & Tenkasi, 1995) require participants to coordinate their perspectives. Schober (1998) proposes that perspectives derive from four sources: (1) a speaker's time, place, and identity (for example, a group member's specific role on the assembly line might result in a unique perspective on the work process); (2) a speaker's conceptualization (for example, a specific characterization of the group's problem); (3) a speaker's conversational agenda (for example, a member may be avoiding conflict because she wants to end a meeting early); and (4) a speaker's knowledge base (for example, a member with expertise in finance is likely to bring a different perspective to discussions from the one brought by the member with expertise in marketing). Boland and Tenkasi (1995) argue that innovation requires perspective taking. We argue that perspective taking as a group norm benefits group effec-

FIGURE 6.4. DIMENSIONS OF GROUP EMOTIONAL INTELLIGENCE.

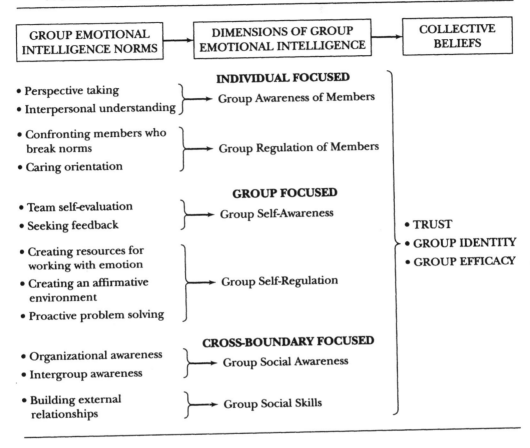

tiveness through two routes. First, it facilitates the successful assimilation of important information. Second, a member who feels her perspective is heard is more likely to trust and identify with her group and its decisions (Ashforth & Mael, 1989; McAllister, 1995) and therefore more likely to give her energy and attention to the group's work (Kahn, 1990).

The second group norm important to Group Awareness of Members is *interpersonal understanding*, the accurate understanding of the spoken and unspoken feelings, interests, concerns, strengths, and weaknesses of group members. This understanding allows members to predict and cope with one another's day-to-day behavior. This argument derives from the research of Druskat (1996), who found that members of high-performing self-managing work teams exhibited significantly higher levels of interpersonal understanding than did members of comparatively low-performing teams. She found that when group norms supported interpersonal understanding, members accurately interpreted one another's nonverbal emotional expressions and behavior and knew whether a fellow team member was having work-related problems or needed to take a break.

Group Regulation of Members. Groups must create a balance between ensuring predictable group member behavior and allowing members a sense of control and individuality. Theorists have argued that, paradoxically, the more a group allows its members to exert their individuality, the more its members will be open to placing their individualism aside for the good of the group (Smith & Berg, 1987). We propose two interrelated GEI norms that when taken together create a balance between regulating member behavior and allowing individual control. The first norm under this dimension is *confronting members who break norms,* and it is defined as speaking up when a member does something considered out of line. It is based on the research of Druskat (1996), who found that members who broke norms were confronted by members of high-performing self-managing work teams more often than they were by members of relatively low-performing teams. The latter often chose not to engage in confrontation out of fear that it would exacerbate problems and hurt relationships. This norm is also supported by the research of Murnighan and Conlon (1991), who found that members of successful string quartets used confrontation more frequently than the conflict avoidance or compromise tactics used more often by less successful quartets.

The second GEI norm vital to Group Regulation of Members is a *caring orientation* (Kahn, 1998; Wolff, 1998), defined as communicating positive regard, appreciation, and respect. Through a caring orientation, group members communicate that the group values the presence and contribution of each member. In a study of sixty-seven work groups, Wolff (1998) found that a caring orientation in a group contributed to group effectiveness by increasing members' sense of safety, cohesion, and satisfaction, which in turn facilitated member engagement in the task. Kahn (1998) argues that a caring orientation builds workplace relationships that provide a "secure base" for individuals and that this base allows them to take risks that facilitate personal learning and development. Both Wolff (1998) and Kahn (1998) indicate that caring does not necessitate close personal relationships. It requires member validation and respect.

Together, the GEI norms of confronting members who break norms and exhibiting a caring orientation help to balance uniformity and individuality in the group. In any group an individual's beliefs, assumptions, and expectations are partially shared with other group members and partially unique to the individual. Thus an important aspect of regulating group members is the group's ability to perceive, surface, and manage the emotional tension that arises from differences between individual and group needs. Smith and Berg (1987) describe the paradox of involvement as a search to "mesh individual needs and wishes with what the group needs and wants" (p. 95). When an individual does not share the same drive to act as the rest of the group yet group norms coerce compliance with group action, *cognitive dissonance* (Festinger, 1957) occurs. Cognitive dissonance creates a negative drive state that must be resolved by the individual. An emotionally intelligent group has the ability to become aware of this tension (through its awareness of members, as discussed previously) and to help the member resolve the dissonance in a way that builds, or at least does not deplete, trust or sense of belonging. A group low in emotional intelligence either fails to recognize and address the tension or addresses it in a way that reduces group member trust and sense of belonging.

Figure 6.5 summarizes the results of some of the ways a group can manage cognitive dissonance and resolve tension. The group can attempt to coerce the individual into acting according to the group's wishes (which is likely to deplete trust); the group can use persuasive argument to bring the individual around to sharing the group's rationale for action (which is likely to have little effect on trust); the group can alter its behavior to be more in line with the individual's thinking (which may create additional tension in other members and thus deplete trust); the individual can decide to become a rebel and act out against the group (which is a way to deplete trust); or the group can confront the member in a caring way that builds consensus and brings shared interpretations and behaviors more in line with each other (which is likely to increase trust and group identity).

An ethnographic study on control practices used in self-managing teams illustrates the need for groups to practice consensus building as a continuous process. Barker (1993) determined that early in the teams' formation, control was rooted in norms based on consensual values. However, over time, circumstances and membership changed, and team control moved away from consensual values and toward a strict and unforgiving form of concertive control. An important contributor to this shift was membership turnover. New members had not been part of the early consensus-building activities and had little sense of ownership of the group norms and values they were expected to follow. Thus rules became increasingly necessary for norm enforcement. Surely, trust and group identity diminished in these teams with the rule-based enforcement of team norms.

As a set the GEI norms of perspective taking, interpersonal understanding, confronting members who break norms, and caring orientation create a sense of social support and social acceptance and help balance group and individual needs. Sarason, Sarason, and Pierce (1990) propose that supported individuals feel that they are worthwhile, capable, and valued members of a group and that the

FIGURE 6.5. MANAGING GROUP
MEMBER COGNITIVE DISSONANCE.

(A) Cognitive dissonance and emotional tension exist in the difference
   between the way the individual believes he should act and the way
   the group actually behaves.

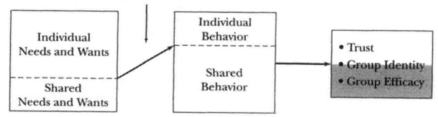

(B) Trust is either used or created in the process of resolving the tension.
   The emotionally intelligent group resolves the tension in a way that builds
   trust, group identity, and group efficacy (for example, by confronting
   members in a caring way).

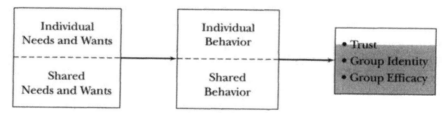

(C) The group that is not emotionally intelligent will either
   (1) resolve tension in a way that drains trust, group identity, and group
      efficacy (for example, through coercion, relenting, or rebellion) or
   (2) will not be able to resolve the tensions.

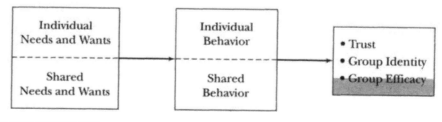

resources they need to pursue and achieve their goals are available to them, either within themselves or through a combination of their own efforts and those of other group members. Theory and research also reveal that social acceptance and a sense of belonging facilitate individual self-esteem (Baumeister, Goethals, & Pittman, 1998; Leary, Tambor, Terdal, & Downs, 1995), reduce anxiety, and enhance interpersonal skills (Sarason et al., 1990).

Managing Emotion in the Group Arena

LeBon (1895/1977) was the first to propose that emotion in a group context can create a powerful force that overwhelms individual differences in emotion and creates a collective group character. McDougall (1920) later labeled the phenomenon *group mind*. At the core of LeBon's and McDougall's controversial theories is the proposition that a group construct can be greater than the sum of its individual parts (Barsade & Gibson, 1998). Three decades after McDougall, Lewin (1948) referred to *group atmosphere* as a similar group-level phenomenon that had a strong influence on group member behavior. Since then, researchers have defined and empirically examined a great number of group constructs that are influenced by emotion and that shape member behavior and attitudes. Samples include group cohesiveness (Festinger, Schacter, & Back, 1950; Gully, Devine, & Whitney, 1995; Whyte, 1943), group emotional or affective tone (Cartwright & Zander, 1968; George, 1990), social support (Campion et al., 1993; Gladstein, 1984), and conflict norms (Jehn, 1995, 1997).

The potentially strong effect of group-level emotion (Barsade & Gibson, 1998) requires that GEI norms facilitate awareness of this emotion and also regulate it. Thus, returning to the outline in Figure 6.4, we propose these two dimensions of GEI in the group arena: (1) Group Self-Awareness and (2) Group Self-Regulation.

Group Self-Awareness. Goleman's theory of individual emotional intelligence (1998b) proposes Self-Awareness as a key emotional competence. Self-Awareness is defined as "knowing one's internal states, preferences, resources, and intuitions" (p. 26). We borrow from this definition and define Group Self-Awareness as member awareness of group emotional states, preferences, and resources. We propose that such awareness can help a group think intelligently about itself and its needs. Indeed, it has been argued that understanding these aspects of an organization's culture can facilitate decisions that support an organization's core competence and thus focus and increase organizational effectiveness (Prahalad & Hamel, 1990; Schein, 1985). We propose the same to be true in a group context.

The first group norm we propose under this dimension is *team self-evaluation*, and it is defined as a group's ability to evaluate itself, including its emotional states and the strengths and weaknesses in its modes of interaction and operation as a team. Research indicates that highly effective teams are more likely than lower-performing teams to hold a norm that supports team self-evaluation (Druskat, 1996; McIntyre & Salas, 1995). Druskat (1996) found that team self-evaluation often manifests itself through the collection of information about other teams and the subsequent comparison of one's own team to those other teams. This behavior is consistent with what Festinger (1954) labeled *social comparison*. Festinger's theory argued that the only way to truly know how good one is at something is to compare oneself to others. To obtain such comparisons the effective teams in Druskat's study often observed and discussed the attitudes and work habits of other teams and used that information to define what was good or bad about their own team.

McIntyre and Salas (1995) propose that Group Self-Awareness is also encouraged by a norm supporting the value of feedback and constructive criticism. Thus, the second group norm in the Group Self-Awareness dimension of GEI is *seeking feedback* and is defined as searching out feedback from external sources. A norm of seeking feedback creates a climate in which continuous improvement can occur. In a review of thirty-three laboratory studies examining the impact of feedback on group behavior, Nadler (1979) concluded that feedback can bring about positive change in a group through its impact on motivation and cuing (that is, calling attention to important issues). He also determined that positive feedback can improve attraction to the group, pride in the group, involvement, and esteem. In her research with self-managing work teams, Druskat (1996) also found that the higher-performing teams were more likely than average teams to seek out and attend to feedback.

Group Self-Regulation. Mayer and Salovey (1997) propose that individual emotional intelligence includes the ability to regulate emotion so as to promote emotional and intellectual growth. We borrow from this definition and propose that GEI involves the group's ability to regulate itself so as to promote group emotional well-being and development. To do this, the Self-Regulation dimension must work in partnership with the Self-Awareness dimension. Group Self-Awareness reveals issues that require the group's attention, but it does not guarantee the group will effectively address those issues. Group Self-Regulation refers to a group's ability to manage its emotional states and create desirable responses. It encompasses what Holmer (1994) refers to as coping with, or managing, *emotional challenge*.

Emotional challenge is the degree of psychological threat perceived in a situation. In his theory of "orientation and response to emotional challenge," Holmer (1994) argues that "the quality of our response to such challenge [defined by Holmer as our *emotional capacity*] clearly affects our perceptions and interpretation of 'the facts' and hence our ability to take appropriate action" (p. 53). A group with low emotional capacity responds to emotional challenge with "self-deception and avoidance of reality" (p. 50). For example, a product development team may miss its deadline because underlying tensions in the team reduce its efficiency. A group with low emotional capacity may choose to ignore the tensions to avoid conflict or its members may blame external causes. A group with high emotional capacity, however, responds with "full awareness and responsiveness" (p. 50): for example, members recognize and confront the problem. The norms of Group Self-Regulation are related to a group's ability to build emotional capacity and mobilize effective responses to emotional challenge. Research and theory suggest three norms are needed for a group to regulate its response to emotional arousal.

The first norm is *creating resources for working with emotion*. A group facilitates effective interpretation of and response to emotional stimuli by providing resources that encourage the recognition of emotional stimuli and that help members discuss how they feel about those stimuli (Levy, 1984). Levy (1984), as we have discussed, argues that people draw upon cultural resources for their ability to process feelings—without such resources, emotion is likely to be ignored or suppressed. In individuals, suppressed emotion leads to dysfunctions such as depression (Kleinman, 1988). In groups, suppressed emotion might manifest itself as apathy or lack of motivation. An emotionally intelligent group accepts emotion as an inherent part of group life. It legitimizes discussion of emotional issues and creates a vocabulary for discussing them.

Legitimizing discussion of emotional issues creates a resource group members can use to examine and cope with their feelings. For example, learning can be associated with risk, uncertainty, and anxiety (Schein, 1993). Unless a group legitimizes these emotional issues and makes time available to address them, learning can be reduced. Duck (1993) described a team responsible for a complex computer conversion that effectively dealt with emotions by scheduling time during their meetings for the expression of feelings associated with the difficulty and stress surrounding the project. This fifteen-minute session was followed by a *brag session* where small victories were celebrated. These discussions resulted in heightened group identity and efficacy, or confidence, that facilitated completing the task well. Team members felt closer to one another, and they felt they were part of a winning team.

Another important resource groups need to create for working with emotion is a common, acceptable language for discussing emotion (Levy, 1984). For example, if group norms limit the use of the word *fear*, group members may interpret the feeling of fear as anger and act accordingly. They may also look for blame, hold unproductive gripe sessions, or try to find ways to retaliate against the source of this "anger." Alternatively, the feeling may be suppressed, which can lead to dysfunction and apathy (Holmer, 1994; Kleinman, 1988). Conversely, sanctioning use of the word fear and labeling this emotion accurately can lead to the type of appropriate response used by the technical team just described.

Once a group has accepted emotion and created resources for working with it, it must channel its energy toward *creating an affirmative environment* that cultivates positive images of the group's past, present, and future. This is the second norm for Group Self-Regulation. As discussed earlier, emotion can be contagious in a group environment (Barsade & Gibson, 1998); thus constructive, positive images can have an important impact on how emotions are ultimately experienced in a group. Research by Cooperrider (1987) suggests that positive images facilitate positive affect, positive behavior, and positive outcomes. For example, in an affirmative environment, group members are likely to interpret an unexpected obstacle as a challenge rather than as a difficulty and thus are likely to mobilize positive energy to manage the obstacle and to generate a sense of group efficacy. Cooperrider (1990) argues that imagery "integrates cognition and affect and becomes a catalytic force through its sentiment-evoking quality" (p. 104). Indeed, the research of Isen and her colleagues shows that positive affect helps create a heightened sense of optimism about the future (Isen & Shalker, 1982) and predisposes people toward acts that are likely to support continued positive affect, such as helping (Isen, Shalker, Clark, & Karp, 1978).

A body of research that supports the power of positive images consists of studies that examine expectancy confirmation, or self-fulfilling prophecy, often referred to as the Pygmalion effect. This research (see Rosenthal & Rubin, 1978, for a summary of 345 studies) reveals that one's expectations about the capabilities of another individual tend to be confirmed. An example is the study in which a teacher is told that one set of students is very bright and able and that a second set is not. In fact, both sets of students have scored equally on standardized exams. Yet when these students are retested at the end of the school year, those students believed by the teacher to be the more able test higher on the exam. In this situation, expectancy confirmation occurs because of the positive or negative image held by the teacher and the way this image influences how he or she treats and works with students throughout the school year. A positive image creates a positive upward spiral of encouragement and success, whereas a negative image creates a downward spiral of discouraging interactions and failure.

Creating an affirmative group environment can be accomplished through norms that guide the interpretation of emotional stimuli. Events that trigger emotion are often ambiguous, thus individuals draw upon cultural norms to help them interpret and make sense of their feelings (Levy, 1984). Interpreting and labeling ambiguous events through positive images can result in self-fulfilling prophecies in groups. For example, failure can be interpreted as a constructive learning opportunity. Indeed, recent research indicates that effective groups are more likely to interpret failures as opportunities to learn (Edmondson, 1999). Negative images surrounding failure tend to result in negative affect and a reduced sense of group efficacy (Fein, 1990), which can create a negative emotional spiral for a work group.

The third norm associated with Group Self-Regulation is *proactive problem solving* (Druskat, 1996), which involves actively taking initiative to resolve issues that stand in the way of task accomplishment. For example, teachers in today's public schools must improve instruction yet stay within a budget imposed by the school district. They can choose to focus on the limitations imposed by the budget or they can engage in proactive efforts such as writing grants to secure additional funds. By taking control of the situation, they create a sense of group efficacy and reduce the emotional challenge experienced by the group (Fein, 1990). In her study of self-managing work teams, Druskat (1996) found that effective teams took proactive control of ambiguous or difficult situations. Members of one highly effective team that was experiencing frequent equipment breakdowns decided that rather than continue to endure the long wait for the maintenance crew to make the repairs, they would watch closely the next time the mechanics repaired the problem and, even though it was against plant policy, repair the problem themselves after that. Other teams with norms supporting proactive problem solving designed new parts rather than tolerate equipment that was difficult to maneuver or use. The result for these teams was an increased sense of control over their environment, a greater sense of group efficacy, and enhanced performance.

Managing Emotion in the Cross-Boundary Arena

Research indicates that group effectiveness also requires networks of relationships with individuals and groups outside a group's boundary (Ancona & Caldwell, 1992; Argote, 1989; Druskat, 1996; Gladstein, 1984). Indeed, Yan and Louis (1999) argue that the cross-functional, cross-boundary communication required for smooth organizational functioning that once occurred through formal hierarchical channels has now become the responsibility of work groups. Thus the third area of GEI involves group awareness of the feelings, needs, and concerns of important individuals and groups in the external boundary. It also involves the social skills required to develop relationships with these individuals and to gain their confidence. Two dimensions of GEI are proposed for managing cross-boundary emotion: (1) Group Social Awareness and (2) Group Social Skills.

Group Social Awareness. Roles and activities in effective groups are directed outward as well as inward so that groups can gain external influence and obtain resources that exist outside of their boundaries (Ancona & Caldwell, 1992; Yan & Louis, 1999). To effectively engage in such activities, a group must first understand the needs and expectations of the broader organizational system and of the specific individuals and groups with whom it must interact (Druskat, 1996). We have identified two GEI norms related to this type of Social Awareness: organizational awareness, and intergroup awareness.

Organizational awareness refers to the ability of the group to be aware of and understand the social and political system of which it is a part. In her study of self-managing work teams, Druskat (1996) found that highly effective teams had a better understanding of the organization's culture including how and why managers made certain decisions. This understanding served the team well when they needed external resources. For example, one team had requested a new piece of equipment that they felt was necessary to their continued smooth operation. When management procrastinated in making the decision to purchase the equipment, they reframed their request and argued that their safety was at risk. They then attended a plant wide safety meeting and stood up in front of the plant and upper management to present the case for their new equipment. This team understood that safety was of paramount importance in the eyes of management. They also understood that by announcing their own safety issue in a public place they were more likely to capture the attention of management. They got their new equipment.

Emotionally intelligent groups also recognize the expectations and needs of other groups in the organization; we label this norm *intergroup awareness*. In a study of thirty hospital emergency units, Argote (1989) found that the most effective units had groups with high levels of intergroup agreement about norms. She concluded that agreement among teams about intergroup norms and processes was more important for unit effectiveness than the specific processes adopted.

Group Social Skills. Being aware of organizational and intergroup issues and expectations is vital yet not sufficient in itself to influence and engage the resources necessary for group effectiveness. A group must also have the skill to develop relationships that help to secure these resources. We have identified the norm of *building external relationships* as representative of this category of GEI.

A study of group boundary management activity and its link to team effectiveness (Ancona & Caldwell, 1992) determined that the most effective teams employed norms and strategies that involved engaging in what the researchers labeled *ambassadorial activities*, for example, communicating frequently with those above them in the hierarchy, persuading others to support the team, and keeping others informed about the team's activities. The least effective teams were those labeled *isolationists*, because they avoided engaging in boundary management activities and did not even communicate with those outside the team about the team's activities. Druskat (1996) also found that highly effective teams build good relationships with other teams. Some of the effective teams in her study went out of their way to help a team that was having equipment problems or was far behind in its production schedule. One team even nominated another team for the organization's Team of the Month award. An important factor here is that these teams knew that their help and respect would be reciprocated. Emotionally intelligent groups recognize they are part of a larger social system and work to develop contacts and relationships that can facilitate their effectiveness.

Developing Group Emotional Intelligence

We have defined GEI as the ability to develop a set of norms. An important question is how these norms emerge and get enforced. *Symbolic interactionism* (see Layder, 1994; Stryker & Statham, 1985) proposes that group norms emerge through group member interactions. Through interaction and negotiation, members actively create expectations about how they should think and act in their group. Sherif (1936) was the first to conduct laboratory experiments examining the emergence of social norms. To study norm formation he made use of the autokinetic effect, which is the visual perception that a small stationary light is moving when it is seen in a dark room. When experimental subjects were tested one-by-one in a dark room, they each established their own consistent estimate of how far the light moved. When the same subjects were placed in a room in groups of three or four and could hear one another's responses, their individual judgments changed, converging into a group judgment. Postgroup tests in the individual condition showed that even when alone again, individuals' thinking continued to be influenced by their former group's norm. The research also revealed the resilience of group norms. In the group condition, even when old group members left and new members entered the group one at a time, the original group norms lasted for four or five generations.

Subsequent research and theory provides important information about the specific processes that occur as group norms develop (see Bettenhausen & Murnighan, 1985; Feldman, 1984; Festinger, 1954; Weick & Bougon, 1986). This research suggests that norms characteristic of group emotional intelligence emerge through a four-phase process. In the first phase of norm development, members come together and base their behavior and expectations on their prior experience in similar situations (Bettenhausen & Murnighan, 1985; Feldman, 1984). Thus, for GEI norms to develop, some individual members need to arrive with the competencies required for emotional intelligence and a belief that behaving in emotionally intelligent ways will serve the group's well-being and effectiveness. If all members have had similar past experiences that lead them to believe in using emotions to think intelligently and in thinking intelligently about emotions, then GEI norms will develop with little need for negotiation or challenge. However, when members have differing expectations, discussion and negotiation will occur in the phases that follow.

The second phase starts as members begin to interact. Through their actions, observations, and reflections, members begin to create and make sense out of common experiences, which in turn start shaping their expectations (Bettenhausen & Murnighan, 1985). According to Festinger's social comparison theory (1954), the ambiguities experienced in this early phase cause members to turn to one another to seek information about the correctness of their behaviors and beliefs. Such social comparisons move the group toward convergence and uniformity by creating comfort and validation for individuals when they behave and think alike. Member sensemaking in this phase also involves experiments with risk-taking behavior and reflections about that behavior's consequences (Weick & Bougon, 1986). Members can learn by participating in such experiments or by merely observing as others take the risks.

An example of the way GEI norms emerge from a series of interactions, observations, and reflections is seen in the relationship-building process (Gabarro, 1987; Golembiewski & McConkie, 1975). Self-disclosure can be important for building close relationships, but it involves a series of reciprocated risk-taking behaviors (Jourard, 1971). One person takes the risk to self-disclose. The second person responds by indicating that the disclosure will not result in harm and then demonstrates approval by reciprocating with his or her own self-disclosure. As the cycle repeats, each person grows to trust the other more deeply through each iteration, and over time the relationship becomes defined through these repeated patterns of behavior. We propose that the same type of iterative, reflective process is involved in the development of group norms that characterize GEI. That is, as members exhibit emotionally intelligent behaviors such as perspective taking, which involves seeking awareness of one another's points of view and emotions, the behavior is reciprocated and eventually, if approved of by the group, incorporated into a norm.

In phase three of the norm development process, members begin to challenge the emerging status quo of the group and to voice alternative preferences (Bettenhausen & Murnighan, 1985). This type of challenge occurred in most of the groups studied by Bettenhausen and Murnighan, who found the challenge could take two courses: it could provoke discussion and negotiation ending in an altered group path, or it could be dismissed, thus confirming the perceived suitability of the group's existing direction. It must be noted that norms develop only for those behaviors and attitudes that are viewed as important by most group members (Hackman, 1976). Thus, if any GEI norms are emerging, they are likely to be challenged during this phase and must come to be supported by a majority of group members if they are to endure. Alternatively, if GEI norms have not emerged, this is an important time for individuals to make interventions in support of GEI norms and to try to influence other group members in that direction.

We propose that five kinds of influence can leverage the importance of emotionally intelligent behavior in the eyes of the group majority: the influence of (1) formal team leaders, (2) informal team leaders, (3) courageous followers, (4) training, and (5) organizational culture. The first three kinds of influence involve interventions by individuals who believe in the importance of GEI norms and who are willing to champion the cause of thinking intelligently about emotions and using emotions to think intelligently. Formal team leaders can use their formal authority to intervene in the group's early norm-building process in order to encourage emotionally intelligent behavior (see Bass, 1990). They can also encourage GEI by providing individual coaching to members who need to build the competencies necessary to support GEI norms. Informal leaders, defined as high-status, influential group members, can play a critical role in developing GEI because members are likely to turn to them when seeking insight into appropriate behaviors and attitudes (De Souza & Klein, 1995; Wheelan & Johnston, 1996). Courageous followers (Chaleff, 1995) are not high-status members but do believe strongly enough in the importance of behaving in emotionally intelligent ways that they are willing to step forward and argue for norms that support GEI. The last two influences come from factors available in the environment. Training programs provided early in a team's development can advocate developing GEI norms and help members build the individual and group competencies necessary to support such norms. Indeed, training interventions have long been known to have an important influence on norm development (see Hackman, 1976). Finally, an organizational culture that supports and rewards emotionally intelligent behavior can promote and reinforce the emergence of emotionally intelligent group norms.

In phase four, the last phase of the norm development process, group members start behaving according to the group's expectations instead of the expectations they came in with (Bettenhausen & Murnighan, 1985). Once norms are formed they are a strong influence on member behavior because deviations are usually met with sanctions (McGrath, 1984).

Conclusion and Implications for Practice

Our full model of the way group emotional intelligence influences cooperation and collaboration is presented in Figure 6.6. This model takes theory on group effectiveness one step closer to explaining how to build effective work groups. Although several current theories describe the kind of behaviors a group needs to

FIGURE 6.6. HOW GEI INFLUENCES COOPERATION AND COLLABORATION.

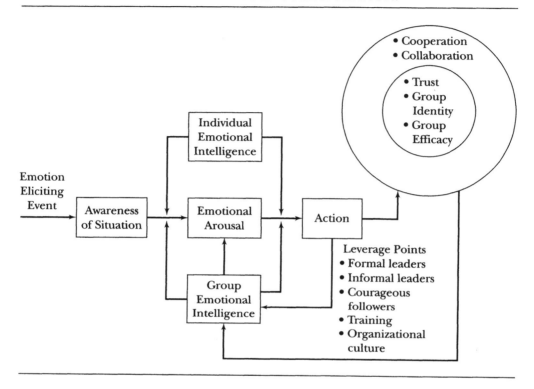

display to be effective, they have not been fully useful for practicing managers interested in knowing how to build those behaviors (Cannon-Bowers et al., 1995; Donnellon, 1996). We propose that building effective groups requires building group trust, group identity, and group efficacy. We further suggest that the way a group deals with emotion in the individual, group, and cross-boundary arenas is critical to building these collective beliefs. This model has several practical implications for managers wishing to develop effective work groups. First, it provides a clear direction toward two main destinations: group emotional intelligence and group member cooperation and collaboration. Second, it outlines our detailed map for getting to those destinations through the group norms and behaviors that support the dimensions of group emotional intelligence.

In sum, like other group theorists (see Cohen, 1994; Shea & Guzzo, 1987; Hackman, 1987; Sundstrom, DeMeuse, & Futrell, 1990), we believe factors in a group's context (reward systems, culture, and educational systems, for example) are important for setting up a group for success. However, we differ from the others in our belief that the current information age emphasis on cross-functional and empowered work teams means that group interaction processes and group member relationships are fast becoming the critical determinants of a group's level of effectiveness. We also believe, as a corollary to this belief, that groups play a role in creating their own contexts by actively choosing and constructing norms that prescribe how members will treat one another, work together, and deal with those outside of the group. By incorporating norms that build group emotional intelligence, groups can create self-reinforcing spirals of heedful interrelating, strong emotional attachments, effective interaction processes, and group effectiveness.

PART TWO

HUMAN RESOURCE APPLICATIONS AND EMOTIONAL INTELLIGENCE

CHAPTER SEVEN

USING HUMAN RESOURCE FUNCTIONS TO ENHANCE EMOTIONAL INTELLIGENCE

Ruth L. Jacobs

As the world economy becomes more global and information based, organizations are finding it necessary to adapt to a quickly changing and more competitive marketplace. Emotionally intelligent organizations are able to leverage the talent of their members to meet these challenges more effectively. These organizations exhibit core competencies such as Teamwork and Collaboration, Adaptability, Achievement Orientation, and Service Orientation; and they tend to be more networked and flexible than traditional hierarchical organizations. As organizations become more networked they require more emotional intelligence among their members than do traditional hierarchical organizations. In networked organizations people more often work together in teams and often team members find themselves managing others who do not report directly to them. Most of the emotional intelligence competencies are critical for this type of organization to perform well. Members must be able to work well with others (Self-Control, Empathy, Teamwork and Collaboration, Conflict Management, Communication), influence others in a collaborative manner (Empathy, Influence, Leadership), and find quicker and faster ways of doing things (Initiative, Achievement Orientation). It is easier to create virtual teams when team members are able to focus on solving problems, creating new ideas, serving customers, or adapting to changes in the marketplace.

The objective of this chapter is to introduce ways that organizations can increase their emotional intelligence through use of standard human resource

(HR) functions—hiring, training and development, and performance management systems—and successfully meet the demands of the changing marketplace.

There are basically two ways to increase emotional intelligence in an organization: (1) hire people who are emotionally intelligent or (2) develop emotional intelligence in current members. Hiring (or selecting) is one of the quickest ways to increase emotional intelligence in an organization; but unless the organization hires a critical mass (usually greater than 20 percent) of emotionally intelligent personnel, it may not see an impact. In addition, if the organization's climate does not support or reward emotionally intelligent behavior, it is likely that the people it is trying to keep will leave. Thus it is important for organizations to develop and maintain emotional intelligence in their present employee populations. This chapter suggests how organizations can use HR applications such as hiring, training, executive coaching, and performance management to successfully select for and develop emotional intelligence in their organizations.

Selecting for Emotional Intelligence

The quickest way to increase emotional intelligence competencies in members of an organization is to select individuals who already demonstrate those competencies and behaviors. Unfortunately, typical HR selection processes tend to focus on what appears on the applicant's résumé: education, skills, and experience. Although these factors are important and often a baseline for adequately performing a job, they rarely differentiate outstanding from average performance (Spencer, McClelland, & Spencer, 1992). Beyond that, hiring decisions are often left to interviewer *hunches* or to *chemistry* between the interviewer and candidate. An inability or failure to categorize *exactly* what is giving the interviewer a positive impression may lead to faulty decisions. Sometimes the good feelings may be due to the candidate's being *like* the interviewer: they may share the same values or work ethic, for example; they may both play golf; they may have similar backgrounds. At best, relying on such similarities may have little impact on job performance. At worst, basing decisions on such feelings may be discriminatory or negatively related to job performance.

The emotional intelligence competencies, although more difficult to detect, have been shown to be the key differentiators between typical and outstanding performers (McClelland, 1998; Goleman, 1998b). If organizations want to increase these competencies in their workforce, the HR hiring process must include a method for identifying these competencies in candidates.

Using the Emotional Intelligence Competence Model

Goleman's revised model, or framework, of emotional intelligence currently consists of twenty emotional competencies distributed in four clusters (Boyatzis, Goleman, & Rhee, 2000). Selecting for all twenty competencies would be an extremely challenging, costly task. Fortunately, David McClelland has demonstrated that competencies operate on a category, or cluster, level and not just individually. Many of us have known intuitively what McClelland advocates—that there is no one single set of characteristics that lead to success; rather there are alternative configurations and combinations of competencies that produce results. "I cannot overemphasize," says McClelland (1994),

> the importance of recognizing that there are alternative combinations of characteristics that lead to success in a particular job. Too many consultants and companies operate on the assumption that we need to discover the *one best set* of competencies that lead to success. We are acting like "cookie cutters." We are trying to find the best competency mold so that we can pick or shape individuals to fit that mold. *Yet everyone who has been in a business for any length of time has observed instances in which the same job has been performed very well by two people who appear to have quite different characteristics. The fact is that often various combinations of competencies lead to success* [italics in original].

McClelland referred to this phenomenon as a formula, or algorithm, for success. Competency model algorithms work on the cluster level. In order to demonstrate mastery of a cluster, the criteria for that cluster must be met. For example, let's create a cluster called Getting Results that consists of the following competencies:

- Self-Confidence
- Achievement Orientation
- Initiative

Let's also say that the algorithm for this cluster requires that the individual demonstrate a certain level of mastery of at least two out of the three competencies. If the individual masters only one of the competencies, for example, Initiative, he would not fulfil the criteria for the cluster and therefore would not meet the algorithm for that competency model.

Understanding Competency Clusters

Some competencies in a cluster may be required as individuals, others may be grouped with other competencies as in the previous example. Richard Boyatzis spells out four different groupings of relationships that may exist between competencies in a cluster: complementary, alternate manifestations, compensatory, and antagonistic.

Competencies that have a complementary relationship enhance a person's effectiveness when used in conjunction with each other. Demonstrating one competence does not interfere with the ability to demonstrate the other. For example, Boyatzis (1999a) explores the relationship between Adaptability and Conscientiousness: "A person can demonstrate flexibility in adapting to situations. His/her demonstration of reliability and consistency (i.e., Conscientiousness) would not interfere with the demonstration of Adaptability, but if the person can use both competencies their effectiveness would increase in many situations. For example, if the situation changed but a reliable response was still needed, the use of Adaptability and Conscientiousness would allow for continued appropriate behavior even in the new situation."

The second competency relationship, alternate manifestations, occurs between competencies that represent the same set of capabilities although each competence possesses behaviors that are situation specific. For example, Leading Others and Change Catalyst are alternate manifestations of Leadership behavior. Leading Others is more general and is seen in traditional leadership roles, whereas Change Catalyst is a manifestation of Leadership specific to organizations undergoing change—as a result of mergers, reengineering, or rapid growth, for example.

Competencies that have a compensatory relationship are able to make up for the lack of use of or weakness in each other. Whether one competence or the other is used, the results are the same. Achievement Orientation and Initiative are examples of compensatory competencies. As Boyatzis (1999a) writes:

> A person can demonstrate a great deal of concern about doing better, contemplating and acting on cost-benefit utility analysis and so forth (i.e., Achievement Orientation). This may drive a degree of innovation and discovery of new and better ways to accomplish things. At the same time, someone else in the same situation may find new and better ways to accomplish things because they are starting things before anyone has thought of them, seeking information in distinctive ways, and so forth (i.e., demonstrating Initiative). While the outcomes are the same, the specific behavior used and the intention underlying the behavior are different.

The fourth and final type of competency relationship is antagonistic. Being very strong in one competence may prevent the use or demonstration of another. Often the person who has the ability to balance the use of antagonistic competencies demonstrates the best performance. In the emotional intelligence competence model, Self-Control can be antagonistic to Initiative. As Boyatzis (1999a) reports: "If someone demonstrates a great deal of Self-control and inhibits their impulses and actions, they would have an increasingly difficult time demonstrating Initiative and starting things before anyone asks."

Creating Algorithms

Algorithms are created empirically through a rigorous process that involves correctly sorting *outstanding* and *typical* performers to an acceptable degree of statistical significance. Algorithms are developed during the process of model building or concept formation, as researchers review behavioral event interview transcripts and code for competencies in the population under observation. After reviewing transcripts and getting a sense of how behaviors work together in the context of the job or role, the researchers develop a hypothesis about how the competencies work together.

For example, a critical aspect of a role might be execution and implementation. After reviewing the transcripts researchers might observe that outstanding implementers were using behaviors associated with *either* Initiative *or* Achievement Orientation *or* Self-Confidence. They might then hypothesize that in order to be outstanding, an individual had to have mastery of least one of these three competencies. To test the hypothesis, they would create a two-by-two matrix that sorted the outstanding and typical performers against this criterion. In this case, if they had a sample of twenty outstanding and twenty typical performers, the distribution might look like that shown in Table 7.1.

TABLE 7.1. COMPETENCIES OF OUTSTANDING AND TYPICAL PERFORMERS.

Demonstrates at Least 1 of the 3 Competencies	Outstanding	Typical
Yes	18	5
No	2	15

Note: Chi-square = 17.29, $p < .001$.

In this scenario the algorithm correctly sorted 83 percent of the sample. Outstanding implementers were correctly identified eighteen out of twenty times, or with 90 percent accuracy. Typical implementers were correctly identified fifteen out of twenty times, or with 75 percent accuracy. The typicals had a false positive rate of 25 percent. These results were statistically significant at $p < .001$.

Sometimes the scenario gets more complex. For instance, a competence such as Self-Confidence may be so critical to success that it has to be mastered regardless of other strengths the individual may possess. At the same time, it may not be sufficient by itself to predict outstanding performance. Thus we could have a scenario in which, in order to be an outstanding implementer, a person would have to demonstrate Self-Confidence and also demonstrate either Achievement Orientation or Initiative. The results of the algorithm for this scenario are shown in Table 7.2. In the new scenario the algorithm correctly sorts 90 percent of the sample. When Self-Confidence is added as a mandatory competence, the outstanding performers are, as before, correctly identified 90 percent of the time. However, the false positive rate for typical performers falls from 25 percent to 10 percent, showing the increased accuracy of the algorithm. This scenario creation process is repeated until the combination of competencies produces the most accurate sort at a probability due to chance of less than 5 percent ($p < .05$).

Through this process, we at Hay/McBer have created algorithms for numerous models, such as the one described by McClelland (1994). This knowledge base is the foundation for the algorithm proposed in Figure 7.1 for Daniel Goleman's competence model of emotional intelligence. I describe each cluster in the following paragraphs.

Self-Awareness. The Self-Awareness cluster consists of one mandatory competence (Self-Confidence) and two compensatory competencies (Emotional Self-Awareness and Accurate Self-Assessment). In order to meet the algorithm for the Self-Awareness cluster—that is, in order to be likely to be an outstanding performer—a person must demonstrate Self-Confidence and either Emotional Self-Awareness or Accurate Self-Assessment.

TABLE 7.2. RESULTS OF USING A MORE COMPLEX ALGORITHM.

	Self-Confidence		Achievement or Initiative		Number Who Meet Algorithm
	Yes	No	Yes	No	
Outstanding	20	0	18	5	18
Typical	2	18	5	15	2

Note: Chi-square = 25.6, $p < .001$.

FIGURE 7.1. THE EMOTIONAL INTELLIGENCE
COMPETENCE MODEL ALGORITHM.

Self-Awareness	Social Awareness
• Emotional Self-Awareness *or* Accurate Self-Assessment • Self-Confidence	• Empathy • Organizational Awareness *or* Service Orientation
Self-Management	**Social Skills**
• Self-Control • Trustworthiness *or* Conscientiousness *or* Adaptability • Achievement Orientation *or* Initiative	• Influence • Leading Others *or* Developing Others • Building Bonds *or* Teamwork and Collaboration *or* Conflict Management • Communication *or* Change Catalyst

Self-Management. The Self-Management cluster consists of a mandatory competence and two groups of additional competencies. Self-Control must be demonstrated, as it is the core of managing oneself and one's motives. A person also needs to demonstrate Trustworthiness or Conscientiousness or Adaptability. Trustworthiness and Conscientiousness may be considered compensatory, or alternate, manifestations of each other. Trustworthiness tends to be associated with executive and management jobs, whereas Conscientiousness tends to be associated with individual contributor and administrative support jobs. Both these competencies are somewhat antagonistic to Adaptability. Whereas Trustworthiness and Conscientiousness are about stability and reliability, Adaptability is about flexibility and openness to change. Finally, a person must demonstrate either Achievement Orientation or Initiative. As mentioned earlier, these two competencies are compensatory. Having strength in one can make up for lack of use of the other.

Goleman originally conceptualized the Self-Management cluster as two clusters: Self-Regulation and Motivation. Self-Regulation involved managing or controlling one's impulses, and Motivation involved energizing or driving one's behavior. A cluster analysis by Boyatzis (Boyatzis, Goleman, and Rhee, 2000) revealed that the two clusters were not distinct. Although the Self-Regulation competencies are antagonistic to the Motivation competencies, it is a balance between the two that maximizes effectiveness.

Social Awareness. At the core of the Social Awareness cluster is the mandatory competence Empathy, an awareness of others' feelings, needs, and concerns. From Empathy are derived the other two competencies: Organizational Awareness and Service Orientation. Organizational Awareness and Service Orientation are alternate manifestations of each other. Organizational Awareness tends to be used in higher-level management and executive positions where understanding and navigating the organization is critical for success. Service Orientation tends to be important in positions relating directly to customers (external or internal). Front-line personnel, customer-service representatives, consultants, salespeople, individual contributors, and the like hold these positions.

Social Skills. The Social Skills cluster contains competencies that tend to be more situation specific than competencies in other clusters, that is, more appropriate to certain jobs or roles. However, the Influence competence is the core of the Social Skills cluster and is therefore considered mandatory. The remainder of the Social Skills cluster is divided into two primary groups. The first group—Leading Others and Developing Others—demonstrates the ability to lead and manage others. The second group—Building Bonds, Teamwork and Collaboration, and Conflict Management—demonstrates the ability to work well with others. The algorithm for this cluster requires that an individual demonstrate at least one competence from each of these groups. In addition, this cluster contains additional competencies—Communication and Change Catalyst—that may or may not be critical (depending on the situation) and therefore are considered optional.

Selecting for Different Types of Jobs

The algorithm depicted in Figure 7.1 is a good overall guide for selecting for emotional intelligence competencies. It may be considered a generic model for emotional intelligence, important for building the overall capability of an organization. However, if you are looking for more immediate, short-term impact, you will need to take into account the competency requirements of the job. As Spencer and Spencer (1993) have shown, "the better the fit between the requirements of a job and the competencies of a person, the higher the person's job performance and job satisfaction will be."

Spencer and Spencer's *Competence at Work* (1993) presented a number of generic models developed from a meta-analysis of over two hundred competency models in the Hay/McBer database. A review of targeted competency models reveals that most of the differences in the models are manifested in the Social Skills cluster. That is because Self-Awareness, Self-Management, and Social Awareness are all building blocks from which the Social Skills competencies arise. Because much of Spencer and Spencer's work is the precursor to Goleman's work, many of their generic models can be mapped to the emotional intelligence competence model.

In the following paragraphs, I have mapped four of Spencer and Spencer's generic models to the emotional intelligence paradigm. These models are for competencies for managers, individual contributors, salespeople, and helping and human service workers.

Managers. The manager model emphasizes competencies that facilitate leading or influencing others (see Figure 7.2). In the Self-Awareness cluster, Self-Confidence becomes particularly salient at the managerial level. In the Hay/McBer database this competence was found to be a critical differentiator of outstanding managers across studies. The same held true for Trustworthiness, also known as Integrity in many competency models. In order for managers to be effective they must consistently act upon their espoused values and beliefs. Achievement Orientation, or setting and meeting challenging goals, was also a key differentiator in Spencer and Spencer's meta-analysis; and Self-Control, the core of Self-Management, has been found in longitudinal studies to predict success in

FIGURE 7.2. EMOTIONAL INTELLIGENCE COMPETENCE MODEL FOR MANAGERS.

Self-Awareness	**Social Awareness**
• Emotional Self-Awareness *or* Accurate Self-Assessment • **Self-Confidence**	• **Empathy** • **Organizational Awareness** *or* Service Orientation
Self-Management	**Social Skills**
• **Self-Control** • **Trustworthiness** *or* Conscientiousness *or* Adaptability • **Achievement Orientation** *or* Initiative	• **Influence** • **Leading Others** *or* **Developing Others** • Building Bonds *or* Teamwork and Collaboration *or* **Conflict Management** • **Communication** *or* Change Catalyst

managers, particularly those high in power motivation (McClelland & Boyatzis, 1982; Jacobs & McClelland, 1994). In the Social Awareness cluster, Empathy and Organizational Awareness are critical competencies for managers. As one moves up in the organization, understanding the underlying issues and politics of the organization becomes increasingly necessary in order to be successful. In the Social Skills cluster the emphasis in managerial jobs is influencing and leading others. Thus, Influence competence along with the Leading Others and Developing Others competencies is considered especially salient. In addition, Conflict Management and Communication have also been shown to be important behaviors for managers to demonstrate.

Individual contributors. One of the most critical differentiators of outstanding individual contributors, professionals, and entrepreneurs has been the achievement motive (McClelland, 1985; Spencer & Spencer, 1993). In the emotional intelligence competence model, behaviors related to the achievement motive are represented by the Achievement Orientation and Initiative competencies residing in the Self-Management cluster (see Figure 7.3). A characteristic of individuals with the achievement motive is that testing themselves against a standard of

FIGURE 7.3. EMOTIONAL INTELLIGENCE COMPETENCE MODEL FOR INDIVIDUAL CONTRIBUTORS.

Self-Awareness	**Social Awareness**
• Emotional Self-Awareness *or* **Accurate Self-Assessment** • Self-Confidence	• **Empathy** • Organizational Awareness *or* **Service Orientation**
Self-Management	**Social Skills**
• **Self-Control** • Trustworthiness *or* **Conscientiousness** *or* Adaptability • **Achievement Orientation** *or* **Initiative**	• **Influence** • Leading Others *or* Developing Others • **Building Bonds** *or* **Teamwork and Collaboration** *or* Conflict Management • Communication *or* Change Catalyst

excellence energizes them. Thus Accurate Self-Assessment, knowing one's strengths and weaknesses, often characterizes this population. In terms of the Social Awareness cluster, Service Orientation is often more critical to individual contributors than is Organizational Awareness, because the former is more focused on helping, consulting, or assisting clients and customers. Lastly, successful individual contributors, particularly professionals, build networks and work well with others. Thus in the Social Skills cluster the Building Bonds and Teamwork and Collaboration competencies are more critical for these people than are the Leading Others or Developing Others competencies.

Salespeople. Like outstanding individual contributors, outstanding salespeople are characterized by a high achievement motive. Thus the same Self-Management competencies—Achievement Orientation and Initiative—are important (see Figure 7.4). However, salespeople differ from other individual contributors in that their main goal is to influence others to buy a service or product. Thus the Influence competence, as Spencer and Spencer have shown, is particularly critical to outstanding salespeople. In order to successfully influence others, salespeople must build on some of the Social Awareness competencies, particularly Empathy and

FIGURE 7.4. EMOTIONAL COMPETENCE MODEL FOR SALESPEOPLE.

Self-Awareness	**Social Awareness**
• Emotional Self-Awareness *or* Accurate Self-Assessment • **Self-Confidence**	• **Empathy** • Organizational Awareness *or* **Service Orientation**
Self-Management	**Social Skills**
• **Self-Control** • Trustworthiness *or* Conscientiousness *or* **Adaptability** • **Achievement Orientation** *or* **Initiative**	• **Influence** • Leading Others *or* Developing Others • **Building Bonds** *or* Teamwork and Collaboration *or* Conflict Management • Communication *or* Change Catalyst

Service Orientation. They must understand the underlying needs and issues of each customer and work to address those needs. In addition, many salespeople actively build long-term relationships with their clients, acting as trusted advisers. This requires the Building Bonds competence from the Social Skills cluster.

Helping and human service workers. Helping and human service workers include social workers, therapists, medical personnel such as nurses and physicians, teachers, and the like. One of the key characteristics of outstanding helping and human service workers is a high socialized power motive, which indicates that these people enjoy having an impact and influencing for the good of others or for the good of an organization (McClelland, 1985). Thus the Influence competence, as well as the Developing Others competence, is particularly critical for those successful in these professions (see Figure 7.5). The nature of these helping positions requires strong social awareness. Empathy is a given, and Service Orientation takes precedence over Organizational Awareness. People in these jobs need to understand and manage themselves well in order to be helpful to others. This requires Self-Control, Self-Confidence, and Accurate Self-Assessment. In addition, they must

FIGURE 7.5. EMOTIONAL INTELLIGENCE COMPETENCE MODEL FOR HELPING AND HUMAN SERVICE WORKERS.

Self-Awareness	**Social Awareness**
• Emotional Self-Awareness *or* **Accurate Self-Assessment** • **Self-Confidence**	• **Empathy** • Organizational Awareness *or* **Service Orientation**
Self-Management	**Social Skills**
• **Self-Control** • Trustworthiness *or* Conscientiousness *or* Adaptability • Achievement Orientation *or* **Initiative**	• **Influence** • Leading Others *or* **Developing Others** • Building Bonds *or* **Teamwork and Collaboration** *or* **Conflict Management** • Communication *or* Change Catalyst

be able to work well with others, using the competencies of Teamwork and Collaboration and of Conflict Management.

Using Selection Tools: The BEI

Once you know what competencies you are looking for, you will need a reliable, valid methodology for measuring them. In Chapter Five, Marilyn Gowing presents some tools that can be used for assessing emotional intelligence. When possible, I recommend using several assessment tools rather than just one, in order to provide a more accurate, reliable picture of the person. However, this may not be economical or practical in many situations. Because the interview process is the most frequently used method of selection, adapting interview techniques to measure emotional competencies can be practical and enlightening.

One of the best and most often used techniques for selecting for emotional competencies is the behavioral event interview (BEI) or critical incident interview (McClelland, 1998). The purpose of the BEI is to reliably capture the behaviors, thoughts, and feelings of a candidate during events that were personally important to her. The BEI is an operant measure designed to capture naturally occurring behavior. By enabling the interviewee to choose the events, the BEI homes in on the competencies that the candidate is most likely to exhibit.

A complete BEI can last for over three hours. It consists of asking the candidate to recall four events in the recent past—two positive and two negative. The interviewer walks through each of the events with the candidate in a storylike fashion, starting from the beginning of the event. The interviewer looks for concrete data that reveal what the interviewee actually *did, said, thought,* or *felt.* Leading questions are avoided. The purpose is to let the candidate talk about what is important to her. The interviewer's role is to obtain specific, detailed information from the candidate. Generalizations (for example, "I usually do . . . ," or, "My philosophy at work is . . .") are discouraged. When a generalization is made, the interviewer may ask, "Can you think of a specific example when you actually did this?"

Again, the goal is to get an accurate snapshot of the person's representative behaviors, something as concrete as a videotaped documentary of the candidate at work—but obtainable in an interview format. Using a rigorous assessment process, trained and reliable coders then transcribe and analyze the BEI for evidence of the demonstration of emotional competencies. The coder extracts a profile from the interview, which provides information on the candidate's strengths and weaknesses. This information is then added to information about the candidate's technical background and experience, resulting in a broader perspective.

The BEI is a powerful tool for executive selection when emotional competencies are particularly critical. David McClelland studied an international organization that adopted the BEI selection technique to reduce its executive turnover rate of 49 percent over two years. The company had estimated the cost of a lost executive to be approximately $250,000. Adding up the monetary value of the loss of sixteen executives annually, the company realized that turnover was costing it over $4 million a year. Two years after the company began using the BEI to select for critical emotional competencies during the hiring process for executives, it discovered that the turnover rate had decreased significantly from 49 percent to 6.3 percent, with an estimated savings of $3.5 million (McClelland, 1998).

Although the BEI is one of the best techniques for selecting for emotional intelligence, it can be costly and time consuming. It is recommended that interviewers be accredited in the BEI technique and that coders be accredited in recognizing the competencies. Ideally, interviewers should not code their own interviews. The BEI is most often used for executive or high-impact positions where it is critical to make the right hiring decision.

There are variations of the BEI that can be used with large groups of candidates. Known as *targeted behavioral event interviews,* they can be done in less than an hour. Targeted BEIs use questions designed to focus candidates on incidents likely to reveal competencies pertinent to the job being filled. For instance, an interviewer looking for customer service representatives might ask, "Can you tell me about a time when you had to deal with a difficult customer?" Although the questions overall are more targeted than those on the complete BEI, the interviewer employs the same basic techniques and probes.

Another time- and cost-saving technique is training the interviewer to recognize and code emotional competencies *during* the interview. Although this technique is less reliable than having an accredited coder analyze a transcribed interview, it still provides useful information. Employing this technique, the interviewer jots down evidence of a competence from the candidate's answers during the course of the interview. The challenge is to find someone very experienced in the BEI technique who is able to handle both the interviewing and coding tasks.

Other organizations have implemented *panel BEIs.* The panel consists of a trained interviewer, the hiring manager, and other relevant parties trained to recognize or code emotional competencies. During the BEI the panel takes notes for *codable* evidence of the competencies. Codable evidence is specific, concrete, and directly attributable to the interviewee. For instance, "We accomplished the goal" *is not* codable, but "I accomplished the goal by doing . . ." *is* codable. After an interview the panel reviews the data and comes to agreement on the candidate's strengths and weaknesses. Although this method is more reliable than that of the single interviewer, the interviewee might find a panel intimidating. As an alternative to the panel interview, one might make a videotape or audiotape of the interviews and have trained coders analyze them later.

Training and Development

Although selection is a relatively quick way to obtain emotional intelligence competencies in the workforce, it can also be costly. New employees need to be trained and brought up to speed in terms of job knowledge, practices, processes, and so forth. Hiring costs may also include such things as recruiting fees and the expense of work time lost in interviewing. Often it is more practical for an organization to increase emotional intelligence in its current workforce through training and development.

Goleman advocates that emotional intelligence competencies *can* be developed. However, development takes time, commitment, and support. Moreover, organizations often hinder rather than foster the process of development. An emphasis on producing immediate results often produces coercive or emotionally unintelligent methods of development, which in turn reinforce bad behavior and take a long-term toll on the health of the organization and its members. Even in the many organizations that routinely provide training, the training model is usually designed to produce a certain technical or cognitive skill level, and Goleman (1998b) notes that "technical training is easy compared to developing emotional intelligence. Our entire system of education is geared to cognitive skills. But when it comes to learning emotional competencies, our system is sorely lacking."

Cherniss and Goleman, with the help of the Consortium for Research on Emotional Intelligence in Organizations, have issued a number of guidelines for developing emotional intelligence training programs that produce measurable change (see Chapter Nine). The following paragraphs explore some of these guidelines that have implications for the ways a human resource function implements training and development programs in its organization.

Create an Encouraging Environment

Different organizations have different levels of readiness for encouraging development and change. Before an organization undertakes a training or development program for emotional intelligence, it must have a strong case supporting its need for this program. The commitment to developing emotional intelligence must be made from the top. As I noted earlier, development takes time and work. If the activity is not seen as important or is not valued by the organization, people will quickly drop out of it, using the time for what seem to be more immediate, pressing needs. Developing emotional competence in organizations will be successful only if the leadership values such competence and communicates the importance of emotional intelligence to its members. Indeed, the process of communicating, as well as developing, a climate that fosters emotional intelligence requires a number of emotional competencies. Successful leaders *model* emotional intelligence. In many of the studies of executives in Hay/McBer's database, a critical indicator of outstanding leadership is either Integrity or Trustworthiness. Organizational members must believe a leader is genuine before they will give the organization their commitment. Outstanding leaders communicate compelling visions that connect with and motivate employees. Doing this well requires emotional competencies such as Leadership, Influence, Empathy, and Communication. When a leader does not exhibit emotional intelligence, members often experience a disconnect. It is difficult to increase emotional competencies in an organization when the leader periodically blows up in public or doesn't listen or doesn't communicate well with others. Building emotional intelligence in an organization starts with the leadership.

HR systems should consider the following steps before initiating an effort to increase emotional intelligence in an organization:

- Ensure leaders understand and buy into the long-term benefits of developing emotional intelligence in the organization.
- Have leaders experience the training or interventions themselves to increase their own emotional competence before the rest of the organization participates.
- Help leaders communicate the purpose and importance of the change effort.
- Provide leaders with ongoing feedback on the development of their emotional competencies and their impact on the organization.

Gauge Readiness

Readiness to change must be gauged at the individual level as well as the organizational level. Boyatzis (1999a) demonstrated that adult learning occurs best when it is self-directed. Individuals are motivated to change when their ideals and aspirations are engaged. Efforts to develop emotional competencies quickly fall flat when the only motivation is that "my boss or organization wants me to." I recommend that any extensive competence development programs be voluntary. Forcing someone to undergo a program when she doesn't want to simply wastes time and money.

Assess the Individual

In order to develop emotional competencies, individuals must first have a clear assessment of their own strengths and limitations. The assessment then becomes the catalyst for the change process, as individuals feel a discrepancy between their ideal self and feedback about their real self. This discrepancy, or cognitive dissonance, energizes and motivates individuals toward an action plan and the implementation of change (also see Chapter Ten). Indeed, adult development is unlikely to occur without such an assessment. This objective assessment may be done through a behavioral event interview, as outlined earlier in this chapter. However, these interviews are time consuming and often not practical for a large number of people. Thus organizations are more often using a 360-degree process to assess competencies. A 360-degree assessment supplies feedback to participants not only from a self-assessment but also from a variety of other perspectives, including those of managers, direct reports, peers, customers, and business associates. This tends to be more helpful than a self-assessment alone as it provides specific feedback about the way the individual is perceived by others and about the impact the individual has on others at different levels in the organization and in different situations. Here are a few guidelines for using a 360-degree assessment to measure emotional intelligence:

Emphasize Development. A 360-degree process that measures emotional intelligence should be conducted for *developmental purposes only*. It is important that this be clearly communicated throughout the organization. Otherwise people often feel there is a hidden agenda affecting such vital areas as their job security, pay, and promotions. In addition, when 360-degree surveys are used for other purposes, people tend to undermine the usefulness of the process by overrating their colleagues in order to protect them. Finally, organizational members are likely to see the process as punitive rather than as an opportunity to get helpful feedback for their personal development and are less likely to truly internalize their results.

Communicate. Informative communication is critical for the implementation of a successful 360-degree assessment. Up-front communication should address these issues:

- The overall purpose of the 360. (How does it fit into the strategy of the organization?)
- What the 360 will be used for. (How does it assist personal development?)
- What the 360 will look like. (How much time will it take? When can people expect results?)
- How confidentiality will be protected. (Who sees the results?) The 360 is likely to be most beneficial when each participant's data remain completely confidential, available only to the participant and his coach. Moreover, it should not be possible to associate a rater with specific data. Thus a standard rule is that

any rater group, other than self and manager, must contain at least three raters before data for the group are reported.

• What the organization expects from the individual. (What degree of improvement is expected? What sort of effort to learn is expected?)

Select Raters. Participants should select a sufficient number of raters with varying perspectives (from among managers, direct reports, peers, customers, and so forth) to provide reliable feedback across rater groups and situations. For an objective, reliable assessment, each participant should have at least seven raters other than self. Raters should know the participant fairly well and have at least some frequent contact with her, otherwise, ratings may have more to do with hearsay than with actual, observable behavior. Participants should be encouraged to select their own raters and to ask these raters personally to complete the 360. This increases commitment and response rate.

Provide Feedback. Feedback should always be given in a facilitated environment because the participant is likely to have difficulty processing discrepancies between his self-image and how others see him. Facilitation also provides a process for moving the participant to recognize and understand his strengths and weaknesses in order to create a development action plan. Facilitation can be conducted one-on-one by an executive coach or an internal or external HR consultant, or it can be accomplished in a workshop environment with trained facilitators to help the participants process their data.

Once participants have received feedback and implemented their development plans, it is helpful for them to report back to their raters. Generally, when you ask someone to take the time to do something, you should give something back. For participants who turn out to have substantial emotional intelligence deficits to make up, the process of approaching raters should be carefully planned with a coach. Otherwise the process could backfire, with raters feeling that their confidentiality was violated and that the participant is taking it out on them. Ultimately, this process should involve a constructive discussion through which raters can help the participant monitor his behavior and his impact on others.

Provide Performance Feedback

Another of Cherniss and Goleman's primary guidelines for enabling change is that people should be offered ongoing feedback and support. Feedback allows people to fine-tune their behaviors and also tells them when they are getting off track. The best type of feedback is immediate, specific, and behavioral. General feedback—statements such as, "You don't have Self-Control"—is vague and demotivating. Instead, use specific statements: for example, "In the meeting this morning you started yelling at one of your employees. I noticed this had a demotivating effect on that person as well as the others. People didn't speak up as much after the incident." This feedback describes a specific incident and illustrates the impact the behavior had on others. Specific feedback helps build Self-Awareness as well as Social Awareness.

Feedback is also important as a motivational tool. As a rule, people spend more time on the things they are measured on. When learning new concepts and skills, they need support and encouragement to continue on against obstacles and to celebrate successes. When people do not receive feedback and support, they tend to become demotivated, or they lose interest in their goals and activities. Training programs in organizations often fail to create sustained change because there are no follow-ups and no systems in place to measure and reward progress once the formal program is over.

To keep organizational members energized around developing emotional intelligence competencies, an organization should, at the minimum, provide feedback nine to twelve months after the initial training program. Research by McClelland (1994) demonstrated that managers who received timely feedback had significant improvements in performance compared to those who did not receive feedback or who received feedback a year after assessment. This feedback may be provided through a 360-degree assessment process, as outlined earlier. Although such postprogram assessment is helpful, it is insufficient for real, sustainable change. For people to successfully practice and tune new behaviors, they need ongoing feedback and encouragement in their daily lives.

Arrange Support

Arranging support is a critical success factor for adult change; however, it is often left out or not attended to in organizational training programs. All too often, after people attend a program there are no further follow-ups or measures or any other steps taken to encourage and track progress. Before implementing training programs for developing emotional intelligence, organizations should consider building in support mechanisms to enable people to practice their competencies, experiment with them, and get ongoing feedback on them. Support can be arranged in a number of ways. Traditionally, executive coaches have offered it. Referent groups are another source of necessary support.

Executive Coaches. Many organizations provide coaches or consultants to meet regularly with executives. Coaches may be especially helpful for high-level executives who may not have peer groups available as a forum for discussing problems, obtaining feedback, and carrying out similar developmental tasks. Coaches can be a sounding board, and they can work with executives on developmental goals and action plans and offer helpful feedback and suggestions.

Although coaching is a powerful tool for development, it can require a significant investment in cost and time. Consequently, these services are reserved mostly for executives or other individuals who have a significant impact on the bottom line of the organization.

How can organizations provide the same kind of feedback for the remaining majority of members? One way is to train and encourage managers to provide behavioral feedback to their employees. Although most managers do not make the time to discuss long-term development with employees, Hay/McBer's research with over three thousand managers has shown that employing a coaching managerial style makes a significant impact on employees' discretionary effort and commitment on the job (Kelner, Rivers, & O'Connell, 1994). In other words, managers who focus on completion of short-term tasks and results have *less effective* organizations than do managers who spend time with employees on their long-term personal development. Unfortunately, the coaching style is rarely employed by managers in most organizations. Increasing the use of the coaching style among managers involves training, providing models (that is, managers' managers need to coach as well), and rewarding managers for developing their employees.

Referent Groups. Another way to provide ongoing feedback is to set up *referent* or support groups for members who have gone through training and have made a commitment to develop certain emotional intelligence competencies. Boyatzis (1999a) demonstrated that these groups were a key factor in developing emotional competencies. Groups should be small, with no more than four members, so there is sufficient time for people to share their experiences, concerns, and successes. They should meet on a regular schedule (once a month, for example) and have the support of the organization. If individual managers or the organization do not see the groups as important, the groups will not survive. Members may come to feel the meetings are a waste of time, and meetings will be canceled as people focus on short-term deadlines.

Referent groups may also be informal. Successful training programs enable program participants to bond. These individuals may contract on their own to keep in touch, share stories, and obtain feedback. A thorough program should provide participants with guidelines for providing feedback to each other. Individuals may also establish "buddies" with whom they can contract for on-the-job feedback after a critical incident. Such feedback should be behavioral—describing what the person *did or said*—and it should also describe the impact the behavior had on others.

Buddies are most effective when they work directly and frequently with each other so they have multiple opportunities to observe behaviors.

So far, we have looked at how to use selection and how to conduct training and development to increase emotional intelligence in an organization. Now let's look at performance management, one of the most widely used methods of judging performance.

Performance Management

Organizations' performance management objectives and methods for implementing the performance management process vary significantly. Although many organizations see the process as a once-a-year performance review that is linked to pay, others incorporate long-term development and coaching into the process. Frank Hartle (1992) incorporates emotional intelligence into his compelling definition of performance management as "a process or set of processes for establishing shared understanding about what is to be achieved (and how it is to be achieved), and of managing people in a way that increases the probability that it will be achieved." For the highest degree of effectiveness, Hartle recommends that performance management systems operate as an integrated process, incorporating elements such as performance objectives, coaching and counseling, performance review, skills training, performance-related pay, and training and development. When performance management integrates setting objectives, ongoing coaching, and training and development in a yearlong process, it can also afford an excellent opportunity to assess emotional intelligence competencies that ultimately lead to outstanding performance, provide feedback on them, and support their development.

However, emotional competencies can be integrated into the typical performance review process as well, which involves setting objectives or business goals, providing feedback on the attainment of these goals, and linking this to pay. When this process incorporates feedback on emotional intelligence, the manager and employee can identify strengths and weaknesses, discussing how the weaknesses might impede attainment of the goals and developing a road map for the employee on how to attain the goals.

The example in Table 7.3 illustrates how emotional intelligence might be integrated into a performance management or performance review process. A business goal is set; in this case, selling $250,000 in services by a certain time. I recommend that rewards continue to be based on the attainment of the business goal. The action steps that the person will need to take to attain her goal are

TABLE 7.3. INTEGRATION OF EMOTIONAL INTELLIGENCE INTO PERFORMANCE MANAGEMENT.

Goal	Timeline	Action Steps	Emotional Competencies
Sell $250,000 in services	By end of 4th quarter	Find new clients Build business with old clients Partner with colleagues	Self-Confidence Initiative Service Orientation Building Bonds Teamwork and Collaboration

decided on. Then the necessary emotional competencies are determined, providing a framework for the types of behaviors needed to successfully implement the action steps. So, if partnering with colleagues is a key action step to building business, the individual will need to demonstrate behaviors related to the Building Bonds and Teamwork and Collaboration competencies. These behaviors may entail sharing information, identifying and encouraging opportunities for collaboration across and within groups in the organization, and broadening and maintaining a network of beneficial relationships with colleagues. In this way, although the performance management process still focuses on the achievement of business goals and the participant is rewarded for this achievement, the emotional competencies add value to the process by increasing the likelihood that the individual will be able to demonstrate the behaviors that will achieve the goals.

Nevertheless, those in HR systems need to be careful when incorporating the process of developing emotional intelligence in individuals into the process of the performance review with its linkage to pay and promotion. According to Boyatzis, adult competency development is most successful when it is self-directed and engages the aspirations of the individual (in other words, when it is intrinsically motivated). Although bonuses and promotions (extrinsic rewards) may provide goal clarity and motivation to work toward specific goals, they are generally not good long-term motivators for adult competency development. Research has shown that such extrinsic rewards or motivators have a short-term effect on behavior, whereas intrinsic motivation predicts long-term *sustainable* behavioral change (Koestner, Weinberger, & Healy, 1988). Because developing emotional intelligence is a long-term endeavor, focusing solely on extrinsic rewards is not sufficient. This is not to say that a rewards system should be based purely on results. It should have a component that takes into account *how* the results were achieved, an issue addressed in the example in Table 7.3. Typically, this component is reflected in a person's bonus compensation rather than in her base salary.

Conclusion

In this chapter I have discussed ways to employ human resource applications to increase emotional intelligence within the organization. The applications focus primarily on selection and on training and development. Although I have also discussed methods to incorporate emotional intelligence competencies into the performance management process, I emphasize the developmental function of these competencies, how mastering them can improve one's performance, rather than their use as an evaluation tool for pay and promotion. Once again, as Boyatzis demonstrated, adult learning and development is most likely to occur when it is self-directed and engages the individual's long-term ideals and aspirations. Even though pay may motivate individuals to work on development in the short term, it is often not enough to sustain development long term. Ultimately, the organization needs to provide an environment that reinforces, encourages, and supports the self-directed development process.

CHAPTER EIGHT

THE CHALLENGE OF HIRING SENIOR EXECUTIVES

Claudio Fernández-Aráoz

Because senior executives have a huge impact on the results and morale of any organization, the criteria for their selection are vitally important to the organization. Yet the traditional criteria for hiring senior executives are dysfunctional because they usually ignore emotional intelligence competencies. It is now time to challenge the whole selection process. This chapter discusses why the process needs to be challenged, where it should be strengthened, what should be measured, and who should be doing the evaluating.

Senior Executive Hiring Has a Huge Impact

Ask any CEO, board member, or senior executive of any large corporation about the most important decision she has to confront. Chances are that her answer will be hiring. Hiring the right executive is the most important challenge because of its impact, its lasting consequences, its irreversibility, its growing complexity, and its increased criticality. This decision adds or destroys a huge amount of economic value for the organization. Whereas the right decision can start or continue a profitable growth pattern and boost morale and motivation, a poor decision may bring the company to the brink of financial distress and even bankruptcy, and start a downward trend in organizational climate, with a dramatic impact on the company's income statement and balance sheet.

Though the impact of hiring the right manager has always been great, this task has become even more urgently important and visible lately. Over the last few years, whenever I have read in the news about a top executive's hiring or departure, I have gone on to analyze the change in market value of the relevant company. In most cases, market value has gone up or down significantly, in some cases by as much as 10 percent in a few hours, which for large companies translates into billions of dollars of shareholder value.

If the bottom-line and balance sheet impact of hiring the right key executive is large even for sizable, well-established corporations, it can be the difference between life and death for start-ups and new ventures. During the recent start-up of a publicly held U.S. telecommunications company, the board concluded that the CEO needed a strong executive vice president and chief operating officer who would complement the CEO's skills. Six months after the new COO joined, the stock price had multiplied fourfold. This 300 percent increase in value, according to financial analysts, was justified by the new manager's track record and credibility, exhibited in rapidly assembling a superior team and speeding promising new products and services to the market. William Sahlman (1997), a leading authority in entrepreneurial finance, put the impact of executive selection on start-ups best: "When I receive a business plan, I always read the résumé section first. Not because the people part of the new venture is the most important, but because without the right team, none of the other parts really matter" (p. 100).

In addition, the rapid rise of private equity funds, which adds significant value by upgrading the management of acquired companies, and the record activity in acquisitions both confirm the crucial impact of bringing the right management into play. Likewise a few recent cases offer unfortunate examples of significant value destruction, when advanced negotiations for major mergers of publicly traded companies collapsed when executive egos or chemistries clashed.

Senior executive hiring decisions are also crucial because they have lasting effects. Once a company is in serious trouble, it usually takes years to bring it back on track, if it ever recovers. Take the case of a venture capital firm with a very poor track record of hiring CEOs for several of its acquired companies. In one of its companies, a service business, four CEOs have been hired and fired in the space of just two years. Given this history, no one qualified for the position wanted to be on that list as the next "victim." The investment firm found itself unable to attract the required talent for over a year. In the end it was forced to exit the business, at considerable loss.

Mistaken hiring decisions are also critical because they are so difficult to reverse. Acknowledging a major mistake on such a critical matter is very hard for most of us. As a result, in many cases the error lingers long after it has been diagnosed, with a compounded decrease in enterprise value. Companies and senior executives then face a lose-lose dilemma: either take the pain of acknowledging a major mistake or continue destroying value. This was the case with another venture capital firm, which concluded after one year that the new CEO of a major acquisition was the wrong choice. The venture capital fund had only eighteen months to go before it was to end its investment role, and it was clear it would take at least six months to bring a new CEO on board. Senior management, unethically, tried to hide the hiring mistake, therefore perpetuating major value destruction in the acquired company and making the error potentially irreversible.

Hiring Is, However, a Very Difficult Task

Just how well has management risen to meet this critical challenge of hiring? Regrettably, the weight of evidence indicates that management has done rather poorly. In his 1985 classic article "How to Make People Decisions," Peter Drucker concluded that top management's "batting average" on promotion and staffing decisions was as low as one third! My own experience is that the situation has not improved since then. Increased turnover at the top, more news coverage of major firings, increased takeover and acquisition activity, and even the growth of the executive search and outplacement professions all point toward poor corporate performance on this major task. Research on the outcomes of senior executive selection and evaluation is very limited; nevertheless, recent surveys indicate that the process is still quite unreliable, with some estimates of overt failure in the range of at least 30 to 50 percent of senior appointments (Ciampa & Watkins, 1999).

Significant research in the field of hiring and particularly in the techniques used to improve candidate evaluation and selection has been conducted and published since 1915. The results of this research are not very promising and confirm the extreme difficulty of the task. Most of the research has been centered on low- to medium-level positions. Even for low-level positions, validities for predicting performance on the job are on the order of .6 for some of the best techniques available (such as a well-structured interview), which implies that less than 40 percent of the performance of the individual hired can be explained by the results of the evaluation (Andersen & Shackleton, 1993; Eder & Harris, 1999a). Not a very promising result, frankly. What about the other 60 percent?

Moreover, even though the task of hiring a senior executive has always been challenging, this challenge has intensified recently. First, the accelerated rate of technological change and the increasing global competition demand much faster accurate responses. There simply might not be a second chance, an opportunity to correct a hiring mistake. Second, new organizational forms and practices are proliferating (such as joint ventures, strategic partnerships, team-based horizontal processes, and flatter organizations). How are organizations to judge the relevance of a candidate's previous experience to a completely different organizational environment and increasingly competitive global world? Finally, there is the growing evidence that what accounts for superior performance in top managers and business leaders is not only their résumés and IQs but also, perhaps more fundamentally, the way in which they handle themselves and their relationships (Goleman, 1998a). Competencies in the domains of Empathy and Social Skills, especially those related to team building, change management, and self-motivation, have become crucial for most senior management roles. These "soft" skills, however, are very hard to evaluate, certainly much more difficult than experience and IQ. Although developments in information technology have made available vast quantities of information about top managers, this information is typically related to their experience and educational background. It can be reliable on some of the "hard" aspects, but it usually says very little (and if it does it is hardly reliable) about the other critical "soft" aspects, such as many emotional intelligence competencies essential for predicting managerial performance.

"Why CEOs Fail," the cover story in a recent issue of *Fortune* magazine, asks, "So how do CEOs blow it? More than any other way, by failure to put the right people in the right jobs—and the related failure to fix people problems in time" (Charan & Colvin, 1999, p. 70). This article confirms not only that senior appointments frequently go wrong but also that one of the main reasons for CEO failure is, in turn, the difficulty CEOs have making effective senior appointments!

To complicate matters further, it is evident now that this new decade has brought with it a global war for top executive talent. This war is fueled by demographic factors that are resulting in a growing mismatch of demand and supply with no countervailing trends in sight (such as the earlier trend to incorporate women into the workforce) and by the increased employment of top corporate talent by small and medium-sized companies (now a bigger group and faster growing than the large companies), including many start-ups in the new economy (Chambers, Foulon, Handfield-Jones, Hankin, & Michaels, 1998).

In summary, hiring a senior executive is the toughest challenge for top management, with ever-increasing, longer-lasting, and frequently irreversible implications. And it promises to become only more complex and critical in the years to come.

The Higher the Level, the Higher the Risk

One of the greatest paradoxes I have found in the world of hiring is that the higher the level, the higher the risk. Given the huge consequences of a hiring mistake at the top, one would expect that appropriate actions would be taken to control the risk. My experience tells me this is not the case.

First, the impact of hiring grows with the level of the position being filled. This is the consequence of two factors: the larger impact of the more senior positions, as discussed earlier, and the larger spread of managerial performance in senior jobs. Conclusive research, a decade old now, has in fact shown a very large spread in managerial performance, a spread that grows exponentially with the complexity of the job. The difference in output between a top and a bottom blue-collar worker on an assembly line may be as high as 300 percent. However, the difference between top and bottom performance grows exponentially as one moves up the hierarchical chain, becoming dramatically larger for top- and bottom-performing CEOs (Hunter, Schmidt, & Judiesch, 1990).

Second, the reliability and validity of the evaluation process tends to decrease for senior positions. Very senior jobs are unique and infrequently filled, making it more difficult to learn from hiring for similar positions. Useful techniques to improve reliability and validity, such as conducting behavioral event interviews with average and top performers to identify the key differentiating competencies, are not easy to implement at the top given the lack of an adequate sample of comparable managers. This often leads organizations into the trap of writing up a set of unique, and also unrealistic, specifications, which only Superman, Spiderman, and Batman could meet—together! A related difficulty is that jobs at the top show little stability, and the nature of the job tomorrow will likely be quite different from its nature today and certainly different from its nature in the past.

An additional reason for the lower reliability and validity of senior executive evaluations is the larger importance for senior managers and leaders of "soft" factors, or emotional intelligence competencies, over experience and IQ, as demonstrated by Daniel Goleman (1998b) in his book *Working with Emotional Intelligence.* These soft factors have a lower reliability of measurement using traditional selection techniques (such as interviews) than harder factors, including experience and IQ, do.

Senior executive evaluations are also compromised by time pressure. In most cases, hirings at the top are made reactively, often in response to the firing or sudden loss of the previous incumbent. The board, key shareholders, and the financial community are all watching anxiously, and it is hard to resist their pressure for a fast solution and instead to take as much time as needed to produce the best solution. And hiring well at the top may take time. First, the organization should invest time in problem definition, identifying and confirming the key competencies required now and in the future, rather than falling into the trap of looking for an executive similar to the previous one but without the previous one's obvious defects. In addition, the organization should take the significant time needed to conduct a systematic internal and external search, to carry out a thorough evaluation of candidates found, and then to recruit and integrate the best one. Resisting time pressure in order to do all this, however, is usually not easy.

Another factor that threatens senior executive hiring is the lack of competence of the typical evaluators involved! When hiring for low-level positions, experienced HR professionals usually follow a well-tried process. They know the job needs, they have a clear process, and they follow it. They are more experienced in hiring than the candidates are in being evaluated. They are also more senior than the individuals being hired, and they can perform well at a high-complexity job (such as evaluating these candidates).

When hiring for the highest levels, however, little of this holds true. The evaluators involved are in many cases ill prepared for this highest complexity task. Because of this evaluation's importance, often the boss wants to make the evaluation personally. Typically, however, this boss is not knowledgeable about the best practices for hiring. Decision makers have not been formally prepared for making this type of decision. Most board members, CEOs, and senior executives, particularly in the Western world, have reached their positions as a result of hard factors, their educational and career experience. Chances are that the CEO of an operating company studied accounting or engineering and perhaps completed an MBA degree and then progressed into general management through a career in a commercial function. The leader of a conglomerate may have progressed, with a similar educational background, through the financial function. It is likely that both have received almost no formal training in choosing executives. They may have had significant practical experience. However, practical experience does not necessarily imply competence in the field of executive selection. Given the importance of the decision, however, top executives still want to make these calls personally. And rightly so.

Nevertheless, untrained and unprepared evaluators tend to rely on unstructured interviews, still the most frequent technique for senior executive hiring despite its demonstrated poor validity. They tend to fall into a rich series of hiring traps, such as taking people at face value and evaluating them in absolute terms rather than in terms of their fit for the specific job and organization. They tend to be naïve about references, they like to hire people similar to themselves, and they often make gaffes in critical parts of the hiring process.

Whereas evaluators of senior candidates are frequently unprepared, the candidates themselves are many times trained in interviewing techniques. In addition, if they are near the top of their fields and currently employed, they are likely to have low tolerance for a thorough evaluation. They are typically self-confident, highly successful individuals, who truly believe in their capability. They have little time available, are not looking for a new job, and are seriously concerned about the confidentiality of the whole process, for which they won't make themselves available for too long or to too many people. They have in short a low level of acceptance of the evaluation process.

Finally, the integrity of the hiring process at the top is usually threatened by political pressures, often complex ones. Take the case of a large industrial corporation that had to fire a CEO because, apart from his poor business performance, he lacked personal stability. The turmoil of daily activity in effect paralyzed him. After a thorough analysis of the top management potential within the organization, the board decided to look for a new CEO outside. At the same time, however, board members were afraid of the impact a public search might have on the business community. Therefore they decided to keep this top management change "within the family" by identifying possible candidates among their own friends and business connections. The names put forward by the various board members were discussed by the whole board, and the long list was reduced to the one person that the board chair (a strong, prestigious personality and an inspiring leader himself) proposed. The forceful recommendation from the chair was enough to get agreement from all board members, and again in order to preserve confidentiality, no outside references were examined for the successful (and only) candidate. In less than a year this newly appointed CEO proved a failure, lacking flexibility and strategic vision, running a one-person show, afraid of appointing strong and competent subordinates. As in this example, hiring at the top is usually plagued by all sorts of political pressures from all categories of stakeholders with all types of open and hidden agendas, who want to push their favorite candidate into a key position.

In summary, then, the forces opposing the reliability and validity of senior executive evaluations are uniqueness of job, lack of job stability, lack of knowledge of key competencies, unreliability of evaluation, time pressure, evaluator incompetence, political pressures, and low candidate acceptance of the process. And the great paradox is that the higher the position level, the higher the risk in hiring, both because of the increasing potential impact of the executive's performance and because of the lower reliability and validity of the evaluation process. Figure 8.1 summarizes this point.

Emotional Intelligence Competencies Are Key for Hiring at the Senior Level

During the last fifteen years I have personally conducted over two hundred senior executive search projects. As the leader of professional development for the fifty-eight offices of our executive search firm worldwide, I have been exposed to the results of several thousand cases of hiring senior executives all around the world. This experience has left me with no doubts about the relevance of emotional intelligence to senior management success. A couple of years ago, moreover, I had

FIGURE 8.1. THE INCREASED RISK IN HIRING SENIOR EXECUTIVES.

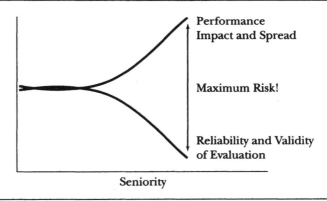

Performance
Impact and Spread

Maximum Risk!

Reliability and Validity
of Evaluation

Seniority

the opportunity to conduct research that dramatically demonstrated this point. This study, which I summarize below, clearly demonstrated that the classic profile organizations look for in hiring a senior executive (relevant experience and outstanding IQ) is much more a predictor of failure than success unless the relevant emotional intelligence competencies are also present. In fact, serious weaknesses in the domain of emotional intelligence predict failure at senior levels with amazing accuracy. Conversely, in the absence of candidates with relevant experience, a combination of high emotional intelligence and high IQ will still function pretty well to produce success.

I first did some research in Latin America on the topic. What I did was to review cases of executives I have known and followed closely over the previous decade, and I classified them as *successes* (true stars, top performers in their categories) and *failures* (not necessarily fired, but at most average or mediocre performers). For each executive, I analyzed the moment of recruitment, looking at the type of alternatives considered as candidates for the position and the executive's relative standing at that time on three dimensions: (1) relevant previous experience, (2) high emotional intelligence, and (3) outstanding IQ.

The relevance of each candidate's previous experience was assessed by considering the situational, functional, and specific industry knowledge required in each case. For each alternative candidate the relative standing on the IQ dimension was assessed on the basis of academic background and on performance, logical reasoning, and problem-solving skills.

No valid and reliable measurement of emotional intelligence was available at the time of the study. So subjective relative assessments of the candidates were made on the basis of information from structured interviews and intensive reference checking. Typical personal emotional competencies discriminated were Self-Confidence, Self-Control, Trustworthiness, Conscientiousness, Adaptability, Achievement Drive, Commitment, and Initiative. The most frequently observed social competencies included Understanding Others, Political Awareness, Influence, Communication, Leadership, and Collaboration and Team Capabilities.

As one would expect, many of the stars were strong in all three dimensions. To force a discrimination, I identified for each executive the two most salient of the three dimensions, again relative to the other candidates considered for the position for which the executive had been hired or to which he had been promoted. Thus for each executive I obtained one or two (maximum) areas of relative strength. Processing the data for all cases, I obtained the typical profiles of successes and failures.

Even though these assessments were relative and subjective assessments, the difference between the success and failure profiles was so strong that I had no doubts about the reliability and validity of the conclusions, which at that point were based on a sample of about two hundred executives in Latin America, most of them in Argentina. When I shared the results with Daniel Goleman, he became interested in exploring two other cultures: Germany and Japan. Three colleagues in those countries (Horst Broecker, Ken Whitney, and Tomo Watanabe) then performed similar analyses. The results were almost identical for the three very different cultures. Aggregating the data for Japan, Germany, and Latin America, a sample of 515 managers, the difference between the success and failure profiles is indeed quite dramatic.

Figure 8.2 summarizes these profiles. For successes, emotional intelligence was found to be the most frequent relevant characteristic, closely followed by relevant experience. Outstanding IQ came last, at a significant distance. For failures the case was even more dramatic: their most frequent relevant characteristic was previous relevant experience, closely followed by outstanding IQ. Moreover, failures almost inevitably had some serious weakness in some emotionally based competencies and therefore a relative weakness in their overall emotional intelligence compared with other candidates for the same position. In other words, if people were hired for their experience and IQ, they were likely later on to be fired for their lack of emotional intelligence! The largest difference by far between successes and failures was in the field of emotional intelligence. Although there are other implications from this research, the relevant point for this discussion is that emotional intelligence competencies are indeed key for senior executive hiring success.

FIGURE 8.2. SUCCESS AND FAILURE PROFILES.

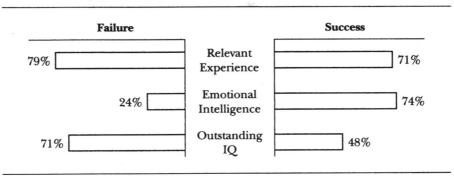

Traditional Hiring Criteria Are Dysfunctional

Traditional hiring criteria for senior positions have emphasized, either explicitly or implicitly, two dimensions: previous relevant experience and high IQ. Typically, potential candidates are first analyzed on paper, and two filters are usually applied to these CVs: relevant previous experience and an advanced educational background (taken to be correlated with IQ). Most hiring processes then continue with unstructured interviews in which most of the focus is on the relevance of past experience and the candidate's ability to respond well to the interviewer's questions. However, the combination of experience and IQ is a dysfunctional set of criteria in the sense that it won't work effectively toward the objective of hiring the manager most likely to turn in the highest performance on the job. The discussion in this section analyzes the implications of this dysfunctional practice from the point of view of an evolving theoretical model of performance, candidate distribution, and decision criteria. Empirical testing of this model would indeed be very welcome.

Outstanding performance in each job is of course the result of a specific set of competencies, unique for each job. If I were to generalize, however, I would argue that as indicated in the profiles in Figure 8.2, success in senior positions requires three components: (1) previous relevant experience or specific expertise, (2) high IQ, and (3) a series of relevant emotional intelligence (EI) competencies. For the purpose of simplifying the model for this discussion, I have collapsed the first two dimensions into one, which I call *experience and IQ*. Research supports this step as there is usually a positive correlation between these two variables in individuals in real life. The model thus analyzes both performance functions and decision criteria on two dimensions: experience and IQ and EI competencies (the relevant set of EI threshold and differentiating competencies for a given senior job in a specific organizational context). For the model I also assume that the two dimensions are synergistic—high levels of both produce an effect greater than the effect of adding their independent contributions. Thus to simplify the analysis, I am assuming that performance is a function of the product of these two variables:

$$PEFFORMANCE = (EXPERIENCE \; AND \; IQ) \times (EI \; COMPETENCIES)$$

Under the assumptions of this model, then, the higher the product of these two dimensions, the higher the expected performance of the manager.

Figure 8.3 presents a series of three curves. For each of these curves, any point of it represents a different combination of both dimensions that would still produce the same level of performance. For example, point Y would be a highly experienced and high-IQ manager with an expected high performance, while point Z would be a manager with outstanding EI competencies and the same level of high expected performance (despite a more limited experience and IQ). The further away from the origin, the higher the expected performance (in fact, performance grows with the square of the distance to the origin). Given the synergy of the two variables, the shape of the curves needs to be convex to the origin because it takes a higher than proportional level of one variable to compensate for a deficiency in the other. The curves of these models are actually equilateral hyperbolae.

FIGURE 8.3. EXPERIENCE AND IQ VERSUS EI COMPETENCIES AS A PREDICTOR OF PERFORMANCE.

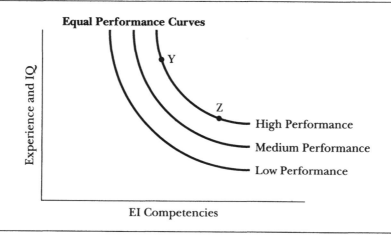

Regarding candidate distribution, I assume that the two dimensions are independent. In other words, candidates with highly relevant experience and high IQ do not necessarily have a high aggregate level of relevant EI competencies. A scatter diagram of candidates represented along these two dimensions would indicate neither positive nor negative correlation among them.

Figure 8.4 adds the set of potential candidates, in the circle, to the performance functions. In a three-dimensional performance model, this circle would be the base of a bell. Most candidates are in the center of the circle, with their numbers diminishing as one moves toward the limits of the circle.

The final element of the performance model is the set of decision criteria for selecting candidates. As can be seen in the success and failure profiles (Figure 8.2), using a set of evaluation criteria that maximizes the importance of the combination of experience and IQ and ignores EI competencies is more likely to produce an executive hiring failure than a success. It implies a model with evaluation lines parallel to the horizontal axis, as in Figure 8.5. If only experience and IQ are used for evaluation, candidates A and B will be considered to have the same predicted performance. And candidate D will be considered inferior to candidate C, who will be evaluated as having the absolute best potential of the whole candidate population. After all, how can you fail if you recruit the most experienced and smartest (in the IQ sense) of all possible candidates?

Figure 8.5 is not just the result of an intellectual exercise. In my opinion it truly represents at least the implicit and sometimes the explicit criteria used for selection at the top. When specifications include, for example, an advanced educational

FIGURE 8.4. CANDIDATES IN RELATION TO PERFORMANCE.

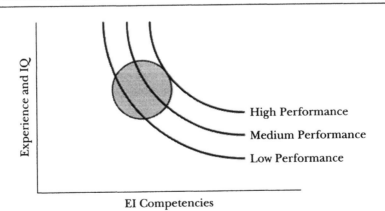

FIGURE 8.5. TRADITIONAL SELECTION.

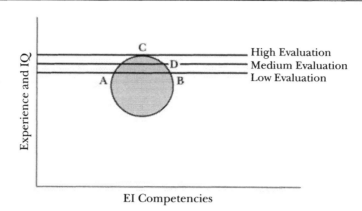

background such as an Ivy League MBA with distinction, then the decision criteria are ignoring EI competencies and implicitly maximizing IQ (still correlated with academic performance in most traditional educational programs). Similarly, demanding specific experience implies that experience is critical but has nothing to do with the emotional intelligence competencies required for the job. And experience, again, does not imply competence for most jobs.

Figure 8.6 identifies the true top performer of the population. This is candidate D (the one tangent to the furthest curve) rather than candidate C (the one who would be chosen as the result of applying a traditional selection model). That is, using the traditional dysfunctional set of criteria, a candidate of significantly lower expected performance would be chosen (remember that the difference in expected performance grows with the square of the curve's distance), probably just an average performer. Also, because a threshold level of experience and IQ is likely to be a consideration, candidate D (again, the best) might not even be considered; he is barely at the threshold level of the dysfunctional criteria.

The model being presented here seems to confirm a series of recent empirical findings that demonstrate that spread in emotional intelligence explains most of the difference in star performance (Goleman, 1998b). This can be clearly seen in Figure 8.7. In the set of considered candidates (those inside the arc above the threshold level), maximizing experience and IQ would mean moving from candidate F to candidate C (the assumed best). However, candidates C and F are in fact almost on the same performance curve level. In contrast, maximizing emotional

FIGURE 8.6. FINDING TOP PERFORMERS.

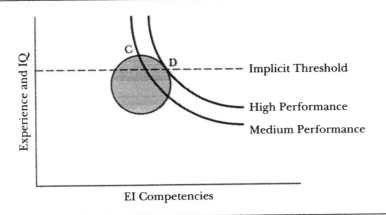

FIGURE 8.7. USING EMOTIONAL INTELLIGENCE TO PREDICT PERFORMANCE.

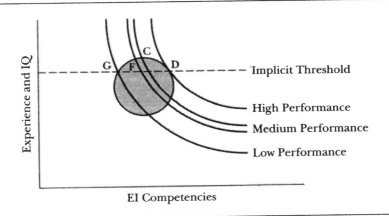

intelligence competencies implies moving from candidate G to candidate D (the true best), whose performance curves are the farthest apart, not only among the subset of candidates considered but almost across the whole candidate population. Again, the performance difference between G and D is proportional to the square of the distance of both curves. After implicit filters have been applied along the IQ dimension (as is the case in practice when a demanding educational background and similar criteria are specifications), it is the emotional intelligence dimension that explains most, and is the best predictor of, superior performance at the top.

So far, I have centered this discussion on one critical consequence of the traditional dysfunctional selection criteria: hiring average performers while aiming for the best. There are other negative consequences of following the traditional process, including overpaying for less qualified management. Given the socially accepted overvaluing of IQ, candidates such as C (the assumed best), extremely intelligent and experienced, would probably be in higher demand than candidate D (the true best, despite being marginally above the threshold level in terms of IQ and less experienced). As a result of following the traditional hiring process, an organization may pay significantly more for a significantly less competent manager! Quite a case of dysfunction in fact.

Finally, there is yet another expensive consequence of the traditional process: it dramatically limits the pool of considered candidates. In the context of the current war for talent, this will indeed be a very costly error. Figure 8.8 demonstrates this point. As mentioned, the candidates considered would be in the top arc above

FIGURE 8.8. LEAVING OUT SOME OF THE BEST.

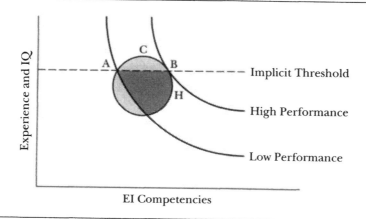

the implicit threshold. However, all candidates in the heavily shaded area below the threshold and above the performance curve of candidate A would have an expected performance higher than that of A. Because the number of cases in this zone is proportional to the volume under the three-dimensional bell above the circle, the implication is that the traditional process clearly leaves out the vast majority of potentially valid candidates. And it certainly leaves out some of the best potential candidates, like H who, despite being significantly below the implicit threshold, are still much better than candidates like C (the assumed best).

In summary, traditional selection criteria are dysfunctional. Although attempting to maximize the expected performance of the hired candidate, they unknowingly overpay average performers, and what is ultimately much more costly to the organization, by ignoring EI competencies they fully leave out of consideration some of the candidates with the best potential for performance.

Suggestions for Changing the Process

So far I have focused mainly on the problems associated with hiring senior executives and the reasons the whole process needs to be challenged. I believe that it should be challenged because it exposes the organization to a major risk by performing with low reliability and validity a process of major impact. As we have seen, traditional selection criteria usually ignore emotional intelligence competencies and result in the hiring of senior executives who are not the best, and may be far from the best, for the job. The remainder of the chapter looks at a few salient points on the way to a solution to this dysfunctional hiring process, addressing where the process should be strengthened, what should be measured, and who should be doing the evaluating.

Where the Process Should Be Strengthened

Hiring is a process which starts, like any decision problem, with a problem definition. It continues with the generation of alternatives and their evaluation and ends with the actual effort to recruit the perceived best. In my experience, although most corporations do reasonably well in two of these four steps (generating candidates and motivating them to join), they frequently underinvest in the first step (defining the problem) and underperform in the third one (evaluating the candidates). As a result, senior hiring goes wrong as often as it goes right.

The first major challenge to be offered to the current process then is to have the discipline to invest significant time and attention in the front end of the process, because a good definition of the problem is half of the solution. Investing up-front in senior hiring is clearly justified by the organizational impact of these positions as well as by their uniqueness, that is, the person the organization is looking for is in many cases quite special. Moreover, this time investment can help organizations avoid many of the usual hiring traps, including the reactive approach (looking for someone similar to the person who had the job previously but without that person's obvious defects), unrealistic specifications, and the similar-to-me effect. Investing time up-front can not only improve the effectiveness of the process by identifying the right target to aim at but also make the process more efficient by focusing in the right direction from the start.

Finally, this initial investment can significantly enhance the integrity of the rest of the process. In practice, because most hiring decisions are still reactive and either a crisis situation or a window of opportunity is exerting time pressure, the first temptation is to jump into the nearest or simplest solution. However, this usually just makes the problem bigger and the consequences larger. To relieve some of the pressure and stick to a disciplined approach to filling the need, those conducting the hiring process need to make some agreements with board members before launching an internal or external search. The potential trade-offs required by different hiring decisions should be clearly discussed (the comparative advantages and disadvantages of internal versus external searches, the likely costs, and so forth), and the underlying strategy, managerial priorities, and essential competencies required should also be confirmed at this stage. Once this consensus has been reached, those ultimately responsible should stick to meeting the confirmed need, bravely resisting all pressures.

An excellent example of the value of this initial time investment and of sticking to the need can be found in the recent recruitment of a CEO for one of the largest international stock exchanges. This stock exchange had been privatized and sold to a group of banks, each one of which had a representative on the board. These shareholders, collectively, represented the market, and therefore most of the potential candidates were either working with or related to one of them. Understandably, each board member was interested in promoting someone he or she knew to be CEO; in some cases the candidate was even a friend or a major client. The president of the stock exchange, to whom the new CEO would report, was, however, extremely forceful in successfully driving the whole process. He made it clear right from the beginning that as the person ultimately responsible for the nomination, he was going to be fully independent and impartial. He developed a clear list of competencies, most of which were so objective that it was quite easy to agree on the measurement of them. He was inflexible in his insistence on leaving out nominees who didn't meet the criteria, despite all sorts of internal and external pressures and in the face of newspaper speculation on potential candidates. He chose a finalist who was initially not interested at all in the position, and with an intense motivation effort, finally brought him on board. The new CEO's outstanding performance at the country level was later on taken to a higher level, as he developed major agreements with other international stock exchanges.

The second point of the process that typically needs to be strengthened is the evaluation of candidates. This in turn implies an improved execution of the right combination of structured interviews and serious reference checking. Assuming that the right homework and analyses have been done at the problem definition level, there should now be an understanding of what needs to be looked for during the evaluation. This understanding needs to be translated into the critical competencies essential for success in the new job. These competencies are capabilities, not just experience. It will be rare to identify more than half a dozen truly critical competencies for any given situation, that is, competencies that can't be supplied by the rest of the organization. These few key competencies should be defined as clearly as possible, *in behavioral terms,* so that it is clear what the person who has the competency should be able to do. Organizations shouldn't rely on general descriptive terms that can have very different meanings to different people. Try asking several people for their own definition of the term *team player* or *leader with a strategic vision.* The answers will be all over the map.

Once the set of clearly defined competencies is in hand, the first improvement to make in the evaluation step is to have the discipline to prepare a proper interview guide, with the best possible set of relevant questions to measure each competence, ideally looking for examples of actual past behavior as the best evidence. And the major challenge for senior hiring is to have the further discipline to follow the structure of the process and the interview guide. Because of very senior candidates' low acceptance of the evaluation process, among many other reasons, hiring at the top requires extremely competent interviewers who can maintain both discipline and finesse in this crucial task.

A second leverage point for improving the evaluation task is taking serious references. The best way to evaluate a person is after the fact, by observing the person in action—by watching what she does, how she does it, and the consequences of her actions in situations similar to those expected in the new job. Because we can hardly have the opportunity to do that, we conduct reference checks, speaking with people who have previously worked with a candidate. However, in the way these references are usually handled they have very limited value, if any. First, referees are usually selected by the candidate. Second, although these referees might be useful for checking for serious misrepresentation (such as outright lies regarding a former employment position or working period), they typically give generous evaluations and are influenced more by worry about their potential relationship with the candidate than by the desire to help someone unknown make a good hiring decision. In addition, if we don't know the person giving the reference, how can we judge the authenticity and reliability of his judgments?

Though superficial reference checking adds no value, proper references are still essential. Whenever possible, the evaluator should try to find someone she knows who also knows the candidate; this may produce more sincerity and openness. If this is not feasible, she should focus on the most reliable sources (typically former bosses), and try to see them personally. During reference checking, the evaluator should not ask for a general opinion of the candidate but rather should describe the situation and expected contribution and try to find out whether the candidate has faced similar challenges before and how he or she performed. Finally, a reliable reference check should include speaking with several people who have worked with the candidate in relevant situations.

What Should Be Measured

In addition to investing in the problem definition and evaluation steps of the process, organizations need to confront the issue of what typically should be measured. Although every situation is unique, a few general considerations can be put forward about the competencies to be included in the ideal profile for the position and subsequently in the evaluation.

First, start with the strategy. The company's mission drives the strategy, and the strategy drives the organization and the senior executive (and particularly the CEO) profile. Without a clear organizational strategy, hiring simply can't get started.

In addition, reference to generic situations can sometimes be of some initial help at this stage. In discussing *strategic selection*, Gerstein and Reisman (1983) argue that most company situations can be classified in one of seven groups (start-up, turnaround, rationalization, growth, redeployment, divestiture, and new acquisition) and that each of these situations has a specific set of major job thrusts that help to define the specific characteristics of ideal candidates. For example, according to Gerstein and Reisman, a turnaround situation has two major thrusts: rapid and accurate problem diagnosis and fixing short-term and ultimately long-term problems. These thrusts imply that the person needed to manage this situation would have a profile with these elements: has a "take charge" approach; has the ability to be a strong leader; has strong analytical and diagnostic skills, especially financial; is an excellent business strategist; has a high energy level; is a risk-taker; handles pressure well; has good crisis-management skills; is a good negotiator.

Helpful though reference to generic situations may be initially, what ultimately matters is to understand the future job of the new manager. A useful strategy for this purpose is to try to identify the managerial priorities of the job for the first couple of years. In other words: How are we going to tell, two years from now, whether the new manager has been successful? What is it that we expect her to do, and how should she go about doing it in our organization? What are the initial objectives we could agree on? If we were to implement a short- and medium-term incentive system, what would be the key variables and parameters?

Yet another valuable exercise is to identify a series of *critical incidents* for the new job, by gathering descriptions of frequently occurring situations in which the new senior executive's actions will demonstrate whether she is an acceptable or unacceptable performer. Various tactics can be used to gather these incidents, such as looking at qualified or partially qualified managers in similar positions and at the reasons for the failure of predecessors.

In addition, as mentioned before, the ideal person who has *all* the knowledge and can do *everything* perfectly well on her own does not exist. An effort should be made to keep the list of truly essential differentiating competencies short. What matters is to identify those essential competencies that condition the implementation of a well thought out strategy and that are neither present in the organization nor available through outsourcing. This was the approach used by the CEO of a large European conglomerate who took the company over in the early nineties, with a bleeding bottom line and many strategic question marks on several of its business units, and accomplished a remarkable turnaround, with dramatic changes in the strategy and composition of the portfolio and with outstanding results in both the balance sheet and the income statement. How did he do it? He found new leaders for all the business units, sometimes through internal promotions, at other times by using his own network, and at still other times by conducting external searches. In all cases, however, he was particularly good at defining the need, at identifying what was required that was not present in the organization, be it knowledge or capability or even personal characteristics. In all cases the managers he appointed were not the popular champions in their industries, but they were bringing in what was needed, and nothing else. And this created enormous shareholder value, uninterruptedly, for the last decade.

Another useful practice for defining what to measure is to explore the job requirements not only downward (looking at the group of reporting managers and the expected bottom-line and balance sheet results) but also laterally (examining the external relations desired both within and outside the organization). Similarly, job requirements should also explore upward. Conflict with their bosses as a result of differences of style and competing agendas is one of the most frequent causes of derailment among newly appointed senior managers. A small investment of effort at this stage can not only clarify the need but also confirm the role and the mandate, both key elements for a smooth integration. Such clarification is crucial when the newer organizational forms such as strategic alliances and joint ventures are involved.

Hiring these days is like hitting a double moving target. How can we predict success in such a complex and dynamic job and organizational environment? The strategy is less complex than the problem: for short-term impact, look for people who, in addition to the relevant managerial abilities dictated by the situation, have also at least a minimum of relevant experience (at least functional and situational). Although experience is not always as essential for success as many emotional competencies are, it accelerates passage through the learning period and the faster results generate credibility. From then on, even more important for a longer-term successful performance is a series of personal and interpersonal factors, the most important of which is the ability to develop good relationships within the first year with key people in the organization (including one's boss and subordinates). These relations, and the new senior executive's adaptability, will facilitate the adjustment to further changing roles and priorities. Hitting a double moving target requires, therefore, focusing on the soft (personal and interpersonal characteristics) as well as on the hard (experience).

Let me end this section on what should be measured with some generalizations regarding trade-offs among the three characteristics of a successful hire: relevant previous experience, high emotional intelligence, and outstanding IQ. What happens when you can achieve only two out of the three? Which pair out of the three is the best combination, and which one the worst? To answer this question, I processed the research data for the success and failure profiles in a different way. Rather than looking for the most salient characteristic, I analyzed the relative frequency with which successes and failures, respectively, in all three cultures for which I had data, presented each possible pair among the three characteristics: (1) experience + emotional intelligence, (2) experience + IQ, and (3) emotional intelligence + IQ. The results are presented in Figure 8.9. The main conclusions to be drawn from this analysis are that when only two characteristics can be achieved at a high level in a hiring, then

- The most powerful combination for predicting success is relevant previous experience and a high level of emotional intelligence. Accepting a moderate level of IQ is the trade-off.
- IQ can be complemented by emotional intelligence in a favorable way when relevant previous experience is not available. In other words the second best combination is EI and IQ.
- The traditional combination of relevant experience and high IQ seems to be, again, much more a predictor of failure than of success when emotional intelligence is low.

FIGURE 8.9. TRADE-OFFS AMONG EXPERIENCE, EI, AND IQ IN RELATION TO SUCCESS AND FAILURE.

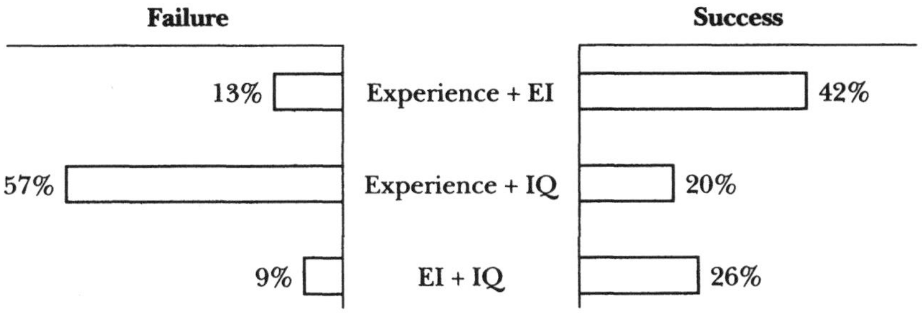

Failure		Success
13%	Experience + EI	42%
57%	Experience + IQ	20%
9%	EI + IQ	26%

Who Should Be Doing the Evaluating

A key issue often neglected is who should be the one evaluating candidates for senior hiring? In my view, researchers and academics frequently miss the point on this crucial issue or fail to communicate their findings to practitioners. Research and the resulting publications tend to focus more on evaluation techniques (even though, as mentioned, all of them are still unacceptably unreliable and invalid) than on the person applying them. However, the spread of validity across different individuals applying a given assessment technique might be higher than the spread of validity across assessment techniques. In other words, choosing the right evaluator might be even more important than applying the "best" technique.

Research on this topic is very limited. In the most recent edition of Eder and Harris's classic *The Employment Interview Handbook,* Graves and Karren (1999) review this point, and present an agenda for future research. They state that only six studies to date have examined individual differences in the validity of interviewers' judgments. However, five of these six studies provide evidence of individual differences in interviewer validity. A similar conclusion applies to individual differences in interviewers' use of information. This should be no surprise given the tremendously complex and demanding challenge of predicting a top executive's future performance in what is typically a dynamic and unique combination of managerial priorities and organizational setting. If, as discussed earlier, performance spread grows exponentially with the complexity of the task, then evaluating a senior manager should be a task at which some people are much better than others.

Despite the overall mediocre track record of top management in this critical challenge, and despite the powerful reasons for that poor record, some business leaders still stand out for their ability to hire or promote. They do it consistently well, time and again, regardless of strong pressures and political crosswinds. In this section I draw on my experience to present a few recommendations on how to choose those who should be doing senior executive evaluation.

Experience alone does not make managers good at evaluation for the reason that the feedback on that experience is neither instant nor clear because many uncontrollable factors affect the performance of the hired managers. In addition, a potentially costly error goes totally unnoticed in most organizations: the error of rejecting a highly qualified candidate. The fact that some people are much better than others at making hiring decisions, however, is not recognized by most organizations. When I ask top leaders and senior managers about creative individuals in their management teams or outstanding planners or strong team players, they immediately have the answers. When I ask who are the best people to evaluate a potential candidate, they always indicate those closest to the position or at the highest levels, regardless of their competency at evaluation. When I ask why they are the best for the job, the usual answer is "because they will suffer the consequences." However, as with any task, motivation alone is not enough for performance.

The most common practice is to involve the future manager's boss, a senior human resource executive, or both. These are not bad choices, provided that the line manager is familiar with and trained in the best evaluation practices (such as the structured, behaviorally based interview) and the HR professional is fully briefed about the organization's specific need. The first recommendation, then, is to make sure that this provision is met.

Next, because being knowledgeable about a task doesn't necessarily imply being competent at it, I advocate evaluating managers on the effectiveness of their hiring, not only for motivational purposes but also to build up a documented history of their track records. This will be useful both for each manager's own learning and for the organization's future decisions about who to assign to this critical task of evaluating. My second recommendation then should be obvious: Assign, whenever possible, those with the best track records to work on this task.

Accountability and motivation are also important for success at evaluation. Those who have a high motivation to do a good job perform consistently better at that job. This is both common sense (we try to choose well whom to marry, given the very personal important consequences), and has been properly documented by research as well (Taft, 1955; Eder and Harris, 1999b).

Finally, when we look at the most common performance characteristics of top evaluators, they show no exceptions to the general conclusion discussed earlier:

although experience and IQ are important, emotional intelligence is absolutely crucial for success. I referred previously to an article that found the main reason for the failure of CEOs to be an inability to put the right people in the right jobs (Charan & Colvin, 1999). Those CEOs were all certainly experienced in making people decisions and smart in the traditional IQ sense. They failed at those key people decisions because of a lack of emotional intelligence. Here is the full passage that I quoted the beginning of earlier:

> So how do CEOs blow it? More than any other way, by failure to put the right people in the right jobs—and the related failure to fix people problems in time. Specifically, failed CEOs are often unable to deal with a few key subordinates whose sustained poor performance deeply harms the company. What is striking, as many CEOs told us, is that they usually know there's a problem; their inner voice is telling them, but they suppress it. Those around the CEO often recognize the problem first, but he isn't seeking information from multiple sources. As one CEO says, "It was staring me in the face, but I refused to see it." *The failure is one of emotional strength* [p. 70, emphasis added].

Emotional intelligence is key not only for dealing with low performers but for all major people decisions, including hiring. Consider these roles of specific competencies:

- Accurate Self-Assessment is essential for superior hiring, in order to look at the problem with a complementary perspective and also to avoid typical evaluation biases such as the similar-to-me effect.
- Self-Control, Conscientiousness, and Trustworthiness are also necessary ingredients for an evaluator who must resist the strong time and political pressures that typically plague the whole process of hiring at the top.
- High levels of Achievement Drive and Motivation are also needed, so as to aim for true excellence in hiring.
- A large degree of Empathy, in the form of Understanding Others, is essential as well, not only for a reliable and valid evaluation but also for the final job of attracting the best candidate.
- Finally, excellent hiring also demands extremely well developed Social Skills, primarily in the form of the competencies of Influence and Communication, both for the evaluation as well as the final process of attracting the desired candidate.

Conclusion

The first sections of this chapter focused on why the entire process of senior hiring needs to be challenged. Traditional selection criteria usually ignore emotional intelligence competencies and are thus dysfunctional for the organization. The latter sections focused on a few salient points on the way to the solution, examining where the process should be strengthened, what should be measured, and who should be doing the evaluating.

Just as the need to develop a hiring process that focuses on candidates' emotional intelligence competencies is the essential message of the first part of the chapter, the employment of highly emotionally intelligent evaluators is my key recommendation for achieving that process.

PART THREE

EFFECTIVE SOCIAL AND EMOTIONAL LEARNING IN ORGANIZATIONS

CHAPTER NINE

TRAINING FOR EMOTIONAL INTELLIGENCE

A Model

Cary Cherniss
Daniel Goleman

We recently heard about a new training program in emotional intelligence. It is being used by some of the largest corporations in the world. The length can vary from one to four days, but virtually all the companies using it to date have opted for the one-day version. As many as thirty people participate at one time. There is one trainer for the program, an individual with no formal training other than an undergraduate major in psychology. And the companies that buy the program are led to expect that it will significantly improve the emotional intelligence of the participants, even though there has been no research conducted on the program's impact. (Participants do report that they "enjoy" the program and find it "useful.")

Is it possible for adults to become more socially and emotionally competent? The people who designed this training program and the companies that are using it apparently believe that it is. In fact they seem to think it is rather easy to do so. However, many business leaders are less certain. For instance, the dean of a major business school, when asked about the importance of emotional intelligence at work, enthusiastically agreed that it was crucial. But when we asked him how his school attempted to improve the emotional intelligence of MBA students, he said, "We don't do anything. I don't think that our students' emotional intelligence can be improved by the time they come here. They're already adults, and these qualities are developed early in life, primarily in the family."

So who is right—the skeptics who believe that nothing can be done to improve individuals' emotional competence after the age of fifteen or the enthusiasts who claim that they can turn emotional dunces into emotional Einsteins in an afternoon? As usual the answer lies somewhere in between. A growing body of research on emotional learning and behavioral change suggests that it is possible to help people of any age become more emotionally intelligent at work. However, the process usually requires more sustained effort than many people realize.

In the first part of this chapter, we present research on some existing training and development interventions. This research strongly suggests that it is possible to help people in the workplace become more emotionally intelligent and effective. In the second major section, we present a model for designing effective programs, based on research on social and emotional learning (SEL) in a variety of contexts.

Effective Training and Development Interventions

Because the idea of emotional intelligence (EI) is relatively new in the world of work, very few well-researched training and development interventions explicitly address it. However, if we recognize that EI consists of a number of emotional and social competencies (see Chapter Two), then we can consider any intervention that has targeted one or more of those competencies. When we redefine the subject of research this way, we discover there have been a number of relevant interventions, going back more than forty years. Here are selected examples of the research conducted on such interventions, showing that we can help employees to become more emotionally competent.

Human Relations Training

One of the earliest examples of a successful EI training effort was a "human relations" training program for supervisors developed in the 1950s at the Pennsylvania State University (Hand & Slocum, 1972). The program, which was delivered numerous times in firms throughout the northeastern United States, targeted several social and emotional competencies, including Self-Awareness, Empathy, and Leadership. The training consisted of ninety-minute sessions given once a week for twenty-eight weeks (a total of forty-two hours). The first phase, which involved primarily cognitive learning, was devoted to a discussion of managerial styles and lasted approximately nine hours. The second phase was primarily experiential, offering numerous individual and group exercises including self-ratings, an in-basket exercise, a listening exercise, and a corrective interview role-play. Thirty hours were devoted to this experiential learning. The final phase of the program, which lasted about three hours, was devoted to discussion of the motivational theories of Porter, McGregor, Herzberg, and Maslow.

Two behavioral scientists conducted a rigorous evaluation study of this program when it was implemented in a specialty steel plant in central Pennsylvania. The research design involved both a trained group of managers and a control group that did not receive training. It also involved pretraining, posttraining, and long-term follow-up measures of managerial attitudes, leadership behavior as perceived by subordinates, and performance as rated by superiors. The posttraining measures were completed ninety days following training, and the long-term follow-up assessment occurred eighteen months after the completion of training. The results indicated no differences between the two groups at the ninety-day posttraining assessment but several significant differences at the eighteen-month follow-up. By that time the trained managers had become significantly more self-aware and more sensitive to the needs of others. Their subordinates also perceived them as having improved in rapport and two-way communication. In contrast the controls did not change in their attitudes, and their subordinates perceived them as significantly less considerate than they had been at the time of the pretraining assessment. Performance ratings also improved for trained managers whereas ratings of the untrained controls declined.

Behavior Modeling Training for Supervisors

Ever since the seminal work of Goldstein and Sorcher (1974), behavior modeling has been used to train supervisory personnel in a number of settings, including health care, communications, education, and manufacturing. The method is based on Bandura's social learning theory (1977), which suggests that people learn in part by observing and then emulating models. The typical behavior modeling training program teaches social and emotional competencies such as Accurate Self-Assessment, Adaptability, Initiative and Innovation, Empathy, and Communication.

The program is divided into modules, each of which teaches specific behaviors for handling various employee problems, such as a conflict between two employees or an employee who is chronically late. A module begins with a short, didactic, content-focused presentation. Learners then view a positive model, a video of a person performing the target skills, and discuss what they have seen. The next step in the process involves extensive role-playing as the learners try to apply and practice what they have seen. After each practice round the learners receive feedback from peers and the trainer on how well they have used the skills. Whenever possible, each half-day (at the most) of training is followed by a couple of weeks back on the job. This gives participants time to practice new skills and to receive feedback on their performance and interventions. Participants then bring these experiences back to the training group to discover what may have hindered the application of their newly acquired skills. The trainer now has an opportunity to reinforce the proper application of the new skills and to show how to break down or go around any roadblocks that seem to be getting in the way (Pesuric & Byham, 1996).

Behavior modeling programs have been subjected to a number of evaluations using experimental designs, and in general the results have been impressive (Burnaska, 1976; Byham, Adams, & Kiggins, 1976; Latham & Saari, 1979; Moses & Ritchie, 1976; Russ-Eft & Zenger, 1997; Smith, 1976). For instance, in one case the program was implemented with a group of supervisors in a forest products company (Porras & Anderson, 1981). The results indicated that within two months following completion of the behavior modeling program, the trained supervisors had significantly increased their use of all five target behaviors. No comparable change occurred in a control group. Further, most of these improvements were maintained or increased during the following six months. Even more impressive, the work groups of the trained supervisors pulled ahead of the controls' work groups in several performance and productivity measures, exhibiting increased monthly production, improved recovery rates, and decreased turnover and absenteeism, for example.

In an evaluation study at a manufacturing firm, employees' lost-time accidents after their supervisors were trained dropped by 50 percent. In addition, formal grievances fell from an average of fifteen to three per year, and the value of plant production exceeded productivity goals by $250,000 (Pesuric & Byham, 1996). Thus behavior modeling is another example of a training intervention targeting EI competencies that has helped individuals to improve work performance.

Self-Management Training for Problem Employees

A program example involving self-management training shows that nonsupervisory employees also can learn how to become more emotionally competent at work. Self-management training was initially developed and used by clinical psychologists (Kanfer, 1986). The underlying premise was that individuals who need to change are more likely to succeed when they are in control of the change process. Rather than have a psychologist apply behavioral principles to bring about change in an individual, the individual is taught those principles and helped to apply them on his or her own. When people take charge of their own change program, they are more likely to feel efficacious, and their change should be more lasting than it is when they feel someone else is in charge. Self-management programs can influence a number of emotional competencies, including Accurate

Self-Assessment, Self-Confidence, Self-Control, Conscientiousness, and Achievement Drive.

One of the first workplace applications of self-management training occurred in a unionized state government agency (Frayne & Latham, 1987; Latham & Frayne, 1989). The participants were employed in a maintenance department as carpenters, painters, and electricians, and they had a record of frequent absences. The training program consisted of eight one-hour weekly group sessions, with a thirty-minute individual session for each trainee following each group session.

The first week's group session was an orientation in which the principles of self-management were explained. At the next session the trainees identified reasons for taking sick leave. Then they learned how to develop a description of the problem behaviors, identify the conditions that elicited and maintained the behaviors, and identify specific coping strategies. The third session focused on goal-setting. The long-term goal was to increase attendance in a specific amount of time, such as one or two months. The short-term goal was to identify the specific behaviors necessary to attain the long-term goal. During the fourth session the trainees learned how to monitor their own behaviors through the use of charts and diaries. In the fifth session the trainees learned how to administer self-selected rewards and punishments. Then they developed rules for assigning the rewards and punishments to specific behaviors. In the sixth session the trainees wrote a behavioral contract with themselves in which they specified in writing their goals, the time frame for achieving them, the consequences for attaining or failing to attain them, and the behaviors necessary for goal attainment. The final segment of the program (sessions seven and eight) covered maintenance. The trainer helped the participants to think about what issues might result in a relapse in absenteeism. Then they planned strategies for dealing with these situations should they occur.

During the weekly individual sessions the trainer helped the employees tailor the training to their specific concerns. Employees also had an opportunity to discuss concerns that they might be reluctant to bring up in the group.

This particular self-management program was evaluated with a pre- and post-training control group design (Frayne & Latham, 1987; Latham & Saari, 1979). Forty individuals initially volunteered for the program and met the eligibility criteria. Half were randomly assigned to receive the training, and the other half served as a control group. Outcome measures included trainee reactions, performance on a test measuring coping skills, and attendance rates. In addition to an assessment conducted three months following the training, there were follow-up assessments at six and nine months.

Results were positive for all three outcomes. First, although many trainees initially were hostile to the training (one accused the trainer of being a spy for management), no one dropped out, and at the end of the program they rated the training experience very favorably. Second, following the training the participants scored significantly better than the controls on a test of their ability to cope with problems affecting attendance. (There was no difference between the two groups on the learning test prior to the training.) Most important, the trained employees had significantly better attendance rates following the training. Prior to the training the employees in the training group clocked an average of 33.1 hours per week (out of a possible 40 hours), and the controls had a similar attendance record. Three months after the training the trainees had improved to thirty-five hours per week, whereas attendance for the controls had dropped slightly. This was a statistically significant change, and it held up over time: at six months the trainees' attendance had improved to 38.6 hours per week, and at twelve months it was 38.4 hours. Meanwhile, the attendance of the control group remained at the same lower level during the same nine months.

What It All Means

There are several other interventions that have been shown to be successful in helping managerial and nonmanagerial employees become more emotionally intelligent at work (Cherniss & Adler, 2000). Taken together, all these interventions demonstrate that it is possible for adults to develop EI competencies. Thus the question should no longer be whether organizations can teach EI skills but rather how they can teach them. We turn to this question in the next section.

Methods for Developing Specific Domains of EI

The ways of enhancing emotional intelligence are endless. In this section we briefly describe just a few of the techniques that have been used in training and development efforts to help people increase their competence in each of the five domains of EI identified by Goleman (1998b). (We are using the old five-domain model in order to provide a richer variety of options.)

Promoting Self-Awareness

There are a number of ways of helping people to a better knowledge of their internal states, preferences, resources, and intuitions, but the most effective approach employs assessment followed by feedback of the assessment results (Boyatzis, 1994). The oldest assessment method for this purpose uses psychological tests such as the Myers-Briggs Type Indicator (Myers, 1987), Minnesota Multiphasic Personality Inventory (MMPI), or FIRO-B (Campbell & Van Velsor, 1985). More recent assessment approaches have used assessment centers, in which learners are observed, evaluated, and sometimes videotaped while engaging in a simulation (Bray, 1976). Also popular is 360-degree assessment, in which a person's boss, peers, and subordinates rate that person on a variety of dimensions. In some training and development programs, ratings by family members and friends outside of work are obtained as well.

Two other methods are used primarily in coaching interventions. The first is *self-monitoring* (Peterson, 1996), in which learners gain insight by "observing" themselves in various ways. For instance, they can set aside time each day to reflect on their feelings and actions. Writing their reflections in a log or diary can enhance the effect. Another approach they can use is to videotape or audiotape themselves in different situations and then study the tapes. The other assessment method employed in coaching is *in-depth interviewing.* The interviewer helps the learner develop Self-Awareness by acting like a mirror and offering interpretations about the learner's thoughts and actions.

The effectiveness of Self-Awareness interventions based on assessment depends on two factors. The first is the validity and credibility of the assessment method. The second is the quality of the feedback process. Both the learner and the trainer (or coach) should have confidence that the assessment data are valid. In addition, the learner should have ample opportunity to digest, integrate, and reflect on the assessment during the feedback process. Providing too much data in too short a period of time can weaken the impact of this approach. The impact will also be diluted if the learner does not feel safe because of the particular person who is providing the feedback or the setting in which it occurs.

One other strategy for increasing Self-Awareness is *meditation.* Many different types of meditation have been taught that can be useful for helping people become more aware of how their emotions affect their behavior. One of the more effective ones is *mindfulness meditation,* which is designed specifically to help people become more aware of their inner experience (Kabat-Zinn, 1990).

Promoting Self-Regulation

Meditation also can be useful in helping people manage their internal states. Methods commonly employed in stress management can be useful as well. For instance, cognitive approaches to Self-Regulation help people learn to modify the beliefs and ideas that trigger undesirable emotional responses (Meichenbaum, 1985).

A good example of using these approaches to develop Self-Regulation can be found in certain anger management programs. In one such program the participants first learn how to become more aware of thoughts and feelings by jotting down their cynical or hostile thoughts as they notice them. Then they learn two techniques for controlling such thoughts: thought-stopping and deliberately substituting reasonable thoughts for cynical, hostile ones during trying situations. Finally, the participants learn ways to empathize with or take the perspective of the other person (Williams & Williams, 1997).

One other approach to promoting Self-Regulation is counterconditioning, in which the individual repeatedly engages in the behaviors that have proved most problematic (Prochaska, 1999). Consider the individual who became anxious when talking with his boss or other authority figures and who thus avoided contact with them as much as possible. With the help of a training program in emotional competence, he began to regularly seek out opportunities to have conversations with his boss. After doing so for about two months, he found that most of the anxiety had dissipated and he was conversing with his boss much more often.

Promoting Self-Motivation

Many of the methods that work for Self-Regulation can also help people with Self-Motivation—the emotional tendencies that facilitate reaching goals. For instance, the same cognitive strategies that help people to modify beliefs contributing to disruptive anxiety can be used to help people persist in the face of discouraging setbacks (Seligman, 1991). Another useful method is the self-management training that we described in the previous section. Here the participants learn how to direct their behavior toward desired goals by using behavioral techniques such as self-monitoring, goal-setting, self-reinforcement, and written contracts (Frayne & Geringer, 2000).

Another method for promoting Self-Motivation is *achievement motivation training,* developed by David McClelland and his colleagues (Aronoff & Litwin, 1971; Miron & McClelland, 1979). In this program learners develop greater Achievement Drive by engaging in a number of different exercises. Initially participants join in small-group discussions to analyze situations in which achievement motivation has been a significant factor. Next the participants become more aware of their current level of achievement motivation by writing stories and then scoring the level of achievement motivation reflected in the stories. They also participate in simulations involving achievement motivation. The participants next practice *achievement thinking* by writing a new set of stories, now trying to saturate them with achievement thinking. Then the participants do the same with a set of business situations. In the last part of the program, participants develop a personal action plan, and faculty members help them identify techniques they can used to increase achievement motivation.

Promoting Empathy

Many of the most commonly used methods for helping people become more aware of others' feelings, needs, and concerns are labeled *sensitivity training*. Unfortunately, these well-meaning efforts are often poorly designed and executed. More effective approaches directly target empathy, the underlying competency. People are shown pictures of actors expressing different emotions, and they try to understand what emotions the actors are expressing. The task becomes gradually harder as different parts of each actor's face are obscured (Rosenthal, 1977).

Interviewing people whose perspectives differ from one's own can also be an effective method for promoting empathy when it is accompanied by well-designed opportunities for reflection. An example is a technique used as part of a project to redesign the Lincoln Continental automobile (Goleman, 1998b). Instead of relying solely on market research data, project engineers spent a week just talking to present owners of Continentals and listening carefully to what they said about the car. They were encouraged to listen especially for people's underlying emotional reactions. The interviews were videotaped, and as the engineers looked at the tapes together, they tried to get in touch with the aspects of the driving experience that created the strongest emotional reactions in the car owners.

Promoting Social Skills

Behavior modeling, described in a previous section, is a particularly effective strategy for helping people develop their ability to induce desirable responses in others (Goldstein & Sorcher, 1974; Latham & Saari, 1979). In this approach the learners first view and discuss a model that uses the skills in a simulation. Next the learners practice using the skills themselves in role-plays, receiving feedback on their performances. Finally, they try out the skills on the job and then return to discuss their experiences and get help in dealing with any problems they encountered.

There are of course other useful methods for developing Social Skills. In fact, because Social Skills build on the other domains of emotional intelligence, all the other techniques we have described can play a useful role in Social Skills training programs.

Doing It Right: The Ingredients of Effective Intervention

The effectiveness of any EI development effort depends not only on the techniques used but also on their design and implementation. A careful analysis of the most effective models can reveal some of the ingredients of effective implementation.

Even more useful is systematic research on the underlying processes of social and emotional learning. Unfortunately, researchers in the training and development field have not focused particularly on SEL. As Tannenbaum and Yukl (1992) note, those who study training "have tended to consider all training the same, without regard to the purpose of the training or the type of learning involved" (p. 401). Where, then, can organizations find relevant research on the ingredients necessary for effective interventions?

We believe there are a number of applicable sources. A particularly rich source of insight is research on psychotherapy and behavioral change. At first glance such research might seem of dubious relevance. After all, there is a big difference between psychotherapy (or counseling) and training and development. Psychotherapy is designed to help individuals who are experiencing significant personal and interpersonal distress. It usually begins with an individual who has an identified problem, and the goal is to eliminate the problem or reduce its severity. Training and development programs—even those that target emotional competence—are usually designed for individuals who are already functioning at a relatively high level and wish to be even more effective.

Despite such obvious differences, there is also an important similarity between psychotherapy, counseling, and training and development efforts directed at aspects of emotional intelligence: all involve social and emotional learning. Thus there is reason to believe that the underlying processes of change will be very similar, if not identical in each case. Furthermore, during the last three decades there has been a significant amount of research on the underlying processes of change in psychotherapy and counseling. We believe that the results of this research, along with some of the research in training and development, can point to the most important ingredients for success in social and emotional learning interventions.

A Model of EI

We have developed an action model based on the research on SEL (see Figure 9.1). This model draws in part from the work of Prochaska (1999). Prochaska's research has revealed that people go through several stages before they are ready to engage in meaningful change efforts. In the *precontemplation* stage, they have no interest at all in change and no plans. In the next stage, which Prochaska refers to as *contemplation*, the individuals are aware of some possible benefits of SEL, but they are not yet sure that it is both desirable and possible for them to work on improving their own emotional competence. They are no longer actively resistant, but they are also not convinced that they should embark on a change effort. Only in the third stage, *preparation*, do people decide that they will undertake a program of personal change and make specific plans for doing so.

FIGURE 9.1 THE OPTIMAL PROCESS FOR PROMOTING EI IN WORK ORGANIZATIONS.

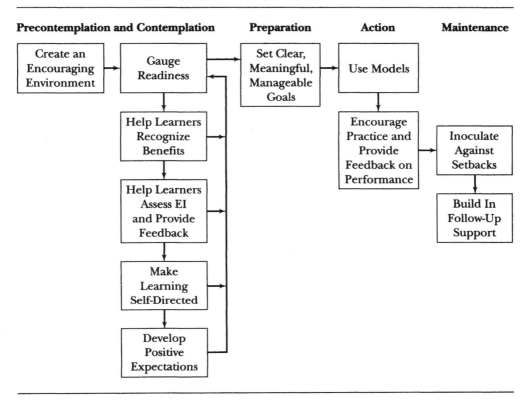

Research on the common factors that contribute to positive change in all types of therapy and counseling has revealed that the client's engagement in treatment is probably the single most important factor in change (Asay & Lambert, 1999; Bachelor & Horvath, 1999; Kolb, Beutler, Davis, Crago, & Shanfield, 1985). Unfortunately, many people who enter change programs are not sufficiently motivated. Prochaska (1999) found that only about 20 percent of the people who need to change are motivated to do so. In the workplace, even people who come to a workshop or participate in a coaching intervention may not be ready to engage in sustained SEL. For example, in one companywide EI training program, many of the participants came because they were part of a regional management team and the regional vice president had decided that everyone would participate. Other participants were new managers, and EI training was a required part of new manager development. Still other participants entered the program because their bosses told them it would be good for them. Moreover, even people who freely choose to participate in SEL programs may be ambivalent about actively engaging in personal change.

Because many individuals who participate in SEL efforts may be resistant or ambivalent, program designers, trainers, and coaches need to devote more attention to strategies for increasing people's motivation and engagement in the change process. Most SEL programs are designed for people who are motivated when they enter the program; they arrive ready to take action to change their behavior in some way. More attention needs to be devoted to monitoring learners' motivation and to building in processes that generate the level of sustained motivation and effort necessary for successful change. The first two stages of the action model contain several such processes.

The optimal change process, as outlined in the model, begins with an appropriate environment. Those who wish to promote EI in organizations need to make sure that the environment will support such efforts. If it won't, then the first step is to create a more encouraging environment. The next task is to gauge the readiness of the learners. If they already have the motivation necessary for sustained effort, then they are ready to set goals. If they are not ready, the model suggests several ways in which one can help learners develop the motivation necessary to move into the preparation phase: one can help learners recognize the benefits of SEL, assess learners' EI and then give them the results, put them in control of the process, and develop their positive expectations for change. After any attempt to increase learners' commitment to change, one needs to gauge their readiness again. When they are ready to move into the preparation phase, a useful process is to help them set specific and challenging but manageable goals for change. Completion of this goal-setting leads the learners into the action phase. At the beginning of this phase the learners need to develop a clear picture of the competencies they wish to develop. Models can be useful in this step. Next, they need to practice the new skills often and receive feedback on their performance. Finally, the learners move into the maintenance phase by preparing for the inevitable setbacks that will occur as they apply what they have learned back in the work environment. Building various kinds of supports into the natural environment also helps learners maintain their changes. We now consider each step of the model in more detail.

1. Create an Encouraging Environment

SEL does not occur in a vacuum. The motivation of the learners is strongly influenced by the social environment of the organization. Everything else that program designers, trainers, or coaches might do will be unconvincing if the environment does not support SEL (Asay & Lambert, 1999).

Leadership sets the tone. Learners look to the organization's leadership to see how much SEL is valued. Actions here speak louder than words. When an EI training program was implemented in two different companies, the company presidents endorsed it in both cases. However, in the first company the president actively participated in the program along with his top managers. Between sessions, he continually referred to ideas covered in the program during meetings with his managers, and he made a visible effort to apply what they all had learned. He also encouraged and rewarded his managers for doing the same. In the second company the president gave a brief introduction to the participants at the beginning of the first session of the program and then left. Even though it was the same program delivered by the same trainer, the results in the two companies were dramatically different. The program was highly successful when the president actively participated, but it was a flop when the president gave it only lip service. Furthermore, as important as leadership is, leaders cannot create the right environment alone. Others in the organization also need to promote an environment that encourages SEL. For example, in the successful company the director of training also assisted by continually checking, prompting, encouraging, and supporting the participants as they applied what they learned.

Research supports the proposition that the organizational environment is key, and it points to specific ways in which people in an organization can create an encouraging environment. For example, Baldwin and Magjuka (1991) found that trainees in a manufacturing firm reported greater intention to apply what they were to learn when they received program information prior to the program, recognized that they would be held accountable by their supervisors for using what they learned, and believed that the program was mandatory. Other research has shown that in organizations where senior management has demonstrated a real commitment to learning by providing intensive and recurrent training, employees show a greater acceptance of it. Also important is the extent to which participants receive follow-ups to see whether they are applying what they have learned (Helmreich & Foushee, 1993).

The emotional competence program at American Express Financial Advisors (AEFA) (see the case study in Chapter Twelve) provides a good example of using intensive and recurrent training to create a culture supportive of SEL. An initial program was offered to veteran financial advisors. It was designed to help them sell more life insurance products by improving their abilities to cope with the emotional strains associated with the selling process. After the first program proved successful, program staff developed a second version for the advisors' regional managers, designed in part to make them *emotional coaches*. Program staff then went even further by encouraging the regional management teams to go through the training together. Eventually, several versions of the program were offered as a regular part of the training and development process for new managers, new advisors, and corporate office management groups.

The learning environment also influences learners' motivation. Particularly crucial is whether the environment feels safe (Boyatzis, Cowen, & Kolb, 1995; Kolb & Boyatzis, 1970a). Many people are likely to approach SEL with a certain amount of apprehension. They are concerned about looking weak or foolish. If the learning environment is not perceived as safe, most learners will not be motivated to engage in SEL. Effective programs include components designed to help learners feel safe. In a program designed to help airline cockpit crews to work more effectively as teams, the crew members develop skills by participating in simulated missions. The simulations are videotaped, and the crew members then observe themselves interacting. The trainers make this learning environment feel safer by erasing the videotapes after each session (Gregorich & Wilhelm, 1993).

An especially important part of the learning environment is the trainer or coach. Research on training and development in the workplace has largely ignored the role of the trainer—particularly the personal characteristics of trainers (Goldstein, 1993). However, research on psychotherapy and counseling has devoted considerable attention to therapist qualities and the relationship between the therapist and the client (Asay & Lambert, 1999). Therapists who are caring, empathic, warm, and accepting create safe learning environments for clients and provide positive models for SEL. These personal qualities (which are aspects of emotional intelligence) are far more important in influencing outcomes than are differences between therapists in professional training or experience (Tallman & Bohart, 1999). Furthermore, this effect has been found in group therapy as well as individual treatment (Bachelor & Horvath, 1999). The research also suggests that whereas the specific techniques and strategies that the therapist or counselor might use in treatment account for about 15 percent of the variance in outcomes, the therapist-client relationship accounts for as much as 30 percent of the variance (Lambert, 1992). Also, client ratings of therapists predict outcomes better than objective ratings do (Asay & Lambert, 1999). Thus the relationship between the therapist and the client seems to be key.

The most effective SEL programs devote considerable attention to the selection, training, and ongoing monitoring of the trainer or coach. The JOBS program, which helps unemployed workers develop the emotional and social competencies necessary to return quickly to the workforce, selects its trainers from the ranks of the unemployed and has applicants "audition" by conducting a brief training session as part of the job interview (Caplan, Vinokur, & Price, 1996). The fact that the trainers themselves have been unemployed gives them credibility and makes for a more positive, trusting relationship between trainer and learners.

In addition to having the personal qualities that create positive relationships, effective trainers engage in specific actions that contribute to a positive learning environment. In AEFA's emotional competence program the trainer often telephones participants before the program begins to find out what they hope to get out of it and whether they have any concerns. In the JOBS program, trainers foster a positive relationship and learning environment through moderate self-disclosure (Caplan et al., 1996). Effective trainers also monitor the emotional atmosphere during the training process by paying attention to their own feelings and those of the participants, and they address problems directly when they occur (Bachelor & Horvath, 1999). In all these ways the trainer works to make the learning environment safe and encouraging.

2. Gauge Readiness

If the environment is supportive of SEL, the next task is to gauge the motivational level of the learners. As noted, many people who participate in SEL programs are not yet ready to engage in active change efforts. If trainers or coaches use intervention strategies more appropriate for the action phase than for the precontemplation or contemplation phases, they can actually increase the participants' resistance (Prochaska, 1999). So the first step is to determine the participants' phase. If they are in the preparation phase, they are ready to move on to the action phase of the model. However, if they are still in the precontemplation or contemplation phases, then they require interventions designed to increase their motivation for change. The following processes are most appropriate for individuals who are in this latter group.

Help Learners Recognize EI benefits. When people are not yet ready for change, they view the costs of change (time, effort, potential embarrassment) as greater than the benefits (Prochaska, 1999). Thus appropriate intervention strategies for people in the precontemplation or contemplation phases involve helping them realistically assess the benefits and costs of change. One such strategy is educational: the trainer provides data, information, and examples that show learners that EI competencies can help them to achieve greater satisfaction in their work and in the rest of their lives and also that such competencies can be taught and learned.

Reluctant learners can often become more motivated if they see a connection between SEL and important performance issues. In AEFA's emotional competence program, the company did research that showed a clear connection between superior sales performance and a high level of emotional competence. At the beginning of the training program, the trainers presented these research results to the participants. The message in effect was, "If you want to be more successful in your job, here is how to do it." Participants were also helped to recognize the relevance of emotional competence through an exercise in which they broke into groups of three and thought together about the ways emotions influence the workplace. Within half an hour many of the skeptical participants discovered for themselves—and helped convince others—that emotional competence is valuable. Prochaska (1999) has suggested a similar though more directive technique. He asks people who are not yet ready to change to identify all the benefits of changing. Typically they list four or five. Then he tells them there are many more benefits and challenges them to increase the number. Usually they come up with many more reasons to change, which helps them to move to a higher stage of readiness.

Another technique that helps participants see the benefits of SEL has been used with male executives at a brokerage firm who participated in a program on how to be more effective mentors to midlevel women managers. Before the first session the trainers interviewed each participant, asking him about current mentoring practices, the factors most important in developing senior-level executives, and the experiences that had led to success for people he knew. They also asked him to identify the qualities of his own mentors. During the first session the trainers presented the interview results to the participants, and the group used them to develop a set of best practices for mentoring. Then, in an assignment for the second session, each participant interviewed a minority employee to learn more about his or her experience in the firm.

Information that generates emotional arousal can be particularly effective in motivating a person to actively engage in SEL (Prochaska, 1999). Fear, inspiration, guilt, and hope cannot by themselves bring about lasting changes in emotional intelligence, but they can generate the motivation and enthusiasm necessary for the person to move from contemplation to preparation and action. Training and coaching activities that generate this kind of emotional response can be especially useful with those hardest to persuade that SEL is desirable for them.

Help Learners Assess Their Emotional and Social Competence and Provide Feedback.
Even after learners recognize the value of social and emotional competencies, they may still not be convinced that they need to work on these competencies until they see how they measure up on them. There are a number of methods for assessing emotional competence for development purposes, including self-monitoring and observation, psychological tests, 360-degree assessments, simulations and assessment centers, and interviews. Different learners find different sources of assessment most credible and compelling. For one person it might be the

boss's opinion of her performance that counts; for another person it might be peer or subordinate views. One learner might find the results of a psychological test most persuasive; another might be swayed by self-observation and monitoring. Sometimes learners need to receive the same message about their competencies from multiple sources before they feel convinced that they should engage in SEL.

The way in which assessment information is provided to the learner is as important as the sources of the information. We have already discussed how crucial it is that the learning environment feel safe. This is especially true when it comes to receiving assessment feedback. Learners will tend to discount or ignore feedback if they are anxious about its consequences. Several studies have found that negative feedback is often rejected. Self-enhancing biases and defense mechanisms lead people to blame others for negative feedback (Born & Mathieu, 1996; Ilgen, Fisher, & Taylor, 1979). Nevertheless, negative feedback is not always detrimental. Although repeated negative feedback often results in decreased effort, lowered goals, and rejection of the feedback, initial negative feedback tends to produce increases in effort (Nease, Mudgett, & Quinones, 1999). Feedback thus should be provided skillfully by a neutral, trusted source and with safeguards built into the process.

Managerial Assessment and Development, a course in the Weatherhead School of Business MBA program, provides an especially good model of assessment and feedback. All first-year MBA students are required to take the course. They spend the first three weeks on assessment exercises, including a learning skills profile, behavioral event interview, group discussion exercise, oral presentation exercise, and values inventory. The next seven weeks are devoted to feedback and reflection. Then the students spend the last four weeks on developing personal learning plans (Boyatzis, 1996; Boyatzis, Cowen, & Kolb, 1995). By the time the students reach the personal action plan stage, they have developed considerable motivation for change, largely as a result of the quality and quantity of assessment data and the careful way in which the course instructors help them to reflect on the results.

Make Learning Self-Directed. Another way to increase learner motivation and commitment to change is by making the learning process self-directed (see Chapter Ten for further detail). Research on psychotherapy and other methods of producing behavioral change suggests that change is more likely to be long lasting in individuals who attribute the changes to their own efforts, and the same is likely to be true for social and emotional learning in the workplace (Lambert & Bergin, 1994). One way to make SEL self-directed is to offer participants more than one learning option, asking them to choose the one they think would be most effective for them (Prochaska, 1999). Change efforts are also likely to be more effective when they teach skills learners can use to achieve outcomes that *they* value. For instance, in SEL programs for airline cockpit crews, participants show a greater motivation for learning when the focus is on issues of particular interest to them, such as "how to get a team off to a good start, how to deal with a change of membership in the cockpit, . . . or how to address conflicts among members constructively" (Wiener, Kanki, & Helmreich, 1993, p. 51).

Develop Positive Expectations for Success. Wanting to change is necessary but not sufficient. Learners also need to believe that it is possible for them to make the changes necessary to achieve the desired outcomes—a phenomenon referred to as *self-efficacy* (Bandura, Adams, & Beyer, 1977; Bandura & Cervone, 1983). It is not enough to recognize that one should change and that there is a way to do it. One also must believe that one has the skills to be successful (Caplan et al., 1996). Research on psychotherapy suggests that after extratherapeutic and relationship factors, hope and expectancy account for the greatest variance in outcomes—about 15 percent, according to Lambert (1992). Expectancy is so powerful that it produces its own effect—the well-known placebo effect. One study of psychotherapy outcomes, for example, found that not only was the average client going through psychotherapy better off than 79 percent of no-treatment controls but the average client going through a placebo treatment condition was also better off than 66 percent of the no-treatment controls (Asay & Lambert, 1999). It is likely that one would find a similar pattern for SEL interventions in the workplace. Frank and Frank (1991) identified four factors that contribute to positive expectancies in psychotherapy (and other types of SEL): (1) an emotionally charged, confiding relationship with a helper or guide who is both hopeful and committed to help; (2) a therapeutic or learning setting that sends the message that the client can expect successful change; (3) a compelling "myth" or therapeutic rationale explaining both why the client is experiencing his or her problems and why a particular form of treatment will help; and (4) therapeutic ritual—that is, the actual procedures used by a therapist.

Self-efficacy can be enhanced in several ways. The most effective is successful action (Bandura & Cervone, 1983). People are most likely to believe they can be successful when they *are* successful. In therapy this experience of success can be accomplished by encouraging the individual to try a very small, manageable step toward the goal. An example is a smoking cessation program in which skeptical participants were urged to take a small step like delaying their first cigarette in the morning for thirty minutes. In many cases success in achieving this behavior increased their self-efficacy enough that they became committed to a systematic program for quitting altogether (Prochaska, 1999).

3. Help Learners Set Clear, Meaningful, Manageable Goals

Setting goals is the primary task of the preparation phase. When a learner is ready to embark on a program of change, setting goals can greatly enhance motivation and help the individual sustain that motivation for an extended period of time (Locke & Latham, 1990). For instance, Kolb, Winter, and Berlew (1968) found that performance in a training program improved when participants set explicit goals for change. The motivating power of such goals can be enhanced through the processes of declaring them publicly and putting them in writing (Heatherton & Nichols, 1994; Prochaska, 1999).

Making the goals specific and manageable is especially important. In general, specific goals are more effective than vague ones in helping people sustain motivation (Locke & Latham, 1990). For example, a student in Managerial Assessment and Development at Weatherhead initially formulated the goal of developing greater self-confidence. Because achieving this goal as stated could be overwhelming, the faculty helped him break it down into manageable steps. First, he came up with a more specific goal of developing the self-confidence necessary for finding a part-time job. Then he broke that goal into a series of manageable steps, beginning with updating his résumé, then moving on to the more challenging goal of contacting people he knew to ask them about jobs, and finally calling potential employers (Boyatzis, Cowen, & Kolb, 1995). The student successfully achieved all of these goals, and his self-confidence increased as a result. If he had not set goals or if the goals had been too difficult, the process might have been aborted.

4. Use Models of Desired Skills

The first task in the action stage is to make sure that learners are clear about what the competencies are and how to do them (Spencer & Spencer, 1993). Giving learners opportunities to observe live models of the skills to be learned can be very helpful. In any kind of learning it is important that the learners be clear about what it is that needs to be learned. In SEL, one cannot rely on words alone to clarify what needs to be learned because the emotional areas of the brain do not use ideas and words. Models provide a way of directly accessing these older parts of the brain that play a crucial role in emotional intelligence (Goleman, 1998b).

The value of modeling has been illustrated in two studies involving medical personnel. In the first, medical residents were taught how to communicate effectively with patients about HIV. One group was taught via a lecture and the other was shown a model. The group that watched the model did better in both knowledge and performance scores (Falvo, Smaga, Brenner, & Tippy, 1991). In the second study, medical students in one group were taught interviewing skills by seeing a videotaped model. A second group viewed a model and also viewed and critiqued their own interviews. A third group viewed and critiqued only their own interviews. The students' interpersonal skills were evaluated through simulations before and after the training. The researchers found that just viewing a model was as effective as viewing a model plus viewing and critiquing one's own behavior. Critiquing one's own behavior without first seeing a model was less effective, although better than no training at all (Mason, Barkley, Kappelman, Carter, & Beachy, 1988).

5. Encourage Practice of New Skills and Provide Feedback on Performance

If the critical tasks for the learner during the first phase involve building sufficient motivation, the most critical task during the second phase involves sustained effort. A common mistake made in planning SEL programs is to think that individuals can increase their emotional competence by participating in relatively brief seminars or workshops or by meeting with a coach for just two or three sessions. Such activities can be helpful but only if they are part of a larger development effort that stretches out over a period of months and that involves active practice of new behaviors by the learner in a variety of situations.

Practice and repetition are valuable in any type of learning but particularly important in SEL because of the parts of the brain involved (Edelman, 1987). Cognitive learning, such as occurs in learning how to create a business plan, involves primarily the neocortex, the part of the brain that uses words and ideas. Such learning usually requires fitting new data and ideas into existing frameworks of association and understanding. At the level of the brain, this means the development of new neural pathways with little interference from older and more established pathways.

Social and emotional learning, such as learning to become more positively assertive with one's boss and peers or more empathic toward one's subordinates, is different. Although the neocortex is still involved, other areas of the brain also come into play. The circuitry in the amygdala and between the amygdala and prefrontal lobes is implicated as well. This is a much older part of the brain, a part that does not process words and ideas. It is an area of the brain that developed before human beings had words or ideas. The only way to train this older part of the brain is through repeated action. Also, unlike much technical training, SEL usually involves unlearning (extinguishing) old patterns of thought, feeling, and action along with developing or strengthening new patterns. This means that at the level of the brain, old neural connections must be weakened and new neural connections, supporting the new repertoire, strengthened. This change requires frequent practice, occurring over a period of months; for only after lengthy practice do the new connections and associated behaviors become the brain's default option—its automatic response even in stressful and demanding situations.

Thus not only is practice important but it should occur repeatedly over an extended period of time. One of the better established laws of learning is that distributed practice is superior to massed practice. Although this law applies to all types of learning, it is particularly true for learning that involves the older parts of the brain. A recent meta-analysis of research on the distributed practice effect found that learners employing such practice outperformed those employing massed practice by almost half a standard deviation (Donovan & Radosevich, 1999). The effect was greatest for simple motor tasks; more complex verbal tasks were less affected. SEL is different from motor learning, but it involves areas of the brain that are close to the motor centers and similar in evolutionary age. Thus it is highly likely that distributed practice is especially useful for SEL as well.

Participants in SEL programs may intuitively recognize the importance of repeated practice for effective learning. For instance, a participant in the American Express emotional competence training program found that after the first two days of training he understood the concepts and could use the skills, but as he said on his course evaluation form, "it still was not something that has become automatic." He did not have a problem using his new skills on the job, but they had not become part of his modus operandi. And he was not using them as often as he might. Another participant echoed this sentiment, stating that the skill "has to be second nature for [people] to use it well. That's why there needs to be repetition."

Finally, as learners practice new skills, they need feedback on their performance. Such feedback provides valuable information that helps the learner gradually improve. It also can be reinforcing, helping the learner remain motivated during the action stage (Goldstein, 1993; Komaki, Collins, & Penn, 1982).

Behavior modeling programs provide an especially good example of the use of the three activities of modeling, practice, and feedback. As we noted, the most effective programs begin by showing the learners a model that depicts the successful application of the social and emotional skills to be learned. Then the learners practice those skills in role-play situations. Following each role-play practice, the learners receive feedback from the other participants and the instructor. The instructor sets the tone by providing feedback in a way that enhances self-confidence—pointing out specifically each positive thing that the learner did and suggesting how she can make her performance even stronger next time. Finally, the learners practice the new skills repeatedly until they reach a high level of mastery and confidence.

6. Inoculate Learners Against Setbacks

Once the learners have mastered the new competencies in the training setting, they are ready to apply what they have learned in the work environment. Unfortunately, things do not always go smoothly in this transition. Research on maintenance following behavioral change efforts suggests that a large percentage of individuals gradually stop using their new skills (Marlatt & Gordon, 1985). Although several factors contribute to such relapses, an especially important one is the way in which the individual responds to barriers and setbacks. In a typical scenario, the learner begins to apply new ways of thinking and acting in the work setting. Although the new behaviors are sometimes successful, at other times situations don't go according to plan. Perhaps the manager who is trying to curb his temper blows up during a staff meeting. Or perhaps he is successful in curbing his temper, but the anticipated positive results do not seem to occur right away. He becomes discouraged and begins to question whether he can really change or whether the change will result in the hoped-for benefits. In a short time he stops trying.

One way to deal with this problem is to prepare learners for it ahead of time. One technique, referred to as *relapse prevention*, helps inoculate learners against relapse by having them anticipate setbacks and consider effective ways of responding to them (Marlatt & Gordon, 1985; Marx, 1982). For instance, in the successful JOBS program, participants are encouraged to identify ahead of time everything that might go wrong when they use what they have learned in actual situations. Then they identify how they might think and feel when things do go wrong. Finally, they develop and rehearse strategies that they can use to handle such setbacks positively (Caplan et al., 1996). Dozens of studies have documented the effectiveness of relapse prevention in behavioral change efforts (Marlatt & Gordon, 1985). Although most of these studies have involved clients in psychotherapy, a few studies have shown that this technique can also be effective in workplace SEL programs (Gist, Bavetta, & Stevens, 1990; Gist, Stevens, & Bavetta, 1991; Tziner, Haccoun, & Kadish, 1991).

7. Build In Follow-Up Support

Even relapse prevention training will not be enough to help people transfer and maintain the skills they have learned unless the natural organizational environment encourages and supports their efforts. We already have noted that the organizational culture needs to support the desired change at the outset of training. In addition, behavioral psychology suggests that *stimulus control* and *contingency management* can be used to help people maintain their newly developed patterns of thought and action. Stimulus control involves "modifying the environment to increase cues that prompt" the desired responses (Prochaska, 1999, p. 243). These cues can be physical or social, and they can be provided by the learners themselves or by others. Contingency management involves setting up a system of rewards and punishments that continually encourages the learner to use the new skills.

For instance, following cockpit resource management training, encouragement and support is provided by check pilots who observe crews during flights and then give them feedback on how well they are using the skills. The crews also return periodically for additional booster sessions and simulator practice (Gregorich & Wilhelm, 1993). Support groups can be particularly effective as a source of follow-up encouragement. As Spencer and Spencer (1993) note, "Learning is better maintained if, after training, learners receive support and coaching from . . . a 'reinforcing reference group' of fellow learners who can support and encourage each other to use the new competency. Ideally training gives the learner membership in a prestigious new group that speaks a new common language, shares new values, and is committed to keeping members' learning alive" (p. 288). Even if only one other person—a coach, mentor, or buddy—is offering support, that can be enough to supply the encouragement necessary for learners to continue to apply what they have learned (Kram, 1996). In one study learners were paired up with one other person who reminded them to use what they had learned and provided ongoing reinforcement for doing so. Results indicated that pairing the learners in this way led to greater transfer of training (Flemming & Sulzer-Azeroff, 1990). Prompts and reinforcement from a learner's supervisor are particularly effective (Baldwin & Ford, 1988; Noe & Schmitt, 1986). In one study, participants in a management training program were more likely to apply what they had learned when, following the training, their supervisors reminded them of their goals and prodded them to use their skills (Rouillier & Goldstein, 1991). Unfortunately, surveys of training and development efforts in industry suggest that such follow-up is rare (Saari, Johnson, McLaughlin, & Zimmerle, 1988).

Though social support is invaluable, learners can provide prompts and cues for themselves. In fact, in some instances, self-reinforcement has been more effective than social reinforcement for long-term maintenance (Prochaska, 1999). An example of how such a strategy might be used in training comes from the evaluation of a stress management program. The researchers found that adding a self-management component at the end of each session significantly improved the program's impact on participants' learning, blood pressure, somatic symptoms, and anxiety. It also reduced posttraining decay over the next six months. The self-management training showed the learners how to monitor their use of the skills they learned and how to reinforce themselves in using the skills.

Applying the Model: The Problem of Resources

The model we have presented can be a guide for those who wish to develop effective social and emotional learning programs in the workplace. One problem with the model, however, is that it can be expensive to follow. For example, the original design for AEFA's emotional competence program would have conformed to the model. There would have been one-on-one coaching for each participant as well as the group sessions, and practice would have been distributed by having one session each week for twelve weeks, with each session lasting one to two hours. Follow-up would consist of three additional meetings every other week and then one meeting per month for two months. Altogether the program would stretch out over eight months. Unfortunately, this program would have been so expensive that the company would not support it. The scaled-back version eventually implemented offered five days of training provided in two blocks separated by about two months, with no follow-ups and no individual coaching. Research showed that the program was still effective, but even in the scaled-back version it was the most expensive training program offered in the company. So the company decided to save more money by cutting back further. A version offered to new advisors consisted of just eight hours of training, and individuals with no special training in emotional intelligence competencies delivered it.

It would be easy to condemn the company for offering such a diluted version of the program, but such a response would not effectively address the resource problem. As long as practitioners think in terms of interventions that are very costly, it is unlikely that many efforts will incorporate all the ingredients necessary for success. The result will be failure and disillusionment. More work is necessary in order to find ways to offer high-quality SEL more economically. One approach is to combine SEL with other types of training offered in organizations. At AEFA, for example, far more money is spent on technical training than on emotional competence training. Some of the technical training is designed to teach advisors how to get new clients and how to sell and market to clients. If emotional competence training could be combined with these other efforts, there would be more resources available for it. Also people throughout the company would be hearing the same message and using the same skills in different contexts, which would facilitate transfer and maintenance. This solution is only one of many that could be used to make SEL more economically feasible. Doing so would make it easier for SEL programs to adhere to the model for effective intervention.

Conclusion: The Need for Research

In this chapter we have argued that theorists and practitioners already know a great deal about promoting emotional intelligence in organizations. Well-documented examples of effective intervention strategies and a large body of research on SEL point to guidelines for practice. However, such work represents only a beginning. Researchers need to continue to evaluate promising new interventions for increasing EI competencies. They also need to focus on theory-driven research that will identify the aspects of the model that are necessary and sufficient for meaningful change to occur. We believe that only a strong research base will prevent applied work in emotional intelligence from becoming just another short-lived fad.

CHAPTER TEN

HOW AND WHY INDIVIDUALS ARE ABLE TO DEVELOP EMOTIONAL INTELLIGENCE

Richard E. Boyatzis

Beyond the benefit of understanding oneself, the appeal of the concept of emotional intelligence is the hope for development. Many researchers of this concept contend that a person can develop the characteristics that constitute emotional intelligence. But few have taken the time to rigorously evaluate change efforts. This chapter presents a model of individual change that draws on years of research on individuals' development of the sets of characteristics now called emotional intelligence. This evidence offers hope that emotional intelligence competencies can be developed. It has emerged from multiple sources, but three in particular: first, the research of David McClelland, David Winter, and their colleagues from the 1960s and 1970s on developing achievement and power motivation; second, the work of David Kolb and his colleagues from the 1960s and early 1970s on self-directed behavioral change; third, the work of numerous doctoral students and my colleagues at the Weatherhead School of Management at Case Western Reserve University in the late 1980s and throughout the 1990s in competency development. This research is reviewed as evidence of a model, or theory, of individual, sustainable change in emotional intelligence.

Emotional Intelligence Can Be Developed

In this chapter, as in all the chapters in this volume, emotional intelligence is defined as the composite set of capabilities that enables a person to manage herself and others (Goleman, 1995a, 1998b). This definition can be made more accurate if we add that the frequency with which a person demonstrates or uses the constituent capabilities, or competencies, inherent in emotional intelligence determines the ways in which she deals with herself, her life and work, and others (Boyatzis, Goleman, & Rhee, 2000). Although the specific labels and conceptualizations of these competencies may vary, they address (1) Self-Awareness, including Emotional Self-Awareness, Accurate Self-Assessment, and Self-Confidence; (2) Self-Management, including Achievement Orientation, Adaptability, Initiative, Trustworthiness, Conscientiousness, and Self-Control; (3) Social Awareness, including Empathy, Service Orientation, and Organizational Awareness; and (4) Social Skills, including Leadership, Influence, Communication, Developing Others, Change Catalyst, Conflict Management, Building Bonds, and Teamwork and Collaboration (Goleman, 1998b; Boyatzis, Goleman, & Rhee, 2000).

Can a Person Improve on EI Competencies?

Decades of research on the effects of psychotherapy (Hubble, Duncan, & Miller, 1999), self-help programs (Kanfer & Goldstein, 1991), cognitive behavior therapy (Barlow, 1985), training programs (Morrow, Jarrett, & Rupinski, 1997), and education (Pascarella & Terenzini, 1991; Winter, McClelland, & Stewart, 1981) have shown that people can change their behavior, moods, and self-image. But most of the studies have focused on a single characteristic (such as maintenance of sobriety or reduction of a specific anxiety) or a set of characteristics determined by the assessment instrument, such as the scales of the MMPI. For example, the impact of Achievement Motivation training was a dramatic increase in small business success, with trainees creating more new jobs, starting more new businesses, and paying more taxes than individuals in comparison groups did (McClelland & Winter, 1969; Miron & McClelland, 1979). The impact of Power Motivation training was improved maintenance of sobriety (Cutter, Boyatzis, & Clancy, 1977).

The current conceptualization of emotional intelligence (EI) poses a challenging question: Can a person change her abilities in the set of competencies that constitute emotional intelligence that have been shown to determine outstanding job performance in many occupations, including management and professional jobs?

A series of longitudinal studies under way at the Weatherhead School of Management (WSOM) of Case Western Reserve University has shown that over two to five years, people can change on these competencies. MBA students, averaging twenty-seven years old at entry into the program, showed dramatic changes on videotaped and audiotaped behavioral samples and questionnaire measures of these competencies, as summarized in Tables 10.1 and 10.2, as a result of the competency-based, outcome-oriented MBA program implemented at the school in 1990 (Boyatzis, Baker, Leonard, Rhee, & Thompson, 1995; Boyatzis, Leonard, Rhee, & Wheeler, 1996; Boyatzis, Wheeler, & Wright, 1997).

Four cadres of full-time MBA students, graduating in 1992, 1993, 1994, and 1995, showed *strong evidence* of improvement (that is, statistically significant improvement in multiple years with multiple measures of the competency) on 71 percent (five out of seven) of the competencies in the Self-Management cluster (Efficiency Orientation, Planning, Initiative, Flexibility, Self-Confidence), 100 percent (two) of the competencies in the Social Awareness cluster (Empathy and Social Objectivity), and 50 percent (three out of six) of the competencies in the Social Skills cluster (Networking, Oral Communication, and Group Management). Meanwhile the part-time MBA students graduating in 1994, 1995, and 1996 showed strong improvement on 71 percent of the competencies in the Self-Management cluster (Efficiency Orientation, Initiative, Flexibility, Attention to Detail, and Self-Confidence), 50 percent of the competencies in the Social Awareness cluster (Social Objectivity), and 83 percent of the competencies in the Social Skills cluster. In a follow-up study of two of these graduating classes of part-time students, Wheeler (1999) demonstrated that during the two years following graduation, they showed statistically significant improvement on an audiotaped, behavioral measure of the competencies in the Social Awareness and Social Skills clusters (Empathy and Persuasiveness) in which they had not shown strong improvement during the MBA program.

These students contrast with the WSOM graduates of the 1988 and 1989 traditional MBA program, who showed strong improvement in only one competency in the Self-Management cluster (in both the 1988 and 1989 cadres, full-time students showed improvement in Self-Confidence and part-time students showed improvement in Flexibility). It is also worth noting that full-time students graduating from the competency-based MBA program showed *strong evidence* or *some evidence* of improvement in 100 percent or all of the emotional intelligence competencies assessed, and part-time students showed strong or some evidence of improvement in 93 percent of the competencies assessed (some evidence is defined as statistically significant improvement in one year or with one measure). In a longitudinal study of four classes completing the WSOM Professional Fellows Program (an executive education program), Ballou, Bowers, Boyatzis, and Kolb (1999) showed that forty-five- to fifty-five-year-old professionals and executives had

TABLE 10.1. EI IMPROVEMENT AMONG FULL-TIME STUDENTS IN OLD PROGRAM AND IN NEW PROGRAM.

Evidence of Improvement	Old Program			New Program		
	Goal and Action Management	People Management	Analytic Reasoning	Goal and Action Management	People Management	Analytic Reasoning
Strong evidence	Efficiency Orientation Initiative Flexibility	Self-Confidence	Use of Concepts Systems Thinking Quantitative Analysis Use of Technology Written Communication	Efficiency Orientation Planning Initiative Flexibility	Self-Confidence Networking Oral Communication Empathy Group Management	Use of Concepts Systems Thinking Pattern Recognition Social Objectivity Quantitative Analysis Use of Technology Written Communication
Some evidence		Empathy Networking	Social Objectivity	Self-Control Attention to Detail	Developing Others Persuasiveness Negotiating	
No evidence	Planning (Attention to Detail and Self-Control were not coded)	Persuasiveness Negotiating Group Management Developing Others Oral Communication				
Negative evidence			Pattern Recognition (verbal)			

TABLE 10.2. EI IMPROVEMENT AMONG PART-TIME STUDENTS IN OLD PROGRAM AND IN NEW PROGRAM.

Evidence of Improvement	Old Program			New Program		
	Goal and Action Management	People Management	Analytic Reasoning	Goal and Action Management	People Management	Analytic Reasoning
Strong evidence	Flexibility		Systems Thinking Quantitative Analysis	Efficiency Orientation Initiative Flexibility Attention to Detail	Group Management Self-Confidence Networking Oral Communication Developing Others Negotiating	Use of Concepts Social Objectivity Use of Technology Pattern Recognition Quantitative Analysis Systems Thinking Written Communication
Some evidence	Efficiency Orientation	Negotiating	Written Communication Social Objectivity	Planning	Empathy Persuasiveness	
No evidence	Planning Initiative (Attention to Detail and Self-Control were not coded)	Persuasiveness Self-Confidence Networking Group Management Oral Communication Developing Others	Use of Concepts Pattern Recognition	Self-Control		
Negative evidence		Empathy	Use of Technology			

statistically significant improvement in Self-Confidence, Leadership, Helping, Goal-Setting, and Action Skills. These were 67 percent of the emotional intelligence competencies assessed in this study.

Why Would People Want to Change?

There are three reasons why a person might want to develop his emotional intelligence. First, a person might want to increase his effectiveness at work or increase his potential for promotion. This could be called a career or professional development objective. Second, a person might want to become a better person. This can be called a personal growth objective. Third, a person might want to help others develop emotional intelligence or to pursue either of the objectives just mentioned.

Effectiveness and success, which are not synonymous, require a good *fit* between the person (that is, his capability or competencies, values, interests, and so forth), the demands of a specific job or role, and the organizational environment, as shown in Figure 10.1 (Boyatzis, 1982). In human resource management, common practice is to identify the competencies needed for effective job performance and then either find people with these competencies and hire them for the job or develop these competencies in people already in the organization (Boyatzis, 1996). The link between the emotional intelligence competencies and performance has been reviewed and summarized in Goleman (1998b). Unfortunately, competencies, even those empirically determined to lead or relate to outstanding job performance and also emotional intelligence competencies are *necessary but not sufficient* to predict performance (Goleman, 1998b). They help us understand *what* a person is capable of doing and what he has done in the past but not what he will do. Competencies explain and describe *how* we perform but not *why* we perform or not. We need to know more about the person's motivation and values to ascertain how his commitment to the organization and his compatibility with the vision and culture of the organization will affect his desire to use the competencies he has. It will also affect his desire to develop or enhance other competencies. In some approaches to competency research, such as those of Boyatzis (1982), Spencer and Spencer (1993), and McClelland (1973), researchers incorporate *intent* in the definition. Although this makes the competency profile for maximum job performance more comprehensive, it still does not address the *will or desire* to use one's capabilities to develop and to enhance others. Looking at competency needs for superior performance in jobs and in roles in life, we are continually drawn back to the need for intentionality; what is the person's intention or reason for using the behavior and ability?

It is the same with behavioral change. Adults change themselves; this is especially true for sustainable behavioral change. In other words, adults decide what

FIGURE 10.1. CONTINGENCY THEORY OF ACTION AND JOB PERFORMANCE.

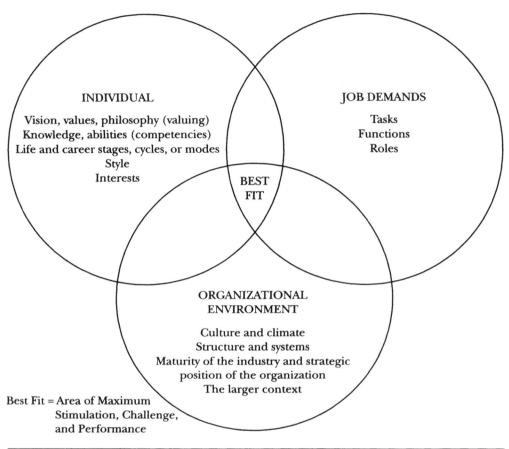

Source: Adapted from Boyatzis, 1982.

or how they will change. This is also evident in learning. People learn what they want to learn. Ideas and behaviors that they are not interested in learning may be acquired temporarily (that is, for a test) but are then soon forgotten (Specht & Sandlin, 1991). Students, children, patients, clients, and subordinates may act as if they care about learning something and go through the motions of learning it, but they will then proceed to disregard it or forget it—unless it is something that they want to learn. Even in situations where a person is under threat or coercion to make a behavioral change, the behavior will typically be extinguished or revert to its original form once the threat is removed. Chemical or hormonal changes in a person's body are not subject to this disregarding or forgetting. But even in such situations, the interpretation of a change and the behavioral comportment following upon it will be affected by the person's will, values, and motivations.

It appears that most, if not all, sustainable behavioral change is intentional. *Self-directed change is an intentional change in an aspect of who you are (that is, your Real Self) or who you want to be (that is, your Ideal Self) or both. Self-directed learning is self-directed change in which you are aware of the change and understand the process of change.* The process of self-directed change and learning is illustrated graphically in Figure 10.2 (Boyatzis, 1999a). This model is an enhancement of the earlier models developed by Kolb, Winter, and Berlew (1968), Boyatzis and Kolb (1969), Kolb and Boyatzis (1970a, 1970b), and Kolb (1971). The remainder of this chapter describes and explains the process, looking at four points of discontinuity and offering learning points for engaging the process. A discontinuity is a part of the process that may not and often does not occur as a smooth, linear event. It is accompanied by surprise. A person's behavior may seem persistent for long periods of time and then it may change quite suddenly. This is a discontinuity. Throughout this chapter, concepts from complexity theory are used to describe the model of self-directed change and learning. A person may begin the process of self-directed change and learning at any point in the process, but it often begins when the person experiences a discontinuity, an epiphany or moment of awareness associated with a sense of urgency. This model describes the process as it has been designed into a required course and into the elements of revised MBA and executive programs implemented in 1990 at the Weatherhead School of Management. Experimentation and research into the various program and course components have resulted in refinement of these components and of the model. For a detailed description of the course, see Boyatzis (1995, 1994).

The First Discontinuity:
Deciding Who I Am and Who I Want to Be

The first discontinuity and potential starting point for the process of self-directed change and learning is the discovery of who you are and who you want to be. This may occur as a decision you make among your choices for your Real Self (Who am I?) and your Ideal Self (Who do I want to be?).

Catching Your Dreams, Energizing Your Passion

Our Ideal Self is an image of the person we want to be. It emerges from our ego ideal, dreams, and aspirations. Research over the last twenty years has revealed the power of positive imaging or visioning in sports, appreciative inquiry (Cooperrider, 1990), meditation and biofeedback, and other psychophysiological

FIGURE 10.2. SELF-DIRECTED CHANGE AND LEARNING PROCESS.

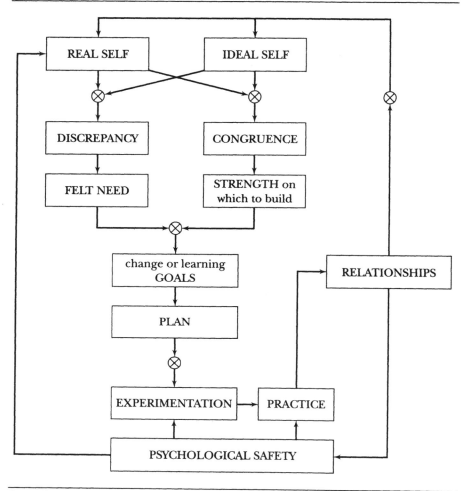

Source: Boyatzis, 1999a.

situations. It is believed that the potency of focusing one's thoughts on the desired end state of one's condition is driven by the emotional components of the brain (Goleman, 1995a). Following in the path of earlier research on approach versus avoidance drives (Miller, 1951) and the power of conscious volition (James, 1892), it has been thought that dreams and aspirations carry with them unconscious drives that are more powerful than conscious thought. The Ideal Self is a reflection of a person's intrinsic drives. Numerous studies have shown that intrinsic motives have more enduring impact on a person's behavior than extrinsic motives (Deci & Ryan, 1994). Our aspirations, dreams, and desired states are shaped by our values, philosophy (Boyatzis, Murphy, & Wheeler, 2000), life and career stages (Boyatzis & Kolb, 1999), motives (McClelland, 1985), role models, and other factors. Research indicates that we can access and engage deep emotional commitment and psychic energy if we engage our passions and conceptually catch our dreams in our Ideal Self image.

It is an anomaly that we know the importance of considering the Ideal Self and yet, when we engage in a change or learning process, we often skip over the clear formulation or articulation of our Ideal Self image. If a parent, spouse, boss, or teacher tells us that something about us should be different, she is giving us *her* version of our Ideal Self. She is telling us about the person *she* wants us to be. The extent to which we believe or accept this image determines the extent to which it becomes part of our Ideal Self. Our reluctance to accept others' expectations or wishes for us to change is one of many reasons why we may not live up to others' expectations or wishes and not change or learn according to their agenda! In current psychology, others' version of what our Ideal Self should be is referred to as the *Ought Self.*

We may be victims of the expectations of others and the seductive power of popular images from the media, celebrities, and our reference groups. In his book *The Hungry Spirit: Beyond Capitalism, A Quest for Purpose in the Modern World* (1997), Charles Handy describes the difficulty of determining his own ideal:

> I spent the early part of my life trying hard to be someone else. At school I wanted to be a great athlete, at university an admired socialite, afterwards a businessman and, later, the head of a great institution. It did not take me long to discover that I was not destined to be successful in any of these guises, but that did not prevent me from trying, and being perpetually disappointed with myself. The problem was that in trying to be someone else I neglected to concentrate on the person I could be. That idea was too frightening to contemplate at the time. I was happier going along with the conventions of the time, measuring success in terms of money and position, climbing ladders which others placed in my way, collecting things and contacts rather than giving expression to my own beliefs and personality [p. 86].

In this and similar ways, we often allow ourselves to be anesthetized to our dreams and lose sight of our deeply felt Ideal Self.

Awareness of the Real: Am I a Boiling Frog?

Our awareness of our current self, the person that others see and with whom they interact, is elusive. It is normal for our human psyches to protect themselves from the automatic intake and conscious realization of all information about ourselves.

These ego-defense mechanisms serve to protect us. They also conspire to delude us into constructing an image of who we are that feeds on itself, becomes self-perpetuating, and eventually may become dysfunctional (Goleman, 1985).

How does this happen in reasonably intelligent, sensitive people? One reason is the slow, gradual development of individuals' perception of their self-image.

The *boiling frog syndrome* applies here. It is said that if one drops a frog into a pot of boiling water, it will jump out due to its instinctive defense mechanism. But if one places a frog in a pot of cool water and gradually increases the temperature, the frog will sit in the water until it is boiled! Slow adjustments are acceptable on the way to a major change, but the same change made dramatically is not tolerated. For a more direct example, consider how people gaining weight or losing their sense of humor often do not see the change in their current Real Self because it has developed through small steps and iterative adjustments. In the recent action-adventure film, *Fire Down Below,* the hero asks a local resident in the hills of West Virginia about smoke pouring out of the ground from an abandoned coal mine. When she tells him that it has been that way for twelve and a half years, he asks if that bothers anyone. She tells him that it does not matter—give it long enough, and anything seems normal.

The greatest challenge to an accurate current self-image (that is, seeing yourself as others see you and in a way consistent with your other internal states, beliefs, emotions, and so forth) is the boiling frog syndrome. Several factors contribute to this syndrome. First, people around you may not let you see a change. They may not give you feedback or information about how they see it. Also, they may be victims of the boiling frog syndrome themselves, adjusting their perception daily. For example, if you haven't seen a friend's child for two years, when you do see him you may gasp over how fast he has grown. Meanwhile, the parent is aware of the child's growth only when she has to buy new shoes or clothes or when a sudden change in the child's hormonal balance leads to previously unlikely behavior.

Second, enablers—those who forgive the change, are frightened of it, or do not care about it—may allow it to pass unnoticed. Our relationships and interpersonal contexts mediate and interpret cues from the environment. They help us interpret what things mean. You ask a friend, "Am I getting fat?" And she responds, "No, you look great!" Whether this is reassuring to the listener or not, it is confusing for your self-image and may not be providing feedback to the question you asked. Of course, if she had said, "No, it's just the spread of age," or "No, it's just the normal effects of gravity," you may not have any more useful information either.

Third, likely in an attempt to be nice or to defend themselves against similar information about themselves, others may foster or perpetuate a delusion about your current Real Self image. Here is a test: Is there something about yourself that you once said you would never let happen but that has? Do you find yourself, for example, gradually taking on more characteristics and mannerisms of one of your parents? Transitions in life or careers may lead to changes in your behavior that may go unnoticed until they abruptly interfere with daily functioning.

In counseling sessions with effective CEOs and managing directors of not-for-profits, I have often been surprised to learn that they do not see themselves as leaders. Others may see them as leaders. Sometimes humility blocks this perception for themselves. Sometimes the interpersonal or cultural context does. When you are just one of the gods on Olympus, you do not stand out because everyone has the same super powers. On the planet Krypton, Superman was just another citizen. Not admitting to yourself that which is obvious to others can also occur when you have prolonged spiritual blackouts, losing sight of your core values and your philosophy.

Challenges and Paths to Awareness of Your Real Self and Your Ideal Self

This point of discontinuity offers two major *learning points* that are helpful in engaging the self-directed change and learning process:

1. Engage your passion and create your dreams.
2. Know thyself!

You put both these learning points into practice by finding and using multiple sources for feedback about your Real and Ideal Selves. The sources of insight into your Real Self may include systematically collected information from others, such as the 360-degree feedback currently considered fashionable in organizations. This source offers construct validity. That is, through listening to the information you collect about how you act and appear to many others (supervisor, peers, subordinates, clients and customers, family and spouse, and so forth), you are forming a consensually validated image of yourself. The degree to which this consensus is an image of *the real you* depends on the degree to which (1) these others see, observe, and interact with you and (2) you reveal yourself to them. Another possible source of insight into your Real Self may be behavioral feedback from videotaped or audiotaped interactions, such as collected in assessment centers. Various psychological tests may also help you determine or make explicit such inner aspects of your Real Self as values, philosophy, traits, and motives.

Sources for insight into your Ideal Self are more personal and more elusive than are those for the Real Self. Various exercises and tests can help by making explicit various dreams or aspirations you have for the future. Talking with close friends or mentors can help. Allowing yourself to think about your desired future, not merely your prediction of your most likely future, is the source of insight that is most difficult to tap into. These conversations and explorations must take place in psychologically safe surroundings. Often the implicit norms of our immediate social groups and work groups do not allow nor encourage such discussion. You may want to search for groups of people who are considering changing their lives; these groups may take the form of academic programs, career development workshops, or programs for personal growth experiences.

The Second Discontinuity:
The Balance Between Preservation and Adaptation

The second discontinuity and potential start of self-directed change and learning may occur when you determine the balance between the aspects of yourself you want to preserve, keep, and relish and the aspects you would like to change, stimulate to grow, or adapt to your environment and situation. Your awareness, or realization, of these components and the balance between them is your readiness to change.

Strange Attractors of Continuity
and Change (Preservation and Adaptation)

The strange attractors of preservation and adaptation, or continuity and change, constitute a yin/yang balance and interaction within ourselves. That is, before you can truly consider changing a part of yourself, you must have a sense of what you value and want to keep. Likewise, considering what you want to preserve about yourself involves admitting aspects of yourself that you wish to change or adapt in some manner. Awareness and exploration of each these parts of yourself exists in the context of awareness and exploration of the other.

All too often, people explore growth or development by focusing on their "gaps," or deficiencies. Organizational training programs and managers conducting annual *reviews* often commit the same mistake. There is an assumption that we can leave well enough alone and get to the areas that need work. It is no wonder that many of these programs or procedures intended to help a person develop result in the individual's feeling battered, beleaguered, and bruised, not helped, encouraged, motivated, or guided. The gaps may get your attention, however, because they disrupt progress or flow (R. Fry, personal communication, April 1998).

Exploration of yourself in the context of your environment (How am I fitting into this setting? How am I doing in the view of others? Am I part of this group or organization or family?) and examination of your Real Self in the context of your Ideal Self involve both comparative and evaluative judgments. A comprehensive view includes both strengths and weaknesses. That is, to contemplate change, one must contemplate stability. To identify and commit to changing parts of yourself, you must identify those parts you want to keep and possibly enhance. Adaptation does not imply or require "death" but evolution of the self.

Your willingness to change, or readiness to change, relies on your articulation of this balance of preservation and adaptation and your understanding of *both* of these factors. In various conceptualizations of readiness to change, Guglielmino (1978) and Guglielmino, Guglielmino, and Long (1987) focus on personal characteristics that precede change and appear to help move the process along. But in the model presented in this chapter, one's readiness to change, and even the desirability of and commitment to the change, is affected by the articulation and balancing of the elements of preservation and of adaptation. This model describes the change process. The subject of the model is not *change*. Change itself is not the object. The ideal or desired end result is the object. This desired end result of the change process may include aspects of the current Real Self as well as aspects of the Ideal Self not as yet achieved.

This result involves juggling the present and future at the same time. That is, preservation and adaptation are present oriented and future oriented, respectively. Preservation requires preserving the core, the stability or, in Fry's term, the *continuity* (Fry & Srivastva, 1992). This is the part of ourselves that we value, enjoy, want to keep; it is often built into our identity, self-image (self-schema), persona, and possibly even our public image. It is in this sense the present. A *continuity story* tells you about your core. You can use a life history or autobiography to generate your core. Meanwhile, adaptation is "stimulating change," or growth, and in aspiring toward some Ideal Self is pursuing something in the future. This personal adaptation is analogous to the forces of adaptation and preservation that Collins and Porras (1994) documented as critical to the change and survival of organizations.

Challenges and Paths to Your Readiness to Change

This point of discontinuity offers two major learning points helpful in engaging the self-directed change and learning process:

1. Identify and articulate both the strengths (those aspects of yourself you want to preserve) and the gaps or discrepancies in your Real and Ideal Selves (those aspects of yourself you want to keep and those that you want to adapt or change).
2. Keep your attention on both sets of factors—do not let either preservation or adaptation become your preoccupation!

Some organizational cultures, as mentioned earlier, encourage a preoccupation with the gaps. Some individuals have philosophies, or value orientations, that push them to focus on areas of improvement (a pragmatic value orientation, Boyatzis, Murphy, & Wheeler, 2000, for example, or a dominant underlying need for achievement, McClelland, 1985). Some individuals have such a low level of self-confidence or self-esteem that they assume they are unworthy; distrusting positive feedback they focus on the negative issues.

To carry out these learning points, build your strengths into any development or learning plan on which you are working. At the same time, do not use a strength as a reason to deny or avoid adaptation and change. Seek a balance.

The Third Discontinuity: The Decision to Change

The third discontinuity and potential start of the process of self-directed change and learning is the decision to change. Prochaska, DiClemente, and Norcross (1992) called this a movement from *contemplation* to *preparation* for change (see Chapter Nine). It is the emotional or intellectual next step once you have achieved awareness of your strengths and weaknesses and of the discrepancies and congruencies between your Real and Ideal Selves, that which you want to preserve and that which you want to adapt. It is during this part of the process that the direction and intention of the change effort is articulated and made explicit (that is, conscious). A major part of this process is setting goals.

Setting Goals

The setting of goals and creating of plans to achieve those goals has been an integral part of models and theories of change processes, and in particular self-directed change processes, for several centuries (Kolb & Boyatzis, 1970b). William James described the importance of conscious volition in personal change. Of course, even earlier, Benjamin Franklin outlined a process for becoming a virtuous person by setting daily and weekly goals to increase one's virtuous behavior. In recent years, McClelland (1965) formulated a motive acquisition process that included goal-setting and planning, and then proceeded to establish the effectiveness of these steps in motive change studies among entrepreneurs (McClelland & Winter, 1969; Miron & McClelland, 1979; McClelland, Davis, Kalin, & Wanner, 1972). Kolb, Winter, and Berlew (1968), Kolb and Boyatzis (1970a, 1970b), Boyatzis and Kolb (1969), and Kolb (1971) began to elaborate the points in the process at which goal-setting and planning are essential for change to occur. Integration of McClelland's steps in motive acquisition and the Kolb and Boyatzis models resulted in a model for the *competency acquisition process* (Boyatzis, 1982; Spencer & Spencer, 1993).

As part of one of the longitudinal studies at the Weatherhead School of Management, Leonard (1996) showed that MBAs who desired to change on certain competencies and set goals to do so, changed significantly on those competencies as compared to other MBAs. Previous literature had shown how goals affected certain changes on specific competencies (Locke & Latham, 1990) but had not established evidence of behavioral change on a comprehensive set of competencies constituting emotional intelligence.

Challenges to Deciding to Change

The third discontinuity offers one major learning point helpful in engaging the self-directed change and learning process:

1. Create your personal learning agenda!

Others cannot tell you how you should change—that is, they may tell you but it will not help you engage in the change process. Parents, teachers, spouses, bosses, and sometimes even your children will try to impose goals for change or learning on you. However, people learn only what they want to learn!

The late 1960s and early 1970s were witness to a widespread program in organizations called *management by objectives*. It was so popular that it spread to other arenas—you could find books and workshops on learning by objectives, teaching by objectives, and so on and so forth. In all these programs, there was one and only one approach to goal-setting and planning taught. It specified development of specific, observable, time-phased, and challenging (that is, involving moderate risk) behavioral goals. Unfortunately, this one-size-fits-all approach lacked a credible alternative until McCaskey (1974) suggested that some people plan by "domain and direction setting." Later, as part of the Weatherhead longitudinal studies, McKee (then London) (1991) studied how MBA graduates planned personal improvement. She discovered four different styles of planning: objectives-oriented planning; domain and direction planning; task- (or activity-) oriented planning; and present-oriented planning. The latter appeared as an existential orientation to one's involvement in developmental activities and could be considered a non-planning style.

The major barrier to engaging in goal-setting and planning is that people are already busy and cannot add anything else to their lives. In such cases success with self-directed change and learning occurs only when people can determine what to say no to and how to stop some current activities in their lives to make room for new ones. Another potential threat to success is the development of a plan that calls for a person to engage in activities calling for a learning style different from their preferred learning style or beyond their learning flexibility (Kolb, 1984;

Boyatzis, 1994). When this occurs the person is likely to become demotivated and often stops the activities or becomes impatient and decides that the goals are not worth the effort.

The Fourth Discontinuity: The Decision to Act

The fourth discontinuity and potential start of self-directed change and learning is to experiment with and practice desired changes. Acting on the plan and toward the goals involves numerous activities. People often engage in these activities in the context of experimenting with new behavior. Typically, following a period of experimentation, the person practices the new behaviors in the actual work and other settings in which he wishes to use them. During this part of the process, self-directed change and learning begins to look like a *continuous improvement* process.

Experimentation and Practice

To develop or learn new behavior, a person must find ways to learn more from ongoing experiences. That is, experimentation and practice does not always require attending courses or a new activity. It may involve trying something different in a current setting, reflecting on what occurs, and experimenting further in this same setting. Sometimes, this part of the process requires finding and using opportunities to learn and change. People may not even think they have changed until they have tried new behavior in a work or real-world setting. Rhee (1997) studied full-time MBA students in one of the Weatherhead cadres over a two-year period. He interviewed, tested, and video- and audiotaped them about every six to eight weeks. Even though he found evidence of significant improvements on numerous interpersonal abilities by the end of the second semester of their program, the students did not perceive that they had changed or improved in these abilities until they had returned from their summer internships.

Dreyfus (1990) studied managers of scientists and engineers who were considered superior performers. Once she documented that they used considerably more of certain abilities than their less effective counterparts, she pursued how they had developed some of those abilities. One of the distinguishing abilities was Group Management, also called Team Building. She found that many of these middle-aged managers had first experimented with Team-Building skills in high school and college and in sports, clubs, and living groups. Later, when they became "bench scientists and engineers" working on problems in relative isolation, they still used and practiced team building and group management in social and community organizations, such as 4-H Clubs, and in professional associations by planning conferences and such.

The experimentation and practice are most effective when they occur in conditions in which the person feels safe (Kolb & Boyatzis, 1970b). This sense of psychological safety creates an atmosphere in which the person can try new behavior, perceptions, and thoughts with relatively less risk of shame or embarrassment and of serious consequences of failure.

Our relationships are an essential part of our environment. Our most crucial relationships are often in groups that have particular importance to us. These relationships and groups give us a sense of identity, guide us as to appropriate and "good" behavior, and provide feedback on our behavior. In sociology, they are called *reference groups*. They create a context in which we can interpret our progress on desired changes and the utility of new learning, and even contribute significant input to formulation of our Ideal Self image (Kram, 1996). In this way our relationships are mediators, moderators, interpreters, sources of feedback, sources of support, and givers of permission for change and learning! They may also be our most important source of protection against relapses to our earlier forms of behavior. Wheeler (1999) analyzed the extent to which the MBA graduates worked on their goals in multiple *life spheres* (work, family, recreational groups, and so forth). In a two-year follow-up study of two of the graduating classes of part-time MBA students, she found those who worked on their goals and plans in multiple sets of relationships improved the most, more than those working on goals in only one setting, such as work or one relationship.

In a study of the impact of the yearlong executive development program for doctors, lawyers, professors, engineers, and other professionals, mentioned earlier, Ballou et. al. (1999) found that participants gained in Self-Confidence during the program. Observers would have said these participants were very high in Self-Confidence even at the beginning of the program, so this was a curious finding! The best explanation came from program graduates' answers to follow-up questions. They explained the evident increase in Self-Confidence as an increase in their confidence that they could change. Their existing reference groups (family, groups at work, professional groups, community groups) all had an investment in their staying the same even though they wanted to change. The Professional Fellows Program allowed them to develop a new reference group that encouraged change.

According to theories of social identity and reference groups and now relational theories, our relationships both mediate and moderate our sense of who we are and who we want to be. We develop or elaborate our Ideal Self from these contexts. We label and interpret our Real Self from these contexts. We interpret and value strengths (aspects we consider our core that we wish to preserve) from these contexts. We interpret and value gaps (aspects we consider weaknesses or things we wish to change) from these contexts.

Challenges to the Decision to Act

This discontinuity offers three major learning points helpful in engaging the self-directed change and learning process:

1. Experiment and practice and try to learn more from your experiences!
2. Find settings in which you feel psychologically safe in which to experiment and practice!
3. Develop and use your relationships as part of your change and learning process!

Comparison to Other Models of Individual Change

The proposed model of self-directed change is consistent with other theories for understanding how people change. There are not many theories of individual change in the professional literature that are based on empirical research or conceptual meta-analysis. In Table 10.3, this model is compared to McClelland's twelve propositions for motive acquisition and change, Prochaska's model, and the model of best practices for developing emotional intelligence compiled by the Consortium for Research on Emotional Intelligence in Organizations. The latter model is a synthesis of the practices in fourteen model programs studied by members of the consortium and found to have published evidence of positive impact on emotional intelligence.

Conclusion

Our future may not be entirely within our control, but most of what we become is within our power to create. It is my intention that the self-directed change and learning process described in this chapter will provide a road map and guidance for increasing the effectiveness of your change and learning efforts. As a concluding thought, I offer a few lines from the 1835 John Anster translation of Goethe's *Faustus: A Dramatic Mystery*. In the Prologue to the Theater, one character declares:

What you can do, or dream you can, begin it,

Boldness has genius, power and magic in it.

TABLE 10.3. COMPARISON OF INDIVIDUAL CHANGE MODELS.

Elements of SDC Process	McClelland's Motive Acquisition[a]	EI Consortium Best Practices[b]	Prochaska's Model[c]
Become aware of Real Self	Improvement in self-image	Gauge readiness of learners Conduct ongoing evaluation research	Precontemplation
Become aware of Ideal Self	Belief that change can, will, should occur Consistent with demands of external reality Improvement on prevailing cultural values	Build positive expectations	Precontemplation
Realize discrepancies or gaps Realize congruencies or strengths		Assess individuals and deliver results with care	Contemplation Contemplation
Identify goals	Clearly conceptualizes changes as improvement in self-image Commits self to achieving goals	Make learning self-directed Set clear, meaningful, manageable goals	Preparation
Articulate a plan	Link desired change to actions Link to events in everyday life		Preparation
Experiment and practice	Keeps a record of progress Setting dramatizes self-study and lifts it from everyday life	Provide practice and feedback Rely on experiential methods Use "live" models	Action
In context of relationships and psychological safety	In an interpersonal atmosphere of warmth, honest support, and respect Persistence of change if new behavior is a sign of membership in a new reference group	Foster a positive relationship between trainer and learner Inoculate against setbacks Create an encouraging environment Build in support	Maintenance

[a]McClelland, 1965.

[b]Cherniss & Adler, 2000 (also includes a number of guidelines addressing assessment and preparation of the organization for the development program or effort).

[c]Prochaska et al., 1992.

CHAPTER ELEVEN

DEVELOPING EMOTIONAL COMPETENCE THROUGH RELATIONSHIPS AT WORK

Kathy E. Kram
Cary Cherniss

There is a growing consensus among scholars and practitioners that in today's context—a world characterized by globalization, rapid technological change, workplace diversity, and constant environmental turbulence—emotional intelligence is essential to effective individual and organizational performance. Although technical and cognitive learning continue to be very important to strategic success in the marketplace, most would agree that they are not sufficient. Numerous studies and essays argue that personal qualities such as self-awareness, self-motivation, flexibility, and integrity, as well as interpersonal skills such as negotiation, listening, empathy, conflict management, and collaboration are critical ingredients for a high-performance workplace (see, for example, Spencer, McClelland, & Kelner, 1997; Spencer & Spencer, 1993; Hall & Associates, 1996; Boyatzis, 1982).

The purpose of this chapter is to examine how individuals can develop essential personal and social competencies through their relationships at work. Although scholars and training specialists have made great strides in defining the parameters of effective training for social and emotional competencies (see Chapters Nine and Ten; see also Cherniss & Adler, 2000; Young & Dixon, 1996; Pesuric & Byham, 1996; Boyatzis, Cowen, & Kolb, 1995), our view is that there is untapped potential for social and emotional learning (SEL) to occur in relationships outside the training milieu. Because time and training budgets are increasingly scarce resources, and because measures of training effectiveness are mixed at best, this is an important avenue to pursue (Morrow, Jarrett, & Rupinski, 1997).

In some respects this perspective is not new. For the last two decades, research on mentoring has demonstrated the value of developmental relationships for personal learning at every career stage (Kram, 1988, 1996; Thomas, 1990, 1993). First, it was recognized that young managers could develop self-esteem, self-confidence, clarity of professional identity, and some of the necessary social skills to advance their careers through relationships with senior managers whom they admired. Then research indicated that senior managers also benefited from these same alliances, deriving self-esteem and personal satisfaction and honing personal and interpersonal skills through the coaching and reflection they offered to their protégés (Allen, Poteet, & Burroughs, 1997). After the first decade of such research, scholars began to demonstrate that relationships with peers could also be sites for social and emotional learning (Kram & Isabella; 1985; Ibarra, 1992, 1993). Most recently, it has been postulated that developmental relationships are being transformed by today's context of diversity and turbulence into relationships characterized by mutual learning, short-term duration, and heterogeneity (Higgins & Kram, in press; Kram & Hall, 1996).

Recent work on women's development supports these findings and further illuminates how and why individuals develop social and emotional competencies through their interactions with others (Fletcher, 1994, Miller, 1991; Jordan, Kaplan, Miller, Stiver, & Surrey, 1991). Scholars of women's development argue that the capacities for self-awareness, self-reflection, empathy, and listening, for example, occur as women build interdependent relationships that provide support and validation as well as model functions (Miller & Stiver, 1997). Development is viewed as a process of understanding oneself as increasingly connected to others rather than as a process of differentiating oneself from others (Fletcher, 1996).

This perspective on growth through relationships implies that relational activity that supports learning is two-way—both parties enter the interaction expecting to be both expert and learner, to give and to receive, to enable and to be enabled. In particular, Miller and Stiver (1997) argue that traditional development theories depicting relationships as one-directional events in which one individual learns and the other teaches and in which the goal is independence and separation (rather than interdependence and connection) are insufficient. They propose instead a relational theory of development that says individuals at every career stage can learn and contribute to others' learning and the overarching goal is interdependence (as opposed to independence). In turn, interdependence supports both task accomplishment and social and emotional learning (Fletcher, 1996; Kram, 1996).

Although relationships can be vitally important and useful for the development of emotional competence, that usefulness depends on the quality of the relationship. Not all relationships will be equally beneficial for the promotion of emotional competence. Some may even be destructive. In this chapter, we thus consider two primary questions. First, how do relationships help develop greater emotional competence and promote social and emotional learning? And second, what are the factors that influence relationships and their capacity to promote social and emotional learning?

Our answers to these questions are summarized in the model illustrated in Figure 11.1. To the far right of the model is SEL. The model suggests that an individual's social and emotional learning will be affected by the quality of her relationships in the work setting. In the first part of this chapter, we describe in more detail how positive developmental relationships can contribute to greater emotional competence through SEL at work. On the left side of the model are a number of factors that influence the quality of relationships and their capacity to promote emotional competence and SEL. On the individual level, there is the *baseline emotional intelligence* that each person brings to the relationship. We argue that a relationship's capacity to promote social and emotional learning depends in part

FIGURE 11.1. FACTORS THAT SHAPE SEL THROUGH RELATIONSHIPS.

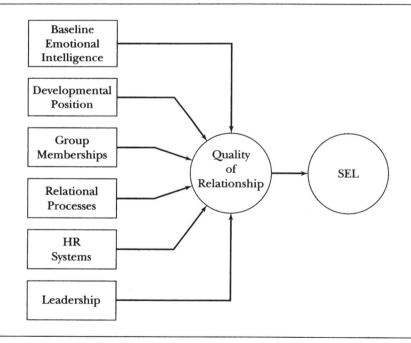

on the participants' baseline levels. In addition, we suggest that an individual's *developmental position* and associated stance toward authority, identity, and competence will influence his willingness and capacity to build relationships that foster SEL.

On the interpersonal and group level the model suggests that *salient group memberships,* such as the race and gender of the individuals involved in the relationship will affect the potential for developing greater emotional competence. A relationship in which one person is African American and the other is European American, for instance, will offer some unique opportunities for developing certain emotional competencies. For example, the opportunity and challenge exists for the individual to enhance her social skills and increase her self-awareness of her biases and values and of the ways her socialization as a black or white person has shaped these biases and values. Differences in group memberships also pose challenges that may make it more difficult to develop certain kinds of emotional competencies. One would anticipate, for example, that empathy is more readily achieved in relationships with those of similar racial backgrounds.

One other interpersonal or group-level factor that is important involves *relational processes.* These are routinized patterns of behavior that are often conscious and intentional, though they need not be. They are part of the model because they can have a significant impact on whether a relationship will promote emotional competence. An example of such a process is taking time at the end of a meeting to reflect on how well the meeting worked and how meetings might be improved going forward. In some groups such reflection on how the group relationship is functioning occurs regularly; in fact it is normative. We argue that when a relational process such as this occurs regularly in a relationship, the relationship has a greater potential for promoting emotional competence.

The last set of factors in the model involves characteristics of the organization. We briefly discuss two that seem to have a significant impact on the developmental potential of relationships. The first is *formal human resource systems,* such as recruitment and selection, training and development, performance appraisal, and succession planning. Formal training programs, for instance, can help people form relationships (as they do in formal mentoring programs, for example) conducive to the development of emotional competence. The second organizational factor is *leadership.* Leaders, through their policy decisions and their behavior, influence the extent to which an organization's culture and reward systems will encourage and reinforce social and emotional competence. This in turn influences the extent to which individuals take the time to build developmental relationships and to regularly reflect on them in order to continually enhance personal and social competencies.

Like all models, ours is overly simplistic in some ways. One of the most notable is that it does not show how these six factors influence each other. For instance, organizational leadership will influence HR systems, and HR systems can encourage the development of relational processes that promote emotional competence. For an illustration of these influences, consider the leader who champions both formal and informal mentoring through modeling mentoring in his relationships with his direct reports and through supporting formal mentoring systems and related training activities. This leader can further promote relational processes that support relationships that promote emotional competence by advocating for a performance management system that monitors, assesses, and rewards such processes on the job. As we discuss the different aspects of the model, we will frequently refer to such interconnections.

We begin our discussion by looking at SEL itself (the far right-hand side of the model as shown in Figure 11.1) and giving some illustrations of the various ways in which individuals can develop specific personal and social competencies through their relationships at work. Then we consider how the multiple factors outlined above (the left-hand side of the model) shape the course of different types of relationships, and in turn the development of emotional competence. Ultimately, our intent is to highlight working hypotheses that can guide future research in this area and to draw practical implications for those concerned with creating positive conditions for SEL in work settings.

Forms of Social and Emotional Learning Through Relationships

Social and emotional learning through relationships takes many forms in the workplace. If we are to systematically consider how to promote such learning, it is useful, first, to delineate the landscape of possibilities. Consider the following examples, which use Goleman's typology (1998b) of personal and social competencies.

Example 1. A young, Asian associate at a large financial services firm is given feedback in the annual appraisal process that she is perceived as not being assertive enough in her dealings with clients. At a dinner meeting with female peers, she listens to other women speak about their approaches with clients, and she clarifies how her style differs. In reflecting on the feedback and what she heard from her female peers, she becomes aware of how her cultural background influences her professional style. She realizes that what is expected and rewarded at the firm is in conflict with her style. She decides that she would like to try to modify her style and enlists the support of several female peers. She also lets her manager know about this new development goal. (The competencies involved are Self-Awareness, Self-Motivation, and Social Skills.)

Example 2. A midlevel professional at a large high-technology firm is experiencing more ambiguity and a multitude of demands and expectations at work. Since a recent downsizing in his organization the scope of his job has expanded significantly. Though he realizes that he is viewed as a high performer—and for this reason has been asked to take on more—he experiences worry and anxiety about how he can possibly do it all. He finally decides to confide his concern in his mentor—a more senior executive who has taken an interest in his development since he took this new position a year ago. His mentor listens and coaches him on how to set priorities, how to do what is most critical and leave the rest—in essence, how to develop an adaptive response. His mentor also encourages him to build exercise and other relaxation habits into his daily life. (He is learning Self-Regulation and Self-Motivation.)

Example 3. A senior executive learns through a 360-degree feedback process that many individuals in his organization perceive him as inaccessible and not particularly interested in their development. After considerable discussion with one of his peers, he decides to talk informally with several junior managers to gather information on what he could do to improve his image and role. He learns that the young white males are relatively content with his coaching and availability—it is the women and minority managers who experience more distance and disinterest. One female manager, in particular, provides specific examples of both actions taken and actions not taken that have undermined his credibility. He actively solicits advice from this manager and suggests they meet again in six months to see whether his actions have become more responsive. (He is working on Self-Awareness, Empathy, and Social Skills.)

In all three of these scenarios the individuals are developing emotional competence through relational activity. Although formal feedback processes are facilitating change in two instances, social and emotional learning is occurring without any formal training or other developmental activity in all the cases. Moreover, it is not difficult to see how the natural relationships in each case could be even more effective teachers than a formal class or workshop might be. The examples also show how relationships can foster any of the basic competencies associated with emotional intelligence, including Self-Regulation, Self-Motivation, and Social Skills and particularly Self-Awareness and Empathy.

The most salient difference among the three scenarios is the nature of the relationships sought out for learning. In the first, female peers are a source of motivation, insight, and strategizing (even though it was the employee's immediate boss who raised the issue and set the reflection process in motion). In the second situation, a trusted, informal mentor is sought as confidante and advisor. In the third, the senior executive consults a trustworthy peer and then solicits input from a number of subordinates. The texture of the relational learning is quite distinct in each instance, suggesting a wide array of possibilities.

The possibilities for SEL through relationships at work can be categorized into four types (see Table 11.1). First, we consider whether the relationship has been formally arranged by the organization or whether it is a naturally occurring relationship that has emerged through the informal interaction of individuals. Second, we consider whether the primary purpose of the relationship is to facilitate personal and professional development or to get work done that contributes to organizational goals. Although a relationship may combine these two objectives, it is usually the case that one or the other will be the primary impetus for the relationship. Although the table simplifies the complex nature of relationships (because a relationship may have dual purposes), it nevertheless provides a framework within which to consider the unique potential and constraints of each type of relationship and the ways in which both individuals and organizations might foster such alliances for the purpose of developing particular social and emotional competencies. Although assessment of the real impact of each of these possibilities has yet to be subjected to systematic evaluation, we draw on related research on mentoring and leadership development as well as our own experiences and observations to speculate about the potential impact.

Formally Assigned Mentoring and Coaching Relationships

During the last two decades the formal assignment of mentoring alliances for the purpose of development has become a common human resource strategy (Kram & Bragar, 1992; Phillips-Jones, 1982; Zey, 1991; Kram & Hall, 1996; Hunt & Michael, 1983). Originally the notion was to make mentoring available to targeted groups of employees who were unlikely to experience naturally occurring mentoring relationships. So, for example, in the late 1970s and early 1980s, a flurry of mentoring programs appeared, designed to bring high-potential women and mi-

TABLE 11.1. TYPES OF RELATIONSHIPS IN ORGANIZATIONS.

	Mode of Initiation	
Primary Purpose	**Formally Arranged**	**Naturally Occurring**
Development	Assigned mentoring relationships Assigned coaching relationships	Emergent mentoring relationships Emergent coaching relationships
Work accomplishment	Supervisory relationships Intrateam relationships	Emergent peer relationships Organizational networks

norities together with senior white male managers for the purpose of giving these employees opportunities for growth and advancement that they had not previously experienced (Kram & Bragar, 1992; Morrison, 1992). Even prior to that, high-potential managers were in general being paired with senior executives as a means of fast-tracking their advancement (Collins & Scott, 1978; Roche, 1979; Shapiro, Haseltine, & Rowe, 1978).

Formal mentoring programs vary in structure and function, and organizations usually provide some guidelines to participants. These guidelines might suggest that the assigned pairs meet regularly to discuss matters of concern to the junior's professional and personal development. They also might suggest a number of topics as a vehicle for getting started. Organizations also generally offer orientation and training to help individuals develop an understanding of the potential of these relationships and in some instances to develop essential interpersonal skills associated with mentoring (for example active listening, coaching, and soliciting and giving feedback); the more comprehensive such formal programs are, the more likely it is that personal and social competencies will be enhanced as a result. In addition, some kind of monitoring process is usually established for assessing the progress of these matched pairs over a defined period of time. This infrastructure of training and follow-up increases the likelihood that relational processes that promote SEL will be established.

Although the learning outcomes of such relationships vary with the personal objectives, career stages, and interpersonal skills of the individuals involved, as well as the quality of the program, the potential for enhancing personal and social competencies is great. Through role modeling and coaching the junior person has the opportunity to acquire new approaches to challenging situations as they are reflected upon and explored in the context of this relationship. Over time, new strategies for dealing with particular situations can be tested and then reviewed in subsequent conversations. Social skills related to handling conflict or effectively leading a team, for instance, can be developed through such alternating periods of action and reflection. Alternatively, Self-Awareness and Self-Motivation can be enhanced as the junior person shares personal experiences and then receives feedback from a more experienced advisor. As trust and rapport grow, the boundaries of what can be discussed expand, and the potential for SEL expands as well.

Although this result is perhaps less apparent, those participating as mentors can develop personal and social competencies as well. For example, the senior manager who is assigned to mentor and coach a less experienced manager has the opportunity to develop skills in listening, giving feedback, and developing others. Alternatively, the mentor who is viewed as a role model by an assigned mentee may be invited to reflect on her experiences and in doing so enhance her Self-Awareness or Self-Regulation. In getting to know the challenges and concerns of the assigned mentee, the mentor may also develop new Social Awareness (such as Empathy) or Social Skills as the new relationship evolves. New mentors may also be more motivated and able to develop social and emotional competencies when they are given the opportunity in a formal program to assess their mentoring skills and to practice those that are essential to initiating and building effective developmental relationships.

Mentoring programs can contribute to enhanced emotional intelligence in less direct ways as well. Managers who become formal mentors and receive training in emotional competence as part of their preparation for the role may use these competencies in other contexts as well. For example, coaching and listening skills practiced in training designed for formally assigned mentors can be used in relationships with subordinates and peers back at work. Similarly, the empathy a mentor develops during the experience of getting to know an assigned protégé of a different race or gender can be helpful in strengthening relationships with other colleagues in his immediate work setting. Ultimately, if a critical mass of individuals has taken part in training that promotes the personal and social competencies necessary for effective mentoring and if the HR systems are in alignment (that is, they recognize and facilitate mentoring and associated relational processes), a mentoring program may contribute to the development of an organizational culture that is generally more supportive of emotionally intelligent behavior.

There is a notable lack of systematic evaluation of mentoring's impact on emotional competence. However, some data suggest that formally arranged relationships tend to remain instrumental, with a focus on helping the junior person prepare for advancement (Noe, 1988). Other studies have demonstrated that such alliances are often correlated with reduced turnover, increased organizational commitment, or career advancement (Scandura, 1992; Ragins & Scandura, 1994; Whitely & Coetsier, 1993; Whitely, Dougherty, & Dreher, 1991). Explicit exploration of the conditions that facilitate social and emotional learning in these alliances has not as yet been completed. It appears that when interpersonal skills training is offered in conjunction with a formal mentoring program and when other HR systems are congruent with the program objectives (offering, for example, 360-degree feedback practices, rewards for taking the time to mentor, development plans that inform and are informed by the assigned relationship), the potential for these relationships to become sites for SEL is enhanced.

In addition to mentoring programs, formal coaching relationships are becoming an increasingly common developmental tool (Kinlaw, 1993; Mink, Owen, & Mink, 1993; Pryor, 1994; Hall, Otazo, & Hollenbeck, 1999). More limited in scope than formal mentoring relationships and generally targeted for use with executives, internal or external coaches are matched with individuals with specific development objectives in mind. Oftentimes, coaches are used in conjunction with a 360-degree feedback process to help executives interpret the feedback they have received and develop new competencies that will enhance their effectiveness in particular dimensions (Hollenbeck, 1992). If the match is effective (that is, trust and rapport are easily achieved, and the coach's style is acceptable to the executive), periodic meetings in which the coach fosters action and reflection can lead to new personal and social competencies.

Emergent Mentoring and Coaching Relationships

In contrast to formal mentoring alliances, emergent relationships are those that evolve naturally out of informal interaction and mutual attraction (Kram, 1988). Interpersonal chemistry sets the relationship in motion, and over time both parties recognize the value of their continued involvement. There are various starting points for emergent mentoring alliances—a shared work project, membership on a task force, advice asked and given on a particular project, or simply an intuitive sense that there are common values and interests to be shared. Regardless of the particular events that set the relationship in motion, it is usually only in retrospect that the parties recognize that a developmental alliance has been formed.

Examination of the process by which emergent relationships evolve suggests that a baseline level of emotional intelligence is a prerequisite for setting such alliances in motion. In the absence of a formal program that legitimizes and facilitates early encounters, both individuals must rely on their willingness to invest in the relationship and their capacities to initiate contact, actively listen, invite and give feedback, and foster ongoing communication. Thus emergent mentoring relationships will evolve only when both parties bring some degree of Self-Awareness, Self-Motivation, Empathy, and Social Skills to the relationship. When that occurs, these personal and social competencies are likely to deepen and broaden over time through various developmental functions such as role modeling, coaching, and counseling.

Unlike formally assigned mentoring relationships, developmental alliances have no apparent limit in number. If organizational conditions are favorable—if the culture values developmental activity and encourages individuals to take time to engage in it—and if individuals have baseline emotional intelligence, then those individuals can benefit from multiple developmental alliances. Indeed, formal mentoring programs are often positioned as a springboard for informal mentoring, a means of increasing emergent relationships back in the work setting by giving individuals a chance to learn the requisite personal and social skills (Kram & Bragar, 1992; Kram & Hall, 1996).

As the workforce has become more diverse and the research on mentoring has accumulated, it has become clear that emergent mentoring alliances are more likely to occur between individuals of similar demographic backgrounds (Kram, 1988; McKeen & Burke, 1989; Thomas, 1990). This is not surprising, because it is often identification with the other that underlies the motivation to nurture a new relationship and that becomes the glue solidifying the new interpersonal bond (Wenger, 1998). In addition, research on cross-gender and interracial mentoring alliances has demonstrated that prior socialization, gender and racial stereotyping, and intergroup dynamics pose special challenges to individuals who want to form relationships with individuals of different backgrounds (Ibarra, 1993; Kram & Hall, 1996; Thomas & Alderfer, 1989; Thomas & Gabarro, 1999).

For example, women are less likely than their male counterparts to form relationships with male mentors (Dreher & Ash, 1990; Ragins, 1989). Several factors make cross-gender alliances more difficult. First, both men and women may experience discomfort in taking the initiative to foster interaction for fear that such action might be misinterpreted. Second, even if the relationship does get established, either party may unknowingly impose gender stereotypes, which limit the potential of the relationship and of the other party (Ragins, 1989; Ragins & McFarlin, 1990; Kram, 1988). A female protégé, for example, may not be offered a particular assignment because her mentor assumes she would not want to do all the traveling involved, or a female protégé may avoid conflict with her mentor because she has been labeled a poor team player for disagreeing on other matters. Finally, due to subtle yet deeply ingrained stereotypes, behaviors that are acceptable and even valued for men in an organization don't always work for women; thus the advice and models offered in cross-gender relationships may be faulty.

Similar dynamics regularly occur in interracial alliances (Thomas, 1989, 1990, 1993; Thomas & Gabarro, 1999). Collusion in stereotypes, for example, may limit the range of acceptable behaviors for the minority protégé. Mutual trust and rapport may be difficult to attain as a result of unspoken assumptions on both sides about interests, values, and personal history. Thus either party may find it difficult to discuss challenging situations that would benefit from reflection and strategizing within the relationship. Either party may unknowingly thwart opportunities to acquire new perspectives as well as new approaches. If, however, both parties are able to transcend these obstacles (through increasing Self-Awareness and Communication skills), their potential for learning from one another is great. In such diverse relationships both can develop awareness of the views held by members of other demographic groups. Such learning increases Social Awareness and Social Skills, and in particular, capacities to lead, manage, and leverage a diverse workforce.

In recent years, organizations have begun to foster emergent mentoring and coaching relationships, particularly among individuals who share demographic characteristics (Hodgetts & Hodgetts, 1996). For example, it is now quite common to create opportunities for women managers to come together periodically to discuss issues of mutual concern. Such events enable women to discover the value of engaging in dialogue with other women who face similar challenges in their work. Over time such dialogue fosters emergent mentoring and coaching alliances that exist for the purpose of growth and development. Some of these homogeneous groups have been convened specifically to support individuals who find emergent mentoring alliances with white male managers to be limited or nonexistent. In these forums, peer alliances that provide similar mentoring functions can emerge (Hodgetts & Hodgetts, 1996; Kram & Hall, 1996; McDougall & Beatty, 1997).

Supervisory and Intrateam Relationships

Many kinds of relationships in organizations exist for the primary purpose of accomplishing work (in contrast to promoting learning and development). Most obvious are relationships formally defined by the strategy and structure of the enterprise. Among all the relationships that exist as a result of the formal objectives and design of an organization, supervisory and intrateam relationships are the most likely to serve as sites for SEL as well.

Traditionally, the primary supervisory responsibilities include allocating work to subordinates and regularly assessing performance against targeted objectives. In recent years the supervisory role has been expanded to include coaching and counseling activities designed to improve employee performance, retention, and development (Pfeffer, 1998; Baird & Kram, 1983). When supervisors expand their roles to engage in activities that assess performance and coach for improved performance, the opportunities to enhance personal and social competencies multiply (see Chapter Seven). Again, it is not just subordinates who are the potential beneficiaries here. In carrying out the expanded role, supervisors may acquire and practice a number of personal and social competencies essential to the work at hand. These positive learning outcomes for supervisors are most likely to occur in organizations where relevant feedback is regularly offered, informally or through a 360-degree feedback process.

Thus, for example, an employee may be asked to actively participate in assessing his performance for the year-end review process. In preparing for the appraisal discussion the subordinate has the opportunity to strengthen a number of personal competencies (for example, Self-Awareness, Self-Motivation, and Self-Regulation). In reviewing this self-assessment with his supervisor, he is given feedback that may confirm or disconfirm the self-assessment and also offer new insights into particular areas of performance that might be strengthened going forward. If open to the feedback, the subordinate has an opportunity to commit to development objectives for personal and social competencies that could be improved as he accomplishes future work objectives. Similarly, the supervisor, in offering effective feedback and coaching, must practice Social Skills that are critical to effectively managing the performance and development of subordinates.

Supervisory relationships can promote SEL throughout the year, not just at the year-end review. When supervisors frame coaching and developing subordinates as central to their work, they are more likely to seize daily opportunities on the job to invite dialogue with subordinates about the work at hand and about the challenges they are facing in accomplishing their objectives. Similarly, when subordinates see relationships as potential sites for learning, they are more likely to seek feedback and advice from their supervisors. Like relationships that have development as their primary purpose, work-centered relationships that encompass learning and development objectives are more likely to exist when the organizational culture encourages, rewards, and recognizes attention to such matters. Thus, when human resource management systems such as performance appraisal, employee development, succession planning, and career planning are effectively designed and easy to use, supervisors are more likely to have the tools and motivation to foster ongoing development. And when individuals at all levels are assessed not only for their technical competencies but also for their personal and social competencies, learning through relationships will be viewed as a central part of the work to be done.

The opportunities for SEL in the context of intrateam relationships are perhaps not as obvious. Yet most individuals work in team-based organizations today and spend a good part of their work time interacting with members of various permanent and temporary groups and teams—product development teams, engineering teams, salesforce teams, departmental groups, task forces, and so on. It is not our purpose here to examine the various team and group structures that may exist. Rather we aim to illustrate that when there is an emphasis on relational learning, interactions with colleagues in these various teams become sites for learning personal and social competencies.

In collaborating with their team colleagues to accomplish work, individuals have several opportunities to develop personal and social competencies. First, they can observe colleagues handling particular situations with customers, peers, and superiors. In doing so they may be exposed to strategies different from their own, which they can add to their behavioral repertoire. Second, they may be asked by their peers for advice and counsel; in responding to such requests individuals have the opportunity to reflect on their own experiences, enhancing their Self-Awareness as well as their Social Awareness or Social Skills. In essence in this situation, team members invite other members to serve as role models and coaches on matters in which they are perceived as having expertise. Finally, when working in teams, individuals regularly encounter challenges related to leading, handling conflict, giving feedback, negotiating, and communicating; thus membership in teams provides a ready-made laboratory for practicing a range of social skills (Bennis & Biederman, 1997).

Like SEL opportunities in supervisory relationships, these opportunities for SEL through intrateam relationships are more likely to happen when the organizational culture encourages, rewards, and recognizes efforts to engage in such relational learning. For example, in one division of a financial services firm, a department manager devoted one morning staff meeting a month to checking in on critical work objectives. During this meeting each individual was expected to give a progress report and to identify current challenges requiring assistance and support. As each individual made a report, other team members listened carefully, asked probing questions, and provided coaching and support based on their own experiences. The department head framed this meeting as one that supported the work of the department. It was designed to support each member in addressing critical work problems and in acquiring new coaching and feedback skills and other Social Skills. This regular department meeting was centered on accomplishing mission-critical work and also facilitated SEL through intrateam relationships.

In another work setting, a high-technology firm, design teams were regularly formed around new product development initiatives. Recognizing the need to actively support new team start-ups, the organizational development department offered a series of team-building activities that helped new teams establish meaningful goals, work procedures, and monitoring systems. Early on in the life of these core teams, it was established that meaningful goals would necessarily include ongoing learning and development objectives for all members of the team. In keeping with this vision for the teams, members described themselves as peer coaches, having the explicit responsibility to help colleagues acquire new skills as the team moved forward in its primary work. Before long, it was clear to team members and consultants alike that in addition to acquiring new technical competencies, members needed to acquire critical personal and social competencies that were required if they were to innovate and deliver in a core team environment.

Emergent Peer Alliances and Organizational Networks

Among all the types of relationships in work settings, emergent relationships with peers and others that make up individuals' social networks are perhaps least likely to be considered sites for social and emotional learning. These alliances generally exist for the purpose of getting work done, and the majority are characterized by less frequent interaction and less emotional involvement than the relationships already outlined. Yet on further inspection it is clear that the instrumental and social support provided by organizational networks can enable individuals to develop particular personal and social competencies.

First, relationships with peers outside the immediate work group or team generally form in order to access information, resources, or support for a particular work initiative. For example, an engineer might seek information and support for a design idea from a peer in the sales organization. Such an encounter can give the engineer an opportunity to further develop certain personal and social competencies. For instance, the salesperson may suggest how to reframe the product idea to be more relevant to customers and also provide coaching on how to position the idea to senior management, thus enhancing the engineer's Communication and Leadership competencies.

Second, when individuals see such peer relationships as sites for learning, they are likely to invest energy in initiating and maintaining them (Wenger, 1998; Wellman, Carrington, & Hall, 1988; Wellman, Wong, Tindall, & Nazer, 1997). To the extent that individuals have this stance toward relationships and that the context rewards learning and relationship building, individuals develop (perhaps unknowingly) a network of relationships that regularly presents opportunities for increasing their Social Awareness and Social Skills. Given that these relationships are started for instrumental reasons and are less readily accessible than the relationship with the immediate work group, we would not expect these alliances to enhance Self-Awareness, Self-Regulation, and Self-Motivation, because learning in these areas seem to require more intimacy and involvement than these alliances afford. However, we hypothesize that those individuals who are willing to self-disclose, reflect, and ask for help from others outside their immediate work group and social support system are likely to develop these personal competencies as well.

The larger organizational network encompasses relationships with colleagues in other departments, divisions, and locations and at various hierarchical levels. Much has already been written about the importance of these emergent alliances in enabling individuals to accomplish work and to have relationships they can leverage for the purpose of obtaining challenging assignments, opportunities for exposure, and prospects for career advancement (Ibarra, 1993; Higgins & Kram, in press). Like emergent peer alliances, this broader array of relationships can provide information and resources as well as instrumental and social support. Although, by definition, these relationships begin in order to achieve a work-related objective, research on mentoring suggests they can evolve into relationships that support personal and professional development as well (Higgins & Kram, in press; Kram, 1988). Like all other types of relationships discussed earlier, these relationships are likely to have as prerequisites members' willingness to see organizational networks as potential sites for learning and a certain baseline of emotional intelligence.

In addition, a number of other factors are likely to shape the nature of emergent organizational networks. Perhaps most important are the demographic characteristics of an organization's workforce, including its representation of gender, racial, ethnic, and age groups at various levels and in various occupational groups. Considerable research indicates, for example, that women are more likely to experience positive developmental relationships with other women in their social networks when there is a relatively high representation of women at senior levels in the organization (Ely, 1994). When this representation is poor, emergent relationships among women are more likely to be characterized by competition and the absence of mutual support. When women and members of minority groups are insufficiently represented in powerful positions, women, people of color, and ethnic minorities are unlikely to find role models and psychosocial support and therefore also unlikely to have opportunities to develop Self-Awareness and other personal and social competencies in relationships with others who share common group memberships.

The demographic characteristics of an organization place unique constraints on women and racial minorities that cause their networks to differ from those of their white male counterparts (Ibarra, 1993). Assuming that individuals make strategic choices about how to build and manage their organizational networks, Ibarra argues that these choices are shaped by the organizational context and that women and minorities generally have structurally limited alternatives. In an empirical study of men's and women's interaction patterns in an advertising firm, men were more likely to form homophilous ties across multiple networks and to have stronger homophilous ties, whereas women evidenced a differentiated network pattern in which they obtained social support and friendship from women and instrumental access through network ties to men (Ibarra, 1992).

Influences on the Quality of Relationships

The examples we used at the beginning of this chapter and the subsequent discussion show how different types of relationships at work can contribute to developing emotional competence. They also suggest several factors that influence the degree to which relationships will provide fertile ground for such learning. We now move to the next part of our model and systematically consider those factors suggested by related research and experience to be most essential.

Baseline Levels of Individual Emotional Competence

The model suggests that a relationship will be more effective in promoting emotional competence if the individuals involved possess a certain level of emotional competence coming into the relationship. We suggested previously that an existing baseline of emotional intelligence is a prerequisite for taking advantage of developmental opportunities in both formal and emergent relationships. In the absence of these competencies many such opportunities are likely to go unnoticed or at best underutilized. The willingness to be vulnerable and the capacity to engage in relationships for the purpose of social and emotional learning are necessary conditions for the potential of relationships at work to be realized. Yet it appears that individuals vary in their willingness and capacity for such interaction.

This proposition raises three questions. First, how much emotional competence is minimally necessary? Second, what particular competencies are necessary? And third, what selection processes would enable organizations to hire individuals who come with critical emotional competencies? We do not know of any definitive research that bears directly on these questions. However, we can at least speculate about the second of these questions and offer some hypotheses, drawing on prior work that clarifies the core competencies underlying emotional intelligence (Goleman, 1998b; see also Chapter Two) and the work on how developmental relationships in the workplace evolve over time (Kram, 1988; Thomas, 1990; Thomas & Gabarro, 1999).

Perhaps the most obvious candidates for necessary competencies can be found in the Social Skills and Empathy clusters—that is, the social competencies. We hypothesize that a moderately high level of Understanding Others, Developing Others, Leveraging Diversity, Communication, Conflict Management, Building Bonds, and Collaboration and Cooperation is necessary for the development of relationships that nurture emotional competence. Moreover, Goleman (Chapter Three) has argued that these social competencies are built on certain personal competencies. Thus we also hypothesize that individuals need a certain level of Emotional Self-Awareness, Accurate Self-Assessment, and Self-Confidence. Also important are Self-Control, Trustworthiness, Commitment (to the relationship), Initiative, and Optimism. The optimal level will depend on the competence and on-the-job requirements (or situational demands). For example, the individual who has sufficient Self-Confidence and Initiative to request feedback from colleagues and also has considerable Self-Awareness is more likely than the individual who is lacking in these personal competencies to benefit from 360-degree feedback practices and informal feedback practices. In contrast, the individual who lacks Self-Awareness, has not engaged in Accurate Self-Assessment, and is not optimistic about the potential of relationships to support learning is less likely to seek out and benefit from such opportunities.

The minimal level of a competency that is necessary depends, in part, on the nature of the relationship. For instance, in certain relationships one might need higher levels of a competency such as Leveraging Diversity in order for that relationship to foster increased emotional competence. Situational factors also play a role: to take but one example, individuals are likely to need greater Initiative and Adaptability to sustain developmentally productive relationships in an organization experiencing downsizing or other forms of turbulence.

Developmental Position

The motivation and initiative required to make relationships sites for learning may be shaped by an individual's developmental position—including life stage, career stage, and ego psychology. We hypothesize that these development characteristics influence individuals' willingness and capacity to build relationships that foster social and emotional learning. From models of adult development and career development, for example, we know that individuals face unique developmental tasks at different periods in their lives and careers (Dalton & Thompson, 1986; Schein, 1978; Hall, 1976; Levinson, Darrow, Levinson, & McKee, 1978; Dalton, 1989; Super, 1957, 1986). These tasks reflect challenges that individuals must address if they are to experience personal efficacy and move into subsequent stages. Each model emphasizes a particular aspect of growth and development. For example, Dalton (1989) points to the roles that individuals play as they move from apprentice to independent contributor to mentor to sponsor. Levinson et al. (1978) emphasize the concept of the life structure, which embodies the relationships with self, work, family, community, and others that exist for the purpose of creating and realizing a life dream. Others, like Super (1957, 1986), emphasize the concept of identity, suggesting that the developmental task throughout a career is developing a clear and consistent sense of self and self-worth.

With this perspective at the forefront, we can speculate that to each relational opportunity individuals bring a certain willingness and capacity that is shaped and limited by developmental position. For example, individuals at midlife and mid-career face a set of developmental tasks generally characterized by reassessment and redirection and often motivated by an internal desire to modify or amplify the life structure built in the first half of adulthood (Levinson et al., 1978; Schein, 1978). Often, individuals at this life or career stage will find new satisfaction in facilitating growth in younger adults (Kram, 1988; Levinson et al., 1978). Indeed, mentoring alliances are often quite engaging and rewarding for the senior members of the pairs precisely because these relational opportunities become sites for addressing their own developmental tasks of this period. In relationships with junior colleagues, individuals at this stage may be particularly available to facilitate Self-Awareness, Self-Regulation, and Self-Motivation and to coach in critical Social Skills; for it is in doing this relational work that opportunities to reflect, reassess, and expand their own repertoire of activities are presented. We can assume that the midlevel professional described earlier found considerable support and coaching in his relationship with his mentor because, in part, his mentor was at a stage of development where engaging in such relational learning would enhance his ability for reassessment and redirection in his own life.

Kegan (1982, 1994) offers a different yet complementary view of individuals' developmental position. His *constructive-developmental* theory suggests that throughout the life course, individuals are engaged in a process of meaning making. This process leads them from being embedded in their own subjectivity to having an increasingly strong ability to take the world, including themselves, as object. This *subject/object dialectic* manifests itself as the degree to which individuals can balance their opposite yearnings for inclusion and for independence. In contrast to phase or stage theories (for example, those of Levinson or of Dalton & Thompson), Kegan's theory argues that developmental position is not strictly aligned with age or career stage, though it may be correlated with them. Development is depicted over time as a helix with movement back and forth between strong desires for inclusion and for separation; managing these opposing needs occurs mostly at the subconscious level, though strongly affecting how individuals approach relationships. At the most advanced stage, the *interindividual* stage, individuals are perhaps most able to engage in intimate, growth-enhancing connections with others.

How well individuals manage the continuous tension between autonomy and connection will therefore influence their willingness and ability to engage in growth-enhancing relationships at work. Kegan's helix model suggests that at lower points on the helix (that is, earlier in time), individuals may be too embedded in relationships (or alternatively too detached from relationships) to reflect objectively on and absorb any lessons that are offered. For example, the theory suggests that the individual at the early "over-included, fantasy-embedded" *impulsive* position will over-identify in relationships and therefore be limited in the Self-Awareness that might be derived from interactions with others. Then, as the individual moves from this position to the next—the *imperial* position—the tension is resolved in favor of autonomy. As the individual moves from the "sealed-up self-sufficiency" of the *imperial* position to the "over-included" *interpersonal* position, the tension between autonomy and inclusion is temporarily resolved in favor of inclusion. As the individual moves from the interpersonal to the "autonomous, self-regulating" *institutional* position, autonomy and distinctiveness become dominant. Finally, in moving to the *interindividual* position (the most advanced position in the development helix), the individual attains a new form of openness in which both individuality and connection are experienced more fully (Kegan, 1982).

In terms of social and emotional learning, we speculate that the texture of learning in relationships at work will change over the life course as individuals move from position to position. We hypothesize that Self-Awareness, Self-Regulation, and Self-Motivation will deepen and that the learning related to both personal and social competencies will be of greater complexity as individuals acquire the ability to be in connection with others while maintaining a sense of self as separate from the context of work and relationships.

Relational models of growth similarly identify the importance of interdependence in building relationships that facilitate growth and personal learning (Miller, 1986; Jordan et al., 1991; Fletcher, 1996). This new perspective on growth and development reinforces the hypothesis that individuals who reach Kegan's *institutional* or *interindividual* developmental positions, and who can maintain a stance of interdependence toward authority yet also have a baseline of emotional competencies including Empathy, Self-Reflection, Flexibility (to move in and out of novice and expert roles), Collaboration and Trustworthiness, are most likely to experience social and emotional learning through relationships at work.

Salient Group Memberships

Another factor that will influence the potential of a relationship to promote emotional competence are the participants' race and gender. There is considerable evidence, for example, that as a result of gender socialization, women have a greater tendency than men to see the potential of growth in connection with others and to have the personal and interpersonal skills to engage in such relational learning (Miller, 1986; Jordan et al., 1991; Kram & McCollom, 1998). For example, the willingness to be vulnerable, to express feelings, to actively listen, to nurture, and to collaborate is behavior more often reinforced in girls and women than in boys and men (Miller & Stiver, 1997). Indeed, these capacities regularly surface in studies of women managers as qualities that help them to be effective in organizational roles (Belenky, Clinchy, Goldberger, & Tarule, 1986; Marshall, 1984; Rosener, 1990). Similarly, Noe (1988), in studying formal mentoring programs in educational institutions, found that women were seen as using their mentors more effectively than male protégés did. In addition, Van Velsor and Hughes (1990) found that female leaders were significantly more likely than male leaders to use learning from other people as a key developmental event. They also reported that women learned more from reflection and self-assessment than did their male counterparts.

It is precisely because of such differences in gender socialization that there is considerable potential for social and emotional learning in cross-gender relationships at work. For example, though women have a tendency to be stronger in some domains (such as Self-Awareness, Empathy, and Self-Reflection), there is some indication that men tend to be stronger in the domain of Self-Regulation (having more Self-Control and ability to manage under high stress and handle multiple demands) (Goleman, 1998b). When individuals who have different emotional competencies form a relationship, each has the opportunity to observe, reflect upon, and consider experimenting with alternative ways to handle challenging situations. When they see relationship as sites for learning, both men and women find it possible to expand their repertoires of personal and social competencies through interactions with one another. Similarly, relationships that cross racial or ethnic boundaries have the potential to enhance personal and social competencies in a number of domains. In interracial alliances, for example, both minority and majority group members have the opportunity to develop Empathy, particularly for the other group's perspectives, and therefore become more effective in building collaborative alliances in the context of a diverse workforce (Kram & Hall, 1996; Thomas, 1990). Research on interracial mentoring also suggests that these developmental alliances offer both juniors and seniors the opportunity to enhance their repertoire of Social Skills—including Empathy, Communication, Influence, and Conflict Management—as they strive to connect with others who bring fundamentally different life experiences and perspectives to the organization (Thomas, 1990, 1993). So, for example, the minority protégé receives coaching and sponsorship for positions of greater responsibility and has the opportunity to acquire new social skills. And while doing so the protégé contributes to the mentor's empathy for and ability to work with individuals from diverse backgrounds.

Although the potential for SEL is great in cross-gender, cross-race, and cross-cultural alliances, these relationships may also hinder learning and development. Such relationships are not readily available in most settings (Koberg, Boss, Chappell, & Ringer, 1994; Cox & Nkomo, 1991), and even when they are available gender and racial stereotyping often infuse them, to the point where individuals are locked into constraining and unproductive roles. For example, Thomas (1989, 1990) has demonstrated how negative archetypes resulting from the history of race relations in the United States going back to the days of slavery still make it very difficult for blacks and whites to form positive developmental alliances with each other. As a consequence, in the context of cross-race alliances black men may be viewed as inadequate and overly aggressive, black women may experience attention from senior white men as demeaning or sexual, and white men may similarly experience great discomfort in relating to their black colleagues. Often, these negative stereotypes operate on an unconscious level, and until they are consciously examined will thwart the development of relationships in which personal learning can occur (Thomas & Alderfer, 1989). Similarly, studies of gender dynamics have illustrated how subtle—and not so subtle—dynamics can prevent developmental alliances between men and women from getting beyond the initiation phase (Kram, 1988; Bowen, 1984; Burke, 1984). Sexual tensions and fears of intimacy make both men and women cautious about spending informal time together, occasions where deeply personal reflection and mutual learning might otherwise take place. In addition, stereotypes about appropriate sex role behavior can lock men and women into roles that limit their effectiveness and learning (Owen & Todor, 1993; O'Leary & Ickovics, 1992; Alderfer, 1983). For example, senior white men may willingly provide more protection to their female protégés than they might to men, and junior women may collude by acting as if they need protection. Although in the short run such protection might be warranted in particularly hostile environments, in the long run it undermines junior women's capacity to establish autonomy and authority.

Clearly, the potential for SEL in relationships that cross gender, racial, and cultural boundaries can be realized only when individuals have sufficient emotional intelligence to recognize how longstanding stereotypes limit their own and others' behavior and learning. Oftentimes awareness and understanding of these obstacles to relational learning become discussible in relationships between individuals of similar backgrounds. Thus women learn about their relationships with senior men in their organization in dialogue with their female peers. And blacks find ways to navigate effectively in a white-dominated organization through their relationships with black peers and mentors. As Thomas (1990, 1993; Thomas & Alderfer, 1989; Thomas & Gabarro, 1999) has found, black managers benefit from a *dual support* strategy—relationships with both black and white seniors.

Although opportunities for same gender and same race network alliances that facilitate SEL may be more limited for women and minorities, it is also possible that with a baseline level of emotional intelligence and the willingness to see relationships as sites for acquiring personal and social competencies, women and minorities will find other benefits in the differentiated network pattern. Although it has yet to be systematically tested, our hypothesis is that when participants are armed with sufficient Empathy and Social Skills, relationships that cross gender, racial, or ethnic boundaries can be sites for significant learning. Both men and women and both whites and minority group members can acquire increased empathy for other groups' perspectives, new social skills derived from observing and modeling the behavior of those who approach situations differently, and increased capacities to effectively communicate, negotiate, and manage with people of different backgrounds.

Relational Processes

Even less is known about the impact of relational processes on relationships that foster social and emotional learning. However, we believe that the potential of relationships to promote emotional competence can be greatly enhanced when the individuals regularly engage in certain patterns of behavior. For instance, consider two hypothetical mentoring relationships. Both exist in the same organization, and the senior and junior individuals in both are very similar in their baseline levels of emotional competence. However, one pair have arranged to meet once a month after work for a couple of hours to talk about the junior person's work experiences. Furthermore, they agree that during the last fifteen minutes of their meetings, they will talk about how the relationship itself is working and whether there are any ways they could make it more productive and meaningful for both of them. As a result of these two relational processes—regular meetings and reflection on the relationship itself—the first mentoring relationship is likely to be a more productive vehicle for SEL.

Whether or not relational processes are used depends in part on other factors defined in our model. For instance, a matching process that takes participants' developmental stages and personal styles and values into account increases the likelihood that formally assigned relationships will be attractive to both parties. Similarly, a training program for mentors and mentees, provided by the organization's HR department, makes it more likely that pairs will use the relational processes suggested in our hypothetical example. Some organizations have experimented with *dialogue groups,* which are created for the purpose of fostering systematic reflection and inquiry about relationships between individuals of diverse backgrounds (Walker, 1996). As a result, enhanced Self-Awareness, Empathy, and Social Skills enable continued reflection and personal learning back on the job. Finally, if an organization's leader periodically sets aside time at the end of meetings to reflect on the group process and encourages other groups in the organization to do the same, it is more likely that others in the organization will adopt this practice.

One task for future research is to identify some of the relational processes that might be most productive for social and emotional learning in relationships and then evaluate whether in fact they have an effect on SEL. Systematic comparisons of learning outcomes for those who participate and those who do not would help identify the relational processes that have significant impact. Another area for research as well as practice is to experiment with ways of encouraging people in relationships to regularly use relational practices. When such interventions are designed as action research projects, it will be possible to identify factors that enhance or undermine adoption of such practices.

Human Resource Systems

Offering training designed to foster effective relational processes is one example of how human resource systems might influence the extent to which relationships contribute to emotional competence. In moving from the interpersonal and group level to the organizational level of our model we focus on systemwide policies and practices that either reward or undermine attention to relationships and development. Particularly important is the degree to which human resource practices encourage attention to learning and development. As Hall (Hall & Mirvis, 1996) suggests, organizations and their leaders need to assess to what extent a range of human resource practices—including performance management systems, training and education programs, developmental practices, team design and development efforts, and leadership development—are helping to create a *developmental culture.*

Most relevant here are the practices directly related to performance management—those systems that monitor and assess performance and provide incentives for behavior that is consistent with strategic objectives. These include standard systems such as performance appraisal, succession planning, and reward and recognition (including but not limited to compensation). When these systems are designed to acknowledge the importance of coaching and counseling, monitor whether individuals are attending to development of their subordinates' and peers' learning, provide feedback to managers on how well this relational work is done, and reward managers appropriately, they contribute to a culture that supports relational learning and development.

For instance, at Eli Lilly an executive mentoring process has been put in place to encourage senior decision makers to actively support the learning and development of high-potential junior managers. A primary objective of this initiative is to actively develop high-potential women and minorities for executive positions. Recognizing that in all likelihood the senior executives needed help in learning how to build relationships across gender and racial boundaries and how to facilitate others' learning of personal and social competencies, the executive development staff has continuously offered training and follow-up meetings that provide this critical support. In this way the human resource component of the organization is contributing to the potential of developmental relationships to enhance emotional competence.

There are a number of other ways in which education and training can facilitate social and emotional learning through relationships. Certainly, programs that support performance management systems by offering training in the critical interpersonal skills of listening, giving and receiving feedback, coaching, and so on have been proven quite useful (see Chapter Nine). Training can also support participants in both formally assigned and naturally occurring mentoring relationships and can help individuals recognize the value of building relationships for the purpose of learning and development (see also Phillips-Jones, 1993; Kram & Hall, 1996). Whether introduced in conjunction with a formal mentoring program or as part of career development, professional development, or diversity initiatives, such forums can help individuals develop the Self-Assessment skills and Self-Motivation to better discern opportunities for building developmental alliances within their work group and beyond. In addition to its focus on personal competencies, such training can be designed to foster Social Awareness and Social Skills, which enable individuals to begin building a network of relationships that support continuous learning.

In more recent years several other developmental practices have been introduced that may contribute to social and emotional learning (see Chapter Nine). Such initiatives—including 360-degree feedback, executive coaching, dialogue groups, assessment centers, and action learning—create opportunities for structured reflection, personal feedback, and skill practice. In the course of participating in any one of these practices, individuals have an opportunity to strengthen the personal and social competencies that can guide them in seizing opportunities to continue learning in relationships at work.

It is likely that innovative developmental practices will continue to emerge to address the pressing need for individuals at all levels in all disciplines to learn continuously, to work in collaboration with others, and to acquire the personal and social competencies that can leverage relationships for both learning and work accomplishment. And although systematic evaluation is lacking, anecdotal information suggests that these practices can make important contributions toward preparing individuals to engage in relationships for the purpose of social and emotional learning.

Leadership

Excellent performance management systems combined with effective training and a range of innovative developmental practices will have their intended impact only when the organization's leadership practices are aligned with them. Senior executives and other organizational leaders must actively model and support the relational learning and development that these human resource practices are intended to foster (also see Chapters Two, Three, and Eight for the importance of leadership). There are too many examples today of large sums being spent on elaborate programs that produce negligible results (Morrow et al., 1997). Often such failures can be attributed to the senior executive team's lack of support for the program and lack of engagement in it. As Schein (1985) and Hall (1994) have pointed out, the extent to which an organization achieves a developmental culture will largely depend on the actions and values of its leaders.

It is not surprising that there is frequently a gap between senior managers' declaration of support for development and their actions, particularly in these times of turbulence, rapid technological change, and increasingly competitive global markets. Although leaders may believe that individual and organizational capacity for continuous learning is an essential competitive advantage, matters in the external environment may consistently take their attention away from this concern. Indeed, in our own experience, executives frequently attest to the importance of mentorship and coaching in their own learning and career development. As a consequence, they espouse the use of these developmental tools in their organizations. Yet when asked to actively mentor and coach their own subordinates, they do not meet the expectations of their subordinates or their own coaches and consultants. Lack of the requisite personal and social competencies and lack of time prevent them from serving as positive role models.

The impact of this gap between espoused goals and factual actions is significant. Time and again we have seen mentoring programs, 360-degree feedback processes, and performance management systems fail to meet expectations because managers find the pressures for short-term results far more compelling than their responsibility to develop subordinates or serve as coaches to their peers. Their perception of what is most important is due in large part to the signals that senior executives send as they too are drawn into spending time on immediate business issues that might otherwise have been spent on coaching relationships with their subordinates. Thus, almost unknowingly, managers and leaders at all levels collude in perpetuating a results-oriented culture that forfeits opportunities for learning critical personal and social competencies through relationships at work.

This dynamic is very difficult to change. In our view, there are major impediments to realizing the potential of individuals (not to mention teams and organizations) to continuously enhance emotional intelligence through relationships at work. Indeed, coming to recognize the gap between beliefs and actions and developing the willingness and skills to develop more action more consistent with beliefs requires considerable Self-Awareness and Self-Reflection, considerable soul-searching (Argyris, 1993; Hall, 1994). Capturing the attention of leaders functioning in extremely demanding circumstances for the purpose of engaging them in personal learning that will ultimately contribute to the strategic success of the organization is a considerable challenge. Fortunately, there has been progress in identifying the conditions that facilitate such work (Argyris, 1986, 1994; Hall, 1994).

Argyris and Schön have demonstrated that unexamined and overlearned patterns of behavior often trap executives in loops of dysfunctional behavior and decision making (Argyris, 1994; Schön, 1990; Argyris & Schön, 1978). What is needed is a clear, simple process through which executives engage in self-learning that can be directly related to their firm's strategic objectives. For example, if senior executives know that an increasingly global and diverse customer base requires a more diverse senior management team, they may be motivated to examine behaviors that may be undermining the development and promotion of women and people of color. Similarly, if continuous learning and efficient product development teams are essential to maintaining a strong position in a particular market segment, they may be motivated to examine how they can encourage and support high-performing, diverse teams. It is up to the human resource professional to design a learning process that is user-friendly and relevant to such current strategic challenges. This process is likely to contain many of the elements already discussed—360-degree feedback, action learning, and a personal coach. In the context of structured opportunities for reflection, executives would enhance personal competencies (that is, Self-Awareness) and also develop the Social Awareness and Social Skills to lead their organizations more effectively. Ultimately, changes in executive behavior that result in the executives' modeling learning through relationships (that is, through coaching and developing their subordinates, coaching their peers, and soliciting feedback from their subordinates) would help to create a culture that values attention to growth-enhancing relationships and supports development.

Beyond the Organization

Although our model ends with organizational influences, it should be clear that the factors influencing SEL through relationships extend beyond the organization's boundaries. These macro-trends—including globalization, rapid technological change, increasing workforce diversity, and persistent economic turbulence (Handy, 1989; Wheatley, 1992; Mirvis & Hall, 1996)—have already resulted in organizational restructurings, downsizings, and dramatic strategic redirections aimed at developing more facile and effective responses to the marketplace (Friedman, 1999). Organizations that are succeeding in maintaining market share and in entering new and more competitive markets are developing flexible and autonomous work structures that empower individuals and teams to respond quickly to changes in the external environment. In the last decade we have seen numerous examples of new work designs and of reengineering and continuous improvement programs, increased numbers of mergers and cross-company ventures for the purpose of reinventing the corporation, and the proliferation of e-commerce (see also Lawler, Mohrman, & Ledford, 1992; Mirvis & Marks, 1992). Terms such as *flexform* (Toffler, 1990) and *3F—fast, free and flexible* (Hall, 1993), are used to describe key design principles of this new workplace.

Clearly, this new environment necessitates a workforce of individuals who have the wide range of personal and social competencies needed to function as continuous learners, build relationships with a diverse population of customers and coworkers, address increasing complexity and turbulence in their immediate job situations, and manage their own development in the face of an uncertain career context. Hall (1986a, 1986b) suggests that this new environment requires successful individuals to possess two *meta-competencies*, two skills of learning how to learn: identity growth (the ability to handle more complexity, self-reflection, and self-learning) and adaptability. These are quite similar to personal and social competencies that Goleman and others have delineated in this volume (see also Goleman, 1995a, 1998b).

What is less clear is how this same environment might pose substantial obstacles to developing these critical emotional competencies, especially through relationships at work. Most important is the likelihood that the rapid pace and increasingly demanding jobs leave little time for building developmental alliances or for reflection. Individuals are experiencing more pressure to produce, and investing time in learning and development may seem a luxury that most cannot afford. In addition, organizational leaders are more consumed than ever with staying abreast of global trends and competitive forces and building strategic partnerships, tasks that distract them from the equally important challenge of building a high-performing learning organization. Indeed, the macro-trends cut both ways—they pressure executives to place a greater emphasis on developing emotional competence at the same time that they erect barriers to carrying out this development.

Conclusion: Implications for Research and Practice

A challenge for scholars and practitioners is to clarify how individuals and organizations can establish conditions for creating a positive cycle of learning through relationships. As we have noted, this challenge has become a strategic imperative. It is now readily apparent that the macro-trends outlined earlier require organizations and their members to be adaptive, flexible, and able to learn continuously from experience if they are to remain viable and seize opportunities in new markets. Building high-performing heterogeneous teams that are innovative despite short cycle times and nurturing a diverse workforce that is innovative because differences are valued and managed effectively are just two of the many tasks that make the acquisition of the personal and social competencies outlined by Goleman (1995a; 1998b) and others (Hall, 1986a; Boyatzis, Cowen, & Kolb, 1995) a necessity.

Our model suggests a number of ways in which relationships can help people to develop these vital competencies. It also suggests a number of questions for future research (see Exhibit 11.1). First, relationships of different types offer unique opportunities to develop particular personal and social competencies. For example, in hierarchical mentoring relationships, juniors have the opportunity to enhance Self-Awareness, Self-Regulation, and some of the Social Skills required to navigate in the organizational world. In these same relationships, seniors have the opportunity to enhance coaching, listening, and feedback skills and also to enhance

EXHIBIT 11.1. AGENDA FOR FUTURE RESEARCH.

Types of Relationships

1. How do *formal* and *emergent relationships* compare in the extent to which they foster SEL?

2. How do *mentoring* and *coaching relationships* compare in the extent to which they foster SEL?

3. How do *peer relationships* foster the development of particular *personal* and *social competencies?*

4. How do *supervisory relationships* enable individuals to develop particular *personal* and *social competencies?*

5. Are there identifiable *patterns of relationships* that enhance particular *personal* and *social competencies?*

Individual Factors

6. What levels of *personal* and *social competencies* are *minimally necessary* in order for individuals to engage in relationships that promote further competence?

7. How does an individual's *developmental position* influence his or her *willingness* and *capacity* to enhance personal and social competencies in relationships?

Interpersonal and Group Factors

8. Under what conditions do cross-gender and interracial relationships serve as sites for developing *Self-Awareness, Self-Regulation, Empathy,* and *Social Skills?*

9. Which *relational processes* enhance the development of emotional competencies in relationships at work?

10. How can *relational processes* be incorporated in work teams in order to promote SEL in intrateam relationships?

Organizational Factors

11. How can *selection processes* be designed so that organizations hire individuals who possess the necessary baseline of emotional competence?

12. How can *human resource development systems*—for example, performance appraisal, training, 360-degree feedback, and executive coaching—promote SEL in relationships?

13. What *intervention strategies* are most effective in engaging leaders in learning that enhances their *personal* and *social competencies?*

14. What *intervention strategies* are most effective in engaging leaders in creating and reinforcing a developmental culture?

15. How can *scholars* and *practitioners collaborate* to invent, evaluate, and learn from interventions designed to foster SEL through relationships at work?

Self-Awareness through sharing their own experiences and to enhance Empathy through understanding the juniors' experiences. In intrateam relationships, opportunities abound for increasing Negotiation, Collaboration, Conflict Management, and Leadership skills as individuals strive to accomplish work objectives in this context.

Our framework suggests that relationships that exist primarily for the purpose of achieving work objectives can also foster social and emotional learning. For example, a range of personal and social competencies might be developed in supervisory relationships. We hypothesize, however, that the evaluative component in supervisory relationships limits the scope of this range. The focus on performance management and the accomplishment of work may conflict with the self-disclosure, self-reflection, and willingness necessary for SEL. In addition, although it has been beyond the scope of this chapter to consider the impact of dysfunctional relationships on social and emotional learning, it seems important to consider how these relationships too might serve as sites for SEL as individuals strive to cope with such difficult situations.

We have also suggested that the potential for social and emotional learning will depend on the emotional competence that the individuals bring to the relationship. A sufficient baseline of emotional intelligence is a prerequisite for setting SEL in motion. Without the willingness and the ability to reflect on experiences, actively listen, and engage in periodic self-assessment, it is unlikely that personal learning will occur. In addition, even when a baseline of emotional intelligence is present, the challenges posed by relationships that cross gender, racial, and cultural boundaries are significant. These heterogeneous relationships have the potential to foster personal and social competencies as individuals learn to build relationships with others who have differing values, perspectives, and personal histories. Indeed, the opportunities to develop Self-Awareness, Empathy for others' points of view, and the Social Skills of Managing Conflict and Leveraging Diversity on a number of dimensions abound in cross-gender and cross-race relationships. Yet research has demonstrated that too often powerful stereotypes rooted in history and socialization interfere with the apparently high potential for growth in these connections (Thomas, 1993, 1989; Kram, 1988; Ragins, 1989). Thus another hypothesis is that racial and gender heterogeneity in relationships will contribute to SEL only when both parties have a high degree of certain competencies such as Empathy.

Similarly, we hypothesize that the developmental position of each individual in a relationship will shape the potential of that relationship as a site for acquiring particular personal and social competencies. Various development theories converge on the hypothesis that individuals' stance toward authority, willingness to be vulnerable in exchanges with others, and current developmental tasks related to their identity at work will shape the extent to which they enter relationships with superiors, subordinates, or peers with the expectation of mutuality, collaboration, and personal learning (compare Levinson et al., 1978; Kegan, 1994; Kahn & Kram, 1994). When, for example, an individual is in an early stage of adult development, it is likely that she will view those in authority as distant experts rather than as co-learners; given this perspective, her learning at this time may be limited to emotional competencies that can be enhanced through one-directional learning (for example, Self-Awareness that is increased through feedback and coaching from a boss or mentor).

We also hypothesize that certain relational processes will enhance the development potential of relationships. Specifically, relationships will contribute to greater Self-Awareness and Social Skills if the individuals periodically set aside time to reflect on their own interactions and then create new norms for dealing with any difficulties such reflection reveals. Similarly, teams that reflect on their process can discover practices that facilitate members' acquiring new personal and social competencies.

The model also suggests that relationships are more likely to promote social and emotional learning when there are human resource systems that support such learning. These systems might include performance management processes that explicitly incorporate social and emotional learning as well as training to support the processes. For example, formal mentoring programs that incorporate training in social and emotional competence should lead to more developmentally productive relationships than programs that lack such learning objectives and related training.

Finally, we have suggested that organizational leadership will influence the degree to which relationships in the organization enhance social and emotional learning. Specifically, we hypothesize a parallel process in which relationships among leaders at the highest level of the organization become templates for relationships at lower levels. If organizational leaders value relational learning and engage in it regularly themselves, others in the organization will be more likely to do so. The importance of attending to the ways in which organizational leaders support or undermine efforts to facilitate SEL through relationships cannot be underscored enough. It is already known that combining opportunities to reflect systematically on experiences, in a context that is user-friendly and directly relevant to critical strategic issues, and 360-degree feedback and personal coaching can be effective in enabling leaders to model the process (Argyris, 1993, 1994; Hall, 1994). Researchers and practitioners will make important contributions to an understanding of the conditions that promote emotional intelligence in the workplace if their efforts to positively engage senior managers in this challenge are grounded in existent research and effective practice and if they then reflect on lessons learned as they go about this work.

Our intention in this chapter has been to push beyond the boundaries of what research has already demonstrated. Interventions designed to promote opportunities for social and emotional learning are a critical next step. In our review of the human resource practices that influence relationships at work, we have suggested that there are many opportunities to enhance performance management systems and training toward this end. In addition, a range of innovative developmental practices—such as 360-degree feedback, dialogue groups, action learning, and executive coaching—have a track record of effectiveness that suggests they can support the objective of creating opportunities for learning through relationships. It seems especially important to consider how to make personal and social competencies explicit goals in such initiatives and to systematically evaluate the impact of these competencies on individuals' behavior, on relationship and team dynamics, and on organizational performance (Cherniss & Adler, 2000).

It is our hope that researchers and human resource professionals will focus on how to maximize the possibility that relationships at work will serve as sites for social and emotional learning. The challenges that we have outlined in this chapter call for active collaboration among scholars and practitioners (Price, Friedland, Choi, & Caplan, 1998; Price & Politser, 1980). Such collaborations can test and evaluate some of the intervention strategies suggested here, invent new approaches not yet articulated, and contribute to an understanding of the ways in which (and the conditions under which) individuals can develop the willingness and capacity to build growth-enhancing connections at work.

CHAPTER TWELVE

IMPLEMENTING EMOTIONAL INTELLIGENCE PROGRAMS IN ORGANIZATIONS

Cary Cherniss
Robert D. Caplan

American Express Financial Advisors prides itself on helping clients develop financial plans that include the purchase of life insurance. But in 1991, the senior vice president in charge of life insurance at American Express Financial Advisors (AEFA) noticed that something was wrong. Seventy-three percent of clients with such plans never followed through with the purchase of life insurance. This is the story of how the vice president's process of inquiry led, a year later, to a novel solution—AEFA would train its financial advisors and their managers in "emotional competence." The year was 1991. Four years later, Daniel Goleman's first book on emotional intelligence (1995a) practically turned the concept into a household word in the halls of corporate America.

How did the AEFA program come about? And what was the impact on sales revenue?

To seek the answers, one of us (Cary Cherniss) visited AEFA corporate headquarters in Minneapolis a number of times in order to learn the history of the emotional competence program. As we studied what we had learned, we realized that this case study has much to teach all of us about how to implement emotional intelligence (EI) programs in large corporations. The lessons highlight both keys to success and some problems and mistakes that can make it more difficult to establish an EI program.

Program Overview

The emotional competence program at American Express Financial Advisors was designed initially to help the company's advisors cope with the emotional reactions that they have to selling life insurance. The advisors learn about the impact of emotions on human behavior, and they learn how to identify and manage their own emotional reactions. Several versions of the program are currently being or have been offered. One version is an integral part of the training that all new advisors receive. Another version is for managers and is a standard part of the new manager development program. A third version is offered to regional management sales teams. There also are versions designed for sales consultants, veteran advisors, and corporate office management teams. In the earliest versions of the program, external licensed psychologists provided the training. Outsiders continue to provide the regional management team, or leadership, versions, but veteran advisors now deliver the program to new advisors.

Two versions of the program have been evaluated. The findings suggest that advisors who receive the training generate more sales revenue than advisors do who are not given it. Furthermore, when regional management teams are trained, their advisors generate more revenue than advisors working in regions where the management teams have not received the training. For instance, one study showed that when group vice presidents and their direct reports received emotional competence training, their advisors generated 11 percent more growth in sales revenue during a fifteen-month period than did advisors whose management team did not go through the training. The company estimated that this difference resulted in over $200 million more in sales revenue. Moreover, the program is well liked: 91 percent of participants report a positive personal benefit, and 88 percent of leaders report that it is relevant to their jobs.

A Brief History

In 1991, the senior vice president in charge of life insurance noticed that few of the clients whose financial plans called for the purchase of life insurance actually bought some. His first thought was that there was something wrong with the product, but his marketing people could not discover any serious flaws that would lead to such a low purchase rate. So he established a *skunk works* team comprising four individuals with different backgrounds, and he told them to take six months to study the problem and come up with a solution. They had complete autonomy and their own budget. The only restrictions were that they must support any conclusions with data, and they should be innovative in their thinking. Although this unconventional approach raised some eyebrows, there was little overt opposition because this executive had a great deal of credibility. He had come to the company a few years before and had quickly established a stellar record. He was viewed as one of the most successful executives in the life insurance industry. Also the company was very profitable at this time.

The skunk works team commissioned a series of studies by an outside consulting firm. The results suggested that many advisors found it unpleasant to sell life insurance to their clients. Selling life insurance made them feel guilty, embarrassed, and even ashamed. They felt that selling was not congruent with their role or values. These negative emotional reactions seemed to be a major impediment to sales. Traditional methods of motivating encouraged the advisors to ignore or override their emotional resistance. However, these methods seemed to make the problem worse, not better.

The "skunks" sought permission to test a theory about why more insurance was not being sold. They proposed conducting a pilot program. This program would teach advisors how to become aware of their emotional reactions and to cope with them in adaptive ways. For instance, in one exercise, participants would learn how to stop and focus in on what they were feeling at that point in time; a list of *feeling words* would help them to identify their feelings. In another exercise, they would learn to become aware of the *self-talk* that led to disruptive feelings like self-doubt or shame and to replace it with more accurate, constructive self-talk. Management gave the skunk works team members permission to conduct the experiment. They designed and implemented the program and evaluated its impact on sales revenue. They found that the advisors who went through the training generated more revenue than a matched group that did not.

After this successful pilot, the first corporate sponsor, the senior vice president in charge of life insurance, decided that the program should become a regular part of the training for advisors. The senior vice president in charge of sales agreed. He had long argued that the sales process was strongly influenced by emotion. He became a staunch advocate for the program, frequently mentioning it in his talks with advisors around the country and encouraging them to sign up for it.

About this time (1994) the skunk works team also changed. Three of the four original members left to assume other responsibilities in the company, and a new person joined the team. Trainers and consultants from outside the company also helped with the planning. The team members now developed a new version of the program for regional management teams. It was intended to teach managers how to be *emotional coaches* to the advisors. Unfortunately, the first session of the program pilot was a disaster. The trainers and their material failed to connect with the trainees. The trainees felt that the trainers were unfamiliar with the process of financial advising and that their material was mostly "psycho-babble." The problem was partly due to the training design and a lack of fit between the trainers' personal qualities and the trainees' expectations. There was too much lecturing, and the trainers presented themselves more as experts than as guides and facilitators. Another difficulty arose from social dynamics within the trainee group. The trainees came from two regional offices that had recently been merged, and there was still considerable tension between the people from the different offices. (As a result of this experience the trainers now find out beforehand about the dynamics of the groups they will work with so that they can take these issues into account during the training.)

Fortunately, two members of the emotional competence team revised the program after the disastrous pilot. They made the material more relevant and business oriented, and they selected new trainers. A third team member used her influence to get a second chance to test the program. The second session went much better, and this leadership version of the program became popular with regional management teams during the next two years.

Over time the program evolved in both design and management. The skunk works team eventually was broken up, and two members were assigned to different groups in the company. One took charge of the leadership versions of the program, and the other focused on the advisor versions. Although there was research suggesting that the program had a positive impact on sales, and the senior VP for sales continued to provide strong support, the initial resistance to the program continued. The program manager in charge of the leadership versions was assigned to other responsibilities and told not to spend time on the emotional competence program. She continued to work on the program in her "spare time," and her performance review suffered as a result. Finally, at the end of 1998, she was told there was no money in the budget for her or the program. Rather than try to secure another position in the company, she decided to leave in order to promote emotional competence training in a more supportive setting. Resistance to the program had persisted because some managers and advisors remained unconvinced that becoming more skilled in handling emotions would lead to more sales.

However, in spite of this resistance, the company continued to offer the program. Within two months after the senior program manager left, the head of training for advisors assigned someone else to oversee it. Six months later the program was more popular than ever, and the company was selling it to other companies. (A chronology of the case is presented in Table 12.1.)

TABLE 12.1. CHRONOLOGY OF
PROGRAM DEVELOPMENT AND IMPLEMENTATION.

1991	A skunk works project is set up by the senior vice president for life insurance to find out why clients are not buying more life insurance. He selects four people to form the team.
1992– 1993	The skunk works team conducts three studies on the role of emotion in the business and reports on the results throughout the company.
1993	The team develops and implements the first training program for a group of advisors.
1994	The team reports on the results of the first training program.
	Three of the original four members of the team leave, and a new person joins the project. Trainers and consultants from outside the company help with the planning.
	The project is shifted from the life insurance organization to the sales training organization; it is now under the sponsorship of the executive VP for sales.
1994– 1995	A version of the program for leaders is developed and piloted with one regional management group. The first module is a disaster. The program is redesigned, the trainers are changed, and the second module is presented to the same group. The outcome is much more positive.
1995	The leadership version of the program is repeated in several other regions. There is much demand for it and positive feedback.
	A corporation-wide training initiative provides resources for offering the program throughout the regions.
	A new version of the program for veteran advisors is designed.
	Training on emotional competence is added to the standard training for new advisors.
	Another version of the program becomes part of the new manager development program.
1996	The veteran advisor version of the program is scaled back from 3 days to 1 day. The results are disappointing.
	The program is offered to corporate office leadership teams.
1997	A version of the program for sales consultants is developed.
	The manager of the program begins to market it to other companies.
1998	The original program manager leaves the company.
1999	A new manager for the program is selected, and efforts to market the program outside the company intensify.
2000	The program continues to be implemented in the company and in other companies as well.

The Case Analysis

Despite continued resistance and a future that remains unclear, the emotional competence program represents a successful implementation in many ways. It was established in a large corporation several years before emotional competence became an "O.K." topic in business organizations, and it has survived for over eight years. We believe the program's success results primarily from two factors. The first is how well it has navigated the three critical stages required for the successful implementation of an innovation. The second is the emotional intelligence of the program's implementers.

Price, Friedland, Choi, and Caplan (1998) have suggested that successful adoption and implementation of innovative practices requires safe navigation through three stages: exploration, innovation and mutual adaptation, and institutionalization. We believe that the American Express Financial Advisors emotional competence program was successful because of the way it navigated these three stages. We also believe that the problems encountered in establishing the program on a secure and lasting basis are related to a failure to achieve some of the tasks associated with each stage.

Stage 1: Exploration

During the exploration phase, a proposed innovative program or practice needs a champion, and that champion must be able to demonstrate that there is a critical need and that the innovation addresses that critical need. In addition, employees who are expected to adopt the new practice must be exposed to convincing evidence that they are capable of adopting the new practice (see, for example, Lawler, 1973). After all, what good is a perfect solution if nobody feels capable of implementing it? All three of these ingredients—a champion, demonstration that the innovation addresses a critical need, and convincing evidence that it can work—were present in the case of the emotional competence program.

Championing the Innovation: Sponsorship from a Powerful Executive. For better or worse, organizations are political entities. The support of an influential executive who can provide political protection and financial backing can make the difference between success and failure for a new initiative that promotes emotional intelligence.

The AEFA emotional competence program had *two* powerful sponsors who helped the program become established and gain widespread recognition. The first was the senior vice president in charge of life insurance. He was the one who brought together the four people who eventually developed the emotional competence program. When they recommended a solution that would train advisors to cope better with their feelings, there was much skepticism and eye-rolling. The vice president often heard comments such as, "Why do you want to allocate money for this touchy-feely garbage?" But he provided the protection that the project's designers needed in order to go on and validate their findings. This executive was a particularly effective sponsor for several reasons. He had come to the company a few years before and had established a solid track record there. At the time he was the head of the fastest-growing life insurance concern in the country, and he was viewed by many as a mover and shaker in the insurance industry. Moreover, he was an actuary by training, and actuaries are viewed as anything but reckless or "flaky." All these credentials gave him a great deal of credibility and clout. With this kind of sponsorship, the new program was allowed to move ahead with its unconventional message. The work of French and Raven (1959) suggests that a sponsor's power will depend on a number of factors, including position in the organization, perceived expertise, and likability. The executive who initially provided sponsorship for the emotional competence program scored high on all of these "bases of social power."

Once the program had been pilot tested and evaluated, the first sponsor handed it off to the senior vice president in charge of sales. He became an even more enthusiastic sponsor of the program. And he too was a powerful source of support. This sales executive had been with the company for twenty years, starting as an advisor right out of college. From the beginning he had been extraordinarily successful. Within a year he had been asked to help train new advisors, and within two years he was promoted to district manager. His district was the top in the country for seven of eight years. He had been the executive in charge of sales for over five years when he became the program's sponsor. He was viewed as an "excellent sales leader," and he was very well regarded in the field and in the home office. Also, he headed up one of the most valued parts of the company; as one person we interviewed put it, "new sales is what generates revenue for the company." The sales VP liked the program. He long had believed that emotions were crucial to selling. He was convinced that his own success had much to do with helping people deal with emotions. He even had written a book in which he discussed the importance of emotions and motivation in sales. Thus when he became the "owner" of the program, he gave it more than just a home and a budget. He became an advocate and gave the program a strong plug every time he spoke to a new group of advisors. Virtually everyone with whom we spoke said that this sponsor's support was crucial for the program's acceptance and survival. As one person put it, "People in the field could have killed it, and would have, without his support."

Demonstrating Need. One of the most important factors contributing to the program's adoption was that it developed as a direct response to a business need. Too many clients were failing to follow up on recommended purchases of life insurance. The marketing people had tried several approaches but nothing made a significant difference. Finally, a marketing study that also studied the advisors led to the idea that advisor empathy was crucial for developing trust with the client. These studies also suggested that advisor self-doubt was a major barrier in selling. Emotional competence training then was developed and offered as a solution to this business problem.

The program's close link to a business need was reinforced by the fact that it was developed as part of a marketing effort rather than as an HR initiative. It was not initially designed as a course to improve the human relations skills of employees. It was the life insurance VP, not the HR VP, who initiated the first work in this area. None of the four members of the original skunk works team came from HR. Later the program was shifted to the VP for sales. A strong research base also strengthened the link between the new program and the business need. The initiator of the emotional competence program expected it to be based on research from the beginning. The members of the skunk works group that developed the program were told that they had almost complete freedom to do whatever they wanted but that, succeed or fail, they should "learn something." One of the few criteria for deliverables was that "recommendations must be supported by research." Consequently, one of the first actions taken by the team was to hire a consulting firm to do a study of the ways emotions entered into the process of buying and selling life insurance. After conducting an initial study focused on the emotions stirred up for the clients, the same firm did a study focusing on the emotions experienced by the advisors when they tried to sell life insurance. The results showed that many advisors felt uneasy about this part of their role. To confirm the study results, the team proposed yet another study to look at the correlation between advisor success and emotional coping ability. When the results suggested that successful advisors in fact were more adept at coping with the emotional side of selling, the team did one more study: it set up an experimental training program designed to teach advisors how to cope better, and it evaluated whether those who went through the program subsequently sold more insurance than a control group.

A number of persons we interviewed confirmed that these studies were important in helping to make the case for emotional competence training. One person said that he initially was skeptical about the whole idea, but when he saw the results of the research, "it was startling." As results became available the team made numerous presentations to different groups in the company. The fact that the studies were done by outside experts with strong academic credentials helped to give the results credibility. However, not all the research was compelling. The first two studies were not especially convincing for many people in the company. Nevertheless, they were strong enough for the team to get continued support for more research and development work. Eventually, the team was able to provide convincing sales data, and that was what had the biggest impact for many. However, qualitative data that struck a "value nerve" were important too. For instance, it deeply troubled some executives to read statements from the advisors study such as, "I feel like a used car salesman when I try to sell life insurance," or, "It makes me feel unethical." Thus the maximum impact was achieved by the combination of hard data on sales and emotionally gripping anecdotes. Of course some managers and executives in the company remained skeptical. One person we interviewed claimed, "The evaluation data haven't been persuasive at all. Everyone knows you can make data say what you want. The data were looked at with suspicion." For this individual and some others, it was more important that the program had the backing of powerful sponsors and that so many participants liked it. Nevertheless, many people in the company were impressed that the program was based on so much solid research.

The planners continued to focus on linking the program to business needs when the program shifted to the regional level. For example, the planners spent considerable time on the phone with each regional vice president in order to learn about the business needs of that particular group, and they were willing to modify the program to meet a region's particular needs. In delivering the program the trainers too focused initially on linking it to business needs. They spent time early in the training on exercises that showed the trainees how emotional competence contributes to the advising process. In this case, really strong support for the program developed only after program advocates *demonstrated* that advisors could learn emotional competence and use it to improve sales.

During the early years of the program, considerable time was spent on demonstrating its relevance for important business needs, but as the program became widely adopted and used throughout the company, the managers and trainers seemed to spend less time on this important task. As a result the company seems to have faltered in the critical third phase of implementation, institutionalizing the innovation. Continued resistance to the program after it had been in existence for several years might have been due in part to this reduction in emphasis on linking it to a business need. Rather than becoming an institutionalized part of the culture, the program seemed like an ongoing request for change, one of the most predictable triggers of resistance to change (Coch & French, 1948).

Providing Evidence That Individuals Can Use the New Practice.
Unlike other innovations that might be introduced into an organization, the emotional competence program was not initially *observable,* and this made it more difficult than

it might otherwise have been for program advocates to convince other managers and employees that the practices taught could actually be used. As a brand-new program created in house, it could be observed by its creators and company executives only through a pilot run. Fortunately, the planners received permission to conduct such a pilot. The successful pilot, with the compelling data showing that the training led to increased sales, convincingly showed that emotional competence training could be implemented in the company.

Stage 2: Innovation and Mutual Adaptation

Once a decision has been made during the exploration stage to pursue a change, teams have to be given considerable freedom to *experiment and explore* in order to innovate and adapt, that is, to discover what works. As general principles evolve, considerable flexibility is still needed to allow the innovator to adapt the innovation to meet the needs and resources of particular implementation sites and contingencies.

Providing Autonomy and Support for Experimentation. In the development of the emotional competence program, using a skunk works team provided freedom and flexibility necessary for navigating the second stage of successful adoption and implementation of innovative practices. Team members developed and pilot-tested more than one version of the program. They monitored each test run closely, and they spent many hours debriefing among themselves and modifying what they had designed. Putting the project in the hands of a skunk works team helped protect it from such *creativity killers* as close surveillance, evaluation, and arbitrary deadlines (Amabile, 1988). Teams with comparatively less formality, more flexible roles, and more open flows of information seem best suited to developing initiatives such as emotional intelligence programs (Kanter, 1989). To put it another way, successful innovation is most likely to flourish in groups based on the principles of the *learning organization* (Senge, 1990). In the formation of the emotional competence program, AEFA achieved these conditions through employing the skunk works technique.

In establishing the skunk works team, the senior VP for life insurance picked four people whom he thought were risk-takers and told them they had six months and half a million dollars to figure out why clients were not buying more life insurance. He also told them to be creative and innovative, even if it meant that they failed. "It's okay to strike out as long as you learn something," was the way he put it at one point. The written charter for the team stated: "The team should bat for the home run every time even if it means we're 0 for 27 at the end. And no bunting! To play it safe, to manufacture a non-breakthrough result for the sake of saying we accomplished something concrete will not be acceptable." Although the team members brought different kinds of expertise and experience, initially there was no leader and no defined roles. The team's first activity was to hire a consulting firm that specialized in creativity training to organize and lead a retreat for them and a few other employees at the company.

Research on innovation suggests that in addition to a high degree of flexibility, development teams need leaders who protect them from outside interference and distractions and set a clear direction without managing too tightly. They also need sufficient resources, encouragement from management, and an atmosphere free of threatening evaluation. Finally, they need a challenge arising from the nature of the problem or its importance to the organization (Amabile & Conti, 1997). The skunk works team had all of these advantages. The life insurance VP provided the time, resources, and protection necessary for the team to innovate and experiment.

The skunk works mechanism itself played a crucial role in the development of the program. Several people we interviewed said that they did not think something as innovative as emotional competence training would have emerged from an existing, traditional group in the organization. In addition to autonomy and the mandate to be creative, a relatively long-term time to work was an important aspect of this skunk works setup. The original charter was extended after the first six months so that the team eventually had almost two years and over a million dollars to incubate the program. Without so much time for learning, reflection, and experimentation, the team probably would not have been as successful in establishing the program.

A skunk works arrangement also works best in combination with some of the other factors we have discussed. For instance, Kanter (1989, p. 219) has argued that "newstream" groups "need to be connected to powerful sponsors in the mainstream organization." She also has suggested that "top management needs to set the context by defining goals to which potential innovators can aspire, allocating resources for experimentation, and then reintegrating the new venture into the mainstream establishment" (p. 221). The senior executive who established the skunk works project at AEFA did precisely that.

Balancing Autonomy and Connectedness. The effectiveness of the skunk works team during the mutual adaptation phase depended in large part on its autonomy and freedom. However, too much autonomy can be detrimental, for it can lead to isolation and marginalization of the group and its activities. A key task for the group is to keep its boundaries with other groups in the organization optimally permeable (Alderfer, 1980). In the emotional competence program case, the skunk works team had considerable autonomy, but it was not completely cut off from the rest of the organization. The group members came from other groups in the organization, and they expected to return to other groups after a certain amount of time. They also worked hard to maintain communication with other groups and to avoid ostracizing them, treating them as unimportant to the work in hand. For instance, when they arranged for a consultant to come in and lead a retreat for them on creative thinking, they invited a number of individuals in the company who were not members of the team to attend it with them.

Some Adaptation Stage Problems. Some of the problems that had to be dealt with during the adaptation stage arose out of group dynamics in the skunk works team, and others were related to the nature of the innovation itself.

The skunk works project, although it proved highly effective in many ways, did have a downside. During much of its existence, internal tension and conflict plagued the group. Part of the problem was that one person was designated the group's "administrator," and another was put on the team because of her "process skills." Yet no one was supposed to be the "leader." Not surprisingly, these two individuals both exerted strong influence and occasionally clashed. Also, the person with the process skills was the only person selected explicitly for social and emotional competence. So in addition to its lack of structure and clear authority, the team overall seemed to lack critical personal and interpersonal competencies that could have helped it deal more effectively with internal tension.

The informality and flexibility of the skunk works team also became liabilities when it shifted into an operational mode and began to design and deliver programs. At that point, the group needed a somewhat more traditional structure. Fortunately, as members of the original team left and were replaced, a more viable structure resulted, with one individual emerging as the clear leader.

Furthermore, although the planners of the emotional competence program enjoyed considerable autonomy, their ability to modify and adapt the program as it evolved was hampered by obstacles inherent in the innovation itself. Successful adaptation of an innovation to a particular organizational setting requires that the innovation be somewhat divisible, easy to install, and user-friendly (Glaser & Taylor, 1973; Heller, 1996; Howes & Quinn, 1978; Klein & Sorra, 1996). The emotional competence program encountered difficulty in meeting all three of these needs. First, the innovation is not easily divisible. After the initial successful implementations of the program, it began to be offered in different forms in different parts of the company. As new groups began to work with it, they tried to scale back the amount of hours required for its implementation. They also tried to use internal training people and even veteran financial advisors with no background in either training or psychology as trainers. These efforts were disappointing. Second, the innovation is not easy to install. It seems to require highly trained professionals with special expertise as well as close monitoring by a program manager. Finally, the innovation has proved to be rather user-unfriendly. The planning team worked hard to make the training experience itself a pleasant one, but emotional competence training cannot be as user-friendly as many other types of training because it involves a high degree of effort and some personal risk on the part of participants and their managers. These three aspects of the innovation limited the extent to which the planners could adapt the innovation to meet the needs of different users.

Despite these problems, the skunk works team ultimately succeeded in launching the new program. In general, the team's high degree of autonomy and lack of structure proved to be an asset during the second phase of the implementation process when research and experimentation were the central tasks.

Stage 3: Institutionalization

Once an innovation has been developed, tested, and refined to fit local needs, planners are ready to move into the third phase of implementation. The challenge for the organization in this last phase is to make the new practice part of the everyday culture, to infuse it throughout the organization. Championship needs to be ongoing and to exist at all levels of management and administration. Although the emotional competence program has made some progress in achieving the tasks necessary for successful institutionalization, there still is much to be done. Evidence for this comes from the fact that many people in the company believe that the program may not survive if its current corporate sponsor leaves. Nevertheless, the program's managers have pursued some strategies that have contributed to at least a degree of institutionalization.

Infusing the Program Throughout the Organization. One way that the emotional competence program has achieved a certain degree of institutionalization is its infusion throughout the organization. Initially the program was designed for advisors. After the pilot the team proposed that a different version be developed for regional management groups. The rationale was that the regional managers met weekly with the advisors, and they could use this time to reinforce emotional competence lessons if they themselves had been exposed to the training. Eventually, an additional version was developed for advisors so that now there is one version for new advisors, which has become a regular part of the new advisor training program, and another version for veteran advisors. Somewhat later, yet a different version of the program was developed for new managers. It too has become a regular part of the training for this group. The next version to be developed targeted corporate office management teams. Finally, a version of the program was developed for sales consultants. These are individuals who provide technical assistance to advisors on a variety of matters. The program manager was able to convince the head of this group that many of the situations sales consultants discussed with advisors had a large emotional competence component. By training the sales consultants to become *emotional coaches,* the company could greatly increase their usefulness to the advisors.

In addition to all these different versions of the program, a program manager found another way to infuse emotional competence into the company. When she was assigned to a high-profile succession planning effort for the company's top executive positions, she found ways to "sneak" emotional competence into the process by making it part of the competencies on which executives were assessed. In short, infusion of multiple program versions throughout the organization has helped emotional competence training to survive for a long time and to become established in the company.

Establishing and Maintaining Quality Standards. Another important task for managers in the institutionalization stage is to set up monitoring, feedback, and reward systems to sustain the change. Quality control becomes particularly important. Quality standards need to be clearly established. Then monitoring and feedback need to detect and correct lapses and deviations from the quality standards. "Booster shots" should be given to avert management and nonmanagement drift away from key practices. Maintaining a high level of quality control is especially important for emotional intelligence programs. If an emotional intelligence program becomes associated with shoddy, superficial work, resistance to it will increase. Opponents of such training need few excuses to kill it. Thus the quality of a new emotional intelligence program will be another factor that affects its implementation. High-quality programs have a better chance of gaining acceptance and surviving.

In the case of the AEFA emotional competence program, the program manager was concerned about the program's quality from the beginning. She was constantly on the lookout for areas in which it might be vulnerable to criticism. For this reason, she monitored the trainers very closely, and she fired more than one because they did not meet her exacting standards. She insisted on employing doctoral-level psychologists as trainers in part because she believed that they would ensure a certain level of quality. During the year following the pilot, the program manager and another member of the skunk works team sat in on every presentation of the program, even though it meant traveling all over the country and spending at least thirty days just observing the program being delivered. After each delivery they devoted several hours to a debriefing with the trainers. Although this close monitoring was expensive, it contributed to a very high level of quality.

One problem, however, has been that this emphasis on quality has never been standardized or formalized to any extent. The only clear quality criterion established concerns the credentials of the trainers: they are, as mentioned, to be doctoral-level psychologists. Everyone has agreed that this is not enough, that trainers need more than just formal training in behavioral science; nevertheless the other qualities trainers need have never been clearly spelled out. Even the requirement that the trainers be doctoral-level psychologists has been questioned. Although the original planning group believed that the trainers should be doctoral-level, licensed psychologists, other managers in the company believe that any effective trainer could deliver this training. This ambiguity and uncertainty has made the innovation more difficult to institutionalize.

Training Individuals to Use the Innovation. Another requirement for the institutionalization phase is that many members of the organization need to be trained to implement the innovation. Controversy over who is qualified to be a trainer and the continued reliance on two outsiders to do much of the training has meant that the emotional competence program has not made much progress on this front either. The program initially relied entirely on outsiders (professional psychologists) with special expertise to deliver it. After two years, some parts of the company tried to implement the program with untrained trainers. In the version that was developed for new advisors, veteran advisors with no special training have been delivering the program. Some of these trainers have not even gone through the program themselves. They were selected because they were part of a pool of veteran advisors brought in to train new advisors. Not until very recently was anyone in the company trained to deliver the new advisors program.

Thus the company has not yet found a satisfactory way to train company employees to deliver the emotional competence program. Neither relying on outsiders nor using untrained insiders will provide the kind of stable foundation necessary for institutionalization of the program.

Routinizing Procedures. Institutionalization of an innovation also requires establishing routine procedures and ensuring that the program becomes a normal part of organizational operations. On one hand the emotional competence program has made some progress on this front. It now is a standard part of training for both new advisors and new managers. On the other hand the level of routinization necessary for institutionalizing the innovation has not yet been achieved. Although the program is part of standard training, it is a separate module that could be easily removed.

Offering Financial Incentives for Innovation Use. One other factor that has hampered institutionalization is the lack of financial incentives. Managers and advisors have few if any incentives to participate, other than the hoped for gains in revenues. In fact, advisors face a strong disincentive because they must give up time and opportunities for selling in order to attend the program.

Thus, although the program continues to flourish, it has not yet successfully navigated the third and final phase of implementation. As a result, the program's long-term survival remains in doubt.

The Emotional Intelligence of Program Planners and Managers

Implementing emotional intelligence programs in organizations depends in part on navigating the three stages described in the previous sections. However, it also depends on *how* these stages are navigated, and this is largely a function of the emotional intelligence of those who orchestrate the implementation effort.

The individuals who implemented the emotional competence program used many social and emotional competencies during all three phases of the process. As mentioned, when the senior VP who set up the project picked four people to work on it initially, one of them was selected specifically for her emotional intelligence—or, as it was described it at that time, her "process skills" and the fact that "she would tell the truth." She eventually became the team leader and the manager in charge of the program. During the next five years, she continued to be the primary person who oversaw its implementation. In promoting the program within the company, this manager displayed many emotional and social competencies.

The competencies of Self-Control, Conscientiousness, and Adaptability were especially important for establishing the new program. As one of the original team members said, "You need to be O.K. with ambiguity and O.K. with failures to do what we did. You need to be able to learn from failures rather than be thrown off by them." The team leader, she said, had this crucial ability. A good example of how the team leader was able to respond adaptively to failure occurred after the first pilot of the leadership version of the program. It was an unmitigated disaster. When the team gathered to debrief at the end of the program, anxiety and gloom filled the air. Most of the team members sat around and blamed the program participants and the lack of time to prepare adequately. No one wanted to work on fixing the problem at that point. The external facilitator quit the project and took an extended vacation. But the team leader quickly pulled herself together and spent her entire Christmas vacation working to revise the design. Then another team member was able to convince a regional vice president to give the program another chance.

The program manager also demonstrated high Achievement Orientation in the way she promoted the program. She established high standards for quality and monitored the program closely. For instance, during the first year or so, she was the one who sat in and observed virtually every day the program was delivered. After every training session she met with the trainers and spent countless hours with them debriefing in order to find ways to improve the program. When the trainers did not meet her high standards, their contracts were terminated.

Most of the people with whom we talked said that the program never would have succeeded without the program manager's visionary Leadership. She assumed leadership early on and inspired others to follow her lead. One of her bosses—an individual who was not particularly supportive of the program—said, "Her passion was compelling." Another person we interviewed who was not a particular supporter said, "If she had to choose between the program continuing and receiving more recognition for herself, she'd choose the program." She herself said, "I'm a servant of the idea." The strength of her leadership and commitment was revealed when, after she had been managing the program for about three years, she was moved to a new position with a new boss who was not supportive of the program. At this time the program management task was split and she became program manager for the leadership versions of the program. This boss gave her other responsibilities and discouraged her from continuing to work on the emotional competence program. In fact, one year her performance rating was reduced because her boss thought she spent too much time on the program. However, she kept managing it anyway, in her "spare time." That kind of commitment inspired others.

The program manager would also score high in Influence. She was constantly thinking of ways to promote the program and generate support for it. For instance, because most of the advisors are male, the manager made sure that they knew that the program taught techniques used by the most successful professional athletes. She even recruited a sports psychologist to be one of the first trainers.

The program manager also was particularly adept at Conflict Management. In talking about how she dealt with resistance, she described how she looked for "common ground" and "win-win solutions." For instance, the skunk works team's approach to the program initially seemed incompatible with the views of the senior VP for sales. Instead of fighting or giving up, the program manager bought the VP's book about selling and read it to see what similarities with the program there were. She found there were many. So team members framed what they were doing more in terms of the VP's work, and he became a powerful sponsor of the program.

One other competence that proved to be important in this effort was Teamwork and Collaboration. The program manager was included in the original team because she was viewed as someone who possessed this competence, and she lived up to her reputation. One member of the team remembered that she was "phenomenal in dealing with process, in helping people to make sense of information and to make decisions." She was good at keeping the group on task, and at the same time, she was very supportive of other people. She also was fair: one team member said, "She never let personal issues affect her as a team member."

Innovators not only need to use many of the competencies associated with emotional intelligence but also need to emphasize different ones at different points in the implementation process. For instance, during the scouting and exploration phase, competencies such as Service Orientation and Organizational Awareness are especially important. During the mutual adaptation phase, Adaptability and Initiative are critical. Finally, in the institutionalization phase, Achievement Orientation and Conscientiousness are especially important. The first manager of the emotional competence program not only had many of the competencies critical for success but also was able to employ them at appropriate times. She could be adaptable and flexible during the exploration and mutual adaptation phases, and she could also exercise strong leadership and stay focused on achievement during the institutionalization phase. In addition, she used Building Bonds, Initiative, and other competencies to enlist the aid of many others who had competencies that she lacked.

Like all of us, the program manager was not perfect of course. She did make mistakes. For instance, her concern for quality sometimes led her to micromanage too much. Her independence and outspokenness got her into trouble more than once. And her commitment and passion for the idea sometimes became liabilities rather than assets. But in general the program benefited greatly from the emotional intelligence and the high level of social and emotional competence that its manager brought to it.

Conclusion: The Role of Timing

This analysis of the implementation of the emotional competence program suggests a number of specific lessons and guidelines for those who wish to implement similar programs in large organizations:

1. Link the proposed program to a business need.
2. Secure the sponsorship of a powerful executive.
3. Provide program implementers with a high degree of autonomy and resources and a mandate to experiment.
4. Establish the program on a strong research base.
5. Monitor the program closely to ensure high quality.
6. Infuse the program throughout the organization.
7. Make sure the implementers have the emotional competencies that contribute to effective performance.

These lessons can help managers, trainers, and consultants to establish emotional intelligence initiatives in work organizations. And one other factor—timing—will always be important as well. At any given time in the life of any organization, conditions will be more favorable or less favorable for the implementation of emotional intelligence training and development activities. The emotional competence program benefited greatly from good timing, that is, conditions were highly favorable at AEFA at the time it was implemented. For instance, when the skunk works project was initially established, the company was doing very well. There was relatively little pressure or turbulence. This meant that the people involved, including the executive who initially sponsored it, could take some risks. If instead they had been concerned about every dollar they spent, something that then seemed as radical as an emotional competence training program probably could not have happened. Timing was opportune in one other way. When the training design team completed the first pilot and was ready to start offering the program throughout the company, a strong, corporation-wide training initiative for the salesforce had just begun. Much money suddenly was available for training, and the emotional competence program was among the offerings from which management groups could choose. This favorable climate for training did not last long; within a year the generous subsidies provided by the corporate office for training began to diminish, and within three years they had all but disappeared. Fortunately, by that time the program had become well established and known throughout the company.

Thus the first task for those who wish to bring greater emotional intelligence to their organizations is to consider whether the timing is right. If it is, the emotional competence program case study offers many valuable lessons.

REFERENCES

Alderfer, C. P. (1980). Consulting to underbounded systems. In C. P. Alderfer & C. L. Cooper (Eds.), *Advances in experiential social processes* (Vol. 2, pp. 267–295). New York: Wiley.

Alderfer, C. P. (1983). An intergroup perspective on group dynamics. In J. W. Lorsch (Ed.), *Handbook of organizational behavior* (pp. 190–222). Upper Saddle River, NJ: Prentice Hall.

Allen, T. D., Poteet, M. L., & Burroughs, S. M. (1997). The mentor's perspective: A qualitative inquiry and future research agenda. *Journal of Vocational Behavior, 51,* 70–89.

Amabile, T. (1988). The intrinsic motivation principle of creativity. In B. Staw & L. L. Cummings (Eds.), *Research in organizational behavior* (Vol. 10). Greenwich, CT: JAI Press.

Amabile, T., & Conti, R. (1997). Environmental determinants of work motivation, creativity, and innovation: The case of R&D downsizing. In G. Raghu & P. R. Nayar (Eds.), *Technological innovation: Oversights and foresights* (pp. 111–125). New York: Cambridge University Press.

American Educational Research Association, American Psychological Association, & National Council on Measurement in Education (1999). *Standards for educational and psychological testing.* Washington, DC: American Educational Research Association.

Ancona, D. G., & Caldwell, D. F. (1992). Bridging the boundary: External activity and performance in organizational teams. *Administrative Science Quarterly, 37,* 634–665.

Andersen, N., & Shackleton, V. (1993). *Successful selection interviewing.* Oxford, England: Blackwell.

Argote, L. (1989). Agreement about norms and work-unit effectiveness: Evidence from the field. *Basic and Applied Social Psychology, 10*(2), 131–140.

Argyris, C. (1986, September-October). Skilled incompetence. *Harvard Business Review,* pp. 74–79.

Argyris, C. (1993). *Knowledge for action: A guide to overcoming barriers to organizational change.* San Francisco: Jossey-Bass.

Argyris, C. (1994, July–August). Good communication that blocks learning. *Harvard Business Review*, pp. 77–85.

Argyris, C., & Schön, D. (1978). *Organizational learning*. Reading, MA: Addison-Wesley.

Aronoff, J., & Litwin, G. H. (1971). Achievement motivation training and executive advancement. *Journal of Applied Behavioral Science, 7*(2), 215–229.

Asay, T. P., & Lambert, M. J. (1999). The empirical case for the common factors in therapy: Quantitative findings. In M. A. Hubble, B. L. Duncan, & S. D. Miller (Eds.), *The heart and soul of change: What works in therapy* (pp. 33–56). Washington, DC: American Psychological Association.

Ashforth, B. E., & Mael, F. (1989). Social identity theory and the organization. *Academy of Management Review, 14*, 20–39.

Bachelor, A., & Horvath, A. (1999). The therapeutic relationship. In M. A. Hubble, B. L. Duncan, & S. D. Miller (Eds.), *The heart and soul of change: What works in therapy* (pp. 133–178). Washington, DC: American Psychological Association.

Bachman, W. (1988). Nice guys finish first: A SYMLOG analysis of U.S. Naval commands. In R. B. Polley, A. P. Hare, & P. J. Stone (Eds.), *The SYMLOG practitioner: Applications of small group research* (pp. 133–153). New York: Praeger.

Baird, L., & Kram, K. E. (1983, Summer). Career dynamics: Managing the superior-subordinate relationship. *Organizational Dynamics*, pp. 46–64.

Baldwin, T. T., & Ford, J. K. (1988). Transfer of training: A review and directions for future research. *Personnel Psychology, 41*, 63–105.

Baldwin, T. T., & Magjuka, R. J. (1991). Organizational training and signals of importance: Effects of pre-training perceptions on intentions to transfer. *Human Resource Development, 2*, 51–65.

Ballou, R., Bowers, D., Boyatzis, R. E., & Kolb, D. A. (1999). Fellowship in lifelong learning: An executive development program for advanced professionals. *Journal of Management Education, 23*(4), 338–354.

Bandura, A. (1977). *Social learning theory*. Upper Saddle River, NJ: Prentice Hall.

Bandura, A., Adams, N., & Beyer, J. (1977). Cognitive processes mediating behavioral change. *Journal of Personality and Social Psychology, 35*, 125–139.

Bandura, A., & Cervone, D. (1983). Self-evaluative and self-efficacy mechanisms governing the motivational effects of goal systems. *Journal of Personality and Social Psychology, 45*, 1017–1028.

Barker, J. R. (1993). Tightening the iron cage: Concertive control in self-managing teams. *Administrative Science Quarterly, 38*, 408–437.

Barlow, D. H. (Ed.). (1985). *Clinical handbook of psychological disorders: A step-by-step treatment manual*. New York: Guilford Press.

Bar-On, R. (1988). *The development of an operational concept of psychological well-being*. Unpublished doctoral dissertation, Rhodes University, South Africa.

Bar-On, R. (1997a, August). *Development of the Bar-On EQ-i: A measure of emotional and social intelligence*. Paper presented at the 105th annual meeting of the American Psychological Association, Chicago.

Bar-On, R. (1997b). *The Emotional Quotient Inventory (EQ-I): Technical manual*. Toronto: Multi-Health Systems.

Bar-On, R. (2000a). Emotional and social intelligence: Insights from the Emotional Quotient Inventory. In R. Bar-On & J.D.A. Parker (Eds.), *The handbook of emotional intelligence: Theory, development, assessment, and application at home, school, and in the workplace* (pp. 363–388). San Francisco: Jossey-Bass.

Bar-On, R. (2000b, May). Paper presented at the Linkage Emotional Intelligence Conference, London.

Barrett, G. V. (2000, April). *Emotional intelligence: The Madison Avenue approach to professional practice.* Paper presented at the 15th annual meeting of the Society for Industrial and Organizational Psychology, New Orleans.

Barrick, M. R., & Mount, M. K. (1991). The big five personality dimensions and job performance: A meta-analysis. *Personnel Psychology, 44,* 1–26.

Barrick, M. R., Mount, M. K., & Strauss, J. P. (1993). Conscientiousness and performance of sales representatives: Test of the mediating effects of goal setting. *Journal of Applied Psychology, 78,* 715–722.

Barsade, S. G. (1998). *The ripple effect: Emotional contagion in groups* (Working Paper). New Haven, CT: Yale University, Yale Graduate School of Management.

Barsade, S. G., & Gibson, D. E. (1998). Group emotion: A view from top and bottom. In D. H. Gruenfeld, B. Mannix, & M. Neale (Eds.), *Research on managing groups and teams: Composition* (Vol. 1, pp. 81–102). Greenwich, CT: JAI Press.

Bass, B. M. (1990). *The Bass and Stogdill handbook of leadership* (3rd ed.). New York: Free Press.

Baumeister, R. F., Goethals, G. P., & Pittman, T. S. (1998). The interface between intrapsychic and interpersonal processes: Cognition, emotion, and self as adaptations to other people. In J. M. Darley & J. Cooper (Eds.), *Attribution and social interaction* (pp. 201–242). Washington, DC: American Psychological Association.

Belenky, M. F., Clinchy, B. M., Goldberger, N. R., & Tarule, J. M. (1986). *Women's ways of knowing.* New York: Basic Books.

Bennis, W. G., & Biederman, P. W. (1997). *Organizing genius: The secrets of creative collaboration.* Reading, MA: Addison-Wesley.

Bettenhausen, K. L., & Murnighan, J. K. (1985). The emergence of norms in competitive decision-making groups. *Administrative Science Quarterly, 30,* 20–35.

Boland, R. J., & Tenkasi, R. V. (1995). Perspective making and perspective taking in communities of knowing. *Organization Science, 6*(4), 350–372.

Born, D. H., & Mathieu, J. E. (1996). Differential effects of survey-guided feedback: The rich get richer and the poor get poorer. *Group and Organization Management, 21,* 388–403.

Bowen, D. D. (1984). The role of identification in mentoring female protégés. *Group and Organization Studies, 9,* 61–74.

Boyatzis, R. E. (1982). *The competent manager: A model for effective performance.* New York: Wiley.

Boyatzis, R. E. (1994). Stimulating self-directed change: A required MBA course called Managerial Assessment and Development. *Journal of Management Education, 18*(3), 304–323.

Boyatzis, R. E. (1995). "Cornerstones of change: Building the path for self-directed learning." In R. E. Boyatzis, S. C. Cowen, and D. A. Kolb (Eds.), *Innovation in Professional Education: Steps on a journey from teaching to learning,* pp. 50–91. San Francisco: Jossey-Bass.

Boyatzis, R. E. (1996). Consequences and rejuvenation of competency-based human resource and organization development. In R. W. Woodman & W. A. Pasmore (Eds.), *Research in organizational change and development* (Vol. 9, pp. 101–122). Greenwich, CT: JAI Press.

Boyatzis, R. E. (1999a). *Developing emotional intelligence* (Unpublished paper). Cleveland: Case Western Reserve University, Department of Organizational Behavior.

Boyatzis, R. E. (1999b). *The financial impact of competencies in leadership and management of consulting firms* (Unpublished paper). Cleveland: Case Western Reserve University, Department of Organizational Behavior.

Boyatzis, R. E., Baker, A., Leonard, D., Rhee, K., & Thompson, L. (1995). Will it make a difference? Assessing a value-based, outcome-oriented, competency-based professional program. In R. E. Boyatzis, S. S. Cowen, & D. A. Kolb (Eds.), *Innovations in professional education: Steps on a journey from teaching to learning* (pp. 167–204). San Francisco: Jossey-Bass.

Boyatzis, R. E., & Burrus, J. A. (1995). *The heart of human resource development: Counseling competencies.* Unpublished manuscript.

Boyatzis, R. E., Cowen, S. S., & Kolb, D. A. (1995). *Innovation in professional education: Steps on a journey to learning.* San Francisco: Jossey-Bass.

Boyatzis, R. E., Goleman, D., & Rhee, K. (2000). Clustering competence in emotional intelligence: Insights from the Emotional Competence Inventory (ECI). In R. Bar-On & J.D.A. Parker (Eds.), *The handbook of emotional intelligence: Theory, development, assessment, and application at home, school, and in the workplace* (pp. 343–362). San Francisco: Jossey-Bass.

Boyatzis, R. E., & Kolb, D. A. (1969). *Feedback and self-directed behavior change* (Working Paper No. 394–69). Cambridge, MA: MIT Sloan School of Management.

Boyatzis, R. E., & Kolb, D. A. (1999). Performance, learning, and development as modes of growth and adaption throughout our lives and careers. In M. Peiperl, M. B. Arthur, R. Coffee, and T. Morris (Eds.), *Career Frontiers: New conceptions of working lives* (pp. 76–98). London: Oxford University Press.

Boyatzis, R. E., Leonard, D., Rhee, K., & Wheeler, J. V. (1996). Competencies can be developed, but not the way we thought. *Capability, 2*(2), 25–41.

Boyatzis, R. E., Murphy, A. J., & Wheeler, J. V. (2000). Philosophy as a missing link between values and behavior. *Psychological Reports, 86,* 47–64.

Boyatzis, R. E., Wheeler, J., & Wright, R. (1997, September). Competency development in graduate education: A longitudinal perspective. Paper presented at the First World Conference on Self-Directed Learning, Group for Interdisciplinary Research on Autonomy and Training, Montreal, Quebec.

Bray, D. W. (1964). The management progress study. *American Psychologist, 19,* 419–420.

Bray, D. W. (1976). The assessment center method. In R. L. Craig (Ed.), *Training and development handbook.* New York: McGraw-Hill.

Bray, D. W., Campbell, R. J., & Grant, D. L. (1974). *Formative years in business: A long-term AT&T study of managerial lives.* New York: Wiley-Interscience.

Brothers, L. (1989). A biological perspective on empathy. *American Journal of Psychiatry, 146,* 10–19.

Bunker, K. A. (1997). The power of vulnerability in contemporary leadership. *Consulting Psychology Journal, 49*(2), 122–136.

Burke, R. (1984). Mentors in organizations. *Group and Organization Studies, 9,* 353–372.

Burke, M., & Day, R. (1986). A cumulative study of the effectiveness of managerial training. *Journal of Applied Psychology, 71,* 232–245.

Burnaska, R. F. (1976). The effects of behavior modeling training upon managers' behaviors and employees' perceptions. *Personnel Psychology, 29,* 329–335.

Byham, W. C. (1977). Application of the assessment center method. In J. L. Moses & W. C. Byham (Eds.), *Applying the assessment center method* (pp. 31–43). New York: Pergamon Press.

Byham, W. C., Adams, D., & Kiggins, A. (1976). Transfer of modeling training to the job. *Personnel Psychology, 29,* 345–349.

Campbell, D. P. (1990, Spring). Inklings. *Issues and Observations, 10,* 11–12.

Campbell, D. P., & Van Velsor, E. (1985). *The use of personality measures in the leadership development program.* Greensboro, N.C.: Center for Creative Leadership.

Campion, M. A., Medsker, G. J., & Higgs, A. C. (1993). Relations between work group characteristics and effectiveness: Implications for designing effective work groups. *Personnel Psychology, 46,* 823–850.

Cannon-Bowers, J. A., Tannenbaum, S. I., Salas, E., & Volpe, C. E. (1995). Defining competencies and establishing team training requirements. In R. A. Guzzo, E. Salas, & Associates, *Team effectiveness and decision making in organizations* (pp. 333–380). San Francisco: Jossey-Bass.

Caplan, R. D., Vinokur, A. D., & Price, R. H. (1996). From job loss to reemployment: Field experiments in prevention-focused coping. In G. W. Albee & T. P. Gullota (Eds.), *Primary prevention works: Issues in children's and families' lives* (Vol. 6, pp. 341–379). Thousand Oaks, CA: Sage.

Cartwright, D., & Zander, A. (1968). Origins of group dynamics. In D. Cartwright & A. Zander (Eds.), *Group dynamics: Research and theory* (3rd ed., pp. 4–21). New York: HarperCollins.

Catholic Health Association. (1994). *Transformational leadership for the healing ministry: Competencies for the future.* St. Louis, MO: Author.

Chaleff, I. (1995). *The courageous follower: Standing up to and for our leaders.* San Francisco: Berrett-Koehler.

Chambers, E. G., Foulon, M., Handfield-Jones, H., Hankin, S. M., & Michaels, E. O., III. (1998). The war for talent. *McKinsey Quarterly, 3,* 44–57.

Charan, R., & Colvin, G. (1999, June). Why CEOs Fail. *Fortune,* pp. 68–75.

Cherniss, C., & Adler, M. (2000). *Promoting emotional intelligence in organizations.* Alexandria, VA: American Society for Training and Development.

Ciampa, D., & Watkins, M. (1999). *Right from the start.* Boston: Harvard Business School Press.

Clarkson, A. (1998). *Relationships at work that get things done: Social capital in organizational settings.* Unpublished doctoral dissertation, Boston University, Boston.

Coch, L., & French, J.R.P., Jr. (1948). Overcoming resistance to change. *Human Relations, 1,* 512–532.

Cohen, S. G. (1994). Designing effective self-managing work teams. In M. M. Beyerlein & D. A. Johnson (Eds.), *Advances in interdisciplinary studies of work teams* (Vol. 1, pp. 67–102). Greenwich, CT: JAI Press.

Coleman, J. S. (1988). Social capital in the creation of human capital. *American Journal of Sociology, 94,* 95–120.

Coleman, J. S. (1990). *Foundations of social theory.* Cambridge, MA: Harvard University Press, Belknap Press.

Collins, E., & Scott, P. (1978, July–August). Everyone who makes it has a mentor. *Harvard Business Review,* pp. 89–101.

Collins, J. C., & Porras, J. I. (1994). *Built to last: Successful habits of visionary companies.* New York: HarperCollins.

Cooper, R. K. (1997). *EQ map overview.* San Francisco: Q-Metrics.

Cooper, R. K., & Sawaf, A. (1997). *Executive EQ: Emotional intelligence in leadership and organizations.* New York: Grosset/Putnam.

Cooperrider, D. L. (1987). Appreciative inquiry in organizational life. In R. W. Woodman & W. A. Pasmore (Eds.), *Research in organizational change and development* (Vol. 1, pp. 129–169). Greenwich, CT: JAI Press.

Cooperrider, D. L. (1990). Positive image, positive action: The affirmative basis of organizing. In S. Srivastva, D. L. Cooperrider, & Associates, *Appreciative management and leadership: The power of positive thought and action in organizations* (pp. 91–125). San Francisco: Jossey-Bass.

Cox, T. H., & Nkomo, S. M. (1991). A race and gender group analysis of the early career experiences of MBAs. *Work and Occupations, 18,* 431–446.

Crant, J. M. (1995). The proactive personality scale and objective job performance among real estate agents. *Journal of Applied Psychology, 80,* 532–537.

Cutter, H., Boyatzis, R. E., & Clancy, D. (1977). The effectiveness of power motivation training for rehabilitating alcoholics. *Journal of Studies on Alcohol, 36,* 1196–1207.

Dalton, G. W. (1989). Developmental views of careers in organizations. In M. B. Arthur, D. T. Hall, & B. S. Lawrence (Eds.), *Handbook of career theory* (pp. 89–109). New York: Cambridge University Press.

Dalton, G. W., & Thompson, P. (1986). *Novations: Strategies for career management.* Glenview, IL: Scott, Foresman.

Damasio, A. (1994). *Descartes' error: Emotion, reason, and the human brain.* New York: Grosset/Putnam.

Damasio, A. (1999). *The feeling of what happens: Body and emotion in the making of consciousness.* New York: Harcourt Brace.

Darley, J. M., & Fazio, R. H. (1980). Expectancy confirmation processes arising in the social interaction sequence. *American Psychologist, 35,* 867–881.

Davidson, R. J., Jackson, D. C., & Kalin, N. H. (2000). Emotion, plasticity, context and regulation: Perspectives from affective neuroscience. *Psychological Bulletin, 126*(6), 890–909.

Davies, M., Stankov, L., & Roberts, R. D. (1998). Emotional intelligence: In search of an elusive construct. *Journal of Personality and Social Psychology, 75,* 989–1015.

De Souza, G., & Klein, H. J. (1995). Emergent leadership in the group goal-setting process. *Small Group Research, 26*(4), 475–496.

Deci, E. L., & Ryan, R. M. (1994). Promoting self-determined education. *Scandinavian Journal of Educational Research, 38*(1), 3–14.

Dirks, K. T. (1999). The effects of interpersonal trust on work group performance. *Journal of Applied Psychology, 84,* 445–455.

Donnellon, A. (1996). *Team talk: The power of language in team dynamics.* Boston: Harvard Business School Press.

Donovan, J. J., & Radosevich, D. J. (1999). A meta-analytic review of the distribution of practice effect: Now you see it, now you don't. *Journal of Applied Psychology, 84,* 795–805.

Dougherty, D. (1992). Interpretative barriers to successful product innovation in large firms. *Organization Science, 3*(2), 179–202.

Dreher, G. F., & Ash, R. A. (1990). A comparative study of mentoring among men and women in managerial, professional and technical positions. *Journal of Applied Psychology, 75,* 539–546.

Dreyfus, C. (1990). *The characteristics of high performing managers of scientists and engineers.* Unpublished doctoral dissertation, Case Western Reserve University, Cleveland.

Drucker, P. (1985). How to make people decisions. *Harvard Business Review.*

Druskat, V. U. (1996, August). *Team-level competencies in superior self-managing manufacturing teams.* Paper presented at the annual meeting of the Academy of Management, Cincinnati, OH.

Duck, J. D. (1993, November-December). Managing change: The art of balancing. *Harvard Business Review,* pp. 109–118.

Dulewicz, V., & Higgs, M. (1998). Emotional intelligence: Can it be measured reliably and validly using competency data? *Competency, 6*(1), 28–37.

Edelman, G. (1987). *Neural Darwinism: The theory of neuronal group selection.* New York: Basic Books.

Eder, R. W., & Harris, M. M. (1999a). Contextual effects. In R. W. Eder & M. M. Harris (Eds.), *The employment interview handbook* (rev. ed., pp. 197–216). Thousand Oaks, CA: Sage.

Eder, R. W., & Harris, M. M. (Eds.). (1999b). *The employment interview handbook* (rev. ed.). Thousand Oaks, CA: Sage.

Edmondson, A. (1999). Psychological safety and learning behavior in work teams. *Administrative Science Quarterly, 44,* 350–383.

Ekman, P. (1980). *The face of man: Expressions of universal emotions in a New Guinea village.* New York: Garland STPM Press.

Ely, R. J. (1994). Organizational demographics and the dynamics of relationships among professional women. *Administrative Science Quarterly, 39,* 203–238.

Falcone, A. J., Edwards, J. E., & Day, R. R. (1986). *Meta-analysis of personnel training techniques for three populations.* Paper presented at the annual meeting of the Academy of Management, Chicago.

Falvo, D. R., Smaga, S., Brenner, J. S., & Tippy, P. K. (1991). Lecture versus role modeling: A comparison of educational programs to enhance residents' ability to communicate with patients about HIV. *Teaching and Learning in Medicine, 3*(4), 227–231.

Fein, M. L. (1990). *Role change: A resocialization perspective.* New York: Praeger.

Feist, G. J., & Barron, F. (1996, June). *Emotional intelligence and academic intelligence in career and life success.* Paper presented at the annual convention of the American Psychological Society, San Francisco.

Feldman, D. C. (1984). The development and enforcement of group norms. *Academy of Management Review, 9,* 47–53.

Fernández-Aráoz, C. (1999, July–August). Hiring without firing. *Harvard Business Review,* pp. 108–120.

Festinger, L. (1954). A theory of social comparison processes. *Human Relations, 7,* 117–140.

Festinger, L. (1957). *A theory of cognitive dissonance.* New York: HarperCollins.

Festinger, L., Schacter, S., & Back, K. (1950). *Social pressures in informal groups.* New York: HarperCollins.

Fiske, S. T., & Taylor, S. E. (1991). *Social cognition* (2nd ed.). New York: McGraw-Hill.

Fleishman, E. A., & Harris, E. F. (1962). Patterns of leadership behavior related to employee grievances and turnover. *Personnel Psychology, 15,* 43–56.

Flemming, R. K., & Sulzer-Azeroff, B. (1990). *Peer management: Effects on staff teaching performance.* Paper presented at the 15th annual meeting of the Association for Applied Behavior Analysis, Nashville, TN.

Fletcher, J. (1994). *Toward a theory of relational practice in organizations: A feminist reconstruction of "real" work.* Unpublished doctoral dissertation, Boston University, School of Management, Boston.

Fletcher, J. (1996). A relational approach to the Protean worker. In D. T. Hall & Associates, *The career is dead: Long live the career* (pp. 105–131). San Francisco: Jossey-Bass.

Folkman, S., & Lazarus, R. S. (1988). Coping as a mediator of emotion. *Journal of Personality and Social Psychology, 54,* 466–475.

Frank, J. D., & Frank, J. B. (1991). *Persuasion and healing* (3rd ed.). Baltimore, MD: Johns Hopkins University Press.

Frayne, C. A., & Geringer, J. M. (2000). Self-management training for improving job performance: A field experiment involving salespeople. *Journal of Applied Psychology, 85,* 361–372.

Frayne, C. A., & Latham, G. P. (1987). Application of social learning theory to employee self-management of attendance. *Journal of Applied Psychology, 72,* 387–392.

French, J.R.P., Jr., & Raven, B. (1959). The bases of social power. In D. Cartwright (Ed.), *Studies in social power.* Ann Arbor: University of Michigan Press.

Friedman, H., & DiMatteo, R. (1982). *Interpersonal issues in health care.* New York: Academic Press.

Friedman, T. L. (1999). *The Lexus and the olive tree: Understanding globalization.* New York: Farrar, Straus & Giroux.

Fry, R. E., & Srivastva, S. (1992). Change and continuity in organizational growth. In S. Srivastva, R. E. Fry, & Associates, *Executive and organizational continuity: Managing the paradoxes of stability and change* (pp. 1–24). San Francisco: Jossey-Bass.

Gabarro, J. J. (1987). The development of working relationships. In J. W. Lorsch (Ed.), *Handbook of organizational behavior* (pp. 172–189). Upper Saddle River, NJ: Prentice Hall.

Ganesan, S. (1993). Negotiation strategies and the nature of channel relationships. *Journal of Marketing Research, 30,* 183–203.

Gardner, H. (1983). *Frames of mind: The theory of multiple intelligences.* New York: Basic Books.

Gardner, H. (1993). *Frames of mind: The theory of multiple intelligences.* New York: Basic Books.

Gardner, H. (1999). *Intelligence reframed.* New York: Basic Books.

George, J. M. (1990). Personality, affect, and behavior in groups. *Journal of Applied Psychology, 75,* 107–116.

George, J. M., & Bettenhausen, K. (1990). Understanding prosocial behavior, sales performance, and turnover: A group level analysis in a service context. *Journal of Applied Psychology, 75,* 698–709.

Gerstein, M. S., & Reisman, H. (1983, Winter). Strategic selection: Matching executives to business conditions. *Sloan Management Review,* pp. 33–49.

Gist, M. E., Bavetta, A. G., & Stevens, C. K. (1990). Transfer training method: Its influence on skill generalization, skill repetition, and performance level. *Personnel Psychology, 43,* 501–523.

Gist, M. E., Stevens, C. K., & Bavetta, A. G. (1991). Effects of self-efficacy and post-training intervention on the acquisition and maintenance of complex interpersonal skills. *Personnel Psychology, 44,* 837–861.

Gladstein, D. L. (1984). Groups in context: A model of task group effectiveness. *Administrative Science Quarterly, 29,* 499–517.

Glaser, E. M., & Taylor, S. H. (1973). Factors influencing the success of applied research. *American Psychologist, 28,* 140–146.

Goldstein, A. P., & Sorcher, M. (1974). *Changing supervisory behavior.* New York: Pergamon Press.

Goldstein, I. L. (1993). *Training in organizations: Needs assessment, development, and evaluation* (3rd ed.). Pacific Grove, CA: Brooks/Cole.

Goleman, D. (1985). *Vital lies, simple truths: The psychology of self-deception.* New York: Simon & Schuster.

Goleman, D. (1995a). *Emotional intelligence.* New York: Bantam.

Goleman, D. (1995b, November–December). What's your emotional intelligence quotient? You'll soon find out. *Utne Reader.*

Goleman, D. (1998a, November–December). What makes a leader? *Harvard Business Review,* pp. 92–102.

Goleman, D. (1998b). *Working with emotional intelligence.* N.Y.: Bantam.

Goleman, D. (2000a). Emotional intelligence. In B. Sadock & V. Sadock (Eds.), *Comprehensive textbook of psychiatry* (7th ed.). Philadelphia: Lippincott Williams & Wilkins.

Goleman, D. (2000b, March–April). Leadership that gets results. *Harvard Business Review,* pp. 78–92.

Golembiewski, R. T., & McConkie, M. (1975). The centrality of interpersonal trust in group processes. In C. L. Cooper (Ed.), *Theories of group processes* (pp. 131–185). New York: Wiley.

Graves, L., & Karren, R. (1999). Are some interviewers better than others? In R. W. Eder & G. R. Ferris (Eds.), *The employment interview handbook.* Thousand Oaks, CA: Sage.

Gregorich, S. E., & Wilhelm, J. A. (1993). Crew resource management training assessment. In E. L. Wiener, B. G. Kanki, & R. L. Helmreich (Eds.), *Cockpit resource management* (pp. 173–198). New York: Academic Press.

Guglielmino, L. M. (1978). Development of a self-directed learning readiness scale. (Doctoral dissertation, Case Western Reserve University, 1978). *Dissertation Abstracts International, 38,* 6467A.

Guglielmino, P. J., Guglielmino, L. M., & Long, H. B. (1987). Self-directed learning readiness and performance in the workplace: Implications for business, industry, and higher education. *Higher Education, 16,* 303–317.

Gully, S. M., Devine, D. J., & Whitney, D. J. (1995). A meta-analysis of cohesion and performance: Effects of level of analysis and task interdependence. *Small Group Research, 26*(4), 497–520.

Hackman, J. R. (1976). Group influences on individuals. In M. D. Dunnett (Ed.), *Handbook of industrial and organizational psychology* (pp. 1455–1525). Glenview, IL: Rand McNally.

Hackman, J. R. (1987). The design of work teams. In J. W. Lorsch (Ed.), *Handbook of organizational behavior* (pp. 315–342). Upper Saddle River, NJ: Prentice Hall.

Hackman, J. R. (1990). Conclusion: Creating more effective work groups in organizations. In J. R. Hackman (Ed.), *Groups that work (and those that don't): Creating conditions for effective teamwork* (pp. 479–505). San Francisco: Jossey-Bass.

Hall, D. T. (1976). *Careers in organizations.* Glenview, IL: Scott, Foresman.

Hall, D. T. (1986a). Breaking career routines: Midcareer choice and identity development. In D. T. Hall & Associates, *Career development in organizations* (pp. 120–159). San Francisco: Jossey-Bass.

Hall, D. T. (1986b). Dilemmas in linking succession planning to individual and executive learning. *Human Resource Management, 25,* 235–265.

Hall, D. T. (1993). *The new career contract: Wrong on both counts* (Technical Report). Boston: Boston University, School of Management Executive Development Roundtable.

Hall, D. T. (1994). *Executive careers and learning: Aligning strategy, selection, and development* (Technical Report). Boston: Boston University, School of Management Executive Development Roundtable.

Hall, D. T., & Associates. (1996). *The career is dead: Long live the career.* San Francisco: Jossey-Bass.

Hall, D. T., & Mirvis, P. H. (1996). The new protean career: Psychological success and the path with the heart. In D. T. Hall & Associates, *The career is dead: Long live the career* (pp. 15–45). San Francisco: Jossey-Bass.

Hall, D. T., Otazo, K. L., & Hollenbeck, G. P. (1999, Winter). Behind closed doors: What really happens in executive coaching. *Organizational Dynamics*, pp. 39–53.

Hand, H. H., & Slocum, J. W. (1972). A longitudinal study of the effects of a human relations training program on managerial effectiveness. *Journal of Applied Psychology, 57*, 412–417.

Handy, C. (1989). *The age of unreason.* Boston: Harvard Business School Press.

Handy, C. (1997). *The hungry spirit: Beyond capitalism: A quest for purpose in the modern world.* London: Hutchinson.

Hartle, F. (1992). Performance management: Where is it going? In A. Mitrani, D. Dalziel, & D. Fitt (Eds.), *Competency-based human resource management.* London: Kegan Paul.

Hay/McBer. (1997, October). *Competency study database.* Boston: Author.

Hay/McBer. (2000). *Research into teacher effectiveness: A model of teacher effectiveness.* Report by Hay/McBer to the U.K. Department for Education and Employment [On-line]. Available: www.dfee.gov.uk/teachingreforms/mcber

Heatherton, T. F., & Nichols, P. A. (1994). Personal accounts of successful versus failed attempts at life change. *Personality and Social Psychology Bulletin, 20*, 664–675.

Heller, K. (1996, May). *Models of community adoption in prevention research.* Paper presented at the fifth national NIMH conference on prevention research, Tysons Corner, VA.

Helmreich, R. L., & Foushee, H. C. (1993). Why crew resource management? Empirical and theoretical bases of human factors training in aviation. In E. L. Wiener, B. G. Kanki, & R. L. Helmreich (Eds.), *Cockpit resource management* (pp. 3–46). New York: Academic Press.

Hemphill, J. K. (1959). Job description for executives. *Harvard Business Review, 37*(5), 55–67.

Higgins, M. C., & Kram, K. E. (in press). Reconceptualizing mentoring at work: A developmental network perspective. *Academy of Management Review.*

Hodgetts, J. L., & Hodgetts, W. H. (1996). Finding sanctuary in post-modern life. In D. T. Hall & Associates, *The career is dead: Long live the career* (pp. 297–313). San Francisco: Jossey-Bass.

Holahan, C. K., & Sears, R. R. (1995). *The gifted group in later maturity.* Stanford, CA: Stanford University Press.

Hollenbeck, G. (1992). *360 degree feedback and development plans* (Technical Report). Boston: Boston University, School of Management Executive Development Roundtable.

Holmer, L. L. (1994). Developing emotional capacity and organizational health. In R. H. Kilmann, I. Kilmann, & Associates, *Managing ego energy: The transformation of personal meaning into organizational success* (pp. 49–72). San Francisco: Jossey-Bass.

House, R. J. (1988). Charismatic and non-charismatic leaders: Differences in behavior and effectiveness. In J. A. Conger, R. N. Kanungo, & Associates, *Charismatic leadership: The elusive factor in organizational effectiveness.* San Francisco: Jossey-Bass.

Howes, N., & Quinn, R. E. (1978). Implementing change: From research to a prescriptive framework. *Group and Organization Studies, 3*, 71–84.

Hubble, M. A., Duncan, B. L., & Miller, S. D. (Eds.). (1999). *The heart and soul of change: What works in therapy.* Washington, DC: American Psychological Association.

Hunt, D., & Michael, C. (1983). Mentorship: A career training and development tool. *Academy of Management Review, 8*, 475–485.

Hunter, J. E., Schmidt, F. L., & Judiesch, M. K. (1990). Individual differences in output variability as a function of job complexity. *Journal of Applied Psychology, 75,* 28–42.

Ibarra, H. (1992). Homophily and differential returns: Sex differences in network structure and access in an advertising firm. *Administrative Science Quarterly, 37,* 422–447.

Ibarra, H. (1993). Personal networks of women and minorities in management: A conceptual framework. *Academy of Management Review, 18,* 56–97.

Ilgen, D. R., Fisher, C. D., & Taylor, M. S. (1979). Consequences of individual feedback on behavior in organizations. *Journal of Applied Psychology, 64,* 349–371.

Isen, A., & Shalker, T. (1982). The influence of mood state on evaluation of positive, neutral, and negative stimuli. *Social Psychology Quarterly, 45,* 58–63.

Isen, A., Shalker, T., Clark, M., & Karp, L. (1978). Affect, accessibility of material in memory and behavior: A cognitive coop? *Journal of Personality and Social Psychology, 36,* 1–12.

Jacobs, R., & McClelland, D. C. (1994). Moving up the corporate ladder: A longitudinal study of the leadership motive pattern and managerial success in women and men. *Consulting Psychology Journal, 46*(1), 32–40.

James, W. (1892). *Psychology: A briefer course.* New York: Holt.

Jehn, K. A. (1995). A multimethod examination of the benefits and detriments of intragroup conflict. *Administrative Science Quarterly, 40,* 256–282.

Jehn, K. A. (1997). A qualitative analysis of conflict types and dimensions in organizational groups. *Administrative Science Quarterly, 42,* 530–557.

Jones, C. (1986). *Programming productivity.* New York: McGraw-Hill.

Jones, C. (1991). *Applied software measurement.* New York: McGraw-Hill.

Jones, G. R., & George, J. M. (1998). The experience and evolution of trust: Implications for cooperation and teamwork. *Academy of Management Review, 23,* 531–546.

Jordan, J. V., Kaplan, A. G., Miller, J. B., Stiver, I. P., & Surrey, J. L. (Eds.). (1991). *Women's growth in connection.* New York: Guilford Press.

Jourard, S. M. (1971). *Self-disclosure: An experimental analysis of the transparent self.* New York: Wiley.

Kabat-Zinn, J. (1990). *Full catastrophe living: Using the wisdom of your body and mind to face stress, pain, and illness.* New York: Delacorte Press.

Kahn, W. A. (1990). Psychological conditions of personal engagement and disengagement at work. *Academy of Management Journal, 33,* 692–724.

Kahn, W. A. (1998). Relational systems at work. In L. L. Cummings & B. M. Staw (Eds.), *Research in organizational behavior* (Vol. 20, pp. 39–76). Greenwich, CT: JAI Press.

Kahn, W. A., & Kram, K. E. (1994). Authority at work: Internal models and their organizational consequences. *Academy of Management Review, 19,* 17–50.

Kanfer, F. H. (1986). Implications of a self-regulation model of therapy for treatment of addictive behaviors. In W. R. Miller & N. Heather (Eds.), *Treating addictive behaviors: Vol. 2. Processes of change* (pp. 272–314). New York: Plenum.

Kanfer, F. H., & Goldstein, A. P. (Eds.). (1991). *Helping people change: A textbook of methods* (4th ed.). New York: Pergamon Press.

Kanter, R. M. (1989). *When giants learn to dance: Mastering the challenge of strategy, management, and careers in the 1990s.* New York: Simon & Schuster.

Kaplan, R. E. (1991). *Beyond ambition: How driven managers can lead better and live better.* San Francisco: Jossey-Bass.

Katz, R. L. (1955, January–February). Skills of an effective administrator. *Harvard Business Review,* pp. 33–42.

Kegan, R. (1982). *The evolving self: Problem and process in human development.* Cambridge, MA: Harvard University Press.

Kegan, R. (1994). *In over our heads: The mental demands of modern life.* Cambridge, MA: Harvard University Press.

Kelley, R. (1998). *How to be a star at work.* New York: Times Books.

Kelner, S., Rivers, C., & O'Connell, K. (1994). *The impact of managerial styles on climate.* Internal white paper, McBer and Company, 1994.

Kemper, T. D. (1978). *A social interactional theory of emotions.* New York: Wiley.

Kinlaw, D. C. (1993). *Coaching for commitment.* San Francisco: Jossey-Bass/Pfeiffer.

Klein, K. J., & Sorra, J. S. (1996). The challenge of innovation implementation. *Academy of Management Review, 21,* 1055–1080.

Kleinman, A. (1988). *Rethinking psychiatry: From cultural category to personal experience.* New York: Free Press.

Koberg, C. S., Boss, R. W., Chappell, D., & Ringer, R. C. (1994). Correlates and consequences of protégé mentoring in a large hospital. *Group and Organization Management, 19,* 219–239.

Koestner, R., Weinberger, J., & Healy, J. (1988). *How motives and values interact with task and social incentives to affect performance.* Unpublished paper, Boston University, Department of Psychology.

Kolb, D. A. (1971). *A cybernetic model of human change and growth* (Working Paper No. 526–71). Cambridge, MA: MIT Sloan School of Management.

Kolb, D. A. (1984). *Experiential learning: Experience as the source of learning and development.* Upper Saddle River, NJ: Prentice Hall.

Kolb, D. A., Beutler, L. E., Davis, C. S., Crago, M., & Shanfield, S. (1985). Patient and therapeutic process variables relating to dropout and change in psychotherapy. *Psychotherapy: Research, Theory, and Practice, 22,* 702–710.

Kolb, D. A., & Boyatzis, R. E. (1970a). On the dynamics of the helping relationship. *Journal of Applied Behavioral Science, 6*(3), 267–289.

Kolb, D. A., & Boyatzis, R. E. (1970b). Goal-setting and self-directed behavior change. *Human Relations, 23,* 439–457.

Kolb, D. A., Winter, S. K., & Berlew, D. E. (1968). Self-directed change: Two studies. *Journal of Applied Behavioral Science, 4*(4), 453–471.

Komaki, J. L., Collins, R. L., & Penn, P. (1982). The role of performance antecedents and consequences in work motivation. *Journal of Applied Psychology, 67,* 334–340.

Kouzes, J. M., & Posner, B. Z. (1999). *Encouraging the heart: A leader's guide to rewarding and recognizing others.* San Francisco: Jossey Bass.

Kram, K. E. (1988). *Mentoring at work: Developmental relationships in organizational life.* Lanham, MD: University Press of America.

Kram, K. E. (1996). A relational approach to career development. In D. T. Hall & Associates, *The career is dead: Long live the career* (pp. 132–157). San Francisco: Jossey-Bass.

Kram, K. E., & Bragar, M. E. (1992). Development through mentoring: A strategic approach. In D. Montross & C. Shinkman (Eds.), *Career development: Theory and practice* (pp. 221–254). Springfield, IL: Thomas.

Kram, K. E., & Hall, D. T. (1996). Mentoring in a context of diversity and turbulence. In E. Kossek & S. Lobel (Eds.), *Human resource strategies for managing diversity* (pp. 132–157). Oxford, England: Blackwell.

Kram, K. E., & Isabella, L. E. (1985). Mentoring alternatives: The role of peer relationships in career development. *Academy of Management Journal, 28,* 110–132.

Kram, K. E., & McCollom, M. (1998). When women lead: The visibility-vulnerability spiral. In E. B. Klein, F. Gabelnick, & P. Herr (Eds.), *The psychodynamics of leadership* (pp. 193–218). Madison, CT: Psychosocial Press.

Kuhn, T. (1970). *The structure of scientific revolutions* (2nd ed.). Chicago: University of Chicago Press.

Lambert, M. J. (1992). Implications of outcome research for psychotherapy integration. In J. C. Norcross & M. R. Goldfried (Eds.), *Handbook of psychotherapy integration* (pp. 94–129). New York: Wiley.

Lambert, M. J., & Bergin, A. E. (1994). The effectiveness of psychotherapy. In A. E. Bergin & S. L. Garfield (Eds.), *Handbook of psychotherapy and behavior change* (4th ed., pp. 143–189). New York: Wiley.

Latham, G. P., & Frayne, C. A. (1989). Self-management training for increasing job attendance: A follow-up and a replication. *Journal of Applied Psychology, 74,* 411–416.

Latham, G. P., & Locke, E. A. (1979, Autumn). Goal setting: A motivational technique which works. *Organizational Dynamics,* pp. 68–80.

Latham, G. P., & Saari, L. M. (1979). Application of social-learning theory to training supervisors through behavioral modeling. *Journal of Applied Psychology, 64,* 239–246.

Latham, G. P., & Wexley, K. N. (1981). *Increasing productivity through performance appraisal.* Reading, MA: Addison-Wesley.

Lawler, E. E., III. (1973). *Motivation in work organizations.* Pacific Grove, CA: Brooks/Cole.

Lawler, E. E., III, Mohrman, S. A., & Ledford, G. E., Jr. (1992). *Employee involvement and total quality management: Practices and results in Fortune 1000 companies.* San Francisco: Jossey-Bass.

Lawler, E. E., III, Mohrman, S. A., & Ledford, G. E., Jr. (1998). *Strategies for high performance organizations: The CEO report: Employee involvement, TQM, and reengineering programs in Fortune 1000 corporations.* San Francisco: Jossey-Bass.

Layder, D. (1994). *Understanding social theory.* Thousand Oaks, CA: Sage.

Lazarus, R. S. (1991). Progress on a cognitive-motivational-relational theory of emotion. *American Psychologist, 46,* 819–834.

Leary, M. R., Tambor, E. S., Terdal, S. K., & Downs, D. L. (1995). Self-esteem as an interpersonal monitor: The sociometer hypothesis. *Journal of Personality and Social Psychology, 68,* 518–530.

LeBon, G. (1977). *The crowd.* New York: Penguin, 1977. (Original work published 1895)

Lees, A., & Barnard, D. (1999). *Highly effective headteachers: An analysis of a sample of diagnostic data from the Leadership Programme for Serving Headteachers.* Report prepared for Hay/McBer, Boston.

Leonard, D. (1996). *The impact of learning goals on self-directed change in management development and education.* Unpublished doctoral dissertation, Case Western Reserve University, Cleveland.

Levinson, D. J., Darrow, D., Levinson, M., & McKee, B. (1978). *The seasons of a man's life.* New York: Knopf.

Levy, R. I. (1984). Emotion, knowing, and culture. In R. A. Sweder & R. A. LeVine (Eds.), *Culture theory: Essays on mind, self, and emotion* (pp. 214–237). New York: Cambridge University Press.

Lewin, K. (1948). *Resolving social conflicts.* New York: HarperCollins.

Lewis, T., Amini, F., & Lannon, R. (2000). *A general theory of love.* New York: Random House.

Lindsley, D. H., Brass, D. J., & Thomas, J. B. (1995). Efficacy performance spirals: A multi-level perspective. *Academy of Management Review, 20*, 645–678.

Litwin, G. H., & Stringer, R. A., Jr. (1968). *Motivation and organizational climate.* Boston: Harvard Business School Division of Research.

Locke, E. A., & Latham, G. P. (1990). *A theory of goal setting and task performance.* Upper Saddle River, NJ: Prentice Hall.

Lusch, R. F., & Serkenci, R. R. (1990). Personal differences, job tension, job outcomes, and store performance: A study of retail managers. *Journal of Marketing, 54*(1), 85–101.

Lutz, C. A. (1988). *Unnatural emotions: Everyday sentiments on a Micronesian atoll and their challenge to Western theory.* Chicago: University of Chicago Press.

Marlatt, A., & Gordon, J. (1985). *Relapse prevention.* New York: Guilford Press.

Marshall, J. (1984). *Women managers: Travelers in a male world.* New York: Wiley.

Martin, J. (1990). *Rapid application development.* New York: Macmillan.

Marx, R. B. (1982). Relapse prevention for managerial training: A model for maintenance of behavior change. *Academy of Management Journal, 35*, 828–847.

Mason, J. L., Barkley, S. E., Kappelman, M. M., Carter, D. E., & Beachy, W. V. (1988). Evaluation of a self-instructional method for improving doctor-patient communication. *Journal of Medical Education, 63*, 629–635.

Mayer, J. (2000, May). Paper presented at the Linkage Emotional Intelligence Conference, London.

Mayer, J. D., Caruso, D. R., & Salovey, P. (2000a). Emotional intelligence meets traditional standards for an intelligence. *Intelligence, 24*, 267–298.

Mayer, J. D., Caruso, D. R., & Salovey, P. (2000b). Selecting a measure of emotional intelligence: The case for ability scales. In R. Bar-On & J.D.A. Parker (Eds.), *The handbook of emotional intelligence: Theory, development, assessment, and application at home, school, and in the workplace* (pp. 320–342). San Francisco: Jossey-Bass.

Mayer, J. D., & Salovey, P. (1997). What is emotional intelligence? In P. Salovey & D. J. Sluyter (Eds.), *Emotional development and emotional intelligence: Implications for educators* (pp. 3–31). New York: Basic Books.

Mayer, J. D., Salovey, P., & Caruso, D. R. (2000). Models of emotional intelligence. In R. J. Sternberg (Ed.), *Handbook of human intelligence* (2nd ed., pp. 396–420). New York: Cambridge University Press.

Mayer, J. D., & Stevens, A. (1994). An emerging understanding of the reflective (meta-) experience of mood. *Journal of Research in Personality, 28*, 351–373.

McAllister, D. J. (1995). Affect- and cognition-based trust as foundations for interpersonal cooperation in organizations. *Academy of Management Journal, 38*, 24–59.

McBane, D. (1995). Empathy and the salesperson: A multidimensional perspective. *Psychology and Marketing, 12*, 349–370.

McCaskey, M. B. (1974). A contingency approach to planning: Planning with goals and without goals. *Academy of Management Journal, 17*, 281–291.

McClelland, D. C. (1961). *The achieving society.* New York: Van Nostrand Reinhold.

McClelland, D. C. (1965). Toward a theory of motive acquisition. *American Psychologist, 20*, 321–333.

McClelland, D. C. (1973). Testing for competence rather than intelligence. *American Psychologist, 28*, 1–14.

McClelland, D. C. (1975). *Power: The inner experience.* New York: Irvington.

McClelland, D. C. (1985). *Human motivation.* Glenview, IL: Scott, Foresman.

McClelland, D. C. (1994, November). *Where do we stand on assessing competencies?* [adapted from a paper presented at the National Conference on Using Competency-Based Tools and Applications to Drive Organizational Performance].

McClelland, D. C. (1998). Identifying competencies with behavioral-event interviews. *Psychological Science, 9*(5), 331–340.

McClelland, D. C., & Boyatzis, R. E. (1982). Leadership motive-pattern and long-term success in management. *Journal of Applied Psychology, 67,* 737–743.

McClelland, D. C., Davis, W. N., Kalin, R., & Wanner, E. (1972). *The drinking man: Alcohol and human motivation.* New York: Free Press.

McClelland, D. C., & Winter, D. G. (1969). *Motivating economic achievement.* New York: Free Press.

McDougall, M., & Beatty, R. S. (1997). Peer mentoring at work: The nature and outcomes of non-hierarchical developmental relationships. *Management Learning, 28*(4), 423–437.

McDougall, W. (1920). *The group mind.* New York: Putnam.

McGrath, J. E. (1984). *Groups: Interaction and performance.* Upper Saddle River, NJ: Prentice Hall.

McIntyre, R. M., & Salas, E. (1995). Measuring and managing for team performance: Emerging principles from complex environments. In R. A. Guzzo, E. Salas, & Associates, *Team effectiveness and decision making in organizations* (pp. 9–45). San Francisco: Jossey-Bass.

McKee (London), A. (1991). *Individual differences in planning for the future.* Unpublished doctoral dissertation, Case Western Reserve University, Cleveland, Ohio.

McKeen, C. A., & Burke, R. J. (1989). Mentor relationships in organizations: Issues, strategies, and prospects for women. *Journal of Management Development, 8*(6), 33–42.

Meichenbaum, D. (1985). *Stress inoculation training.* New York: Pergamon Press.

Miller, J. B. (1986). *The new psychology of women.* Boston: Beacon Press.

Miller, J. B. (1991). The development of women's sense of self. In J. V. Jordan, A. G. Kaplan, J. B. Miller, I. P. Stiver, & J. L. Surrey (Eds.), *Women's growth in connection* (pp. 11–27). New York: Guilford Press.

Miller, J. B., & Stiver, I. P. (1997). *The healing connection: How women form relationships in therapy and in life.* Boston: Beacon Press.

Miller, N. E. (1951). Comments on theoretical models illustrated by the development of a theory of conflict behavior. *Journal of Personality, 20,* 82–100.

Mink, O. G., Owen, K. Q., & Mink, B. P. (1993). *Developing high performance people: The art of coaching.* Reading, MA: Addison-Wesley.

Miron, D., & McClelland, D. C. (1979). The impact of achievement motivation training on small businesses. *California Management Review, 21*(4), 13–28.

Mirvis, P. H., & Hall, D. T. (1996). New organizational forms and the new career. In D. T. Hall & Associates, *The career is dead: Long live the career* (pp. 72–101). San Francisco: Jossey-Bass.

Mirvis, P. H., & Marks, M. L. (1992). *Managing the merger.* Upper Saddle River, NJ: Prentice Hall.

Morrison, A. M. (1992). *The new leaders: Guidelines on leadership diversity in America.* San Francisco: Jossey-Bass.

Morrow, C. C., Jarrett, M. Q., & Rupinski, M. T. (1997). An investigation of the effect and economic utility of corporate-wide training. *Personnel Psychology, 50,* 91–119.

Moses, J. L., & Byham, W. C. (Eds.). (1977). *Applying the assessment center method.* New York: Pergamon Press.

Moses, J. L., & Ritchie, R. J. (1976). Supervisory relationship training: A behavioral evaluation of a behavior modeling program. *Personnel Psychology, 29,* 337–343.

Murnighan, J. K., & Conlon, D. E. (1991). The dynamics of intense work groups: A study of British string quartets. *Administrative Science Quarterly, 36,* 165–186.

Murray, H. A. (1938). *Explorations in personality.* New York: Oxford University Press.

Myers, I. B. (1987). *Introduction to type: A description of the theory and application of the Myers-Briggs Type Indicator.* Palo Alto, CA: Consulting Psychologists Press.

Nadler, D. A. (1979). The effects of feedback on task group behavior: A review of the experimental research. *Organizational Behavior and Human Performance, 23,* 309–338.

Nease, A. A., Mudgett, B. O., & Quinones, M. A. (1999). Relationships among feedback sign, self-efficacy and acceptance of performance feedback. *Journal of Applied Psychology, 84,* 806–814.

Noe, R. A. (1988). An investigation of the determinants of successful assigned mentoring relationships. *Personnel Psychology, 41,* 457–477.

Noe, R. A., & Schmitt, N. (1986). The influence of trainee attitudes on training effectiveness: Test of a model. *Personnel Psychology, 39,* 497–523.

Nygren, D. J., & Ukeritis, M. D. (1993). *The future of religious orders in the United States.* New York: Praeger.

O'Leary, V. E., & Ickovics, J. R. (1992). Cracking the glass ceiling: Overcoming isolation and alienation. In U. Sekaran & F. Leong (Eds.), *Womanpower: Managing in times of demographic turbulence* (pp. 7–31). Thousand Oaks, CA: Sage.

Orioli, E. M., Trocki, K. H., & Jones, T. (1999). *EQ Map technical manual.* San Francisco: Q-Metrics.

Orioli, E. M., Trocki, K. H., & Jones, T. (2000). *EQ Map technical manual.* San Francisco: Q-Metrics.

Owen, C. L., & Todor, W. D. (1993). Attitudes toward women as managers: Still the same. *Business Horizons, 36,* 12–16.

Pascarella, E. T., & Terenzini, P. T. (1991). *How college affects students: Findings and insights from twenty years of research.* San Francisco: Jossey-Bass.

Pesuric, A., & Byham, W. C. (1996). The new look in behavior modeling. *Training and Development, 50*(7), 25–33.

Peterson, D. B. (1996). Executive coaching at work: The art of one-on-one change. *Consulting Psychology Journal, 48*(2), 78–86.

Pfeffer, J. (1998). *The human equation: Building profits by putting people first.* Boston: Harvard Business School Press.

Phillips-Jones, L. (1982). *Mentors and protégés.* New York: Arbor House.

Phillips-Jones, L. (1993). *The mentoring program design package* (2nd ed.). Grass Valley, CA: Coalition of Counseling Centers.

Pilling, B. K., & Eroglu, S. (1994). An empirical examination of the impact of salesperson empathy and professionalism and merchandise salability on retail buyers' evaluations. *Journal of Personal Selling and Sales Management, 14*(1), 55–58.

Porras, J. I., & Anderson, B. (1981, Spring). Improving managerial effectiveness through modeling-based training. *Organizational Dynamics,* pp. 60–77.

Prahalad, C. K., & Hamel, G. (1990, May–June). The core competence of the corporation. *Harvard Business Review,* pp. 79–91.

Price, R. H., Friedland, D. S., Choi, J. N., & Caplan, R. D. (1998). Job-loss and work transitions in a time of global economic change. In X. B. Arriaga & S. Oskamp (Eds.), *Addressing community problems: Psychological research and interventions* (pp. 195–222). Thousand Oaks, CA: Sage.

Price, R. H., & Politser, P. (Eds.). (1980). *Evaluation and action in the social environment.* New York: Academic Press.

Prochaska, J. O. (1999). How do people change, and how can we change to help many more people? In M. A. Hubble, B. L. Duncan, & S. D. Miller (Eds.), *The heart and soul of change: What works in therapy* (pp. 227–258). Washington, DC: American Psychological Association.

Prochaska, J. O., DiClemente, C. C., & Norcross, J. C. (1992). In search of how people change: Applications to addictive behaviors. *American Psychologist, 47,* 1102–1114.

Pryor, S. E. (1994). *Executive coaching: Sign of stigma or success?* (Technical Report). Boston: Boston University, School of Management Executive Development Roundtable.

Q-Metrics. (1996/1997). *EQ Map interpretation guide.* San Francisco: Author.

Ragins, B. R. (1989). Barriers to mentoring: The female manager's dilemma. *Human Relations, 42,* 1–22.

Ragins, B. R., & McFarlin, D. B. (1990). Perceptions of mentor roles in cross-gender mentoring relationships. *Journal of Vocational Behavior, 37,* 321–339.

Ragins, B. R., & Scandura, T. (1994). Gender differences in expected outcomes of mentoring relationships. *Academy of Management Journal, 37,* 957–971.

Rahim, M. A., & Psenicka, C. (1996). A structural equations model of stress, locus of control, social support, psychiatric symptoms, and propensity to leave a job. *Journal of Social Psychology, 136,* 69–84.

Rhee, K. (1997). *Journey of discovery: A longitudinal study of learning during a graduate professional program.* Unpublished doctoral dissertation, Case Western Reserve University, Cleveland.

Rice, C. L. (1999). *A quantitative study of emotional intelligence and its impact on team performance.* Unpublished master's thesis, Pepperdine University, Malibu, CA.

Roche, G. R. (1979, January–February). Much ado about mentors. *Harvard Business Review,* pp. 14–28.

Rondina, P. (1988, October). *Impact of competency-based recruiting techniques on dropout rates in sales training programs.* Paper presented at the McBer twenty-fifth anniversary symposium, Boston.

Rosen, R. (1998). Leadership in the new organization. In M. K. Gowing, J. Kraft, & J. C. Quick (Eds.), *The new organizational reality: Downsizing, restructuring and revitalization* (pp. 221–238). Washington, DC: American Psychological Association.

Rosener, J. (1990, November-December). Ways women lead. *Harvard Business Review,* pp. 119–125.

Rosenthal, R. (1977). The PONS Test: Measuring sensitivity to nonverbal cues. In P. McReynolds (Ed.), *Advances in psychological assessment.* San Francisco: Jossey-Bass.

Rosenthal, R., & Rubin, D. (1978). Interpersonal expectancy effects: The first 345 studies. *Behavioral and Brain Sciences, 3,* 377–415.

Rosier, R. H. (Ed.). (1996). *The competency model handbook* (Vol. 3). Boston: Linkage.

Rouillier, J. Z., & Goldstein, I. L. (1991, April). *Determinants of the climate for transfer of training.* Paper presented at the annual meeting of the Society for Industrial and Organizational Psychology.

Rousseau, D. M., Sitkin, S. B., Burt, R. S., & Camerer, C. (1998). Not so different after all: A cross discipline view of trust. *Academy of Management Review, 23,* 393–404.

Russ-Eft, D. F., & Zenger, J. H. (1997). Behavior modeling training in North America: A research summary. In L. J. Bassi & D. F. Russ-Eft (Eds.), *What works* (pp. 89–109). Alexandria, VA: American Society for Training and Development.

Saari, L. M., Johnson, T. R., McLaughlin, S. D., & Zimmerle, D. M. (1988). A survey of management training and education practices in U.S. companies. *Personnel Psychology, 41,* 731–743.

Saarni, C. (1997). Emotional competence and self-regulation in childhood. In P. Salovey & D. J. Sluyter (Eds.), *Emotional development and emotional intelligence: Implications for educators* (pp. 69–91). New York: Basic Books.

Sahlman, W. A. (1997, July–August). How to write a great business plan. *Harvard Business Review*, pp. 98–108.

Saks, A. M. (1995). Longitudinal field investigation of the moderating and mediating effects of self-efficacy on the relationship between training and newcomer adjustment. *Journal of Applied Psychology, 80,* 211–225.

Salovey, P., & Mayer, J. D. (1990). Emotional intelligence. *Imagination, Cognition, and Personality, 9,* 185–211.

Salovey, P., & Sluyter, D. J. (Eds.). (1997). *Emotional development and emotional intelligence: Implications for educators.* New York: Basic Books.

Sarason, I. G., Sarason, B. R., & Pierce, G. R. (1990). Social support: The search for theory. *Journal of Social and Clinical Psychology, 9*(1), 133–147.

Scandura, T. A. (1992). Mentorship and career mobility: An empirical investigation. *Journal of Organizational Behavior, 13,* 169–174.

Scheier, M. F., & Carver, C. S. (1982). Cognition, affect, and self-regulation. In M. S. Clark & S. T. Fiske (Eds.), *Affect and cognition: The 17th Annual Carnegie Symposium on Cognition* (pp. 157–184). Mahwah, NJ: Erlbaum.

Schein, E. H. (1978). *Career dynamics: Matching individual and organizational needs.* Reading, MA: Addison-Wesley.

Schein, E. H. (1985). *Organizational culture and leadership.* San Francisco: Jossey-Bass.

Schein, E. H. (1993, Winter). How can organizations learn faster? The challenge of entering the green room. *Sloan Management Review*, pp. 85–92.

Schober, M. F. (1998). Different kinds of conversational perspective-taking. In S. R. Fussell & R. J. Kreuz (Eds.), *Social and cognitive approaches to interpersonal communication* (pp. 145–174). Mahwah, NJ: Erlbaum.

Schön, D. A. (1990). *Educating the reflective practitioner: Toward a new design for teaching and learning in the professions.* San Francisco: Jossey-Bass.

Schulman, P. (1995). Explanatory style and achievement in school and work. In G. Buchanan & M. Seligman (Eds.), *Explanatory style* (pp. 159–171). Mahwah, NJ: Erlbaum.

Schutte, N. S., Malouff, J. M., Hall, L. E., Haggerty, D. J., Cooper, J. T., Golden, C. J., & Dornheim, L. (1998). Development and validation of a measure of emotional intelligence. *Personality and Individual Differences, 25,* 167–177.

Seligman, M.E.P. (1991). *Learned optimism.* New York: Knopf.

Seligman, M.E.P., & Csikszentmihalyi, M. (2000). Positive psychology: An introduction. *American Psychologist, 55,* 5–14.

Senge, P. (1990). *The fifth discipline.* New York: Doubleday, Currency.

Shapiro, E., Haseltine, F., & Rowe, M. (1978, Spring). Moving up: Role models, mentors, and the patron system. *Sloan Management Review*, pp. 51–58.

Shea, G. P., & Guzzo, R. A. (1987, Spring). Group effectiveness: What really matters? *Sloan Management Review*, pp. 25–31.

Sherif, M. (1936). *The psychology of social norms.* New York: HarperCollins.

Silver, W. S., & Bufanio, K. M. (1996). The impact of group efficacy and group goals on group task performance. *Small Group Research, 27*(3), 347–359.

Sloan, S., & Spencer, L. M. (1991). *Participant survey results.* Salesforce Effectiveness Seminar. Atlanta, GA: Hay Group.

Smith, K. K., & Berg, D. N. (1987). *Paradoxes of group life: Understanding conflict, paralysis, and movement in group dynamics.* San Francisco: Jossey-Bass.

Smith, L. (1993, December). The executive's new coach. *Fortune,* pp. 126–134.

Smith, P. (1976). Management modeling training to improve morale and customer satisfaction. *Personnel Psychology, 29,* 351–359.

Specht, L., & Sandlin, P. (1991). The differential effects of experiential learning activities and traditional lecture classes in accounting. *Simulations and Gaming, 22*(2), 196–210.

Spencer, L. M. (1986). *Calculating human resource costs and benefits.* New York: Wiley.

Spencer, L. M. (1997, September). *Project management competencies.* Paper presented at the annual meeting of the Engineering Construction and Contracting Association, San Diego, CA.

Spencer, L. M., McClelland, D. C., & Kelner, S. (1997, October). *Competency assessment methods: History and state of the art.* Paper presented at a meeting of the Consortium for Social and Emotional Competence in the Workplace, Boston.

Spencer, L. M., McClelland, D. C., & Spencer, S. (1992). *Competency assessment methods.* Boston: Hay/McBer Research Press.

Spencer, L. M., & Morrow, C. C. (1996). *The economic value of competence: Measuring ROI.* Paper presented at the Conference on Using Competency-Based Tools and Applications to Enhance Organizational Performance, Boston.

Spencer, L. M., & Spencer, S. M. (1993). *Competence at work: Models for superior performance.* New York: Wiley.

Steele, C. M. (1997). A threat in the air: How stereotypes shape intellectual identity and performance. *American Psychologist, 52,* 613–629.

Sternberg, R. J. (1996). *Successful intelligence: How practical and creative intelligence determine success in life.* New York: Simon & Schuster.

Sternberg, R. J. (1997). The concept of intelligence and its role in lifelong learning and success. *American Psychologist, 52,* 1030–1045.

Stryker, S., & Statham, A. (1985). Symbolic interaction and role theory. In G. Lindzey & E. Aronson (Eds.), *The handbook of social psychology* (3rd ed., Vol. 1, pp. 311–378). New York: Random House.

Sundstrom, E., DeMeuse, K. P., & Futrell, D. (1990). Work teams: Applications and effectiveness. *American Psychologist, 45,* 120–133.

Super, D. E. (1957). *The psychology of careers.* New York: HarperCollins.

Super, D. E. (1986). Life career roles: Self-realization in work and leisure. In D. T. Hall & Associates, *Career development in organizations* (pp. 95–119). San Francisco: Jossey-Bass.

Sweeney, P. (1999, February 14). Teaching new hires to feel at home. *New York Times,* p. C4.

Taft, R. (1955). The ability to judge people. *Psychological Bulletin, 52,* 1–23.

Tagiuri, R., & Litwin, G. H. (1968). *Organizational climate: Explorations of a concept.* Boston: Harvard Business School Press.

Tallman, K., & Bohart, A. C. (1999). The client as a common factor: Clients as self-healers. In M. A. Hubble, B. L. Duncan, & S. D. Miller (Eds.), *The heart and soul of change: What works in therapy* (pp. 91–132). Washington, DC: American Psychological Association.

Tannenbaum, S. I., & Yukl, G. (1992). Training and development in work organizations. *Annual Review of Psychology, 43,* 399–441.

Taylor, G. J., Parker, J.D.A., & Bagby, R. M. (1999). Emotional intelligence and the emotional brain: Points of convergence and implications for psychoanalysis. *Journal of the American Academy of Psychoanalysis, 27*(3), 339–354.

Thomas, D. (1989). Mentoring and irrationality: The role of racial taboos. *Human Resource Management, 28*(2), 279–290.

Thomas, D. (1990). The impact of race on managers' experiences of developmental relationships: An intra-organizational study. *Journal of Organizational Behavior, 11*, 479–492.

Thomas, D. (1993). Racial dynamics in cross-race developmental relationships. *Administrative Science Quarterly, 38*, 169–194.

Thomas, D., & Alderfer, C. P. (1989). The influence of race on career dynamics: Theory and research on minority career experiences. In M. B. Arthur, D. T. Hall, & B. S. Lawrence (Eds.), *Handbook of career theory* (pp. 133–158). New York: Cambridge University Press.

Thomas, D., & Gabarro, J. J. (1999). *Breaking through: The making of minority executives in corporate America.* Boston: Harvard Business School Press.

Thorndike, E. L. (1920). Intelligence and its uses. *Harper's, 140*, 227–235.

Thorndike, R. L., & Stern, S. (1937). An evaluation of the attempts to measure social intelligence. *Psychological Bulletin, 34*, 275–284.

Thornton, G. C., III, & Byham, W. C. (1982). *Assessment centers and managerial performance.* New York: Academic Press.

Tjosvold, D., & Tjosvold, M. (1994). Cooperation, competition, and constructive controversy: Knowledge to empower for self-managing work teams. In M. M. Beyerlein & D. A. Johnson (Eds.), *Advances in interdisciplinary studies of work teams* (Vol. 1, pp. 119–144). Greenwich, CT: JAI Press.

Toffler, A. (1990). *Powershift.* New York: Bantam.

Totterdell, P., Kellett, S., Teuchmann, K., & Briner, R. R. (1998). Evidence of mood linkage in work groups. *Journal of Personality and Social Psychology, 74*, 1504–1515.

Tziner, A., Haccoun, R. R., & Kadish, A. (1991). Personal and situational characteristics influencing the effectiveness of transfer of training improvement strategies. *Journal of Occupational Psychology, 64*, 167–177.

U.S. General Accounting Office. (1998). *Military recruiting: DOD could improve its recruiter selection and incentive systems.* GAO/NSIAD-98-58. Washington, DC: Author.

U.S. Office of Strategic Services. (1948). *Assessment of men: Selection of personnel for the Office of Strategic Services.* Austin, TX: Holt, Rinehart & Winston.

Van Velsor, E., & Hughes, M. (1990). *Gender differences in the development of managers: How women managers learn from experience.* Greensboro, NC: Center for Creative Leadership.

Walker, B. A. (1996). The value of diversity in career self-development. In D. T. Hall & Associates, *The career is dead: Long live the career* (pp. 265–277). San Francisco: Jossey-Bass.

Wechsler, D. (1940). Nonintellective factors in general intelligence. *Psychological Bulletin, 37*, 444–445.

Wechsler, D. (1943). Nonintellective factors in general intelligence. *Journal of Abnormal Social Psychology, 38*, 100–104.

Wechsler, D. (1952). *The range of human capacities.* New York: Hafner.

Weick, K. E., & Bougon, M. G. (1986). Organizations as cognitive maps. In H. P. Sims, D. A. Gioia, & Associates, *The thinking organization: Dynamics of organizational social cognition* (pp. 102–135). San Francisco: Jossey-Bass.

Wellman, B., Carrington, P. J., & Hall, A. (1988). Networks as personal communities. In B. Wellman & D. Berkowitz (Eds.), *Social structures: A network approach* (pp. 130–184). New York: Cambridge University Press.

Wellman, B., Wong, R. Y., Tindall, D., & Nazer, N. (1997). A decade of network change: Turnover, persistence and stability in personal communities. *Social Networks, 19*, 27–50.

Wenger, E. (1998). *Communities of practice: Learning, meaning, and identity.* New York: Cambridge University Press.

Wheatley, M. J. (1992). *Leadership and the new science: Learning about organization from an orderly universe.* San Francisco: Berrett-Koehler.

Wheelan, S. A., & Johnston, F. (1996). The role of informal member leaders in a system containing formal leaders. *Small Group Research, 27*(1), 33–55.

Wheeler, J. A. (1999). *Organizational and environmental supports and opportunities for self-directed learning following graduate education.* Unpublished doctoral dissertation, Case Western Reserve University, Cleveland.

Whitely, W. T., & Coetsier, P. (1993). The relationship of career mentoring to early career outcomes. *Organization Studies, 14*(3), 419–441.

Whitely, W. T., Dougherty, T. W., & Dreher, G. F. (1991). Relationship of career mentoring and socioeconomic origin to managers' and professionals' early career progress. *Academy of Management Journal, 34*, 331–351.

Whyte, W. H., Jr. (1943). *Street corner society.* Chicago: University of Chicago Press.

Wiener, E. L., Kanki, B. G., & Helmreich, R. L. (1993). *Cockpit resource management.* New York: Academic Press.

Wiener, R. L. (1999, June). Extending Daubert beyond scientific expert testimony: Technical and other specialized knowledge must be reliable to be admissible. *Psychological Monitor, 30*(6).

Williams, D. (1994). *Leadership for the 21st century: Life insurance leadership study.* Boston: Hay Group.

Williams, V., & Williams, R. (1997). *Lifeskills.* New York: Times Books/Random House.

Williams, W. M., & Sternberg, R. T. (1988). Group intelligence: Why some groups are better than others. *Intelligence, 12*, 351–377.

Winter, D. G., McClelland, D. C., & Stewart, A. J. (1981). *A new case for the liberal arts: Assessing institutional goals and student development.* San Francisco: Jossey-Bass.

Wolff, S. B. (1998). *The role of caring behavior and peer feedback in creating team effectiveness.* Unpublished doctoral dissertation, Boston University, Boston.

Yan, A., & Louis, M. R. (1999). The migration of organizational functions to the work unit level: Buffering, spanning and bringing up boundaries. *Human Relations, 52*, 25–47.

Young, D. P., & Dixon, N. M. (1996). *Helping leaders take effective action: A program evaluation.* Greensboro, NC: Center for Creative Leadership.

Zey, M. G. (1991). *The mentor connection: Strategic alliances in corporate life.* New Brunswick, NJ: Transaction.

Zipkin, A. (2000, May 31). The wisdom of thoughtfulness. *New York Times,* pp. C1, C10.

NAME INDEX

SUBJECT INDEX

A

Ability model. *See* Mental ability model

Ability scales, 93–107, 129–131. *See also* Mayer-Salovey-Caruso Emotional Intelligence Test; Multifactor Emotional Intelligence Scale

Ability tasks, 130

Ability to manage emotion, 95, 96

Ability to stay open to feelings, 94, 95, 96, 97

Academic performance, 194

Account managers, performance distributions for, 49, 52

Accountability, executive hiring decisions and, 204

Accurate Self-Assessment, 108; individual contributor selection for, 169; for making hiring decisions, 205; performance and, 33; as prerequisite for developmental relationships, 270; self-management training for, 212–213

Achievement Drive, 20, 29, 87; Emotional Quotient Inventory

compared with, 108; for making hiring decisions, 205; in outstanding performers, 32, 35; performance and, 35; self-management training for, 213

Achievement (EIC cluster), 54

Achievement motivation, 248

Achievement motivation training and development, 216, 234; effects of, 70, 235

Achievement Orientation: in competency model algorithm, 162, 164, 165; for emotional competence program managers, 301–302; individual contributor selection for, 168–169; Initiative and, 162, 164, 165; manager selection for, 167; salespeople selection for, 169; scale of, 87, 88; Self-Confidence and, 164

Achievement thinking, 216

Achieving Society, The (McClelland), 35

Acquisitions, executive selection and, 183, 184, 200

Action learning, 80, 278, 280, 285

Action plan, 175

Action stage, in social and emotional learning (SEL) model, 220, 221, 223, 253

Action steps, in performance management, 179–180

Adaptability, 17; in competency model algorithm, 165; Conscientiousness and, 162; for emotional competence program managers, 301; in Emotional Quotient Inventory, 108, 109, 111; as meta-competency, 281; in outstanding performers, 32, 35; performance and, 34; as prerequisite for developmental relationships, 271

Adaptation-preservation balance, 246–248

Adult development, developmental relationships and, 271–273

Adult learning, self-direction in, 174, 180, 181, 225, 239–240. *See also* Self-directed change

Advanced Intelligence Technologies, 125

Adverse impact, 46

Affect, friendship and, 134

14406634R00205

Made in the USA
Lexington, KY
26 March 2012